PUBLICATIONS
OF THE
ARMY RECORDS SOCIETY
VOL. 12

MILITARY MISCELLANY I

The Army Records Society was founded in 1984 in order to publish original records describing the development, organisation, administration and activities of the British Army from early times.

Any person wishing to become a Member of the Society is requested to apply to the Hon. Secretary, c/o the National Army Museum, Royal Hospital Road, London, SW3 4HT. The annual subscription entitles the member to receive a copy of each volume issued by the Society in that year, and to purchase back volumes at reduced prices. Current subscription details, whether for individuals living within the British Isles, for individuals living overseas, or for institutions, will be furnished on request.

The Council of the Army Records Society wish it to be clearly understood that they are not answerable for opinions or observations that may appear in the Society's publications. For these the responsibility rests entirely with the Editors of the several works.

Daniel George Robinson as a 2nd Lieutenant in the Bengal Engineers
(pastel, by Peter Overton, 1844)

Private Collection

MILITARY MISCELLANY I

Manuscripts from the Seven Years War,
the First and Second Sikh Wars and
the First World War

Editors

ALAN J. GUY, R.N.W. THOMAS and GERARD J. DeGROOT

Published by
SUTTON PUBLISHING LIMITED
for the
ARMY RECORDS SOCIETY
1996

First published in the United Kingdom in 1997
Sutton Publishing Ltd · Phoenix Mill · Far Thrupp · Stroud
Gloucestershire

British Library Cataloguing in Publication Data

A catalogue record for this book is available from the British
Library

Typeset in Ehrhardt
Typesetting and origination by
Sutton Publishing Limited.
Printed in Great Britain

Contents

I

George Durant's Journal of the Expedition to Martinique and Guadeloupe, October 1758–May 1759

Introduction	3
Section 2 The Durant journal	17
Notes	58

II

Daniel George Robinson: Letters from India 1845–1849

Introduction	71
The Letters of Daniel George Robinson	79
Appendices 1–4	200
Appendix 5 – Gazetteer	226
Notes	239
Bibliography	260

III

The Reverend George S. Duncan at GHQ, 1916–1918

Acknowledgements	266
Abbreviations	267
Introduction	269
Note on Editorial Method	275
Section 1 1916	277
Section 2 January to May, 1917	317
Section 3 May to December, 1917	352
Section 4 1918 and after	402
Notes	411
Biographies	429
Bibliography	435

Index	437

I
George Durant's Journal of the Expedition to Martinique and Guadeloupe, October 1758–May 1759

Edited by
ALAN J. GUY

I
Introduction

'. . . whoever makes a Campagne in the West Indies earns
fairly all he can get'.
> Colonel George Haldane, brigadier
> in the expedition, March 1759[1]

'Pretty pickings, I warrant, abroad.'
> Samuel Foote, *The Commissary* (1765)

The Durant Journal

The *Journal* of George Durant, Deputy Paymaster to the British
expedition to the French Antilles in 1758–59, is contained in three small
notebooks, each measuring 11 × 18 cm, with soft marbled covers. The
notebooks have passed through the family, by direct descent to their
present owner, together with a small quantity of related Durant Papers
[DP]. I wish to place on record my gratitude to the owner, who has
allowed me to examine the manuscript *Journal* and to reproduce it here;
also to Professor Ian Beckett for bringing Durant's *Journal* to my
attention.

The first of the three notebooks, beginning in the weeks immediately
prior to the departure of the expedition, covers the period from 10
October 1758 to 23 January 1759 and continues without a break into the
second volume, covering the remainder of 23 January until 9 April 1759
inclusive. The third volume spans the period 10 April to 30 May 1759.
There are blank pages at the end of this notebook. It was evidently
Durant's intention to write an entry, however brief, every day, and the
only breaks occur between 30 October and 11 November 1758, when the
expedition had been driven back to Portsmouth by bad weather and there
was nothing of interest to report, and from 22 to 25 March 1759, when
Durant was very poorly. His clerkly hand is legible for the most part,
although his phonetic approximations of proper names on first hearing –
'Pharmouth' for Falmouth, or 'Baster' for Basseterre (Guadeloupe) for

3

example – are sometimes confusing, and where this is likely to be the case, I have corrected them, indicating this by the use of square brackets. In other instances, such as the occasional 'Gardaloup', or 'Sylla' (signifying the Isles of Scilly) Durant's original spelling has been retained, as well as his punctuation.

It has been possible to identify nearly all the individuals mentioned by Durant in his *Journal*, but not every one: at this stage of his career he was an obscure personage and his close friends, such as 'Powell' or 'Fowler' [*Journal*, 22 Oct 1758], were men of like degree. Some identifications remain very tentative, such as 'GH' [*Journal* 29 Jan 1759], who might be General Hopson, the force commander, General Haldane, one of his brigadiers (Durant had sailed with both men to the West Indies aboard the *St George* man-of-war, and would have observed them closely) or quite possibly someone else, as he usually gives an officer's abbreviated rank, which would have been 'Gen¹' in both cases.

There is in the Durant Papers a fair copy of the *Journal*, possibly by a later hand, covering the period up to 4 March 1759, after which the scribe apparently lost interest. It is a useful guide to some obscure readings in the original manuscript, and occasionally offers alternative renderings of individual words.

Although he apparently wore a red coat [*Journal*, 3 Feb 1759] George Durant was a civilian, not a soldier, and whilst the point ought not to be pushed too far, he lacked the jaunty brutality cultivated by men of the sword as a shield against the horrors of war, according to which people torn apart by grapeshot or dying in a mess of bloody excrement were deemed to have been 'knock'd on the head' or to have 'receiv'd their *quietus*'. Nor did Durant create for himself a purely literary space of safety – unlike his fellow eye-witness of the campaign, Captain Richard Gardiner of the Marines. Gardiner embellished his text (which he must have had ready for publication almost as soon as he came ashore) with quotations from Virgil and Horace, at one point first quoting Addison and then translating him into Latin.[2] Durant's *Journal* by contrast was an intimate account, part prompted by romantic yearnings, and when he saw something shocking, he gave an unvarnished account of it, underpinned by the morality of the clergy house where he had been brought up. Further evidence of the latter tendency can be detected in his keen interest in sermons preached by various divines aboard the *St George*, some of whom he found greatly wanting in virtue, humility and address.

Aside from Captain Gardiner, George Durant's *Journal* is one of only a few contemporary accounts of the Martinique/Guadeloupe expedition available in print. Robert Beatson served as Practitioner Engineer in the campaign, but his recollections only appeared many years later, embedded in his general survey of British military history.[3] Sir John Fortescue's (posthumous) account of the expedition, based on papers of Colonel George Haldane, a brigadier in the expedition, was published in 1934.[4] Official despatches to and from the home government were published by Gertrude Selwyn Kimball in 1906.[5]

I have been fortunate in being able to supplement these accounts with unpublished material in the Barrington Papers, housed until very recently in the Suffolk Record Office and latterly at the British Library. They include important private letters from Major-General John Barrington, who took over command of the expedition in February 1759, to his brother William, Viscount Barrington, the Secretary at War, and an illuminating letter from Colonel Haldane, also to Viscount Barrington. I am most grateful to the Board of Trustees of the British Library for permission to use these papers and to Mr Robert Smith of the Department of Manuscripts who kindly made them available to me at short notice. (I have cited the old SRO calendar numbers for these documents in my footnotes to the Durant *Journal*.)

I take pleasure in acknowledging encouragement and assistance received from five of my colleagues at the National Army Museum: the Director, Mr Ian Robertson; Dr Peter Boyden, Dr Linda Washington, and Miss June Hicks and Miss Kate Plowman who between them expertly typed the manuscript. I am also particularly grateful for information provided by Dr Robin Thomas.

The Career of George Durant, Esq, to 1758

George Durant, born in 1731, baptized on 20 November that year and subsequently educated at St. Edmund Hall, Oxford, was the second son of the Reverend Josiah Durant, Rector of Hagley in Worcestershire, in the advowson of the powerful Lyttelton family, who resided at nearby Hagley Hall.[6] Sir George Lyttelton, the 5th baronet, although not a politician of the first rank, had close connections with the power brokers of the 'Whig Supremacy' – the Pelhams, the Temples, the Grenvilles and the Pitts. His contemporaries all agreed that he was a most amiable man, but also that he was lacking in understanding of the way of the world.[7]

Lyttelton's beloved first wife, Lucy Fortescue, whom he had married in 1741, died in childbirth in January 1747. Lyttelton was desolated and in his search for a proper replacement he settled upon an intimate friend of Lucy's – Miss Elizabeth Rich, daughter of General Sir Robert Rich,

Governor of the Royal Hospital, Chelsea. It seems, however, that although Miss Rich, or Lady Lyttelton as she became in August 1749, was accomplished in languages, music and painting and graced with a lively, satirical wit (she later became a friend and correspondent of Horace Walpole), her tastes and temper were poles apart from her husband's. She quickly became bored with the society Sir George was happy in and at last with him also. By the autumn of 1756, Sir George and Elizabeth Lyttelton had, as the family historian quaintly puts it, 'agreed to take their pleasures apart'. The baronet carried on his rather ineffectual politicking in London while his lady dwelt at Hagley, under the supervision of his brother, Dr Charles Lyttelton, Dean of Exeter, who clearly detested her and watched her like a hawk.[8]

That September, as the Dean gleefully reported to another of his brothers, William Henry Lyttelton, young George Durant came to Hagley to visit his father, the rector:

'The very first hour after his arrival at the parsonage, he came down to the hall and was admitted to a private audience with the lady in her closet, as he was 3 or 4 times afterwards. From the time of his coming to Hagley Hall 'till Sir George's return in the beginning of October, her Ladyship spent the whole day and evening, except meal times, at the parsonage, and at last invited herself to dinner there . . . Nor was this all; for every attention that could be shewn to the greatest guest that ever entered the house was shewed to the parson and his family, and all kinds of neglect to everybody else and downright rudeness to *me* on every occasion.

'Thus things went on 'till the good man returned from town, the whole country, the parish, and even the servants at the house clamouring loudly without reserve. As soon as he came home we thought it our duty to acquaint him with all the particulars, upon which he first determined to part with her. Happy had it been for her if he had; but being prevailed upon to see her, when she fell on her knees and humbled herself beyond what I thought her haughty spirit would ever submit to, he consented to let her continue with him, acquitting her indeed of actual guilt, but charging her with every thing short of it. He ordered the young man to be sent immediately away and has assured her good Ladyship that if she is ever guilty again of an indiscretion of this kind, and does not behave in a very different manner than she has done both to his family, his friends, and his neighbours, he will absolutely part with her.

'You may easily imagine this was a thunderstroke to her and must necessarily affect her spirits as well as her health too much to admit of her coming to town . . . so she was left at Hagley shut up in her own chamber ill in body and worse in mind; and by the last post we hear she has been confined to bed with an eruption of the erysipelas kind, but not in danger of her life, tho' it would be happy for her and all that belong to her if this illness put a period to it.

'This affair has now got wind and all the town talk of it; report you may suppose has exaggerated the circumstances, and 'tis generally said her Ladyship was caught abed with the young man . . . Her infernal temper has left her so few friends that I don't hear of a single person who speaks in her favour, or that abuses Sir George or his family for the part he has taken. On the contrary, his enemys ascribe great merit to him for his behaviour in this delicate business. I thank God he is pure well and his mind pretty much at ease with regard to his private and publick disappointments'.[9]

While Lady Elizabeth bore the brunt of the Lyttelton family's displeasure, Lord George (as he became in November 1756), rather than dismissing Durant out of hand (it was potentially too humiliating to do so), obtained for him a clerkship in the Pay Office.[10] This patronage, improved by George's undoubted ambition, his astuteness in interpreting the wishes (spoken and unspoken) of his superiors, a robust constitution and an eye to the main chance, was to be the making of him – in the material sense at least.

The eighteenth century Pay Office was the British Army's domestic bank and its chief, the Paymaster General, a junior minister, was the Army's banker. He received, mostly from the Exchequer, money voted by Parliament for military expenditure, as well as incidental income, such as that obtained from the sale of old stores. He issued money to the army, either personally, or via Deputy Paymasters, among whom were officials assigned to expeditions overseas.

During the time in which public money remained in the Paymaster General's hands, from the day he received it until the granting of his *Quietus* (or final discharge) his private estate remained liable, without limit of time. Before a *Quietus* could be allowed, it was necessary for the Paymaster's accounts to be audited by the Auditors of the Imprests but this process, as was so often the case before the advent of 'economical reform' in the 1780s, was subject to protracted delay. Meanwhile, the Paymaster had a chance to invest any balances remaining on his hands for his own benefit. During periods of burgeoning military expenditure, these balances could be substantial indeed, and so the job of Paymaster General was looked upon as one of the most lucrative of all public appointments. In a calculated gesture of disinterested patriotism one recent Paymaster, William Pitt, had declined to make use of these balances: others were less scrupulous.[11]

By degrees, the Paymaster General's opportunities to finger the public treasure extended to all those entrusted with delegated responsibility for it. In the case of a Deputy Paymaster, besides speculating with balances locally, possibilities for self-enrichment included withholding payments, extorting percentages or other kick-backs in exchange for prompt payment, or buying-in local currency at a cheap rate and paying the soldiers at a higher one.

George Durant's arrival at the Pay Office in 1757 coincided with the appointment of Henry Fox as Paymaster General. Fox (1705–74), son of Charles II's Paymaster General, Sir Stephen Fox, was a parliamentary manager who was several times within reach of the premiership itself, but somehow lacked the spirit to undertake it. Severely shaken by the uproar over the fall of Minorca in July 1756, when he had been Secretary of State for the Southern Department, Fox chose the Pay Office as a safe haven, where he felt it could never again be supposed that he had a public share in measures or power. He remained Paymaster General under successive administrations until May 1765, having been created Baron Holland of Foxley in April 1763.[12]

Fox was a highly capable organizer and among his friends and patrons were men of the highest character, but for close associates he selected political buccaneers or dubious, even sleazy, men of business, such as John Calcraft the regimental agent,[13] Samuel Touchet (a Manchester manufacturer who was involved in just about every field of public and private finance before evading bankruptcy in 1763 only by virtue of parliamentary privilege),[14] and – most importantly from George Durant's point of view – the father and son Peter Taylor and Robert Paris Taylor.[15]

Peter Taylor, a silversmith in Cecil Court, the Strand, had by 1755 become a close confidant of Calcraft and Fox. In 1758, Fox procured for him an appointment as Deputy Paymaster to the army in Germany, much to the displeasure of the Secretary at War, William, Viscount Barrington, who had long since taken Taylor's measure.[16]

Peter Taylor served with 'His Britannick Majesty's Army in Germany' until the end of the Seven Years' War in 1763. This was a major theatre of operations with thousands of British troops engaged, and it was believed that at the height of the conflict, £150,000 a month had passed through Taylor's sticky fingers. He came back to England with a large fortune – £400,000 it was said – and a reputation for financial opportunism matched only by his candour in speaking about it, although this was not the case initially. His letters from Germany bewailed the fact that his 'great profits' were making him enemies at home; that he had discovered that he was 'not a Favorite' at the Treasury, or that there seemed to be growing prejudice against him at the War and Pay Offices. He rather querulously insisted that he was ready '. . . to Stand the Strictest Enquiry of my whole Conduct', or that he was '. . . ready to undergo the strictest Scrutiny', hoping meanwhile '. . . for a peace for the good of mankind[.] I wish it on my own Account [–] purchaceing riches at the Expence of my Constitution is a bad Exchange'.[17] Meanwhile, his son, Robert Paris Taylor, had been given a clerkship in the Pay Office by Fox, followed by Deputy Paymaster appointments – first to the luckless expedition to the coast of France commanded by Lieutenant-General Bligh (August–September 1758)[18] and subsequently to the army in Germany, where he became an unreliable subordinate and a constant worry to his father.[19] This did not prevent 'Paris' from coming home with a handsome fortune but, in time, his slapdash methods caused his accounts to be queried.[20] He spent the last twelve years of his life imprisoned in the Fleet for debt, and died in 1792 under the shadow of madness – a condition which may have been the result of the dissipated life he had led whilst following the army as a young man.[21]

Although the circumstances are obscure, it is likely that George Durant's progression to a Deputy Paymastership in the expedition sent against the French Antilles in 1758 was not unconnected with Fox's desire to gratify the Taylors. As Calcraft told Peter Taylor, it had been thought neither advisable nor practicable to send Robert Paris Taylor to the West Indies. The cash for the expedition was being issued in Spanish silver so, at first sight, there seemed to be little chance of making much money out of it by exchange. The climate of the West Indies was unhealthy and in any case there was barely time for Paris to join the departing fleet, '. . . So Durant of the Office goes'.[22] Robert Paris Taylor had been preserved for better things.

Some years later, the Hon. Thomas Lyttelton, son of Lord George, gave another version of Durant's advancement;

'. . . he was left, I believe, by our family patronage to look for any future promotion from his own industry, the chance of succession, or the casual boon of fortune. The latter was disposed to smile upon him, or, it might be said with more propriety, to reward the prudent modesty with which he retreated from her first advances to secure her greater favours. In the usual course of promotion he had an acknowledged claim to succeed to a vacant place of no inconsiderable profit. On this occasion, Lord Holland, for some particular reason which I have forgotten, or perhaps never heard, wished to make an irregular appointment in favour of some other person; and to comply with his lordship's wishes Mr [Durant] wisely waived his right of succession. That nobleman, who never suffered a good office to be long unreturned, soon after procured him to be commissary general [sic] to the expedition then preparing to attack the French West Indian islands'.[23]

Whatever the exact interconnection of these personalities and public employments might have been, it is not hard to imagine how Pay Office affairs were managed under the benevolently cynical guidance of Henry Fox. Yet to George Durant's credit, at the commencement of his adventures he had sound notions of how the public treasure and the rights of the humblest participants in the expedition *ought* to be protected; [*Journal*, 23 Dec 1758].

Failure at Martinique and the Reduction of Guadeloupe, November 1758–May 1759

There is no need to endorse uncritically the neat strategic framework devised, after the fact, by Sir Julian Corbett to appreciate that the expedition launched from Britain against the French West Indies in the autumn of 1758 represented a new departure in the Seven Years' War. In so far as an attack on the sugar island and privateering base of Martinique would damage French trade, hit their revenue and reduce their ability to fight, the objective was a traditional one, but the Pitt–Newcastle administration had more ambitious aims in view – a development of the general offensive that had recently resulted in the capture of Louisbourg (Cape Breton) and the opening of the River St. Lawrence. If Louisbourg was to be retained at the peace, then it became expedient to seize territorial bargaining points in the Caribbean, which later on could be set against the Mediterranean fortress of Minorca, lost in humiliating circumstances at the beginning of the war. If it proved difficult or impossible to bring this about, then there existed the fall-back position of inflicting maximum damage on French assets – robust tactics which appealed greatly to the planter inhabitants of the British-held islands, who had no desire to have their French neighbours competing with them, whether inside or outside of the Empire.[24]

Six regiments of foot were ordered on the expedition; the 3rd, 4th, 61st, 63rd, 64th and 65th, together with detachments from the 38th, long resident in the Leeward Islands. The little army was subsequently reinforced by Highlanders from the newly-raised second battalion of the 42nd Regiment, 300 or more slaves to do heavy duty as pioneers, 350 volunteers from Antigua, Montserrat and St. Kitts, while 700 Royal Marines and parties of seamen from the squadron occasionally participated in actions ashore. An artillery train was furnished by a company of the 2nd Battalion, the Royal Regiment of Artillery. Robert Beatson reckoned the actual striking force to be around 4,444 men.[25] It was more likely something over 5,000 strong, to which must be added the all-important naval landing parties.

After lengthy debate, command of the land forces was given to Major-General Peregrine Hopson, an experienced and distinguished regimental officer, who had recently served as governor and commander-in-chief in Nova Scotia. Arrived in the West Indies, however, it soon appeared that Hopson lacked the moral resources for such a challenging command: as Major-General John Barrington (his second in command) and Colonel George Haldane complained, Hopson neither listened to nor followed their advice, and never visited the forward positions.[26] His miserable death from a flux on 27 February 1759 was, as Durant's *Journal* reveals, unlamented in the army. It was fortunate that John Barrington, although occasionally crippled by gout, proved more than equal to the situation.

The naval armament, an amalgam of vessels sent out from home and the locally-based squadron, all under the command of Commodore John Moore, senior naval officer on the Leeward Islands station, eventually consisted of ten men-of-war, six frigates, four bomb-ketches, a sloop, a hospital ship and sixty or so transports, most of them, in the words of Sir John Fortescue, 'bluff-bowed old brigs which sailed like haystacks'.[27]

After an initial delay caused by bad weather, the expedition sailed from England on 12 November 1758, making contact with Moore at Barbados, the traditional base for English operations in the West Indies, on 3 January 1759. Initial attempts on Martinique between 15 and 19 January were thwarted, however, thanks to a combination of strong local resistance, atrocious terrain and formidable fixed defences. Accordingly, it was resolved to leave Martinique alone (the place would eventually fall to an expedition commanded by Major-General Robert Monckton and Rear-Admiral George Rodney in 1762), and proceed northwards to Guadeloupe, an even richer sugar island than its neighbour. For the moment, however, there was a powerful sense of frustration and humiliation aboard the fleet, as George Durant reveals [*Journal*, 19 Jan 1759]. In Robert Beatson's opinion, Martinique 'was not attacked as briskly as it ought, and brought no kind of credit to our arms'.[28]

Guadeloupe, sixty miles or so to the north of Martinique, actually consisted of two islands lying side by side and separated by a passage one hundred feet wide at its narrowest point. The western island, although mountainous and rugged, was known as 'Basseterre'. The town of the same name, with its citadel of Fort Royal, was the only settlement of real importance. The adjacent island, although flat, low and smaller in area, was known as 'Grandeterre'.

Lieutenant-Colonel William Cunninghame, Hopson's chief engineer, who was sent on ahead to look into Basseterre, at first considered the place to be impregnable. Commodore Moore, however, relied on the tactical doctrine that any fortification which could be approached to within about half a cannon-shot by the broadside of a British man-of-war was doomed. All day on 23 January Moore's warships pounded the French batteries; then, at dusk, his four bomb-vessels, *Infernal*, *Granada*, *Kingfisher* and *Falcon*, stood in for the shore. Throughout the night they hurled shells and carcasses into the town and citadel where, as Captain Gardiner aboard the *Rippon* observed; 'The Houses and Churches were every where soon in Flames, the Magazines of Powder blown about the Enemy's Ears, and the whole at ten o'Clock blazed out in one general Conflagration' – fuelled by immense quantities of rum and sugar stored in the town.[29] Moore, who at first seemed to have favoured just such a destructive operation, later stated that the bombs had set the town on fire contrary to his wishes. As it was, the place blazed all next day.[30]

Characteristically, Captain Gardiner summed up these terror tactics (which would be repeated in a holocaust of dwelling houses and sugar canes as long as the issue of the campaign remained in doubt) with the aid of a Latin quotation: '*Et circumtonuit gaudens Bellona cruentis*'.[31] The more impressionable civilian Durant, bereft of the turn of phrase which would have enabled him to cloak brutal reality in classical drapes, was appalled by the scale of the destruction. His breathless description of shattered and looted Basseterre and the havoc wrought aboard the fleet by the defenders' cannon is among the most striking passages of his *Journal*, and does him credit [*Journal*, 25 Jan 1759].

Even while the distressed inhabitants of Basseterre were being transformed into 'real Objects of Pity'[32] in the eyes of their conquerors, French soldiers and militia took up a strong position inland, defied General Hopson's summons to surrender, skirmished incessantly with the British outposts and waited for what Gardiner called 'the Disorders of the Climate' to do their deadly work. (A similar course of action had served the French very well when the English had attacked Guadeloupe without success in 1703).[33] Durant himself became intermittently quite seriously ill: poor stalemated Hopson fell sick and died. John Barrington, taking over the command, found himself in 'a very delicate Situation'. Six hundred sick had already been sent away to Antigua, and there were 1,649 more waiting to be embarked. On 2 March 1759 he could only muster 2,796 men fit for duty, and when the necessary camp guards and reliefs were deducted, this only left him a tiny army fit to march against the enemy.[34]

Barrington's solution to his difficulties was to exploit the sea-borne mobility of his forces by carrying on a war of detachments – forcing the French to disperse their troops to defend threatened points around the coast, yet achieving decisive superiority wherever his two most energetic brigadiers, John Clavering and Byam Crump,[35] put ashore to ravage their settlements, destroy their goods and impound their slaves.

On 1 May 1759 the French capitulated on generous terms and after their earlier hardships they prospered greatly under British rule until the Peace of Paris in 1763, when Martinique, Guadeloupe and the nearby island of Marie Galante, which had been occupied in late May 1759, were all restored to the French Crown.

Durant's concluding entry records that he was 'Still Sick but rather mending' [*Journal*, 30 May 1759]. When his illness allowed, he explored the island and socialized more than a little; he made a duty visit to neighbouring Dominica to raise funds and creditably performed his twin tasks of disbursing subsistence money to the regimental paymasters and making up his accounts. With hindsight, two cryptic entries might lead us to infer that he had begun to contemplate, if not actually to explore, techniques of enriching himself over and above the customary perquisites of his appointment [*Journal*, 18 & 21 Feb 1759].

Looking back on these events some years later, Thomas Lyttelton maintained that the success that had attended the expedition, '. . . together with the regular profits of [Durant's] appointment, placed him in a situation, with respect to fortune, with which, it may be imagined, he was more than satisfied; and I have been told, that he looked no farther'.

Durant was active in the islands to the close of 1759 or early 1760; raising money for the garrison, liquidating debts at five per-cent commission and perfecting those arts of financial obfuscation which would shortly put him on a par with the masters of his craft.[36]

George Durant's Later Career, 1759–1780

George's intimate *Journal* reveals that he kept in touch with 'my Dst. E.', presumed to be Elizabeth Lyttelton, during the campaign and that for a time at least he received letters from her [*Journal*, 4 Feb 1759], but the pair were not to be reunited, even though Elizabeth and George Lyttelton formally separated in the summer of 1759. Lord George suspected that besides her liaison with Durant, Elizabeth had exchanged love letters with an Italian opera singer and had flirted with a naval officer, but he could obtain no proof of either, so their separation was amicable. Lady Lyttelton lived on for another thirty years, coolly drawing £600 per annum from the Lyttelton estate.[37]

Meanwhile, far from being deterred by his first taste of warfare in the Caribbean, George Durant solicited and obtained from Henry Fox the appointment of Deputy Paymaster to the great armament sent against the Spanish fortress city of Havana, Cuba, in 1762. Fox promised Durant that he could remain with the army throughout the campaign, informing Lieutenant-General Lord Albemarle, commander designate of the land forces, that it would not be worth George's while to undertake the employment on any other terms.[38]

Durant returned from Havana a very rich man, a change in circumstances he never tried to hide – quite the reverse in fact. In 1764 he purchased the estate of Tong Castle, Shropshire, from the Duke of Kingston and rather than demolishing that decayed edifice he extensively restored and renewed it, the word *castle* being, as Thomas Lyttelton sarcastically put it, a 'sounding word'.[39] He built a fine town house in Portman Square, became an officer in the Shropshire Militia and was elected MP for Evesham in 1768, holding the seat until 1774. He married a Quaker girl of eighteen, daughter of the London merchant Mark Beaufoy, rather than the lady of noble title and great connections which Thomas Lyttelton, with all the detestation that a member of the landed élite could summon up for a monied upstart, thought would be most appropriate for the gothic pile at Tong.[40] George Durant died on 4 August 1780.

In an important article in the *Journal of the Society for Army Historical*

Research in 1954 T.H. McGuffie estimated that something like £300,000 in public funds had passed through George Durant's hands during the Havana expedition, speculating besides that he had profited from the administration of the immense sums of prize money allotted to the army after the conquest. Such was the mortality among the troops (largely the result of disease) that only a small proportion of them survived to claim their share – a splendid chance for pickings, as Sir Lewis Namier concluded in his biographical notice on Durant for *The History of Parliament*. Yet the precise origins of Durant's riches are likely to remain a puzzle.[41]

On the personal side, tantalising evidence survives of Durant's increasingly strained relationship with the Lytteltons. During May 1762 he travelled to Jamaica, where Lord George's brother, William Henry Lyttelton, was now Governor, to investigate the tardy recruitment of slaves to labour for the Havana army. Thomas Lyttelton believed that Durant had threatened to create difficulties at home on this matter, and that this in turn had caused his father, the head of the Lyttelton clan, great unease.[42] It would appear that the Lytteltons' former client, creature and thwarted swain was now in the process of emancipating himself from their control and biting the hand that once had fed him. He would shortly build a country residence fit to rival Hagley itself. 'That George should have been elevated to a situation wherein he could repeat what was called an insolent menace to one of the Lyttelton family', reflected Thomas Lyttelton, 'will never be remembered without much mortification, and therefore can never be forgiven'.[43]

2

The Journal of George Durant, 10 October 1758–30 May 1759

10th. October
1758   Appointed Deputy Paym^r. by Mr Fox.

19th.   Spent in Counting my Money in the City, & in pre-
20th.   paring necessaries for my voyage[1]

21st.   Set out from Town at 5 o'Clock with several Friends & lay at an infamous Inn at Kingston [upon Thames].

22^d.   Dined at Godalmin[g] & there parted with a heavy heart from my very honest Friends Powell & [Fowler?].

23^d.   Arrived at Portsmouth – was press'd to draw upon the Paym^r. for £300 [–] flatly denied, & had my refusal approved of – also ship'd my money.

24th.   Came on board the St George[2] wth. Genl. Hopson[3], the Masts & riging were man'd, a Band of Musick was playing & we were received with three loud huzzas.

25th.   Fell down to St Helens[4] & in the evening sailed – painfully parted with D^r. [HF?].

26th.   A vast swell of Sea & every appear^{ce}. of foul Weather.

27th.   The Storm begun – run hard for Torbay, but the wind meeting us in the Teeth were drove back & forced from every other Port.

28th.   Both Wind & Sea increased, our head got loose & our Mast gave way – the land appeared close to us, several

Wrecks past by & the Officers were apprehensive of Danger – In the Evening we had much Rain & soon after the Wind decreased, the Sea abated its Swell & the Sky lightened & seem'd to promise fair Weather.

29th. The Whole day fine & in the Evening returned to St. Helens.

30th. Went to Portsmouth – lodged on the Parade – lived a retir'd life & continued on Shore without any remarkable Event 'till Saturday the 11th of Novr. 1758.

Novr. 11th. Came on board the 2^d. time at Spithead & lay that Night at Anchor.

12th. Set Sail with little wind & in mild weather.

13th. Fine weather continued & we got on moderately.

14th. Reach'd Plymouth – lay to for the Transports coming out – saw them under sail thro' a glass & got on our way with a tolerable fair wind.

15th. A High Sea & rough Wind – The Genl. & most of His Officers Sea Sick.

16th. The weather Mild – the Ship rather steadier[,] the wind against us & sickness still prevailing.

17th. A Dead Calm – saw several Fish on the surface of the Water (called Bluber)^5 which is held a certain sign of a Storm. In the Evening a fresh gale – drove back from Lizard point to [Falmouth].

18th. Wind Contrary – sea high – weather cloudy cold, dark & rainy – lost sight of most of our Transports & spoke to a [Falmouth] Privateer who gave us Intelligence of 6 Ships of the line & four Frigates being sailed out of Brest in order to intercept us.

19th. The wind blew Hurricanes, the Sea roll'd mountains high, the day dreadfully dark, & the heavy cloud that hung over us pour'd down Cataracts of Rain – the Ship loosen'd her head, we sprung our fore-Mast & split our main Sail – the Weather still threatening & the Transports being unable to keep at Sea, the Fleet tack'd about & sail'd for Torbay.

20th. Toss'd to & fro in the Channel – in the Evening a fair wind & moderate weather.

21st. A Sunshiny day, the wind favourable but very gentle so that with crowding all our Sails we made but little Progress.

22^d. Got off Sylla [*sic*] at the Mouth of the Channel – fair weather & all the Cabin in high spirits – M's[6] excellent stories revived [memories] of the Family at the Hawldene [–] of his Robin Hood Orations & of his facetiously eating up the kind Presbiterian's Pudding [.] Saw arrogance properly punished & Impudence herself forced to hide her face.

23^d. A Strong S. Wind & rough Sea – the Transports being unable to bear against it, we changed our Course, & made for Ireland.

24th. Weathered Ireland, the Wind & Sea exceedingly violent, some little rain, a heavy Fog, the Transports dispersed & upwards of thirty missing.

25th. More rain – drove to Leeward of the Fleet, foul weather as before, & but 20 Transports in Sight.

26th. A dreadful Night & most dismal day, the Ship in constant violent motion, & the Sea beyond description – rough & Stormy.

27th. The Morning black & rainy, in the Evening a strong gale & at Night a Calm – the Swell of the Sea immense, the ship roll'd incessantly, & all the furniture in the Cabin broke several times from their Lashing & before they could be secured some [of] the Gentlemen were hurt & many of the chairs broke to pieces – lay a third Night sick & sleepless expecting to lose our Mast or to be drove under water – the constant cr[e]acking of the Ship so loud as it was impossible to hear a person Speak at a yards distance & the very force of the Sea beating against our Stern, made the Cabin feel every instant as if it was shivering into Atoms.

28th.   At four in the Evening a fair Breeze [–] got under Sail with the appearance of good Weather.

29th.   A fine wind, went at the rate of seven Knots an hour – Obliged to lye to for two Frigates that bore down to us – Capt. Gambeer[7] came on board us, who informed the Genl. that he had taken a Dutch Merchantman laden with French goods from Martinico, but as they were not very rich & he did not chuse to weaken his Crew[,] with the Commodore's[8] approbation he let her go untouch'd: The Captain of her told Gambeer of our Destination, & assur'd him that the french had long expected us, & rather wated for us with impatience, as they had everything prepared for a warm reception & even held us cheap in point of Numbers: the Frigates that made to us were bound home-wards, were just come from a Cruize & in want of Provisions; by them we had an Opportunity of sending our antedated Letters to England – this day all the Transports came in Sight except two, which are supposed to be either lost or much damaged, as they were heard to run foul of each other in the Night when the wind blowed hardest; this I suppose was on the 25th. instant.

30th.   Fine weather & a fair wind & sail'd at the rate of 7 Knots 4 fathoms an hour, which is 181 Miles 5 fathoms in the space of 24 hours.

Decr.
1st.   Perpetual changing of winds & a low'ring day.

2^d.   Much Wind in the Night – in the morning an entire Calm & a high Sea – the Transports being widely dispersed, & not having weight to carry them thro' the Swell of the Sea were obliged to lay to [the] greatest part of the day, tho' the wind rose & blow'd fair at Noon.

3^d.   Sailed on moderately but were oblig'd to bring to for a Transport who sprang all her Masts by rolling – This accident happen'd to a Bomb & two other ships but the weather being fair we were not hinder'd much as the Men of War took them in Tow & they were refitted as they sail'd in Company with the Fleet.

4th.   Very dark & rainy – the wind coming one way & the swell another gave the Ship so much Motion that it was very seldom we could either stand or sit; this frequently was the Case, & as it deprived us of the pleasures not only of reading & writing, but even of Conversation, it made a Sea life, which God knows at best is bad enough, more abundantly uncomfortable.

5th.   A Strong fair Wind [–] sail'd upwards of 7 Knots an hour – saw a vast black Fish called a Grampus[9] which play'd about the Ship all Morning, & as often as it breathed above water threw up as much Steem as would rise from a large Furnace: the Figure of them is much like a Whale; they generally measure about 50 or 60 feet long, but as they roll about on the Surface of the Water & draw the Waves after them they appear considerably longer: it's not a Fish of prey & is of no value but for its Bluber of which it affords great Quantities: they are catched with an Harpoon & strong Rope in the same manner as a Whale, & have such vast force in their Tales that they will stave any Boat, or small Vessel by beating it against them; for this reason, whenever they are caught they always contrive to cut off their Tales before they pretend to draw them out of [the] water.

6th.   Fine Winds & Weather – lived upon Deck – almost distanced by the Commodore tho' we sailed the whole day near Nine Knots an hour.

7th.   Perpetual Sunshine – found the Climate much warmer, the Sky a great deal clearer & the day above two hours longer than in England – Spoke with a Transport in distress & lay to while her Forces were removed to another Ship.

8th.   A still smooth Sea, little wind, a serene Sky & enlivening Sun.

9th.   Fair weather & sailed on prosperously.

10th.   All calm & quiet – spent the morning in no unpleasing retrospection & hear an excellent Sermon from the Captain's Chaplain.[10]

11th.   A fresh Gale & a dusky Sky – fell again in solitary reflections & suffered my reason to be bewildered & my Spirit oppressed by inquiring too far & by indulging certain passions which tinge our every action & temper the very Soul.

12th.   Reached the Latitude of the Madeiras, & fell in with the Monsoons or Trade winds – read myself Ill & Stupid, walked afterwards 'till I could hardly stand & afterwards Composed my weary mind & body on the Captain's Couch.

13th.   Little wind & the weather close & Sultery.

14th.   Fresh breeze but excessive hot – writ a Long Letter to the General tho' very unfit for the employ, as I was rather sick with the heat & had several little Fits of the Headache.

15th.   A glorious wind & day but excessive hot – made the Ship Comfortable by putting up her awning, which is a very commodious & handsome kind of Canopy, which is stretched over our heads about 9 feet from the Deck, & secured from the violent heat of the Sun; a Covering in the same Nature goes the whole length of the Ship, so that it not only keeps us from the Sun, but occasions a most refreshing & constant draught of air, which I believe is not less agreeable than healthy.

16th. Nothing Material[,] the wind Continuing & heat sensibly increasing.

17th. Went to Prayers & turned sick with heat – hear'd a Weak Sermon from a Weak Divine[11] whose ignorance nothing could equal but his Impudence – retired to my little Office in [a] dudgeon, & ruminated much on the Cruelty of the World, who unjustly stigmatize & ridicule a whole Order of valuable & worthy men, because there are some few such assuming <u>Illiterate</u>, such mere unmeaning Rants, such gorging Priestly Cubs, & very Calibans in Orders.

18th. Rose by six – had my Cott cut down at that hour by one of the Lieutenants upon guard, a very droll, but a most extraordinary young Fellow, whose Character I shall hereafter mention. The morning dark, but very warm – at twelve we pass'd the <u>Tropicks</u>, & I began to consider myself in another world <u>divided</u> from my Dst. E by every Element, where no blind believing Man has fix'd in his Weak Barrier, but where a whole Ocean Rolls between us, & the very Heavens interpose –

19th. A wet close Foggy day, writ & read from morning to night, & by that means kept myself from the horrors, which I seem'd much inclined to, & the weather greatly incouraged.

20th. Little air & a burning Sun, in y^e. evening the Commodore, Genl. Barrington[12] & Col^o. [Clavering][13] came on board; also Capt. LaCras[14] & sev^l. other officers paid the same Compliment to the General.

21st.   Brought to at 7 in the morning when a signal was made for all Masters of Transports to come on board the Commodore – all the Fleet drew up together, & we had a little levee of officers from 8 to 12:- [I] saw this day a Multitude of Flying Fish pursued by Bonetos[15]; the Flying fish is very small & but an indifferent swimmer, so that whenever he is in danger from the Boneto, he takes to his wings & flies as long as they are wet, which generally carry him about 2 or three hundred yards; the Boneto is of a silver white (the same Colour as the Flying Fish) & but very little bigger, so that when ever the one takes to his wings the other, to see which way he flies, makes vast jumps above water, but before he can get up with him, the flying Fish has wet his wings & is ready for another flight; In this manner they skim above the surface of the water 'till the one is taken, or the other wearied in the pursuit.

22d.   Very hot, no wind but several dense Fogs & more Showers of Rain – about 4 o'Clock the Weather cleared[,] the sky brighten'd & we had a gentle Breeze; as we sail'd along I was greatly surprized & entertained with the sight of a Dolphin that kept playing about the Ship above an hour, in the most sociable & agreeable manner; Its Colours are the brightest I ever beheld & its shape perfectly Corresponds with its other beauties & not only exceeds what I have ever seen, but whatever I could have conceived or believed from description or Relation; Its head, as low as its Gills, is chiefly Yellow with many <u>long shades</u> of different browns about the opening of the Mouth, & an infinite Number of small spots of various colours beautifully interspersed: from the head, almost down to the Tale, is of a pale but dazzling blue, not unlike the back of a Kingfisher when <u>fresh killed</u> or the extreme flame of Sulpher the first moment it is lighted; the sides are also streaked with different Colours & have small spots of a deeper blue, red & brown running down the streaks; from the lowest Finn to within about an Inch of the Tip of the Tale is a Clear green, but where it breaks from the Back the green is very dark but grows lighter & lighter 'till you seem to see [through] it; the Finns & the Tip of the Tale, which is Forket like a swallows is absolutely transparent; the little prickley Fibres of which are of a deep Coral red & the sort of web between of a pale Pea bloom with a distinct regular row of crimson drops running down the Middle of every Web: each side of its belly is of an amber yellow, & all the rest of the brightest white – Either these Dolphins must be of <u>Sea Mens creating</u>, or else the Ancient Printers have done them cruel Injustice for the Picture they are pleased to give of them really no more resemble <u>them</u> than a whale or a Lobster; I wish I had the skill of my D^r. E in drawing & then what my Pen cant describe my Pencil should express: But yet, I hope, a greater pleasure will be mine, that of <u>seeing one by degrees</u> brought to light under my Directions –

23^d.   Hard Rains – lay awake the whole night dying with heat & saw a very ridiculous unmeaning vision, which hardly consisted of anything else, but a Mans deliberately walking into the Cabin, directly making for my Cott & then feeling for something in my waistcoat Pocket which lay upon a table by my Bedside: he took nothing out but look'd steadfastly in my Face & then turned from me, mighty unconcern'd & marched off as leisurely as he came in: all this time I was leaning with my elbow on the pillow, most certainly with my eyes open[,] for about two Minutes before I had taken a Pencil from my Pocket, & writ several words upon the wainscoat that was near me, for it was light enough to write or read anything. That such a Figure was really in the room I no more believe than that the Pope was there, but that such a Vision entered my brain with my

understanding waking is as certain as I am now living: I
was not at all surprised at the Sight or disapearance of
this Gentleman, nor have I dwelt upon it a Moment
since, as I must either attribute it to a disturbed
Imagination, or to the influence of a Superior Being; if
the one, without any meaning at all, if the other with a
certain Meaning beyond human Comprehension: my
chief reason for summarising it is that I may remember
it & observe whether this <u>visible Dream</u> bears the least
affinity to any future accident, or has the most distant
relation to any one circumstance that may happen
hereafter:- at Eleven this morning I was present, will
you believe it, at the Disciplining of two Marines,
whose Crimes were by no means equal to the severity
of their Punishment, the one having only sold his
allowance of Wine, & the other having defrauded the
Purser[16] of a few ounces of Tobacco: For these, their
first offences, in spite of the most affecting Prayers, [&]
earnest Intreaties, were they in a manner suspended by
their arms, & received twelve strokes each upon their
naked Shoulders with that dreadful Instrument of
cruelty a Cat o'Nine Tales: If the Cap[t].[17] had had a
spark of generosity or one grain of humanity he surely
would have remitted one half of their punishment, but
instead of this he cried out every moment for them to
be struck harder, & threaten'd the Executioners, who
seemed disposed to lenity, with the same punishment,
tho' he saw in the Countenance of these poor Sufferers
the strongest Expressions of the utmost torture: nor
were these violent strokes, every one of which sunk into
their Flesh, the worst of their punishment for their
backs were afterwards beathed in brine to prevent a
Mortification & stanch the Blood. Surely this severe
correction for such trivial offences cant be right; it may
make them more secret in their petty Frauds but not
prevent them, & I should imagine it would either push
them to greater Crimes when they know that if they

should chance to be detected their punishment cant well be severer: If a Soldier is so hardened of heart & so corrupt of Morals, as neither to be won upon by mild usage, nor corrected by a sense of Shame, stripes will have little affect, & be no longer had in rememberance than while the smart [remains] upon his Sholders. The subtle Minister that preys upon his Country to feed his vices & support his luxury is seldom, very seldom, disgraced, but often loaded with honors; while the Soldier that hazards his life, ruins his health, & spends his very Marrow in the defence of our Liberties is wantonly put to torture for the disposing of <u>his own</u>, or for taking what custom has made essentiall to his very being, & what thro' poverty he was not able to Purchase. The Capt. who <u>sentenced them to my knowledge</u> [has] defrauded the Public; & the Purser, <u>who complained</u>, daily robs the Ship's Crew of one fourth of their provisions & cheats them enormously ten thousand other ways: Yet these are the wretched who are our rigid dispensers of Justice, who unfeeling stand by to direct the Scourge & in a manner triumph at their right of [inflicting] that Exquisite Miserey, which they themselves have more abundantly deserved. Surely such barbarities cannot go unnoticed! – Injustice may indure for a time, but the hour of redress, methinks, is now at hand, when the poor Sufferers shall rejoice & these inhuman Workers of Injustice receive their reward & experience those bitter agonies themselves, which, with every Circumstance of Agrevation, they have inflicted on others –

24th. A fine day & a fresh wind – attended the Service of the Church but profited little, being offended at the awkward unbecoming Indolence of one Chaplain, who read Prayers; & not a bit better pleased with the affected Airs & indecent Inattention of the other, who Preached: kept most of the day close to my office &

[thought] at least, with the Moralist, that I am never less alone than when by <u>myself</u>; but this joy is by no means perfect, for so long as I am absent from my E, I seem divided from <u>myself</u>: how blest will be that hour, when this joy is entire, & hands as well as hearts are united! –

25th. The day clear & fine, the wind fresh & the air Comfortable – retired to my office & kept my Christmas day in London, where I usually kept it, & felt unspeakably happy – may my O[wn] L[ove] see many returns of this Season, & may Heaven reverse our Fate that I may <u>really</u> be present at all! –

26th. Fine weather – M[orse?] in great disgrace but by common consent returned from Coventry.

27th. Saw many Nameless Fish – walk'd much upon Deck with Mr Holmes[18] & heard a short history of his Travels.

28th. Writ all day – had a little head-ache – blunder'd often thro' absence, & at last grew mightily dissatisfied with myself.

29th. Began to be in Charity with myself – was <u>pleased</u> with what before <u>displeased</u> me, & healed myself with reading a Letter from my Dst. E.

30th. Began sorting my Money & found it short of which I expected.

31st. Heard an old Sermon from a young Divine who made bad Doctrine appear worse by an ungracefull Delivery.

Jan^{ry}. 1st. Rose early [–] prayed particularly for my D^r. E & 1759 wished her, with an over flowing heart, many, very many returns of happy years –

2^d. Went thro' two Chests of small silver, was horridly fatigued, but [thought] myself rewarded, as I found several curious little Coins, which I reserved for my E.

3^d.

A hot close Morning, rose before 6, was refreshed by a cooling Shower [–] at 8 the Panther[19] (who went ahead of the Fleet) discovered Land [&] hoisted her Colours – Received Orders from the General to prepare myself for going to shore, as soon as we came to Anchor, in order to consult the Governor of Barbadoes[20] upon several Occasions relative to my business – at four in the Evening came to an Anchorage in Carlisle Bay – went immediately with Capt. Townsend[21] to the Governor [–] was Saluted as we pass'd thro' the Fleet & received wth. the utmost civility. Had letters of particular recommendation to the Treasurer of the Island & the Collector of the Customs, who lived in Bridge Town & entertain'd us with the greatest Magnificence. Saw nothing but one continued Scene of Inchantment some little acco^t. of which, when I am more at leisure, I purpose to mention, being at present entirely taken up with Consultation with the Genl. & the Regimental Paymaster[s] & in making out various Forms of Business.

4th.

Came on board the St. George from Shore, found a Levee of officers & with the Genl. who held a Council of War, much fatigued with my hurries on Shore, & fully employed in perpetual Computations.

5th.

Rec^d. Warrants for paying the Troops, & [was] confined to my office the whole day.

6th.

Continued my payments & got thro' most of my hurry.

7th.

Unexpected Pay^{mts}., which kept me entirely to business – went on shore for an hour in the Evening – saw the Church & the Negro's Festival.

8th.

Rec^d. Orders for paying the Genl. & Staff Officers [–] obliged to stay on board tho' all the Troops were landed & the whole Island collected together to see them. The inhabitants of this small Island are computed at 120,000, tho' it measures only 24 miles long & about 19 broad.

9th.   Kept on board the whole day & employ'd as usual.

10th.   Went to see the Troops land on the Beech near Barbados, where all the Ladies of the Island were assembled, & some 1000 Negros.

11th.   In the evening on shore where I bought all the <u>first Fruits of</u> the Island for my E [–] nor did I forget my Father for whom I procured with great difficulty a large vessell of Spirits, which I hope will agree with him better than the horrid hot Spirits he usually drinks.

12th.   All agreably surprised by a Detachment of Highlanders from L^d. J^{no}. Murray's Roy^l. Reg^t coming in.[22] Paid 'em their Subs^{ce}., & found Maj^r. An.[23] had obtained the Command: in great confusion all Morning, having much to do, & unfortunately at that time had both my offices pulled down to make ready for action. Left Letters with Mr Husband, Secretary to the Island, for England – supped at Mr Caddells & took leave of his Familly.

13th.   At Eleven this Morning Sailed from Barbados & heard by Accident of a rich worthy name sake, who lived about 7 Miles in the Country, & is not less famous for the Evenness of his Disposition & honesty of his heart than for the beauty of an only Daughter, who will inherit her Fathers wealth, as she possesses & gives lustre to all his Virtues. Left him my Comp^s. & promised to pay him a Visit if I returned to the Island.

14th.   At 8 saw the Island of S^t. Lucia near Martinico, & in the Evening sailed along the Mountainous & fertile shore of Martinico.

15th.   Came into the Bay at one o'Clock & were Fired upon from Pidgeon Island[24] & several other Forts: the Wind falling off our Ships were forced to Leeward, & only tack'd about the Bay without any intention of coming to an Engagement: Many of the Transports bearing near the shore, the Inhabitants were apprehensive we were going to Disembark, & kept a smart firing from all the Forts the whole Night, tho' I believe none of their Shot took plaice, for as we saw all their Shot drop short in the day time, I suppose we took care, in some degree, to measure the distance, & just to keep out of reach.

16th.   Exactly at Eight the Bristol[25] (Capt. Leslie)[26] bore down & came to anchor against Port Niger,[27] & in 40 Minutes pour'd in such dreadful broadsides as drove all the Men from their Quarters, dislodged the Battery, & scoured all the Country round about; he then Mann'd his Boat[s] with Marines, who row'd to shore under Cover of his Cannon, struck the French Colours, & hoisted our own: At nine the Woolich[28] came down upon another Fort, behind which was a large Magazine & strong intrenchments, & after he had engaged it about 10 Minutes the Winchester[29] & Roebuck[30] came down & anchored by him & for about half an hour they all kept up a constant, dreadful & most distructive fire, so that at last their Batteries were knocked down[,] their intrenchments deserted & their Magazine blown up: all the rest of the morning the several ships kept firing as they saw occasion & parties came near them, & at four Two Brigades[31] landed between the Fort we had demolished, without the least Disorder, loss, or opposition. The First Fort consisted of 8 Two & Thirty Pounders, & about 100 Men; the last of only 4 Thirty Two Pounders but of 1,000 Men; the Cannon were left spiked & the men flew up into the woody Mountains & carried their killed & wounded along with them.

17th.   At 6, the third Brigade[32] landed & joined the other

Troops, who were then marching up some rising ground in order to get possession of an advantagious spot, which at the same time would be commodious for a camp, secure a free & easy passage to our Fleet & over-look that stupendous & threatening Pile Fort Royal;[33] the French seem'd sensible of the Consequence of this Point & had posted large bodies of irregulars in every pass so that our Troops could not March 10 paces without considerable loss, nor did our firing in Platoons do much Execution, as the Enemy were not only hid & secured by large Trees, thick Bushes & Plantations of Cane but had also thrown up Entrenchments which were imperceptable to us & with some loss & the utmost Difficulty forced: These Difficulties surmounted we gain'd the Summit, drew up several Field Pieces & Mortars & turned the one against the Woods, & the other against the Neighbouring Villages & Plantations of Sugar Cane; by which means the woods were Scower'd & the whole Island in a bright Blaze, for all the Houses are built with Wood, & the Canes burnt like Pitch, so that wherever a shell dropt, a fierce Flame & immense Columns of bloody smoak instantaniously succeeded: thus everything went prosperously 'till the heat & fatigue o'erpower'd our Troops, & they had gained more ground than they were able to maintain from want of numbers: When the French perceived this they redoubled their vigour & pour'd [in] fresh Forces, so that when the night came on it was thought adviseable to re-embark our Troops; this was accomplish'd about 8, with great regularity, & without any loss, tho' the Enemy took possession of the Ground they had left, & for a considerable time kept firing upon us. The loss on our side was about 60 killed & near 200 wounded.

18th. Came to a Resolution of leaving Port Royal & attacking St. Pierres,[34] & set sail accordingly.

19th. Arrived at S^t. Pierres, which is a most beautiful Town situated by the side of the Sea – one Ship attack'd <u>three Forts</u>, while <u>three</u> Bombs were looking into the Town which in two hours they might have reduced to ashes; In the Evening [we] politely left the Place undemolish'd, & set sail for Gardaloup – affairs began to look very mysterious & horridly villainous, & the more I saw or Inquired, the greater reasons I found for noble Contempt, just Disapprobation, & unavailing Discontent Sorrow & resentment! –

20th. A dead Calm, at Night a Slight Breeze, which gave us some little life tho' nothing could raise our Spirits after shamefully turning our Backs on that glorious happy Island, which, had our Courage & Conduct been equal to our force, most certainly must have been ours.

21st. Sailed close by the Shore of the Island of Dominico – 'Tis, or ought to be, a Neutral Island[35] but the french have lately made large Settlements, & are in reality its haughty Masters; the rest of the Inhabitants are Chiefly Indians, tho' there are scatter'd up & down a few English, or more properly a few Creole Familys, but I believe even they are entirely Frenchafied & therefore no Friends to our Interest.

22^d. Sailed by three small Islands, thinly Inhabited called the Saints[36], & saw at a considerable Distance the sight of Gardaloup directly before us – in the Evening fetch'd the Harbour & prepared for action, but the Winchester, who was sent before to reconoitre the Coast, not being able to come up 'till late, we were obliged to desist, but most of the Captains received Orders for Battering the Town & Forts as soon as it was light the Next day: The St. George being included in these orders Genl. H & all his Officers left the Ship & came on board Captain Randall[,][37] Commodore of the Transports.

23^d.

At break of Day the Signal was made for Seven Men of War, first & 2 rates to form a line of Battle & bear down against the Forts [–] this was done with the greatest regularity & exactness, & as they all kept an equal Distance from each other, & sailed a direct line, it afforded a most Noble Prospect to us, tho' a most dreadful one to the Poor Inhabitants of the Island: As soon as they perceived we were beginning to attack, many of the Religious broke from their Convents & flew up into the Mountains, the Peasants drove their Cattle from the shore, the Slaves were removing their little Properties & the Planters raised Fires along the Hills, collected all their Force, & either thro' wild Despair or in the vain hope of terrifying our Fleet, Crowded along the Shore, & in vast numbers pour'd into the Forts. The Town (which has a fine appearance from the Bay) soon catched the alarm, & in order to keep us at a Distance, set Fire to 8 of their Vessells which lay in Harbour, & let them [drift] amidst the Fleet: but this availed them little as we had sea room enough to keep ourselves clear & came to a close Anchor about Nine o'Clock From that hour 'till Seven at night most of the ships were engaged & the Island seemed to shake & the very Seas to roll back at the perpetual thunder of opposing Cannon; after the first Broadside the ships themselves were hid, & the Town[,] Cittidel & Forts were either constantly enveloped in curling clouds of Smoak, or in flashing Sheets of Fire. At 7 all the Batteries were silenced except that from the Cittidel, which still kept playing upon two of our first rates that lay against it: as soon as it grew dark four of our Bombs sailed in & threw a vast number of Shells into the Town & Fort which intirely finish'd the work as it set the one on fire, threw the other into Confusion & put the Enemy to Flight. Our loss this day was pretty Considerable, tho' by no means as great as it might have been expected in so long & so

warm an Engagement, for out of all the Ships we had
not more than 150 killed & 200 wounded During the
heat of the action a Lieu[t]. with a party of Sailors row'd
close to the Beech, & cut from their Moorings thirty
eight Sail of Privateers & French & Dutch
Merchantmen; amongst the latter was a Ship
completely leaden with Sugars supposed to be worth in
Sterling £1,000: this was carefully brought off, all the
rest had holes bored throw them & turned a drift to
Sea: by this precaution probably our Fleet was Saved,
for 'tis thought it was the fix'd resolution of the
Owners to have set them all on fire & then to have
drove them amongst our Fleet in the dead of night.

24th.   Rose before it was light & beheld the very shocking
Sight of twenty Shells & Carcasses blazing thro' the air
at once, while at the same time [the] greatest part of the
Town was wrapt in the fiercest flames:- The Garrison
seeming to be Evacuated & the Town Deserted[,] the
Signal for landing was made about four o'Clock, which
was immediately obeyed & happily affected without
any Disorder or the loss of a single Man.

25th.   Waited upon the General on shore & wandered [the]
greatest part of the day, thro' one Continual scene of
wide Desolation; The Shore for a mile in length was
covered with the ruins of Houses & with vast Beams of
burning Timber; the Streets were in the same
condition, the Trees, which run on each side the
Streets & afforded once a most grateful shade, were
strip'd of all their honours, had only their mere Trunks
& a few Straggling Branches remaining, which were
burnt as black as Charcole, & were every instant falling
upon your head; the Ground was covered with glowing
Ashes & in many places scorched your feet in so violent
a degree that it was impossible to pass; in several
Streets the mere Shells of the Houses remained while a
dreadful blaze from burning wines, spirits &c was

issuing from every Door & Window; in one part of the
Town (where the Merchants kept their valuable
Liquors in vaults) the pavement was absolutely red hot,
& in others where the Warehouses stood you was often
intercepted by Streams of liquid Sugar, which
generally run about 50 or 60 yards & appeared like
o'erflowing Rivers of melted Pitch:- the only Building
of Consequence which I found intire was the Church,
which indeed had a grand appearance, notwithstanding
I saw it at great disadvantage, as it was covered with
Rubbish, & left in the utmost Disorder: The Isles [*sic*]
were full of Trophies & Relicks, the Pews were every
where scattered with Beads & Books: the <u>vesteries</u> on
each side [of] the Chancel, were a foot deep in Papers,
Prayer Books, Musick, wax Lights, massy Candlesticks
& ten thousand nameless Trinkets & all within the
communion rails was crowded with those gaudy trifles
which are held most sacred; so it was impossible to stir
a Step without trampling on the blessed Virgin Mary
or kicking before you a wooden apostle or a maimed
crucified Jesus. From this Strange Scene of Folly &
Confusion I went into the Suberbs of the Town, & was
there more sensibly affected with the real Miseries &
horrid ravages of a vigerous, & consequently of a
Destructive War. This Part of the Town had entirely
escaped the violence of the Flames, but unhappily was
almost as much destroyed by the barbarous plundering
& mischiefous wantonness of the Soldiery & Sailors.
The Streets, in general, were well built & very regular,
& the Houses lofty, commodious airy & spacious; those
few that were here of any sort of Fashion, were built of
Stone, & divided within into separate Apartments with
a single Deal board: the Shape of most of the rooms,
was Square, & those on the ground floor, which were
entirely for use, were paved with black & white
chequer'd Marble, [&] had carved & painted Roofs: &
the Sides were either whiten'd & covered with vast

looking glasses & an infinite variety of tolerable
Paintings, or else hung with Damask, or a sort of
unfigur'd Silk that to me wants a name: at the Back of
every House you have a long covered Gallery which
they call a Balcony; this always placed towards the Sea
for the Benefit of the Morning & Evening breeze &
usually o'erlooks a Romantick well-cultivated Garden
which sloops [sic] down to the Sea; & is full of little
white marble Boys & gods, which are placed at the
Brink of Spouting Basons of Water, or interspersed
amidst Fairy Groves of all those fragrant Ever-Greens,
which we so tenderly nurse in our Hot-Houses in
England: From hence I went the Cittidel which is not
only the largest, but the Strongest Fortification I ever
saw; It is situated on the Top of a vast Rock, which
rises about 200 feet perpendicular from the Surface of
the Sea; the Walls are about 8 feet high & 10 feet thick
& the Batteries are raised Bastion above Bastion so that
between the bottom & the Top there is not less than 7
tiers or rows of Guns; upon every Story or Platform,
there are several Circular Ridouts, each Ridout
containing from 5 to 12 Guns, those on the Middle
[ramparts] most of the way up, are Two & Forty
Pounders, but all the rest on the sides, are of every rate
from 9 to 36. In the whole Fortification I could find but
two Mortars tho' I counted (& agreed with an Engineer
who had the same Curiosity) 70 Embrasures & 80
Cannon. I suppose the Supernumerary 10 Guns were
reserved least [sic] any of the other should fly or be
dismounted, or perhaps were meant to erect a Batterie
in some other place as occasion might require: The
Garrison was well provided with Water, Stores &
Provisions, but all the Wells were Spoiled by their
throwing in their Dead, & no account can yet be given
of the Quantities of Stores. From the Garrison I stroled
about the neighbouring Country & took a slight Survey
of several adjacent Villas: but even here Rapine, Ruin,

wanton Cruelty & excelling Desolation had reigned
Triumphant: as soon as I came into the Garden, I
found the Shrubs torne up, the out Houses stained
with Blood, & strew'd with the warm carcasses of
Dogs, Cats, Pigs, Sheep, Goats & all sort of Domestick
Animals, which the Soldiers or Sailors had killed or
wounded & were not able to carry away, being leaden, I
am afraid, with richer plunder. Amidst this scene of
Murder & Confusion, were torne Parchments, bundles
of Linnen, Remnants of Silk, broken Drawers,
shatter'd looking Glasses, frames of Pictures, large
pieces of Japan & all sorts of Ornamental & Kitchen
Furniture thrown promiscuously about. The Rooms
within were in as great Disorder, as it was impossible
for you to move from place to place without treading
upon Rich hangings, heaps of Glass, broken Chinea,
Embroider'd Shoes, Children's Stockings, piles of
Books, Boxes of French & Italian Liquors broken to
pieces & swimming along the floor, with 10,000 little
pieces of elegant Furniture, which the Plunderers not
liking, or having taken enough of, had dashed against
the Pavement & shiver'd to atoms. Sick of such sights
of wretchedness I made again for the town, but every
Street bore some resemblance to what I have already
described, & there hardly a single House but what you
found blood before the Door & our Cannon Balls with
the wreck of their furniture lying in the Street. Quite
Dispirited & fatigued I hurried to the Beech, took a
boat & went on board y^e. St George, where I hoped my
mind would be more at rest & I should find some little
Comfort amongst a few of my Friends; but here too
Death had been Familiar & Horror prevailed, for it was
this Ship that lay against the Fort, & received the
greatest Damage, so that most of the men that were
kill'd in action & hurried over board with little or no
ballast, had rose again & were now swimming on the
surface of the Water; this struck me much; nor, when I

came on board, was I less affected, for the Quarter Deck was absolutely steep'd in blood & gore, & the Worthy Son of a Gentleman I knew, I hear'd was the first that fell, & was smashed to pieces by Cannon Shot.

26th.   Went again on Shore – spoke with the Gen¹. – found Mr B³⁸ had very gently taken Possession of my House; look'd for another & could find none so large so commodious, or so elegently furnish'd; however fix'd upon another & return'd on board the St George in the Evening.

27th.   Went to my Quarters at [Basseterre], where I fatigued myself greatly with doing nothing, & at last was forced to go to bed to be out of the way.

28th.   Rumaged all Morning – dined with Col⁰. Cunningham³⁹ & spent the Evening with Gen¹. Barrington.

29th.   Brought my Office on Shore, & with difficulty properly secured it – took a little huff at G[eneral].H[opson?]. & made a Stout & very virtuous Resolution.

30th.   Settled in my Quarters – heard of an Express going immediately to England, & sent several Letters by Capᵗ. Townsend, which I hope my Correspondents will like better than myself, otherwise I am very sure they will hardly have Patience to give them a reading: Grumbled much at being put in a hurry, & seem'd to lament nothing so much as my [sore] want of Brains.

31st.   Wandered from Church to Church, saw only one Picture that I liked & made a resolution to steal it & form'd my Plot accordingly.

[February]
1st. [1759] Cheated the centinel in the dead of night, got into the Church, scrambled up the walls[,] brought down my

Picture & carried it off without further Accident or Expence than a few broken Shins.

2^d.   Look'd about for fresh Plunder, but found I turn'd Robber just in time, for all the Churches were turn'd into Barracks for the Negros, & there was not a single thing left of Moveables, but what was unfit for every thing but fuel.

3^d.   In the Evening walk'd up to the Fort, where I saw an Engagement, between an English & French Party, over a vast Gully; tho' I had several Officers along with me, I could neither keep my Countenance nor hold my Tongue, for both Parties took pretty good Care to be out of <u>harms way</u>, & if a man had been kill'd on either side, I should have imputed it to nothing less than a Miracle. As I thought myself pretty Secure, I took the liberty of Standing upon the Ramparts, & undesignedly exposed myself to more Danger than any of my brethren for the French seeing a Red Coat upon the Walls got as near as they could & fired several shot, & I had the pleasure of hearing their Balls whistle <u>about me</u> tho' I am persuaded none of them could reach me by an hundred yards.

Quite out of conceit with myself & every body else [I] stroled up to this <u>Daring Party</u> of ours & that I might say hereafter that I once in my life pull'd Triger in Anger, I fired a shot at a <u>white jacket</u> I saw crawling on the other side of the Gully, & I verily believe that if the Muskit would have carried [but] <u>a mile farther</u> I should have kill'd my Man – or Woman. After I had observed their Situations, mark'd the ground, & from experience convinced myself they were not likely <u>to do one another prejudice</u> I [thought] proper to Decamp, & felt not a little happy that I was so much Master of my own time & actions, as neither to be forced to be childish at any bodys Will but <u>my own</u>, nor constrained to play the fool except I liked it myself.

4th.

At three o'Clock this morning we passed the Gully, I reconoitred the day before with 200 Men; out of which by strange Misconduct 135 were kill'd or wounded:- In the Evening went on board the Commodore,[40] & saw an unknown Ship, which I found was the Lancaster[41] just arrived from England; full of hopes of hearing from my E[,] I hurried to my Quarters, where I had the vast Satisfaction of receiving all the Letters she writ from H[agley?] supposing me at Portsmouth, & soon afterwards I fetched my Parcel which my D^r. L[ove] little imagined would be received at Basse Terre in Gardaloup.

5th.

Sorted my Letters from England, gave them a second reading, & disposed of them indorsed & numbered in a small Oak Box, with my name writ in Tin on the Top & the N°. 6.

6th.

Went up into the Fort as soon as it was light, to see several Detachments from our Reg^{ts}. take possession of two small Batteries that were perpetually firing upon every Party that went that way & also prevented our Fleet from watering; at first the resistance was trifling, but as soon as they had time to recover their Surprise & Collect their Forces, they boldly marched down to our Main body, that was cover'd by the Walls of the Fort, & even attack'd our Soldiers in their very Intrenchments: for this they must have suffer'd very considerably, for our Men reserved their Fire 'till they came within ten yards of them, & then kept up a constant fire in Platoons for about 15 Minutes, when the Enemy began to Slacken their Fire & to retreat towards their Intrenchments which were not more than a mile from ours: this they effected, for as the way was rocky & covered with Bushes, it was impossible for any Party of ours to intercept their retreat – Had we lost every Man we had we should richly have deserved it, for tho' we had been in possession of the Fort fourteen days, we had not a single Gun we could fire, for those that were left, we found by fatal experience, were unfit for use & ours were very providentially huddled together on board the Ordinance [*sic*] Vessells. This the Enemy must have been informed of as he approached by hundreds within Pistol shot of our main Batterie, & threw several Cannon shot & some 1000 Muskit Balls in or over the Fort: What greatly contributed to our success was the firing of some small Cohorns⁴² which were luckily left in the Garrison; these threw numberless Shells amongst them, & intirely clear'd one of their Batteries consisting of three Guns, which we spik'd, dismounted & threw down the rock, after which we fairly kept our ground while the Enemy appear'd, but when they flew to their Entrenchments, we retreated to the Fort, or dispersed to our several Encampments.

7th.   Kept House the whole day & heard of nothing done <u>so remarkable</u> as my <u>killing a humming Bird</u>.

8th.   Nothing done or likely to be done – thought much of our great Leaders, & their Noble Design, & at last closed my <u>brown Study</u> by reading the <u>Mountain in Labour</u>.

9th.   Rose early, breakfasted, Dined, Supp'd & went to bed; & in a manner lived <u>yesterday</u> over again, & pre-enjoy'd <u>tomorrow</u>.

10th.   Heard Men of sense <u>reason</u> like Idiots, & very Idiots <u>Act</u> like wise Men.

11th.   Built Castles in the Air, – supposed myself first Minister – made strange havock in the Navy & Army, & then sent half the force on this Expedition & took possession of Martinique.

12th.   Made a good wish without knowing it, put a poor Creature in Abrahams Bosom, & saw everything in a better Channel; – felt pleased at this imaginary Disposition, not only as it tended to the public good, but as it would serve an Interest & Income to myself, that would make my life easy & any Enemies, appear little & Contemptible.

13th. Writ to the Genl. & went to Sleep.

14th. Idled away the <u>morning</u> in doing business & at <u>night</u> pray'd heartily that Commanders might have more Brains or Paym^{rs}. more Patience.

15th. Read my Cash Book by way of amusement, – kill'd a flea in Wrath – spit Venom like a furye all the morning & in the Evening fell ill of a Flux.

16th. Bill[ious], Blister'd, Plagued & Purged to pieces – took nothing, went nowhere, amused the Mind, laughed at all these <u>petty Evils</u>, & by force of Spirits only got the better of my Disorder.

17th. <u>Made love</u> to a French Negress, & found a Black at Gardaloup & a white in Drury Lane differ'd only in Complexion, as their Sentiments & <u>winning ways</u> seem'd pretty much the same:- took my E still nearer my Soul & wished the mind only could form the Body & make the Person lovely, then would my Dst. L[ove] be more an Angel, & these impure Harbingers of Leudness, be as like the Brutes in Figure as in action.

18th. Hurried, [bustled], & broiled to Death – sent 5,000£ to Barbados, & paid it in such a way as saved the Public near Cent per Cent, as upon this Sum only I saved 2,331£: In that Island every thing goes by weight, & in all the rest by Tale[,] therefore I paid them by weight in such Coins, as would have pass'd by Tale <u>here</u> for half their value only.

19th. At home the whole day, where I had a particular acco^t. brought me of the success of our Troops on the other side of the Island, & of the utter Distruction of Fort Louis.[43]

20th.
Dined on board Cap[t]. Leslie, & put a Beast out of Countenance by improving a beastly speech.

21st.
Examin'd a hidden Treasure, made [a] most honest Proposal, & received a most rascally reply – grew tired of performing my Duty, as I found Officers in Trust had rather gain 5 shillings, & let the public lose 5 thousand, than see the public gain 5 thousand & they themselves nothing at all.

22[d].
General rejoicing for the taking of Goree[44] – the whole fleet was man'd & saluted the Fort, the Fort discharged all her Cannon, the Walls were lined & gave three Volies, each of which was returned with the greatest exactness from all the other Reg[ts]. in their several Encampments – this was done in the close of the Evening, & afforded a most dreadful sight to the Enemy who crowded down the hills in the greatest astonishment, & not only were witness of such awful Clouds of Fire, bursting all around them, but also saw four of their principal Forts blown up into the Air, with a blaze that reach'd the very heavens, & with an explosion that shook the very Island.

23[d].
Breathed at home without any one occurance or transaction in life that could make the day remember'd & convince me hereafter that I had lived.

24th.
Went to the Kings Auction[45] & bought some mere Books of amusement at a very extravagant rate; look'd over every thing in hopes of finding some one Lot that might be fit for my E but to my great Disappointment I saw nothing portable but arrant Trumpery.

25th.
Read Idle Books for want of better, & found I had no time to spare tho' I had nothing to do.

26th.   A Genl. Allarm – Great hurry & bustling at the Head Quarters & at Camp, occasion'd by the appearance of 50 Drunken Negros reeling out of the wood; – when we had muster'd all our Force together & stood for some two hours upon our <u>defence</u> the Allarm ceased & the Negros reel'd back again.

27th.   Disturb'd at 4 o'Clock when a Servt. came over to inform us of the Death of Genl. Hopson; – tho' I have no sort of connexion with him, nor had received any Favours at his hands, yet I could not help feeling much compassion for him & real concern for his very undeserving & worthless Familly: One great comfort to me was, that the Public had receiv'd no loss[,] for a Man so Weak & obstinate so self-partial, & self-interested, was never yet [trust'd] with so important a Command. Those who sent him have much to answer for, for it was as impolatic as it was wicked to put the lives of so many thousands into the hands of one who neither knew how to save them with credit nor to let them fall with honour.

28th.   Dined by particular invitation with our new Commander in Chief, was admitted into his Familly, & was received with all the marks of real Esteem & true politeness.

March
y^e. 1st.
[1759]   Receiv'd advice that a Ship was going immediately for England, – began the very laborious business of Copying all my vouchers & acc^{ts}., all [of] which I was obliged to go thro' myself, my assistant being wholly taken up with the affairs of the present & the Deceased General, & my Clerk[46] at the same time lying dangerously Ill with a Fever & a Flux.

2^d.   Writing Day & Night without either meat or drink.

3^d.   Finished my Abstract to my great Satisfaction [&] found everything right.

4th.

Order'd to leave money in the Garrison & to send more on board the Commodore [–] Conversed with the Captain on business & got into a wrangle designedly for the sake of exposing a Man to himself – In the Evening at Home & saw a French Spy carried to Execution.

5th.

With much difficulty & great hazard sent my Chief military Chest on board, & sat up the whole Night in Expectation of a boat that was promised me to carry all my things off before the Troops began to embark.⁴⁷

6th.

Brought into the greatest Distress by the forgetfulness of a Lieu^t. & by mere Chance & good Fortune preserved my Baggage, & perhaps saved myself from being taken prisoner, tho' I was obliged to leave several things behind, that were infinitely useful tho' not very valuable; Got off at last in a flat bottom'd boat⁴⁸ with the Troops & came safe on board Capt: Randall, but had my baggage scatter'd amongst several Transports.

7th.

Weigh'd anchor & set sail for Fort Louis – had an unusual Disorder in my head, & violent pains in my Bowells Breast & Back & at last fell down with the bloody Flux.

8th.

Terrible Griping – no appetite, no ease no Spirits no rest! –

9th.

Kept my Bed without a moments ease, without Sleep, without Sustenance.

10th.

Still in perfect Misery – at Night by great good fortune fell in with a Man of War which had been dispersed abroad, with the whole Fleet, & by chance made the same Tack – hail'd her, & got the Capt. to send his Surgeon on board, who gave me an Opiate wch. hush'd my pains for the present & put me to sleep.

11th.

Rose better, saw Grand-terre, & reach'd Fort Louis in

the Evening, close under which we ancher'd & had the pleasure of finding several Men of War had got there before us. Sent to the Physician Gen[l].[49] of the Army, who unluckily lay Ill of the same Complaint, but however he sent a proper Person to take care of me, tho' when he had the List of my Complaints he prescribed himself.

12th.   So low, & so weak, I was unable to speak or stand, however after Bleeding, Vomitting & Sweating I was obliged to take a Purge, which was very near putting an End to my Disorder & my life together.

13th.   Allowed to rest, as I took only composing Pills & Draughts – my Pains with my Complaint greatly abated but was seized with an ugly short Cough, which did not less hurt my health than affect my Spirits – hear'd of Nine Sail of the French Fleet off Barbados – completed all our Men of War with our Soldiers,[50] the General with his one half of Staff Officers came on board our Transport, & we the other were obliged to shift to the Rhuby.

14th.   Lost every Symptom of my Disorder, & was in danger of dying of nothing but hunger: The Commodore sail'd out of Harbour with every Man of War except the Roebuck, & two Transports, which were once Frigates, & which upon this Occasion he put into Commission.

15th.   Quite well but absolutely Starving, as nothing Solid had passed thro' my Lips during my Illness, & I had been obliged to fast two days before I embark'd thro' absolute Necessity [–] dined in Publick & enter'd upon business.

16th.   The Gen[l]. settled in the Roebuck, & we went on board the Exchange (the Rhuby being sent upon an other Service) – taken Ill with many Complaints all owing to the want of Perspiration & other Evacuations – went to

Doctor Brooke, did all that was advised, took medicines immediately but without any sort of effect.

17th.   Purged excessively – full of pain – my head Splitting, my heart aking, & my bladder bursting; void of all Comforts, without either Strength or Spirits, beraved [*sic*] of every blessing & almost lost to hope! – Settled all my affairs & began to think seriously & – not to fear Death, but to tremble for my E! – at Night used fomentations & under went several other disagreeable & painful Operations.

18th.   At two this morning everything had the desired effect, & I was relieved from a Burthen that was painful to bear; rose weak tho' easy & was well enough to go upon Deck to see an Engagement near Fort Louis from whence the Cannon did considerable Execution.

19th.   Settled in the Generals Family on board the Roebuck – low in Spirits, Ill in health, my head constantly aking & my Eyes much inflamed.

20th.   Grew worse – just shew'd myself at Dinner & lay in Darkness all the rest of the day.

21st.   A long & painful night – rose with Pains in every Limb, with my Eyes swell'd out of my Head, & in a burning Fever. – the Roebuck receiv'd Orders for joining the Commodore, therefore in this wretch'd Condition I was obliged to leave the Ship & come on board the John & Mary Transport.

22^d., 23rd., Burning in a Fever; fainting, raving distracted, blind!
24th., 25th., Raw with Blisters, wrack'd with Pains, plagued with
26th.   Fools & tortured by Barbarians –

27th.   Rose for an hour, refresh'd & almost kill'd with shifting – once more had the vast satisfaction of opening my Eyes, & of seeing the chearful light of day.

28th.   Much better, got up several times, & my Fever intermitting I began taking the Bark.[51]

29th.   Lived in the Cabin most of the day, took my Medecines regularly & found no returns of my Fever.

30th.   Very weak but mending – Our Fleet return'd from St Ann's & St. Stephens [*sic*],[52] & informed us of the Distruction of those beautiful places, & of the whole Country's being laid wasted for 14 Miles round about: the same day a party was Detached from Fort Louis, which scoured all the woods along the Coast for 4 miles, burnt every House, Leval'd several Intrenchements & Destroy'd Two Batteries of Cannon[,] One of 4 Eighteen Pounders & another of 3 two & thirty Pounders, which last were just brought with infinite labour about 15 Miles out of the country, were hid in a Wood, were charged & Direct[ed] upon our Fleet & Camp, & that very night were intended to play upon them: In this attack Capt. Gunning[53] was shot thro' the head & died universally lamented; his Person as well as Character was uncommonly amiable, & by his engaging Manner & manly behaviour, he not only made himself beloved in his own Corps, but gained the affection & admiration of the whole Army. At his interment there was not an officer in the Reg^t. nor a private soldier in his Company, whose face was not bathed in Tears – I knew this worthy Gentleman a little, & saw & admired his Extraordinary Qualifications; when I heard of his Death I thought myself happy that I did not know him better, for I was much affected even from a short acquaintance, & when I saw the becoming sorrow of his Friends, I could not help painting to myself the intolerable Misery of a beautious & virtuous Woman whom he had lately married & who had despised the Wordly [*sic*] Toys of Rank & Fortune, from her inviolable attachment to this most accomplish'd Soldier.

31st.   Ventured upon animal Food without suffering, walked upon Deck for the first time & enter'd upon business.

April 1st. Well, but low, dull & Faintly; tired myself with Cleaning,
[1759] & got into a poor dispirited way of thinking.

2^d. Not worse & no better, tired of a sick Cabin, & weary of my own thoughts; left my bed entirely, eat Moderately, & was persuaded to go into the World immediately.

3^d. A good Night & a quiet Morning; dressed with some difficulty & happily returned to my real Friends & old manner of life.

4th. Read writ & rambled from morning to night.

5th. A small relapse; – rather low tho' not dispirited; took fresh Courage from a mere trifle, & nursed myself with double diligence.

6th. Better, or at least fancied myself so; read without weariness, & work'd without fatigue.

7th. Went for the first time on Shore, & began a most pleasing work for my O[wn] L[ove], but had my Dst. E seen me I believe she would have been Angry, as I got wet from head to foot by the waves of the Sea beating against the shore, thro' my eagerness to Collect some Shells, which I fancied she would like, before the succeeding Waves carried them back again.

8th. Much better; kept chearful in a very dull day, & had an agreable Surprise by hearing from a very old Friend at S^t. Kitts.

9th. Rose by break of day, & went a[-]Shelling, fishing & shooting but with very little success.

10th. Hurried with business – writ the whole day, & from an absurd Anxiety lay awake all night.

11th. Finish'd my Payments, settled 1000 little Matters & enjoied a few hours of leizure peace & Satisfaction.

12th.   Still happily quiet – Made myself some work, & began it (as it was for my E) with my usual eagerness.

13th.   Went on Shore with Col[o]. Skene[54] to all the Advanced Posts, where we had the honour of having a 1000 Shot fired at us from the Enemy, tho' happily they all miss'd us tho' we hear'd every Ball pass us, & saw them Cut the Trees & Strike the ground above & below & on all sides of us – at last [we] took shelter under a miserable Breast Work raised with loose Stones, which the French, on the other side of a Gully, entrench'd up to their Chins, fired upon incessantly for above an hour: We were obliged, all this time, to lay flat with our Faces to the ground for the Wall was not a yard high & at the top was so excessive thin that the Balls often came thro', & some time[s] shatter'd the Stones before us. As soon as the fire slacken'd we Crept down a Hill that would in some Measure keep us from their Shot, but while we were effecting this, the Enemy got sight of us, & we had several Volies from the whole line in the Entrenchments before we could get out of their reach. One would almost think it absolutely impossible that so many Balls should pass you so closely & yet not touch you; the French, in general, are but bad marksmen, but here they have a mistaken Notion that a Ball falls, therefore they always elevate their Pieces, so that they Commonly shoot over your head, or strike you very high; for we have hardly an Instance of a Man's being touch'd lower than his Breast, & I have always remark'd that when our People have march'd up against them, & reserved their Fire, 5 Muskits have been shatter'd upon their Shoulders to every Man that was kill'd: To this false Principle of theirs, I believe I owe my safety, but what ever occasion'd it I am truly thankful for it – dont bleam me for this ramble upon my honour, I knew nothing of the Danger, but when I was once lead into it, it was impossible to retreat, without my Friend, therefore I e'en went thro' it as cautiously as I could.

14th. Attended my Friend a Second Time to Shore, but upon the other Island, where Genl. Clav[ering]: & Col^o. Cr[ump]⁵⁵ had laid waste to one of the Richest & most romantick Countries I ever saw for 20 Miles together: to describe its beauties would fill a Volume, but as the Prospect is strongly painted in my Mind, When I have leisure & opportunity offers I dont despair of giving you some idea of it.

15th. Enjoied this day happily by myself – lived over again many past days & tasted of various substantial pleasures yet to come.

16th. <u>Obliged my Friends</u> by going Abroad & <u>obliged myself</u> by returning home early as possible.

17th. Pester'd with your great little people, who plague all they know, live entirely upon prattle & are never pleased but when they hear their own insipid nonsense, or are making false Comparisons in favour of themselves.

18th. Received a Packet of Letters from England, but to my great Grief not a line from my E. I hear'd how ever she was well, & with this [thought] I endeavour'd to comfort myself.

19th. Went down to [Petit Bourg]⁵⁶ with the Genl. & received his Directions for going immediately to Dominico: Saw Genl. C[lavering]: & was much pleased at his Particular Politeness.

20th. Hear'd of a sloop going to Dominico, & got myself in readiness for going next Morning.

21st. Expected to sail every Moment & in that uncomfortable unsettled Situation wasted away the whole day.

22nd. Rose at Gun firing, went on board the Britania Sloop, & set sail about 6 o'Clock with very unpromising

Weather, & with as an unpromising a Companion had a great swell, contrary winds, & Stormy weather the whole passage – kept my bed with Sea Sickness & rose almost devour'd by ten thousand voracious Insects.

23^d.   At Eight o'Clock reach'd Dominico – found most of my Friends well, & some dead; got the better of my Illness & waited on the polite Commodore, whom I found with the Principal Inhabitants of the Island, who had brought their New Governor in order to Introduce him to the Commandant.[57] – Got my business dispatch'd immediately, & had a Man of War order'd on purpose to carry my <u>honour</u> to Fort Louis' Bay.

24th.   Summon'd by the Commodore's <u>first</u> Lieu^t. to go on board the Griffin,[58] Capt: Taylor Directly: took a short leave of my Friends & hurried away as fast as possible & flew from Prince Rupert's Bay to Grandeterre in less than Eight hours.

25th.   Went at day Break to the General's Quarters at Petit Bourg & was most agreably surprized by hearing that we had taken 400 Prisoners, that 1,300 Blacks were come in, & that the Genl. was then treating at St Mary's with Mon^s. [du Treil?][59] & Mr Danfield the Acting Governor, upon Terms of Accommodation for Guadeloupe, or that part call'd Basseterre.

26th.   Went down again to Petit Bourg, heard the Genl., the Gov^{nr}., & all the Chiefs of the Island were together, that there was a Sessation of Arms for four days, but could not hear one Single Article of the purported Capitulation.[60]

27th.   The Inhabitants of Grande terre promised to accept the Terms of the Capitulation but did not sign it – Breakfasted with the Dep^t. Commodore[61] & the French Officer who carried the Treaty under a Flag of truce.

28th.   Received Orders for attending the General, when the

Officer returned & waited for him from morning till night.

29th.

Set sail from Fort Louis with a whole Crew of French Officers & landed at L'Ance S^t. Sauveur[62] about 4 o'Clock – a dreadful shore & most horrid Surf.

30th.

Settled this day with the Genl. at Mon^s. [Poyen's] at [Bois de Bule?] Capesterre[63] – Held a long conversation with the Genl. on Money Matters – found I was under the necessity of going to Antigua & S^t. Kitts & had some distant hints that I ought to stay here 'till business was brought into a regular Channel – Went into the Country to Pay a visit to Ma^d. [Roger?] & to carry her some Presents from the General.

May 1st.
[1759]

Took a long ride with Brigadier Crump into the Country & found the Prospects most Noble & romantick – Saw Hills whose tops reach'd the Clouds cover'd with Stately Woods of ten thousand different shades of Green, & with Flowers in shape something like the [phlox?] but of various lively Colours, hanging amongst the foliage; in the midst of which were little rivers tumbling down the Rock fifty or sixty feet perpindicular, & at the bottom of these Hills a rapid river, which rushes down a Stoney Channel & in many places forms large basons of water & Noble Cascades which has the finest appearance when you look full upon it, & see 8 or ten falls one above the other & the Banks on each side as rich as our English Meadows, or covered with Shrubs that are no where else to be equal'd – rid into Groves of Lemons Oranges & Limes, & was absolutely sick with such a profusion of Sweets – Saw nothing but was agreable except a Monstrous Serpent, which indeed, tho' he was amazingly handsome & quite inoffensive I could not help shuddering at 'till I recollected my E liked them.

2^d.

Reason'd with myself upon a thing that entirely

depended upon the Will of another & made myself unhappy by reflecting upon an important uncertainty.

3ᵈ.   Kept writing to prevent thinking & finish many Letters I could not bear to read, for England.

4ᵗʰ.   Drank Drams with a French Lady – & walk'd myself off my Legs to oblige Strangers.

5ᵗʰ.   Rode into the woods to gather Limes – saw many wonderful Scenes, & wish'd without ceasing for my E by my side.

6ᵗʰ.   Came by Land from Mr [Poyen's?] to Petit Bourg, & from thence to Grande Terre.

7ᵗʰ.   Busy all day on board the Roebuck – heard the News of the Escape of the French Fleet & that ours was following them into the Bay at Martinique.[64]

8ᵗʰ.   Continued with the Fleet & employ'd in writing.

9ᵗʰ.   Settled my affairs & came to my Quarters at Petit Bourg.

10ᵗʰ.   Rambled about the Country, form'd strange Projects & perplex'd myself much by contriving a thousand ways to carry them into Execution.

11ᵗʰ.   Read the whole day, & lost a good dinner to avoid bad Company.

12ᵗʰ.   [Rose] by Gun firing [–] went out an airing [–] call'd in [on] several French Famillys & rode to the place where we first landed at the farther end of Capesterre.

13ᵗʰ.   Went with Colᵒ. S[65] & Majʳ. H[66] to the Head Quarters, had the Genˡ.s Orders for settling at Petit Bourg, & for bringing all my Money Baggage &c from Fort Louis Bay, & Dominico.

14ᵗʰ.   Spoke to Capᵗ. Uvedale[67] to carry me to the Fleet, writ to our Depᵗ. Commodore who sent Orders for his Sailing immediately.

15th.   Horrid Sickness with a sudden Complication of Disorders – In two hours fell Ill of the Flux, & went to bed with every unpromising Symptome.

16th.   Rose Miraculously recover'd, went thro' a vast deal of polite fatigue at the earnest request of my Friends, & unhappily brought on a return of my Disorder. Again upon the Recovery, forced into a quiet Party, & lost Two & Fifty Dollars at Whist.

17th.   Positively refused my Gaming Friends & lock'd myself up to enjoy my greatest Treasures, the Presents of my E.

18th.   Dream't of the only things that could make me Superstitious & lived in the painful Expectation of some bitter Misfortune.

19th.   Lived under the pressure of an unknown Misfortune, & trembled at the approach of Every dismal face or distant noise.

20th.   Cooled by Storms but eat up with Insects, – read much[,] understood little, conversed with My E & cursed this Country & Climate.

21st.   Rec^d. a Letter from Uvedale, acquainting me that the Wind & Weather was fair & that he should sail the Instant I came on board. Road [*sic*] up to Fort Louis, found every thing in readiness, but unluckily the wind vered about & blew much against us, however we set sail & was determined to beat up.

22^d.   Sail'd 50 leagues to gain One, a large sea & fresh Breeze, saw several French Privateers, & met the Transports returning under Convoy from our Marygalante Expedition.⁶⁸

23^d.   In the Morning a fair Wind, but in the Evening a Calm; as we were in sight of Dominico the Ships Crew
24th.   mann'd the Boats & tow'd her into Prince Ruperts Bay

just by day light: waited on the Commodore & lay on board the S^t. George.

25th. Had a Message from y^e. Co^m. that the Winchester was order'd to attend me immediately; The Capt., LeCras, came to fetch me but the wind not Serving we did not sail 'till Night.

26th. Got sight of Grandeterre at about Six o'Clock, & in the Evening Ancher'd in Fort Louis' Bay.

27th. Came in a long Boat full of Money & Baggage to Petit Bourg, – had a horrid disagreable Duty in Escorting it to my office – found the House full of Officers & the Town full of Soldiers.

28th. Went to the head Quarters; heard a queer Tumble upon Bills, found the Genl. out of humour – had a disagreable Letter put into my hands from ye Co^m. to him, with the Gen^{ls}. desire to answer it, did it immediately & very happily to his entire satisfaction. Received Orders for going to Antigua in three days, & in the Meantime had Directions about managing a 1000 things at Petit Bourg.

29th. A day of hurry & fatigue – much out of order without having power to do what was right.

30th. Finish'd my Payments & in the Evening set off for the Head Quarters at Capesterre – Still Sick but rather mending.

Notes

Unless otherwise stated, place of publication of works cited is London.

Notes to Section 1

1 British Library, Barrington Papers; HA174/1026/36/4, Colonel George Haldane to William, Viscount Barrington, [27 Feb–3 Mar] 1759. (For the dating of this letter, see note 26 below.)

2 Captain Richard Gardiner, *An Account of the Expedition to the West Indies, against Martinico, Guadelupe and the other Leeward Islands, subject to the French King, 1759*, 1st edn. (1759).

3 Robert Beatson, *Naval and Military Memoirs of Great Britain from 1729 to 1783* (1804), Vol. II, pp. 228–62; Vol. III, pp. 209–20.

4 Sir John Fortescue, 'Guadeloupe, 1759', *The Last Post*, Edinburgh (1934), pp. 295–320.

5 Gertrude Selwyn Kimball, ed., *Correspondence of William Pitt, when Secretary of State, with Colonial Governors and Military and Naval Commissioners in America*, New York & London (1906).

6 Sir Lewis Namier & John Brooke, *The House of Commons, 1754–1790* (1964), Vol. II, pp. 370–1, 'Durant, George'; Durant Papers [DP], Typescript, 'The Durants of Tong Castle'.

7 Namier & Brooke, *op. cit.*, Vol. III, pp. 74–5, 'Lyttelton, Sir George'; *Dictionary of National Biography*, 'Lyttelton, George, first Baron Lyttelton'.

8 Maud Wyndham, *Chronicles of the Eighteenth Century: Founded on the Correspondence of Sir Thomas Lyttelton and his Family* (1924), Vol. I, pp. 241–2; Vol. II, p. 271. For Dean Lyttelton, see *DNB*, 'Lyttelton, Charles'.

9 Wyndham, *op. cit.*, Vol. II, pp. 271–3.

10 Thomas Frost, *The Life of Lord Lyttelton*, (1876), p. 38.

11 Lucy S. Sutherland & John Binney, 'Henry Fox as Paymaster of the Forces', *English Historical Review*, Vol. LXX, April 1955, reprinted in R. Mitchison, ed. *Essays in English History from the English Historical Review* (1976), pp. 231–59.

12 Namier & Brooke, *op. cit.*, Vol. II, pp. 461–6, 'Fox, Henry'.

13 *Ibid.*, Vol. II, pp. 170–4, 'Calcraft, John'; Alan J. Guy, 'Regimental Agency in the British Standing Army, 1715–63: A Study in Georgian Military Administration', *Bulletin of John Rylands University Library of Manchester*, Vol. LXII (1980), pp. 423–53; Vol. LXIII (1980 pp. 31–57); 'Minions of

Fortune: The Regimental Agents of Georgian England, 1714–1763', *Army Museum '85*, National Army Museum (1986), pp. 31–42.

14 Namier & Brooke, *op. cit.*, Vol. III, pp. 533–6, 'Touchet, Samuel'.

15 *Ibid.*, Vol. III, pp. 517–18, 'Taylor, Peter', & 'Taylor, Robert Paris'.

16 The Hon. Shute Barrington, *The Political Life of William Wildman, Viscount Barrington* (1814), pp. 35–9.

17 BL Add. MSS.54485, Letter Book of Peter Taylor, May 1760–March 1761. See in particular folios 2, 14–15; PRO.WO 79/25, Letter Book of Peter Taylor, Dec 1761–Dec 1762, in particular Peter to William Taylor, 12 Jan 1762.

18 PRO.PMG 2 (Army Establishment Ledgers)/2/197. See also BL Add.MSS.17494 f. 51, Calcraft to Peter Taylor, 1 Dec 1758.

19 '. . . [I] beg of you to take care of your money[.] I am sure I have given you a fair opportunity in order to keep you thereon . . . I desire & insist that I keep clear of you & your acc^t. [–] you can't displease me more than not exactly conforming to this . . .'; BL Add.MSS.54484 f. 18, Peter to Robert Paris Taylor, 26 Sept 1760; *ibid* f. 31, same to same, 19 Dec 1760, '. . . I shall do my Duty by Calling on you for the Several acc^{ts} of payments on the money given you for different publick services [–] your Demand on me as you Claim does not arise by any mistake of mine or my Office but from y^r own . . .'; PRO WO 79/25, same to same, 18 March 1762, '. . . I cant help it [if] you are most certainly the worst young man I ever knew . . .'; *ibid*, same to same, 24 March 1762, '. . . what an unhappy, idle young man you are . . .'

20 PRO.PMG 2/4/344; PMG 2/5/346, Robert Paris Taylor, Accounts for 1760 and 1761.

21 BL Add.MSS.54485, f. 8, Peter to Robert Paris Taylor, 3 July 1760, '. . . the life you have led since this four years I rather wonder you are alive[.] I suppose you have undone a very good Constitution then your whole life is one Continual Scene of Misery and what is worst intail diseases on your posterity and this is not the worst part of a Debauched life[.] I pointed this out to you long since [–] you will take my advice when tis to [*sic*] late . . .'

22 '. . . Paris is sent for to Town, His Business being over for the Present, But I presume next Summer will Produce more work of this Sort, Now nothing is thought of but Hopson's Expedition which is going on in all haste; a Deputy goes with that, but order'd in such a hurry that had it been advisable to send Paris he cou'd not have been up in time, Tho' as the money is to be issued in Spanish Silver, & what is more, the Climate to which they are destin'd not very healthy; Both M^r. Fox & I thought it more advisable not to send him in your Absence, cou'd he have been ready in time; So Durant of the Office goes with Morse, Hopson's Secretary, for his Assistant . . .'; BL, Calcraft Papers, Add.MSS.17494/36–37, Calcraft to Peter Taylor, 19 Oct 1758. Later on in the Calcraft Papers there is a cryptic reference to Robert Paris Taylor's being sent out to the army in Germany. Fox evidently consulted Calcraft, who had assumed the role of Paris's sponsor during his father's absence

abroad, about what would be best to do with the young man; BL Add.MSS.17494/102, Calcraft to Peter Taylor, 26 May 1759.

23 Frost, *op. cit.*, p. 38.

24 Standard accounts of these operations are given by Sir Julian Corbett, *England in the Seven Years' War*, 2nd edn. (1918), Vol. I, pp. 371–95; Sir John Fortescue, *A History of the British Army*, Vol. II (1910), pp. 353–63; Lawrence Henry Gipson, *The British Empire before the American Revolution*, Vol. VIII, *The Great War for the Empire: The Culmination, 1760–1763*, New York (1953), pp. 83–105 and Marshall Smelser, *The Campaign for the Sugar Islands, 1759: A Study of Amphibious Warfare*, Chapel Hill [NC] (1955). Richard Middleton, *The Bells of Victory: The Pitt-Newcastle Ministry and the Conduct of the Seven Years' War, 1757–1762*, Cambridge (1985), re-interprets the strategic picture. Important background material can be found in Richard Pares, *War and Trade in the West Indies, 1739–1763* (1963), and Richard Harding, *Amphibious Warfare in the Eighteenth Century: The British Expedition to the West Indies, 1740–1742* (1991).

25 Beatson, *op. cit.*, Vol. II, pp. 230–1.

26 BL, Barrington Papers: HA174/1026/36/4, Haldane to Viscount Barrington, 27 Feb–3 Mar 1759 (Haldane's letter is dated 3 March, but refers to Hopson dying 'this morning', so it must at least have been begun on 27 Feb); BL, HA174/1026/36/5, John Barrington to Viscount Barrington, 3 Mar 1759.

27 Fortescue, *The Last Post*, p. 297.

28 Beatson, *op. cit.*, Vol. II, p. 235.

29 Gardiner, *op. cit.*, p. 27.

30 'The Commodore . . . thought it would be of great Service to the English sugar Colonies to destroy the Town of Basseterre in the Island of Guadeloupe, and to endeavour to reduce that Island'., Major-General Hopson to William Pitt, 30 Jan 1759, Kimball, *op. cit.*, Vol. II, pp. 22–3. See also Commodore Moore to Pitt, 30 Jan 1759, *ibid.*, Vol. II, p. 30. 'This inconsiderate step', maintained Robert Beatson, 'ruined many innocent people: nor has time ever been able to discover, what purpose the burning of the Town of Basse-Terre was intended to answer, as, when this wanton bombardment took place the batteries were silenced, and the place giving no sort of annoyance to the shipping'; Beatson, *op. cit.*, Vol. II, p. 239. George Durant, it will have been noted, reported that some guns in the citadel were still in action at dusk [*Journal*, 23 Jan 1759].

31 Gardiner, *op. cit.*, p. 34.

32 *Ibid.*, p. 37.

33 There is a succinct account of this little known operation by C.T. Atkinson, 'Queen Anne's War in the West Indies: Part 2, The Windward Sphere', *Journal of the Society for Army Historical Research*, Vol. XXIV (1946), pp. 183–97.

34 Barrington to Pitt, 2 Mar 1759, Kimball, *op. cit.*, Vol. II, pp. 45–50.

35 For Clavering and Crump, see Section 2, notes 13 & 55. Barrington and
Haldane shared a poor opinion of two of the other brigadiers, Cyrus Trapaud
and Robert Armiger. Haldane in particular thought that Armiger was an
'Ideot' and not to be trusted; BL, Barrington Papers, HA174/1026/36,4,
Haldane to Viscount Barrington, [27 Feb–3 Mar] 1759. With Clavering sick,
John Barrington was grateful to Haldane, the governor-designate of Jamaica,
for staying with the command, but he had doubts about him too; '. . . he does
his best, but to say the truth he talks better over a bottle upon Military affairs
than in Practice'; BL, HA174/1026/36/5, John Barrington to Viscount
Barrington, 3 Mar 1759.

36 Frost, *op. cit.*, pp. 39–40; DP, 'Addition to the Report of M^r. Durant's Claim,
in Answer to his Observations upon it', *n.d.*; *c*1769? PRO.PMG 2/3/172;
Durant made his last payments of subsistence to the troops occupying
Guadeloupe to 24 December 1759; bills drawn by him were dated no later
than 13 March 1760. He settled his balance for the Guadeloupe campaign
(£143 2s.) on 21 July 1769.

37 Wyndham, *op. cit.*, Vol. II, pp. 279–82. Elizabeth, Lady Lyttelton, died on 17
September 1795. Her husband pre-deceased her by many years, dying at
Hagley on 22 August 1773, aged 64.

38 Namier & Brooke, *op. cit.*, Vol. II, pp. 370–1, 'Durant, George'.

39 Durant purchased Tong Castle from the Duke of Kingston for £44,000,
together with furniture valued at £150; DP, Agreement between Kingston
and Durant, 1764; Frost, *op. cit.*, pp. 40–1.

40 *Ibid.*, pp. 41–2.

41 T.H. McGuffie, 'A Deputy Paymaster's Fortune: The Case of George
Durant, Deputy Paymaster to the Havana Expedition, 1762', *JSAHR*, Vol.
XXXII (1954), pp. 144–7. Durant acted as agent for the Havana army in
association with William Adair (the regimental agent of Pall Mall) in the
distribution of prize money. The five dividends made by Durant and Adair
totalled £367,981 15s.6½d.; 'General Account of all receipts and payments for
the fleet's moiety of money, goods and ships surrendered with the Havana on
the 12th of August, 1762' [London, 7 March 1772], David Syrett, ed, *The Siege
and Capture of Havana, 1762*, Navy Records Society, Vol. 114 (1970), p. 313.

42 Frost, *op. cit.*, pp. 42–3; Pares, *op. cit.*, pp. 256–7; William A. Foote, 'The
American Independent Companies of the British Army, 1664–1764',
unpublished Ph.D. Thesis, University of California, Los Angeles (1966), pp.
471–4. William Henry 'Governor' Lyttelton was appointed Governor of
South Carolina in 1755 and Governor of Jamaica in 1760. He did not actually
arrive in the island until January 1762; Namier and Brooke, *op. cit.*, Vol. III,
pp. 76–7, 'Lyttelton, William Henry'; *DNB*, 'Lyttelton, William Henry, third
Baron Lyttelton'; Syrett, *op. cit.*, p. 63; *ibid.*, pp. 122–3, Lt-Gen George, Earl
of Albemarle to Governor Lyttelton, 18 May 1762. The original plan had
been for Jamaica to furnish the Havana army with a 500-strong battalion of
free Negroes and 2,000 slaves. Unsurprisingly, the free Negroes were

unwilling to enlist and risk enslavement if captured, whilst the planters put a thousand obstacles in the way of parting with any of their valuable slave labour force; *ibid.*, p. xviii.

43 Frost, *op. cit.*, p. 43. For Thomas Lyttelton, see in addition to Frost's biography, Namier & Brooke, *op. cit.*, Vol. III, p. 76, 'Lyttelton, Hon. Thomas' and *DNB*, 'Lyttelton, Thomas, second Baron Lyttelton'.

Notes to Section 2

1 On 16 October 1758, pursuant to a Treasury direction, cash to the value of £28,190 9s. 4d. was paid to Arnold Nesbitt and James Colebrooke on account for the use of Hopson's expedition '. . . and to be by them paid over to G^{eo} Durant Esq. Deputy Paymaster'; PRO.PMG 2/2/200; Nesbitt and Colebrooke were major Government bankers, underwriters and contractors; Namier & Brooke, *op. cit.*; Vol. II., p. 237; Vol. III, pp. 194–5.

2 The *St George* man-of-war, commanded by Captain Clark Gaton, RN, was, at 90 guns and a crew of 750, the largest vessel in the expedition. Durant was carried on the list of supernumeraries, 'Born for Victuals only', with effect from 23 Oct 1758; PRO.ADM 36/5734/123, Muster Book, the *St George*.

3 Major-General Peregrine Thomas Hopson was a veteran of Marlborough's wars; he obtained his first commission as early as 1703. He was commissioned captain in the 14th Foot in 1718, major in the regiment in 1739, lieutenant-colonel of the 48th in 1741 and of the 29th in 1743. He became colonel of the 29th Foot in 1748 and was appointed governor of captured Cape Breton; he was commissioned colonel of the 40th in 1752 and governor and commander of the forces in Nova Scotia that same year. He was appointed major-general in February 1757. He died in Guadeloupe at one o'clock in the morning on 27 February 1759.

4 St. Helen's Roads, the sheltered anchorage and assembly-point for convoys off the Isle of Wight.

5 By 'Bluber', Durant probably means a form of marine mammal (see his *Journal* entry for 5 Dec).

6 'M'; probably Mr Leonard Morse, a War Office clerk, who served in the Expedition as General Hopson's secretary and George Durant's assistant; BL, Add.MSS.17494/36–37, John Calcraft to Peter Taylor, 19 Oct 1758.

7 Captain James Gambier, RN, of the *Burford* man-of-war, 70 guns.

8 Captain Sir Robert Hughes, RN, led the convoy to Barbados, where Commodore John Moore assumed command.

9 A grampus, one of several kinds of blowing, spouting, dolphinoid marine mammals.

10 The Reverend Sir Richard Temple was chaplain to the *St George*; PRO.ADM 36/5734.

11 Possibly the Reverend Mr Tatchum, General Hopson's chaplain; PRO.ADM 36/5734/123.

12 Major-General John Barrington, Hopson's second-in-command. His brother, William, Viscount Barrington the Secretary-at-War, had been alarmed at the prospect of John succeeding to the command of the expedition. 'Nothing is so unfortunate' he told Lord Ligonier, the Commander-in-Chief, 'as being placed at the head of a great enterprize, to which one is not equal. Though Colonel Barrington served all the last war, it was as captain, aid de camp or volunteer. He has a good understanding, and is very much resolved to do his duty; but I do not think him qualified for the important office of a commander-in-chief'. William took care to ask, however, that his brother should go out as a major-general rather than as a brigadier; Barrington to Ligonier, 14 Oct 1758, Shute Barrington, *op. cit.*, pp. 44–6. John Barrington was colonel of the 64th Foot, which was assigned to the expedition, and Pitt had particularly wanted him to go. As it turned out, the victory was to be credited chiefly to his efforts. He was rewarded with a substantive major-general's command and the colonelcy of the late Hopson's 40th Foot on 9 June 1759. He died in Paris in 1764.

13 Lieutenant-Colonel John Clavering of the 2nd, Coldstream, Regiment of Foot Guards commanded the 2nd Brigade in the decisive weeks of the campaign and greatly distinguished himself. John Barrington considered that '. . . his Judgment Coolness and activity is equal to few in the Profession'; BL, HA 174/1026/36/5 John Barrington to William, Viscount Barrington, 3 Mar 1759. (See also Barrington to Pitt, 9 May 1759, Kimball, *op. cit.*, Vol. II, p. 102). Clavering brought news of the victory to England and was rewarded with the appointment of aide-de-camp to the King in June 1759, taking rank as a colonel in the Army; see *The London Gazette* (Extraordinary), 14 June 1759. He later served in Bengal, and was an opponent of Warren Hastings, dying of sickness in India on 29 or 30 August 1777.

14 Captain Edward LeCras, RN, of the *Winchester* man-of-war.

15 The 'Bonito' or 'Bonnetta' – the striped tunny-fish.

16 Mr Berry Spiller; PRO.ADM 36/5734.

17 'The Capt.': Captain Clark Gaton, RN.

18 Probably Lieutenant Lancelot Holmes, RN, 5th Lieutenant of the *St George*; PRO.ADM 36/5734.

19 The *Panther*, man-of-war, Captain Molyneux Shuldham, RN, carried 60 guns and a crew of 420.

20 Charles Pinfold, LLD.

21 Captain Roger Townshend, Hopson's aide-de-camp, who sailed aboard the *St George*; PRO.ADM 36/5734/123. Townshend carried the expedition's initial despatches to England; see Durant's *Journal* entry for 30 January 1759 and *The London Gazette* (Extraordinary) 7 March 1759.

22 Lord John Murray's Royal Regiment of Foot. In all, seven companies of the recently raised second battalion of the 42nd Foot were assigned to the expedition; two hundred of the Highlanders joined the fleet at Barbados. The remainder, delayed in Scotland for want of transports, joined at Guadeloupe.

23 Captain (acting Major) Robert Anstruther died of fever at Guadeloupe; *The Historical Record of the Forty-Second, or the Royal Highland Regiment of Foot,* (1845), p. 54.

24 Pigeon Island, a fortified position on the southern approach to Fort Royale Bay, Martinique.

25 The *Bristol,* man-of-war, carried 50 guns and a crew of 350.

26 Captain Lachlan Leslie, RN, commanding the *Bristol.*

27 'Point Niger': Point Negro, a battery at the northern outer extremity of Fort Royale Bay. It was a priority target, as the ships could go no closer to the citadel of Fort Royale than this point; Smelser, *op. cit.,* p. 42.

28 The *Woolwich,* frigate, Captain Daniel Deering, RN, 44 guns.

29 The *Winchester,* man-of-war, Captain Edward LeCras, RN, carried 50 guns and a crew of 350.

30 The *Roebuck,* frigate, Captain [?] Lynn, RN, 40 guns.

31 Hopson's little army was organized in three brigades, formed from his six complete regiments of foot: the 1st Brigade, commanded by Lieutenant-Colonel Cyrus Trapaud, (3rd Foot) comprized the 3rd and 63rd Foot; the 2nd Brigade, first commanded by Colonel George Haldane, (3rd Foot Guards and governor-elect of Jamaica) and then successively by Clavering and Lieutenant-Colonel Byam Crump, comprized the 4th and 64th Foot; the 3rd Brigade, commanded by Colonel Robert Armiger (65th Foot), comprized the 61st and 65th Regiments. The battalion of the 42nd, under Major Anstruther and subsequently Captain Francis Maclean, fought separately, and it is not clear whether the elements of the 38th Foot, the Leeward Islands garrison unit, commanded by Major Robert Melville, were brigaded or not; Smelser, *op. cit.,* pp. 22–3. On 16 January, Haldane's 2nd Brigade landed first, closely followed by Trapaud's 1st Brigade.

32 Colonel Robert Armiger's 3rd Brigade.

33 'Fort Royal': Fort Royale, chief naval base of Martinique, with its citadel of the same name.

34 'S^t. Pierres': St. Pierre, a coastal settlement and anchorage, to the northward of Fort Royale.

35 Dominica, situated between Guadeloupe to the north and Martinique to the south, was one of the so-called 'Neutral Islands' (St. Lucia was another) given quasi extra-national status at the Peace of Aix-la-Chapelle in 1748. As Durant says, although occupied by a set of folk who wished to avoid any sort of government, they were largely pro-French in their sympathies.

36 'The Saints', located between Dominica and Guadeloupe, were two small French islands, Terre de Bas and Terre de Haut, with an islet in between, forming a fine roadstead for shipping. To the east was the larger French island of Marie Galante.

37 Captain James Randell, Agent to the Transports.

38 'M^r. B': possibly Mr William Matthew Burt, the Crown's fiscal agent attached to the expedition; see note 39 below. Burt had sailed to the West Indies with Durant aboard the *St George*; PRO.ADM 36/5734/123.

39 'Col⁰. Cunningham': possibly Lieutenant-Colonel James Cunningham, Quartermaster-General to the expedition or, perhaps, Lieutenant-Colonel William Cunninghame, Chief Engineer.

40 Captain, later Admiral Sir, John Moore was born in 1718 and probably first went to sea in 1731 under the command of Captain George Anson, who was First Lord of the Admiralty at the time of the Martinique/Guadeloupe Expedition. Moore served under Rear-Admiral Edward Hawke during the War of the Austrian Succession, greatly distinguishing himself, and in February 1757 he was a member of the Court Martial on the unfortunate Admiral John Byng, defeated off Minorca in May the previous year. Shortly after, he was appointed commodore and commander-in-chief on the Leeward Isles station. Moore returned to England in 1760, was made rear-admiral in 1762 and was thereafter promoted steadily, despite failing health, until his death on 2 February 1779.

41 The *Lancaster*, man-of-war, commanded by Captain Robert Man, RN, mounting 66 guns, had arrived that day, 4 February 1759.

42 'Cohorn' mortars: portable, small-calibre weapons for throwing grenade-size projectiles, were named after their inventor, the Dutch military engineer, Baron Menno van Coehorn.

43 'Fort Louis': a bombardment and assault on Fort Louis, the major strongpoint on the south-west coast of Grandeterre, took place on 13 February 1759. There were many casualties among the attackers, but the capture of the place cut communications between the two parts of Guadeloupe: Smelser, *op. cit.*, pp. 102–4.

44 News of the capture of the French slaving station at Gorée, on the west coast of Africa, by Commodore the Hon. Augustus Keppel, RN, arrived on 22 February 1759, and, as Durant describes, a *feu de joi* was made by the fleet and the troops on shore.

45 General Hopson's last official act had been to authorize an auction of captured goods, which took place under the auspices of the King's fiscal agent attached to the expedition, Mr William Burt. The sale continued between 24–28 February 1759: all tangible wealth, except the captured slaves, was disposed of, but, as Durant confirms, it was of small value – little more than £350, in six different coinages; Smelser, *op. cit.*, p. 99.

46 By '. . . my Clerk'. Durant may mean Leonard Morse, although he usually mentions 'M' when it is likely that he means to identify Morse. There had been another clerk aboard the *St George* listed, like Durant and Morse, among the supernumeraries; a Mr J. Garton; PRO.ADM 36/5734 f. 123.

47 Durant was now caught up in Barrington's drastic re-orientation of the campaign, which began on 28 February, when he ordered the army to hut in its present positions – a ruse intended to persuade the enemy that he intended to remain on the Basseterre side of Guadeloupe. The hutting was completed on 1 March, but on 2, 3 and 4 March, Barrington embarked his artillery, baggage and sick; on 5 March he blew up the batteries in the town,

and before daylight on the 6th he drew in his outposts and collected most of his army aboard the transports, leaving a garrison of the 63rd Foot and Royal Artillery in Fort Royale, covered by two men-of-war. Durant was evidently among the last to embark.

48 Special flat-bottomed boats were devised for assault landings from April 1758, and were first employed in raids on the French coast that summer, techniques of command and control being quickly developed; Major Hugh Boscawen, 'The Origins of the Flat-Bottomed Landing Craft, 1757–58', *Army Museum '84*, National Army Museum (1985), pp. 23–30.

49 Dr Thomas Brooke, MD, TCD (1753), FRCP, Lond. (1764), Physician to Hopson's army, had arrived from Barbados with the hospital ship on 24 January 1759, having been feared lost at sea; Gardiner, *op. cit.*, p. 29. George Haldane declared Brooke to be 'an excellent Physician . . . I believe that there is no instance of so many sick, and so many recover'd, but all his art could not save our Generall[.] I believe the old fool died of a broken heart, for he found himself unequall to the command, which brought on his flux, and prevented medicine haveing the least effect', BL, HA174/1026/36/4, Haldane to Viscount Barrington, [27 Feb–3 Mar] 1759. Brooke later served as a physician with the army in Germany (1760), going on half-pay in 1761. He died on 11 October 1781; Colonel Alfred Peterkin, ed., *A List of Commissioned Medical Officers of the Army*, Aberdeen, (1925), Vol. I., p. 29, no. 534.

50 Durant here refers to the crisis of Barrington's campaign which, for a time, deprived him of naval support. Rumours that a French relief expedition had put to sea had dogged the expedition almost from its commencement, [*Journal*, 18 Nov 1758]. At the beginning of March, it was discovered that a squadron of eight ships of the line and three frigates, under the command of *Chef d'Escadre* Maximin de Bompart, carrying a battalion of Swiss, had arrived at Martinique. Commodore Moore called in his cruisers, and removed to Dominica, to the windward of Guadeloupe, thus putting himself in the best position to prevent Bompart reinforcing the defenders of Grandeterre. The *Roebuck* was left behind to guard the transports, but in a calculated risk, Barrington's manpower was further reduced by re-embarking all the Marines, as well as 300 men from his line regiments to replace sick seamen. It was at this time that George Haldane left the army to assume his governorship of Jamaica; Smelser, *op. cit.*, pp. 113–17.

51 'Bark': Durant probably refers to the so-called 'Peruvian Bark', the bark of the Cinchona tree, from which quinine was obtained.

52 Undeterred by the departure of Moore's squadron, Barrington pursued an aggressive campaign against coastal settlements on Grandeterre. The landings between St. Anne and St. François, (Durant's St. Stephen's?) under the command of Brigadier Crump, were among the most destructive. The attackers re-embarked with minimal loss of life; Smelser, *op. cit.*, pp. 123–4.

53 The eastward concentration of French forces to resist Crump's incursions

facilitated operations carried on simultaneously at Gosier, on the south coast of Grandeterre, and at nearby Fort Louis, where the concealed battery was taken and Captain-Lieutenant William Gunning of the 61st Foot killed.

54 Captain Robert Skene was Adjutant-General to the expedition, with the rank of lieutenant-colonel.

55 Lieutenant-Colonel Byam Crump of the 4th Foot commanded the 2nd Brigade in succession to Haldane and Clavering and greatly distinguished himself at Guadeloupe. 'His merit is infinite', reported John Barrington, 'both as a Soldier and a Man of Judgment; He is of this part of the World, understands the Trade, Customs and Genius of the People, and is besides, possibly the Man who thinks the noblest, and the most disinterestedly; Neither would he have accepted on the Government [of Guadeloupe] but in hope of pushing himself in the Army by that means: and I cannot say how very usefull, and how much our Successes are owing to his Bravery, good Conduct and great Zeal'; BL, HA174/1026/36/9, John to William, Viscount Barrington, 9 May 1759. In a letter to Pitt on 21 July 1759 Crump protested his 'incapacity for Civil Government, especially under the present Circumstances of these Islands, yet as General Barrington did me the honour to appoint me to that task, I cou'd not decline accepting of it, 'till his Majesty's pleasure could be known . . . Civil Government has never been the object of my Attention, my thoughts have been wholly applied to the military, in which Service I shall always be ready to devote my life for the public good . . .', Kimball, *op. cit.*, Vol. II, p. 141. Crump assumed his government in earnest when Barrington sailed for England on 24 June but died less than a year later on 11 March 1760: he was '. . . seized with an ague fit about 4, and died about 5, in strong convulsions'; *The Gentleman's Magazine*, Vol. XXX, 1760, p. 249.

56 The settlement of Petit Bourg on Basseterre was taken by Clavering on 13 April from the landward site, in conjunction with a bombardment from the *Granada* bomb-ketch; Smelser, *op. cit.*, pp. 130–2.

57 Commodore Moore's intention was to oblige the French inhabitants of Dominica, who had sent reinforcements to their compatriots in Guadeloupe, to stick to a strict neutrality and he succeeded in doing so as long as he was around to enforce it; Pares, *op. cit.*, p. 215.

58 The *Griffin*, frigate, Captain Thomas Taylor, RN.

59 As mentioned in the Introduction, Durant's phonetic spelling of names unfamiliar to him is occasionally perplexing, and it is by no means clear here whom he means to identify by the names of 'Mons. Capey' or 'Mr. Danfield'. In the case of the former, some important personnage is implied, and I suggest that he means M. Nadau de Treil, the French governor of Guadeloupe. The ambassadors who went under a flag of truce to Clavering's headquarters in occupied St. Marie on 21 April, with du Treil's tacit consent, were Messrs. Dubourg de Clainvilliers and Duquerey.

60 Articles of capitulation were agreed on 1 May, and the final details settled the

following day. The inhabitants of Guadeloupe benefited greatly from the removal of the Royal Navy's stranglehold on their trade. Gardiner, Beatson and the *Gentleman's Magazine*, Vol. XXIX, 1759, pp. 275–7 all print the terms in full: Smelser, *op. cit.*, pp. 140–2, summarises them.

61 Durant probably means Captain Sir Robert Hughes. At the end of May, Moore divided his squadron into two divisions, the Red and the White, with Hughes as Commodore of the White; Smelser, *op. cit.*, p. 155.

62 L'Anse St. Sauveur: a bay to the south of Capesterre, for which see note 63.

63 This signifies both the settlement of Capesterre, on the south-east coast of Basseterre, and the name of the richest and most fertile zone of the island. When Clavering's forces broke into Capesterre, French resistance collapsed. Barrington had temporarily established his headquarters *chez* Mons. Poyen.

64 Scarcely had the capitulation of the island been agreed when news arrived that de Bompart had given Moore the slip and had appeared off St. Anne, Grandeterre, on 27 April where he landed his battalion of Swiss, but being advised that all was lost, he re-embarked his troops and returned to Martinique. Moore struggled against contrary winds to intercept him, but on 6 May he learned that Bompart had gained the safety of Fort Royal Bay; Smelser, *op. cit.*, pp. 143–7.

65 'Col°. S': probably Durant's friend, Lieutenant-Colonel Robert Skene.

66 'Maj'. H': possibly Major Shuckborough Hewitt, officer commanding the 3rd Foot.

67 Commander Samuel Uvedale, RN, of the bomb-vessel *Granada*.

68 The island of Marie Galante surrendered in the late May without resistance.

II
Daniel George Robinson
Letters from India
1845–1849

Edited by

R.N.W. THOMAS

From Brian Bond (ed.) *Victorian Military Campaigns*, Hutchinson, 1967.

Introduction

Daniel George Robinson (1826–1877), the writer of these letters, was an officer of the Bengal Engineers, a corps which traditionally chose the most talented cadets who applied for commissions to the East India Company. He was later to become Director General of Telegraphs in India 1865–77. The letters form an important source of information on attitudes and personalities in the Punjab following the First Sikh War, since Robinson was serving there at a climactic time in the history of India. There is much detail on events in Hazara during the Second Sikh War, and this assists in filling a notable gap in our knowledge of events there which have received so little attention in the literature dealing with this period. Robinson's colleagues in the Punjab included many of the well known administrators of mid-nineteenth century India, such as Henry and John Lawrence, James Abbott, John Nicholson and Herbert Edwardes, all of whom are mentioned in the letters. It was largely due to their efforts, for better or worse, that India remained a part of the British Empire for a century after these letters were written.

Daniel Robinson was educated at the Royal Naval School near Camberwell until the age of fourteen, and it was there that he developed a marked aptitude for mathematics and scientific subjects.[1] Coming from a service family, it was no doubt due to his father's limited resources, and the influence of his uncle John Ward Harding (who had retired from the Madras Army in 1837), that a career in India was chosen in preference to the Queen's forces. His talents were most suited to one of the technical branches of the service, possibly as a result of his mother's engineer forbears, and a career in the Bengal Engineers was decided upon. By Robinson's time, all artillery and engineer officers in the East India Company's forces were required to undergo training at Addiscombe Military Seminary, entry to which was by recommendation from a member of the Court of Directors, followed by a competitive examination. Robinson entered Addiscombe at the age of fifteen, having first attended the crammer of Stoton & Mayor at Wimbledon, and remained there for two years before passing out as first engineer of his term. Having been commissioned a Second Lieutenant in June 1843, he received further training at the Royal Engineers depot at Chatham before embarking for India just after Christmas 1844 on the ship *Tartar*.

The voyage to India took over four months, during which time Robinson would have celebrated his nineteenth birthday. His first duties were as an Assistant to the Civil Architect and Garrison Engineer at Fort William, Calcutta, during which time he lived with Thomas Cadogan, a contact of his father's friend Charles Kerr. This was followed by a two month journey up the River Ganges to the Bengal Engineers' depot at Meerut, though any thoughts of a peaceful life in cantonments were soon dispelled with the outbreak of the First Sikh War, during which Robinson saw active service and was present at the battle of Sobraon (10 February 1846) as an Assistant Field Engineer with Lord Gough's army. It is unfortunate that we have no letters relating to the campaign, though as Robinson himself wrote in late April 1846, 'I have been moving about so much since last September that I really have not had time to write to any one previous to the battle of Sobraon.' We do, however, have a mention of the brief siege of Kangra (20-29 May 1846), during which Robinson commanded three companies of Sappers.

The Treaty of Amritsar (16 March 1846) at the close of the First Sikh War transferred Cashmere to Maharajah Gulab Singh, and Robinson was appointed to survey the boundary between this province, the land under the administration of the Lahore Durbar and the East India Company's territories. This task was completed between April 1846 and September 1847, when Robinson was placed under the Resident at Lahore as superintendent of the Hazara Survey. He was engaged on this at the commencement of the Second Sikh War, and thus participated in the operations conducted against the Sikh forces in the province. Robinson subsequently commanded a force of Jammu irregular troops and was present at the battles of Chilianwala (13 January 1849) and Gujerat (21 February 1849), for which he received the thanks of the Commander-in-Chief and the Governor General.[2]

The Second Sikh War (1848-9) had its origins in the murder on 20 April 1848 of two British officials, Patrick Vans Agnew and William Anderson, who were visiting the fortress of Multan in order to make new fiscal arrangements and install a governor to replace Dewan Mulraj.[3] The gravity of this event was compounded by the mutiny of the escort and the lack of sufficient troops in the vicinity to restore order. However, the enterprise of Lieutenant Herbert Edwardes, a political officer on the North West Frontier, ensured that by early July the rebels were confined within the fortress of Multan. Although the Multanis fought under the nominal leadership of Mulraj, it is clear that neither he nor his chief subordinates initiated the unrest, which appears to have been entirely spontaneous in its origin, and was confined to the vicinity of Multan. The situation markedly changed, however, with the defection on 14 September of Raja Sher Singh, who was commanding a column of Sikh troops which had been sent against the rebels. Sher Singh raised a force which included many soldiers from the Sikh army defeated during the conflict of 1845–6 and united them with a call to expel the British from the Punjab. It was against these men that the Anglo-Indian army led by Lord Gough fought the principal engagements of the Second Sikh War.

Meanwhile, events in Hazara had also undergone a serious deterioration. The province had originally been transferred to Gulab Singh according to the terms of the Treaty of Amritsar, but the resistance to his rule was significant amongst several of the Muslim chieftains. Viewing it as something of a liability, Gulab successfully persuaded the British to arrange for its exchange in May 1847 with some territory adjoining Jammu belonging to the Lahore Durbar. The Durbar installed Sirdar Chattar Singh as governor and commander of the Sikh troops in Hazara. As head of the powerful Attariwala family, Chattar Singh was concerned about any circumstances which might lessen the influence of his clan at Lahore, especially since his daughter was engaged to Maharajah Dalip Singh. By the late summer of 1848 Chattar Singh felt threatened, and his grounds for feeling so were not unjustified. He conceived that the British were blocking the marriage of his daughter and the young Maharajah, and indeed that they even wished to remove Dalip Singh from the throne at Lahore. The mutual mistrust existing between him and Captain James Abbott, the Assistant to the Resident at Lahore with responsibility for Hazara, was a further important factor. Abbott had suspected that Chattar was seeking to enlist the aid of Maharajah Gulab Singh in a rebellion against the British and, not having more than a handful of regular troops at his disposal, commenced to raise a force of levies from amongst the local tribesmen. It was against this background that the first armed confrontation occurred in Hazara, when Abbott surrounded the capital at Haripur with his levies on 6 August. Inside the town was an American artillery officer in Sikh service, Colonel Canora, who refused to deploy his guns against Abbott and was shot for his pains. Faced with the possibility of having his jagheer and Nazimship confiscated for this, Chattar Singh considered that he had nothing more to lose and so threw in his lot with the rebels.

Abbott withdrew to Nara and Robinson was despatched to the

Margala Pass where it was hoped that he would be able to block the progress of Chattar Singh's troops on their route to join the main Sikh army. Meanwhile, Lieutenant John Nicholson (who was serving as an Assistant to the Resident at Lahore) began raising his own force from the local populace and managed to secure the fort of Attock. Abbott, Nicholson and Robinson succeeded in delaying Chattar Singh's forces for a month – a creditable achievement given that their tribal levies were numerically inferior to the regular Sikh troops of the Pukli Brigade. However, on 11 September the Sikhs managed to force their way through the Dhamtaur Pass, sweeping aside the tribesmen in the process. Operations in Hazara now centred around Attock, which was besieged by a mixed force of Afghans, from whom Chattar had called for assistance, and Sikhs. It was finally taken on 2 January 1849 after a siege of two months, which enabled Chattar Singh to join the main Sikh army commanded by his son, and operations in Hazara came to an end.

Elsewhere, the Anglo-Indian army had been split into two parts, with a division under Major-General Whish proceeding against Multan and the main force under Lord Gough acting as the field army. Whish eventually obtained the unconditional surrender of Mulraj on 22 January 1849 and set off to join Lord Gough, whom he reached on 20 February, the day before the battle of Gujerat. This was the final engagement of the war and ended in the defeat of the Sikhs and their pursuit across the River Jhelum by Major-General Gilbert. Their formal surrender at Rawalpindi on 14 March left only the Afghans in the field, but they hastily retired through the Khyber Pass before Gilbert's pursuing force, which entered Peshawar on 21 March thus effectively ending the Second Sikh War. The conflict resulted in the annexation of the Punjab on 30 March 1849 and the establishment of a Board of Control under the presidency of Henry Lawrence to manage its affairs.

It is clear from these letters that Robinson was ambitious. He was a member of an élite corps with a considerable degree of responsibility on detached duty and could reasonably expect to obtain further advancement in the political sphere. His frustration at the appointment of Sir Frederick Currie ('a cold hearted unfeeling civilian') in the place of Henry Lawrence as Resident at Lahore was marked, and it is probable that Robinson and his military colleagues were sceptical of their chances of advancement in a civilian dominated régime. Coupled with this, the Earl of Ellenborough, who had been Governor-General from 1842 to 1844, had been noted as favouring military men over civilians, and his successor, Sir Henry Hardinge, was himself a Lieutenant-General in the

Army at the period of his tenure in India. Career prospects for the Company's military officers under the Earl of Dalhousie, who became Governor-General in January 1848 may, therefore, have appeared less certain than under his predecessors.

Robinson's views on some of the military officers are also enlightening. He met Lord Gough in December 1848 and described him as 'a very kind hearted old man, without many brains & much altered since I saw him three years since looking very old, very seedy & it seemed to me that his mind was apt to wander at times.' What some of the officers thought of being commanded by Gough in some of the heaviest engagements ever to take place in India may be imagined. Robinson was equally scathing about others. Whish is described as 'an old woman' and Robert Napier as 'wanting in dash & so amiable that he always gives in to the advice of others.' Napier later became Commander-in-Chief in India between 1870 and 1876. During an age in which promotion depended to a great degree on seniority, junior officers in the Company's forces must have felt justifiably frustrated at their slow advancement, though in contrast to this, Robinson had a marked admiration for the Lawrence brothers, Herbert Edwardes and John Nicholson.

One other feature of the letters are the frequent references to money. According to the cashbook of Daniel Robinson senior (which is in the possession of the family), the cost of equipping his son and sending him to India was £510, a not inconsiderable sum in 1844. This comprised £310 for his 'outfit', £100 for the passage, £10 cash and £90 credit in India. The debt would have been compounded by the frequent requests for additional items including stationery, a theodolite, pistols, a saddle and a telescope. It is highly likely from references in the letters that Daniel was expected to repay his father, though it is unknown to what extent he managed to do this and it is almost certain that he never managed it before his father's death.

This introduction would not be complete without some further details of Robinson himself and the members of his family who are mentioned in these letters. He did not marry Adine Edlmann, possibly because her father refused permission on the grounds of the young man's uncertain future and lack of funds. Adine lived to a fine old age, but never married. In September 1851 Daniel Robinson married Jane Amelia Graham at Mussoorie. The couple had nine children, of whom six of the boys followed in their father's footsteps by joining either the British or Indian Armies. His father, who was also called Daniel Robinson, had served in the Royal Marines between 1807 and 1812 when he transferred to the

Spanish Army. He eventually retired in 1830 with the rank of Colonel, having been awarded a Spanish knighthood for services in Mexico, and died in 1849. His sister Ninetta, to whom many of the letters are addressed, married the Reverend Robert Agassiz in August 1849 and had three children. Her husband died in 1858 and she subsequently married the Reverend William English, having one more child by this marriage. The wayward Charles, his younger brother, had a precarious career in the Royal Navy, during which he reached the rank of Lieutenant before he jumped ship and was dismissed the service. After a spell at home, during which he was a bad influence on his younger brother John, their father died and this brought about the 'difficulties which opened his eyes' (see number 17). Sadly, at the age of 23, whilst staying with his maternal uncle in Cape Colony, he went on an expedition up the Limpopo River. His companion returned without him, saying that he had been taken by a crocodile. In complete contrast, Daniel Robinson's youngest brother John served as a Clerk in the House of Lords and Examiner for Standing Orders for many years and eventually retired to Jersey.

The series of letters is obviously incomplete and it is noticeable that only one is dated after the death of the writer's father, despite the fact that Daniel George Robinson continued to serve in India for another eighteen years. It is probable that the letters were kept by Ninetta as a demonstration of the marked differences in character and achievements between Daniel and his brother Charles, some of whose letters have also been preserved. Charles was a source of constant worry to all the other members of his family. The obvious imbalance in the number of letters retained by year is also unaccounted for, since nearly half were written in 1848. Some of the letters were written on tracing paper which would have been supplied for survey purposes. Others were written crossways in order to save money on postage, so that some pages had writing in one direction before the sheet was turned and filled with another 'page' of writing at right angles to the first, as was frequently done at this period. The letters are not foliated and are listed here in date order. Where there is no date or postmark, internal evidence has been used to place the letter concerned in sequence, and a footnote to this effect has been made. The entire text of each letter has been presented, and no words or sections omitted.

The letters represent only a brief snapshot of Robinson's career, and reference may be made to Appendix 4 for further details of his subsequent service and the documentary records relating thereto.

On matters of style, I have referred to Daniel George Robinson in the footnotes as 'DGR' for the sake of brevity and to avoid confusion with his father. Details of the places mentioned will be found in the Gazetteer comprising Appendix 5. In cases where the nineteenth century spelling differs from that of the early twentieth century, a footnote has been inserted after the first occasion on which the place name is mentioned so that the reader may find the Gazetteer entry more easily. In practice, this applies to the majority of the places mentioned, though for reasons of space footnotes have not been used for subsequent uses of the same place name. A more complete explanation of the methods used to identify place names will be found in Appendix 5.

It should be noted that the regimental affiliations of officers mentioned in footnotes to the text refer to the units they joined first, and subsequent exchanges into other corps have not been noted. Squared brackets have been used to mark or suggest words which are illegible in the original letters and, when preceded by 'sic', to suggest what Robinson probably meant to write when this is not altogether clear. Some passages of letters 41 and 42 dating to the Second Sikh War are in Greek characters. These have been placed in italics in the transcriptions. Robinson's spellings have been left unaltered, but [sic] has been used to identify cases where his sentence construction is ungrammatical. It should be noted in mitigation that many of the letters were written in a great hurry, as Robinson noted on 7 November 1847, 'Altho' desperately tired & it is late at night I hasten to scribble a few lines in hopes of not missing the mail.' The conditions in which he found himself could also be trying, as he remarked on 31 December 1847, 'It is now so cold that I can hardly hold my pen.' It is therefore unsurprising that the letters are not, and were never intended to be, works of literature; their grammatical faults convey an immediacy which informs the reader in much greater detail of the conditions under which he worked than if they had been rewritten subsequently.

The work of editing the letters could not have been completed without the considerable assistance received from a number of people. Firstly, I must register heartfelt thanks to my Mother, Mrs B.R. Thomas, for allowing publication of the letters which are in her possession. The challenging nature of transcribing mid-nineteenth century manuscript will be well-known to all those who have experience of it, and her help in deciphering the more difficult passages allowed a much more complete work to be submitted for publication than would have been the case otherwise. Dr David Greathead kindly allowed me to include the letter (number 50) of 17 June 1860 in his possession. I must also thank Dr

Andrew Cook of the Oriental and India Office Library and Records for his many hours spent in assisting me with the place names, gazetteers and maps which were all necessary in order to trace Robinson's original maps in the collections under his charge. His colleague, Miss Shabana Mahmud, very kindly translated the passages in Urdu script. I received a considerable amount of help from my friend Dr Alan Guy of the National Army Museum, who painstakingly read through the entire manuscript and provided a wealth of advice on editorial style and matters of detail. The manuscript benefited greatly from his care and attention. Transcripts from Crown copyright documents in Oriental and India Office Collections of the British Library appear by permission of the Controller of Her Majesty's Stationery Office. Finally, I would like to thank the staffs at the Oriental and India Office Library and Records and the National Army Museum for their help during my research.

The Letters of Daniel George Robinson

Daniel George Robinson to his sister[1]

[Postmarked Madras
April 25 1845]

My dear Sister[2]

I write this so as to send it off upon our arrival at Madras which
we expect to see in about 2 days more. As you will see by the letter
I send with this to my father most of the occurrance[s] of the
voyage I will say nothing about them here.[3]

The weather is dreadfully hot, so much so that one cannot go
into the sun at all and even in the shade the perspiration off the
body and head whilst sitting still is so great as to surpass that
arising from great exertion in England. If even here it be so hot
and there is a little air what must it be like on shore without a
breath of air & such an intollerable quantity of dust.

After leaving England we had a very heavy gale in the bay of
Biscay and so we had whilst of[f] the Cape but I must say the
descriptions one gets of these things on shore are very erroneous.
As for the sea being compared to mountains it it [*sic*] is quite
ridiculous. Certainly no waves we saw could have been above fifty
feet high and to see the gulls hovering about the stern and to hear
the wind howl in the rigging certainly made it unpleasant but still
there was something extremely pleasing & grand in it. It also
afforded very good practice in shooting as the ship pitching made
the aim uncertain. We after that had fine weather and before
crossing the line we caught a great many fish, Bonita and
Albacore[4] and now and then a small shark but though we saw

Caricature 'Morning Dress'.

Y^{rs} obed^{tly}
D.G. Robinson

many flying fish we never got any. The albacore & bonita are large fish. I caught one that must have weighed nearly 1 cwt and we saw some large dolphins but only caught small ones. The flying fish are very small, not more than 6 or 8 inches & they fly along the water like a swallow but never more than a few yards at a time and only then because they are chased by the before mentioned fish. The extraordinary thing is that the flesh of all these fish is quite black.

When we got off the Cape we saw a great many birds amongst the most conspicuous of which were the albatross and the Cape hen. The first bird is much larger than a swan. We caught some when becalmed with a fish hook and when got on board they were let loose on the deck off which they were not able to fly & indeed could hardly run. One I caught I measured and he measured 13 feet from wing to wing and the mass of feathers on his body was enormously thick & soft so I tried to preserve the skin but it was so oily that I was soon glad to get rid of it. However I have got the skeleton of the head. The Cape hen is a much smaller bird of a brownish color & sometimes variegated like a common fowl. I shot a good many of them but could not get the bodys to see what they were like. The albatross have got 4 joints to their wings whilst other birds have only three. I suppose the Milfords[5] have returned to Laugharne long ago. Remember me kindly to them when next you write as well as to all friends & relations. Taking all things into consideration I have been pretty happy all the time I have been on board. Strange to say there has been very little quarrelling but that I account for owing to the paucity of ladies.

April 28th 1845

My dear Sister
We arrived here last night & I came on shore this morning being obliged to report ourselves & was immediately ordered off to Palaveram[6] – 15 miles – nolens volens and I write this in the Adjutant General's office[7] as the mail leaves in a few minutes. Excuse the wretched scrawl above and believe me,
Your affect Brother
DG Robinson

P.S. I should & wished to have written more but for time pressing.

2

Daniel George Robinson to his sister[8]

My dear Sister

I am sorry that time will not allow of my saying all I could wish to say & therefore you must forgive the shortness of this epistle & the hardship of the country. I am sorry to hear fresh bad accounts from Laugharne but as the children are young & there are still some left I think that regret should not be too great for the poor little things are saved. Many of the miseries of this world here mean deaths are so frequent & generally after only a few hours illness one is obliged to look upon it thus. Ever this. I hope however that the shock has passed over & that Uncle & Aunt[9] are themselves again. Had I but time I would gladly write to them but you will say everything that's kind for me.

You would be surprised to see the pale faces here especially of the ladies on whom there is not the slightest tinge of colour, not even rouge, but they in general are good looking. I get a gallop every evening from 6 till 8, or rather the last part is generally a fight between the horse and I for the mastership. I have always succeeded as yet and I dare say shall continue so to do. I have [been] but to one ball since I have been here which was at the Governor General's on the Queen's birthday when there were about 900 people present.[10] You would be saying it must have been very hot when the thermometer stood at 90° but there were punkahs going all over the Rooms just above our heads. These punkahs are large frames of would hung from [the] sealing like the accompanying figure. They are generally about 20' long and 4 deep & they are pulled backwards & forwards like a large fan.

Thus they give a delightful draught. The houses here are all done more than 2 stories high & every room has a punkah in it. The rooms average about 17 feet high and 16' square for the bed rooms, the drawing and dining rooms [are] 36 feet by 24 feet. All the rooms open into one another by two or three doors so as to make a through draught. Here, in this my bed room, there are 6 doors all folding & 2 windows & all about 10 feet high. How does father mean write me a long letter next time & never mind the postage for once.

'Large frames of would hung [from] the sealing . . .' Robinson's drawing of a punkah.

Remember me kindly to all friends & ask Agnes if she has forgotten her promise to write to me. I should write to her had I time.

I must now say adieu & with kind love to Jack[11] & all others believe me

Your affect. brother
Daniel G. Robinson

3

Daniel George Robinson to his sister and father

Calcutta Augt 7th 1845

My dear Sister
Your letter does not contain news quite sufficient to break my heart although you talk of Mary Shield[12] being married to a schoolmaster whose name however you do not mention and also

that the pretty Agnes will marry no one with less than £5000 per annum. I hope she will not lead a life of single blessedness but I am afraid that unless she moderates her terms, she will. However, commend me kindly to her.

I am still living with Mr Cadogan,[13] Mr Kerr's[14] friend, and here I shall remain until I go up country in about another month – but in this country as your servants always go with you even out to dinner the trouble you give the person you are staying with is considerably less than under corresponding circumstances it would be in England. As your own servants make your bed and wait on you [at] dinner &c, & at the same time whatever meat leaves the table after dinner is unfit to eat the next day, indeed it is always killed at 10 or 11 in the morning and eaten at 7 or 8 in the evening.

The climate of Calcutta also is extremely damp especially in this the rainy season when even old mahogany tables become quite white with mildew and every thing made with English glue falls to pieces. One would think that when the weather here is called cool here the Thermometer in doors would stand something lower than 84° and in the hot weather the Thermometer stands at 90° in the same room. As soon as ever the sun is up then the peons[15] commence shutting all the windows and doors (on the outside of the house) to keep the heat out. This is generally about half past seven in the morning and the house is not opened again until 7 in the evening when it is cool again. At 8 o'clock it is quite dark again. No body ever walks here (i.e. that is to say Europeans) unless it be between half past four and six in the morning before the sun is up. To walk 200 yards in the middle of the day is nothing short of madness & sure to bring on a fever. I have perfectly recovered now from the effect of the one I was labouring under for a fortnight. They treat their diseases pretty immediately here [with] linctus and bleeding every day and nothing stronger than sago and arrowroot made with water & never books allowed to be read even when convalescent. When you go to a ball or to Church there is always a punkah going a few inches above your head and in the churches which are built in as open a form as possible the pews are merely divided by the desk in front supported by stanchions about 5 feet apart and instead of sitting on a bench as one does in England each person has an arm chair. No chairs are to be seen in this country but arm chairs with cane bottoms & the rooms excepting the drawing rooms have all mats laid down instead of carpets excepting in the drawing room where a piece of handsomest carpet is put down under the table. Every person here even Milliners keep a carriage of one kind or another and all single men a buggy (no slang word here) or cab, or a horse. Every office has an office jaunt a species of patent safety cab for 4 people belonging to it for the convenience of the people belonging to the firm. I have in this new Railway [have] been very readily taken and I think this new propeller company will be well supported but beyond these 2 things there are very few schemes in India but perhaps it is all for the better for you never hear of failures here. I hope by this time that Aunt and Uncle will have got over the serious loss of so many beautiful children. I get on pretty well with the language although I do not study it but all my servants and indeed every good servant in Calcutta speaks nothing but Hindustanni. A servant who speaks English being sure to be a greater thief than the others who all are thieves also. The manner of punishing servants here is rather curious some people beat them and I am not surprised at it for they try the patience of a saint and although a horsewhip in the room with you is extremely useful they are much better punished by fining them of their pay. If a man is stupid fine him and he soon brightens up again and they never say anything. One servant I had when I was ill when sent for the medecine used to get get [*sic*] drunk and never came back till the next day I dared not dismiss him then because he had my keys in his possession but when well I sent him off minus one half his month's pay. With love to Jack now farewell.

Your affect. Brother
Daniel G. Robinson

My dear Father
The wine trade here is in a dreadful state. The best they will not sell for above R18 per dozn and the market is over stocked with that an[d] fell to a dreadful extent. Saunders & May[16] still hold & I should say they are talking of raising the wine duty. The import trade here I should think was all bad. From my present position I

am not at all thrown in the way of seeing passengers or people going home. I shall be delighted to leave this most extravagant of places and to get a few more rupees monthly pay – the present one being a disgrace to the company & entirely rising out of a mistake.

Yr affect. son
DGR

4

Daniel George Robinson to his sister

Arawul[17] NW Provinces
November 1st 1845

My dear Sister

This as you perceive is dated from Arawul, a diminutive village of mud huts and thievish inhabitants somewhere about 40 miles beyond Cawnpore and where we are for this day encamped. Moreover, there is a post office here from which if in time this letter will proceed to Calcutta, if not it must go viâ Bombay on the 20th, that being now the most direct route and by which route all future letters ought to come.

I am marching up as I before wrote and I have had the good fortune to fall in with a Major Laurenson[18] of the horse artillery who was proceeding to Meerut[19] in the same steamer with me and he said he should be glad of my company and being well acquainted with the country and its manners he has been of great assistance to me in the matter of a drill &c as also saving me great expense at least £20. Well on arrival at Allahabad he told me what I should want and Capt. Laughton[20] of our corps asked me to his house and lent me his servants and gave me advice as to whom I was to employ etc. (which in this country where every native is a thief is invaluable) and so I procured there a good strong horse, got one of his own grooms, a couple of tents & other things complete and after having been one week at Allahabad we started for Cawnpore which we reached after 8 days, the average time being 10 or 11. This was considered tremendous marching, the servants being almost knocked up by it although the distance was one [sic] 124 miles which a man might

86

easily accomplish in England in 4 days. So much for this delightful climate. Well at Cawnpore I stopped a week with Woodcock[21] and there we laid in a fresh stock of provisions, potatoes even not being procurable in this part of the country & proceeded towards Meerut having received another addition to the party in Miss Laurenson, the Major's only daughter, a very small & very nice girl but unfortunately by no means pretty so that there is no prospect of my making a settlement for life in that quarter. And since that period we have been marching up here. The first part of the march the Major was very ill and his <u>bearer</u> i.e. valet got a fever but fortunately when in Calcutta I bought a medecine chest and some books on medecine by which means I cured the bearer in a day or two and the Major is hardly well yet. Our staff is pretty considerable consisting of a cook and his scullion, 3 <u>khitmatgars</u> (men who wait at table), 3 <u>bearers</u> [or] valets, and [an] <u>Ayah</u> or ladies <u>maid</u>, 2 sweepers with their families, 2 <u>chokadars</u> or constables, 5 horses, a buggy with 5 grooms and 5 grasscutters, 6 bullock <u>hackeries</u>, a peculiar species of cart to each of which there is a driver, 2 <u>bheesties</u> or water bearers, 2 <u>dhobies</u> or washermen, 1 <u>durzi</u> or tailor, not one of which can properly be dispensed with. Besides these there are 4 tent pitchers who are hired only for the march so that you see there is some considerable expense for marching in addition to which 6 chokadars are nightly obliged to be hired from the nearest village to to [*sic*] protect us from being robbed and which is a species of black mail, all chokadars being themselves robbers and every morning there are 6 coolies required to carry on the beds as we generally start from one set of tents before daylight which are then struck and put on three hackeries and on arriving at the new place of encampment we find the other tents ready but as bullocks don't travel [more than] 2 miles an hour they never come up with the first set of tents till 3 o'clock in the afternoon. I generally go out of an evening at about 5 o'clock (it is dark at 6) to see what I can shoot for the pot. Once I got a peacock, a brace of teal & some pigeons all in one day which was rather [a] change from the constant meal of fowls & eggs. Some of the large cities are very peculiar places. Benares, the holy city, exterivity (i.e. on the banks of the river) is very beautiful being one continual line of temples and Ghauts,[22] some very beautiful.

Murzapore[23] also was very pretty but the prettiest scenery I have as yet seen is the Rajmahal hills and the rocks of Galcong.[24]

These upper provinces are dreadfully dry and dusty, the very opposite of Calcutta, and I find that most of my English things are enclined to fall to pieces. My chest of drawers have warped most awfully [and] the joints are all coming loose. Likewise my writing desk. The only things that are peculiarly good being the bullock trunks. My pistol box although in another box has come to pieces but the gun box remains entire. All the country up here is in a most splendid state of cultivation but unfortunately we Europeans cannot eat of the produce [since] every species of food that [the] natives eat being much worse than raw garlic with the exception of rice and a few of the fruits. I expect to be at Meerut about the 24th of this month when my pay will be 220 rupees a month instead of 163 & when I can pass the examination in the language which I hope soon to do I shall get command of a company and consequently an additional 50 rupees per mensem.[25] I find the accent the most difficult portion of it natives allways express things by gesture rather than by speech and until perfectly master of that mode of expression I shall never be able to converse with them in [the] best best [sic] possible manner. Moreover they never speak grammar [sic] nor express any thing in the way it is written. Thus they allways say "we is" instead of "I am". Although "thee" is such an expression in their language. The weather is now much cooler than it was and one requires a blanket and counterpane now at night & I always am glad of warm clothing when riding in the morning. My horse is a very nice little one, very strong & pretty good tempered but very lazy & unmanageable without a very sharp pair of spurs. He is not so handsome nor so large as I should like but the price of horses here are so tremendous that I shall be obliged to wait some years before I can get a good one which will cost between 100 & 200 pounds & then not be so good as an English horse which would cost £50. The one I have now cost me 400 rupees or £40 and I could buy one like him in England for 12 or even less so that you see although with what in England would be a splendid pay here in India one is obliged to screw in every possible manner to avoid running into debt. I think I now see my way pretty clear although Taylor[26] is 2000 rupees in debt already & could not avoid it and has not got half the things to show for it that I have for I have got a set of tents and clothes and stores enough for the next two years and I believe have at present very little more to buy but still Meerut is a dreadfully expensive place to live in especially at this season of the year. Sir Henry Hardinge[27] will be there soon about 5 days before we shall and I expect there will be nothing but reviews [and] other equally troublesome things for some time to come. The Punjaub seems to have got a little quiet[er] again and it is very improbable that there will [be] any war there this year which we were all rather in expectation of.

I cannot say that I am by any means sorry that you have not moved into the house that you spoke of for to tell the truth I don't like it. I should rather prefer the other side of London or else Dulwich a little more open and countrified but I do not like Camberwell nor the inhabitants as a whole, though I believe there are a few nice people. So Agnes has returned to Laugharne unmarried maybe she will wait for my return but I fear that will only be in case of sickness or never to return to India again as on a whole I do not dislike India and it agrees with me very well & I like the manners of the Europeans very much. It is now time I should write to Father whose health I hope still remains unimpaired. And therefore with my best love & wishes to you and kindest regards to all friends.

Believe me
Yr affect. Brother
Daniel G. Robinson

5

Daniel George Robinson to his sister and Mary Shirley Miller

Camp Jindree[28] near Pathânkote[29]
Lat 31.50 N Long 76 E [30]
[April 20th 1846]

My dear Sister

I perfectly agree with you that Mary Miller[31] did on the 1st of February write a great deal of nonsense but being natural I

89

suppose she could not help it. Still I did once think that those
<u>Epsom Spinsters</u> to use her own phrase were a more grave and
sedate race. May be that trip to Sidmouth gave her the infection
but I hope she will soon recover and write me a rational letter that
there will be some satisfaction in reading & whilst you are about it
during the next three months you may write just as long letters as
you please for I pay no postage for any thing being about a
hundred miles beyond the reach of any of those respectable
individuals yclept postmasters. And Agnes you say too has gone
mad. I really thought she had some sense but girls are soon spoilt
especially at Laugharne. I am afraid you will never recover [from]
the fever you caught there. I am now a regular wanderer on the
face of the other [*sic* earth] travelling every two or three days 8 or
10 miles further & surveying the boundary as we move along.
There is certainly an excess of work but my horse is strong & we
get over the ground pretty fast. I shall start at 3 or 4 in the
morning, ride 5 or 6 miles to the work & then survey till about 10
and then with an umbrella over my head to keep the sun off
journey home where I generally arrive and breakfast at about 11.
At three I start again, work till dark and then come home again
then dine on fowl roast or boiled no vegetables but sometimes rice
& curry and between 8 & 9 am [*sic*] generally fast asleep. I must say
I like it much for it is all out of door work and the climate and the
scenery is so lovely that it really is quite a delicious trip. We are at
the foot of the hills sometimes a little in them and about 30 miles
off are the snowy mountains which with the sun shining on them
is beautiful beyond all belief. In addition to this my day tent altho'
very old is very cool and large 18 feet square inside with double
Kerrisants[32] or walls four feet apart to keep the air inside the tent
cool. I will explain to you the means of construction of these tents
which in India are absolutely necessary. 1st there on the inside is a
large pole between 18 and twenty feet long about three feet from
the top the inner fly coincidence which is composed of 4 pieces of
cloths the inner one being a chintz ornamented with flowers &c
and giving the same appearance to the inside of the tent as
papering does to a room. Above these four cloths but anchored
together so as to form one is another fly of three cloths leaving a

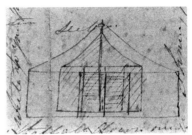

Robinson's sketches of tents, Letter 5.

space of between two & 3 feet between the two so that the suns beams after penetrating thro' the upper fly has [*sic* have] to pass through two or three feet of air before it reaches the second fly. Inside connected with the fly are the four walls or Kerrisants of the tent which also are composed of four & 8 cloths respectively but separated so as to make a verandah all around the tent of 3 or 4 feet. You may perhaps twig this from a sketch.

The doors are flaps of canvas that fall down over the opening & inside there are chicks a kind of network of rushes or cane so close as to allow the air and light to enter freely but to prevent flies also all those horrid insects from finding their way in. There is also a good carpet inside and the walls being 6 feet high and the middle about fifteen feet there is a very comfortable room to live in. These two last days we have had nothing but heavy thunder storms during all this time the outer fly has been wet thro' but the inner one has been perfectly dry & consequently so have we.

The sepoys tent[s] are very much like Gypsies in a large scale. From this we go on towards Noorpore[33] where we have one regiment of Native-Infy[34], thence across a little to the westward of Bimbur[35] & so on skirting the hills nearly up to Peshawur.[36] The object of this is to fix the boundary between our own, Goolab Sing's & the Lahore government['s territory], this will therefore oblige us to go almost to the summit of the Himalayas to mark out the Hill boundary. This will be a pleasant trip won't it.

It is almost needless to state that the part of the country we are now in has never been visited by Europeans much less by Government officers employed in enquiring about the villages and boundary, so that [the people] understand nothing at all of our system and moderation. The consequence is they begin my [sic by] making presents to the chuprassis (literally heart plate men i.e. men who wear a cross belt with a plate on it indicating who & whose servants they are) in hopes of not being plundered by them. They then present the sirdars or heads of the department[s] with sisifens[37] or presents from the inferior to the superior. This being with a hope that their fields will be less [sic more] lightly taxed originally but now so much a matter of course that they give it now as a kind of tribute. Now by the last India Company's order all such presents are forbidden to be accepted excepting such trifles as fruit, flowers & eatables, the consequence is that whenever I hap near a village and I pass such dayly they make me a present of sweetmeats, <u>rupees</u> & a goat or horse or something of the sort and they cannot understand the refusal and immediately fancy that I am angry and disgusted at the Nuzur[38] being so small. The consequence is [that] most ludicrous scenes sometimes ensue and it takes much persuasion on the part of the sepoys who speak the language of course better than I do to pacify them. One jemadar or head of the village the other day offered me a goat. I was busy at the time taking an observation so that I did not attend to him until one of the sepoys told him that a goat was not enough for a village like his and it must be a horse. The poor old gentleman got very frightened and assured me that he was but a very poor man. Indeed he was, that it had never been the custom at that village to give more than a goat but that it was the jemadar of the next village who belonged to the same jagheer[39] always gave a horse, but that the sweetmeats were making and should be sent the next day. I then touched his rupees with my hand to signify that I accepted and returned them. Another poor villager of one of the villages where we encamped was told by one of my sepoys to make a wooden saddle for him. When it was made he brought it to the sepoy who somehow or other took it immediately and refused to pay for it and on the other man expostulating abused him. The villager than came and complained to me and said he had been struck. I therefore enquired into [it] thro' my orderly and the man then said he had not been struck but only abused. Well to stop all further trouble I asked him the value of his sadle he said one <u>pice</u> or the 1/4 of one anna. I gave him therefore one anna which is high and is something less than 3 halfpence. The man stared prostrated himself on the ground and offered me back the 3 pice. After much trouble I convinced him that the whole anna was for himself; no he couldn't understand it. At last he was convinced and before leaving the tent gave me the sadle. I told him I didn't want it & after more trouble I got rid of him but even then he wanted [to] give one pice to the orderly who had let him into my tent. You ask if any of the Robinsons have written to me since I have been in this country. I am sorry none of them have. Indeed I believe it is partly my fault but I have been moving about so much since last September that I really have not had time to write to any one previous to the battle of Sobraon.[40] I believe I did not write to you for two months. Since that I have had as much as I could manage to do until these last two days and tomorrow will commence again. This has been principally owing to three days of thunder storms such as one does not often seen in England or even of such long duration in India. Give my love to all at home, keep Jack quiet & believe my dear sister Yr affectionate Brother

D.G. Robinson

Camp Jindree April 20th 1846
somewhere near Pathankote
Lat 31.50 N Long 76 E

My dear Mary

Your congratulations are so kind and as Ninetta says your letter is so full of nonsense that I cannot resist the opportunity of answering it in order to put your head straight again. It is now so many months since I have seen an Englishwoman and even then those that I did see were so perfectly different in manners, class and general appearance that I began to think that you were in England a kind of divinities only to be regarded after ten years of searching in these arid plains. But unfortunately you who I really had a good opinion of have quite broken the spell and led me to think that women are still mad at times. I suppose it is like the hares in March periodical for I do remember the last time we met. However to make a short story as we say in this country I am neither married, smitten nor is there the least probability of my being so for two years <u>certain</u> during which time I shall be employed on the frontier or rather beyond the frontier for at the end of the time I mention I shall most likely be somewhere about Peshawur. At the time you wrote there were some possibilities of being shot which you hint at. They say mad people have a presentiment of this kind but "be that as it may" I am still alive & got a medal for the campaign and battle of Subraon and had the satisfaction of being one of the first to enter Lahore and Mirritsir[41] and seen much more of the country and real life than most people see in the first ten [years]. I heard from Harry[42] about three months since. He was then at Kurachee[43] but I have been so hard at work since that I have never had time to answer it.[44] However the rains will start in about another six weeks and then I shall of [*sic* have] plenty of rest & shall write & tell ma[ ]d I think I shall enclose to him your epistle on the strength of which we may manage to get a de lunatico ingendered on your body the mind being supposed to have flown. However as Polonius in Hamlet says your madness seems to have a method in it & indeed it would be hard to conceal from any enemy that you are smitten somewhere most probably unrequited affection as you talk of the cold and you desire to emigrate to change the scene. But joking apart think twice before you act. You may approve of Calcutta but Calcutta is no more India than the West End of London is to Johnny Groats house. In Calcutta the houses <u>are all palaces</u> magnificent as a whole beyond any part of London. The society & manners of Calcutta are English every thing is English even provisions, but up the country for there you mean to go I suppose when you start you will live for months on fowls unvarying fowls called <u>Leadden deaths</u> and chaupatties a kind of heavy pastry biscuit only soft & much like what dogs are fed on. I have not tasted bread these three months. But ladies certainly do not live much in tents excepting when marching from station to station. This kind of life I like beyond any thing & hate a house. I have now lived since last September in tents marching about the country shooting sometimes but always with out of door work & more than enough to occupy the mind and having command of a company detached I am never in want of a guard or men for any purpose. Give my love to all at home & congratulate Sarah for me. When you come to Calcutta give me timely warning that I may be prepared. In your disgust of the heat you do not know what it is [to] sit with almost nothing on with the mosquitos bighting thro' your socks and the <u>perspiration</u> flowing from every pore in <u>streams</u>. Anne I think was only in India in the cold weather, she never tried the hot. With many wishes for your recovery. Believe me yr. affectionate cousin

Daniel G. Robinson

6

Daniel George Robinson to his father

Camp Nr. Noorpore[45]
June 15th 1846

My dear Father

My last[46] I believe was dated from Kangra and [*sic* an] exceedingly strong hill fort which has resisted many sieges of great length even when conducted by the renowned Runjeet Sing and which we also were besieging or rather commencing the siege but unfortunately they gave in just as all the difficulties were over.[47] It is strongly situated by nature being almost totally inaccessible but otherwise is of small importance in holding the district in which it is situated being rather a higher one than otherwise. From Kangra we marched across (i.e. my company) the hills towards Noorpore and took possession of Kotla on the way a fort something like Kangra very securely situated but nothing like so strong. The gallant defenders of this strong hold who against the orders of their own government [which] refused to give up the place, bolted long before our arrival, considering it preferable to escape than to have the chance of hanging. From Kotla we came here and here we mean to pass the rains and are busy building huts for that purpose for the men and ourselves. Noorpore (i.e. the city of light) is a colony of Cashmerians driven from their own country in consequence of their continued troubles being one year conquered by Tartars, and then by Afghans & perhaps the 3rd by the Sikhs and as almost all Cashmere seems to be employed in making shawls and scarfs, so do all the inhabitants of Noorpore spend their time in the same employment. At Lahore and Amritsir[48] I have seen some beautiful and some expensive ones but still these are very beautiful and cheap being seldom more than 20 or 25 pounds the pair. The scenery is wild in the extreme but desolate – there being so little water that herds of cattle or goats are scarcely to be seen any where. In Noorpore they have 360 dry wells and 4 with water [in] them. The consequence is that all the water has to be brought from the river up some 500 or 600 steps principally carried by women who seemed to be looked upon as naturally the slaves and consequently the drudges of man. To beat a woman severely is looked upon as something good rather than otherwise and I was considered to deal very harshly with a sepoy the other day who I punished for severely beating a woman in the camp. They are bought and sold sometimes, and if a man complains to a magistrate of another man seducing & running away with his wife he would say she cost me 60 rupees and what I [*sic*] am I to do now without any body to bring my water, sweep my house and make my chauppattis. At the same time they make a great fuss of their marriages, no man marrying his daughter to a man of lower caste generally speaking instead always to a higher caste. The inhabitants of these hills being poor, the means of subsistence small and principally Rajpoots and Brahmins (the highest castes) they find great difficulty in providing their daughters with husbands. The marriage expenses being so heavy & a man of higher caste difficult to obtain they therefore murder nearly every female child as soon as it is born and women thus becoming scarce <u>each wife has 4 or more husbands</u>. Suttee also is excessively common in these hills and when we took possession of them they positively petitioned in very large numbers to be allowed to continue both it and infanticide of course they were told that both crimes would be punished as murder. At this answer they looked very glum. They are nevertheless delighted with their change of masters and are exceedingly civil on all occasions. The last overland is now in but I have as yet received no letters by it. I should be glad to receive letters twice a month from England for now that we are beyond our own territory and far beyond that of European civilization a letter from old England comes more agreeably than ever. I think I told you of my having got an increase of 200 rupees a month which keeps my funds not only in a flourishing condition but in one that is already rapidly regenerating and I hope at the end of the year to have made the 1st instalment to England of £200, 50 of it goes to Calcutta as soon as ever I can get drafts and I fancy the other money will rapidly follow as we shall draw our batta in another month my share of which is a trifle more than £100 and against which I am happy to say I have no claimants. I also want to increase my stud not with expensive but with hard working quiet horses. I have now a horse and a pony but they cannot stand half the work required of them as I am sometimes in the saddle from daylight to sunset and sometimes required to ride 40 or 50 miles which 2 horses could not do in this climate with any thing like speed. I think I wrote to you about a Peat's saddle.[49] I wanted a medium size with all the appurtenances for pistol holsters saddle bags &c to rise much in front for a high withered horse and at the same time to be light. The stirrup irons to be the spring safety and the saddle of the description called the infantry mounted officers, to be 1' 7" long from front to rear measured on the saddle and 1' 8" when measured in the end viz direct from front to rear. I believe some where about the same time I wrote for a prismatic compass which I hope is out by this time. Millington's book arrived some time since but where it is I have not a notion. I knew it was at Allahabad but whether it has moved from there or not I am in perfect ignorance of. I believe the mercantile houses in Calcutta are not quite so healthy just now as they were, one house commission sale agent having failed for 5 lacks and upwards. I have merely heard the 1st hinted, the latter I know to be true.

I am very much vexed and have no doubt that you are with the disgraceful manner the rich members have been behaving in the house of Commons. In India every body came forward willingly with their mites and I believe raised by no means an inconsiderable sum of money. Then surely Irishmen ought to do something for their own country and their own estates. What a pity Dan O'Connell[50] was not hung whilst they were about it. I believe we are to have an army of exercise the next cold weather on the S[ou]th bank of the Sutledge seemingly to manoeuvre in those large plains and jungles where our late battles were fought [but] really more as an army of observation and to keep all quiet at Lahore and in the Punjab. I am now going to write to Ninetta and other friends in England which this rainy weather gives me an opportunity of for once. Farewell my dear Father.

Yr affect. Son
Daniel G. Robinson

[P.S.] Ralph Young[51] my companion late of the free Irish Garrison & Rich sends his best respects. Why? I don't know.

7

Daniel George Robinson to his sister

Camp Noorpore June 18th 1846

My dear Sister

I am sorry to find no letters by this last mail for me from England. I wish you would write twice a month & never mind the expense as if you cannot I can very well afford to pay the postage. I suppose you have heard of my having got a staff allowance of 200 a month extra making my pay something upwards of Rs 450 a month in all and now instead of having to screw in every way I am saving money and living as comfortably as one can under canvas and getting vegetables and meat when we can. Our food generally speaking being oatmeal cakes, eggs and fowls the latter yclept leaden deaths from the rapid method in which they are disposed of when required for even fowls in England are generally considered luxuries here they are so small that 7 a day for two persons is nothing uncommon and I have known one person eating as many as 9 a day. Now don't laugh because this is fact. We are here in a most lovely country w[h]ere there [are] only woods about it and the sun less hot. It is beautifully wild with the snowy mountains apparently quite close and successive ranges of hills between [?beyond] us and then some 4000 feet above the sea the next range 7000 the next 12000 to 15000 and the next something higher somewhere between 18000 and 20000 so that were we masters of our movements we might choose the climate most congenial to our feelings, but as we cannot we can only look and wish. In your last letter you say Mary and Kate Shield were staying with you surely the former might have sent one of her <u>saucy</u> scribblings. I certainly should have enjoyed them and should have laughed much at the attempts to [be] sarcastic which is all that I suppose Mary aims at.

You also say Miss Agassiz[52] wrote to enquire about me. I am much obliged to her for it and hope that you will write and thank her for me. Do you ever go to see them or do you ever correspond with them. You know I have a hope I have some friends there who I should be glad to hear of, so mind that in your next.

Annie also is or was a great friend of mine and often promised to write me letters and so indeed she did till she was married.[53] They have never written to me once from Jersey and I think they ought to have.

Agnes you said has taken to flirting and a f[st] beau so I suppose there's nothing coming from there. I have more charity however than you and believe it is all lightness of heart rather than anything else. She certainly is a mischievous little thing but whose fault is it.

We are encamped here in this "the city of the light" where the rains are regularly set and the quantity of water that falls on the tent would fill it in a week w[h]ere it watertight and turned topsy turvy. The inhabitants sole employment seems to be making the celebrated Cashmere shawls made of the <u>under</u> wool of a peculiar breed of goat that runs wild in the snowy hills not far from here. They make them very beautifully and very cleverly and the prices are by no means very expensive so that I might be tempted to send you a scarf or shawl or something of the sort but the distance from

Calcutta is so enormous that the carriage would be more expensive than the shawls and when they arrived they would very probably be spoiled. I can fancy you and your lady friends getting one that would cost in this country about 25 to 150 £ and exclaiming what a duck of a delightful little shawl. I see you have got a literary gazette at Camberwell or something of the sort which you say are for the ladies and <u>gents</u>. Pray who are those last named individuals. When I was in England they were generally supposed to mean certain shop boys, post boys &c in their Sunday best smoking bad cigars and drawling in what would be a melodious tone where it left to the said shop boy to judge.

Why does not Charly write.[54] Does nobody ever hear from that ship. Surely they cannot be so situated as to [be] unable to write at least once in two months. I sincerely hope he is not running wild but I must say I have great fears that way at present. Please God next mail will give better accounts. And master Jack I suppose is quite busy with <u>the</u> house.[55] I wish they would do something there for Ireland instead of fighting amongst themselves. People in India are disgusted but I have no doubt that were they themselves there they would fight as hard as any of them.

We are I believe to have peace here for the next four or five months and then I should not [at] all be surprised if we have another row in the Punjab. There is no telling any thing though at present beyond this that the present Sikh government are in the midst of a thousand difficulties from which I much doubt if they will ever be able to extract themselves. They have no exchequer, every body is grumbling, and the moment our troops are withdrawn there will be the same scenes as before and I suppose an equal number [of] Sirdars heads cut off. I shall write two or three more letters to England if possible this mail but if I have not time give my love to all friends and believe me my dear sister.

Yr affect. Brother Daniel G. Robinson

[P.S.] Don't forget to let me know about the E[dlmann]'s at Bromley.[56] I have particular reasons for wishing to know which if you are discreet you shall know too some day.

8

Daniel George Robinson to his sister

Camp Nr. Noorpore Augt. 8th 1846

My dear Sister

So you've had a great flare up & turned the house inside out. Thank God I was [not] at home to witness such absurdities. It is now some months since I have seen a lady & I am turned rather a misanthrope in the female line. Tell Mary so & say it was all the fault of her letter. Gipsy life I have often much admired in England but they haven't half a notion of comfort there really. There is something delightful in swanning about amongst this beautiful scenery somethimes awfully grand at other times sweetly soft. If you only knew the comfort of swanning alone & meditating on [it] you would never again wish for society. The only thing that vexes one is the damage done to ones cattle. Since I last wrote I have bought the most beautiful chestnut poney I have ever seen. When mounted his action and fire are so grand that every one takes him [at] a little distance for a full sised arab horse. Well he's now laid up & likely to be so for the next 10 days from a cut on the rocks, just as soon as my other poney had got well & my horse Peter my first in the country & a very great favorite has been laid up for the last three weeks & heaven knows when he'll get well from a thorn in the fetlock joint & so it is with every body's horses. However out of the three I almost always have one fit to ride & as this is the rainy season I have not much work to do & only ride for pleasure. I hope your party went off well I should certainly have liked to have been at the feed but I do [not] think the ladies would have admired my breeches & jack boots or gaiters.

I am glad to hear there is at last a chance of Charly's return home soon. I think he has been quite long enough away from home & six months study at home might fit him for passing his Lieutenant examination. If he has not got too old and unused to study he ought to be able to get up his work easily in 6 months & then he would be ready to receive his lieutenantcy as soon as Government pleased. I don't know whether I asked you to write & thank Miss Agassiz for her kind enquiries. I would do so myself but this being the last day for the post I have not time.

It is by no means improbable that we shall pass this winter in peace at any rate an army of exercise as it is called is to be assembled on the Sutledge & I have no doubt but that in the event of serious disturbances in the Punjab we shall take possession of it especially as it is the wish of a large portion of the inhabitants of the country even of such as are Sikhs. The latter form but a very small proportion of the inhabitants by far the greater part being mussalmans and Hindoos. The assimilation of the Sikhs to the latter is certainly very great they both believing in the same deities &c but the Sikhs try to destroy the prejudice of caste & so quarrel with both Hindoos & mussalmans indeed there is a bitter hatred between them and the latter it is like the Christian half caste who is utterly despised by the blacks & despised with pity by us. They call them John's Christians & go to church to sleep for they cannot understand English at all & have no knowledge of the bible or indeed of any religion whatever added to which they even if of good family & educated as gentlemen are denied access to the army either as officer or soldier they can only be drummers & they are a beastly dumb set when thus.

So I see that Jenkin Jones has gone to Bombay.[57] Was that his own choice or was he sent there. In former times I believe that was the favourite presidency but in our corps there the promotion is dreadfully slow & he will necessarily enter very low indeed. Burke who is a son of Sir John Burke is still only a second Lieut. & he has been at least seven years in the service.[58] Their death steps[59] [are] certainly likely to be rapid for they've got back that delightful place Scinde which Bombay was always wanting & we ever always wanting to get rid of.[60] Henry Miller did not however seem very anxious to go there. I got Jacks scribble some time back & will write to him the first time I have time but I have as much always on my hands as I can manage & were this not the rainy season I doubt if I should be able to write an over land at all this mail. Give my love to Mary and thank her for her last epistle which contained a little more of the <u>rationale</u> than any of her previous. I should have been glad to have seen Earby [?] Cook up here where he would see finer scenery than he ever did in Europe. Every tree & waterfall would be run after in England to be made a sketch of.

Every thing is natural nothing stiff. Whether he ever came to Ferozepore I am unaware if he did but he ought to have visited Simla, Missouree,[61] Agra, Delhi, Lucknow and all that part of India where the ruins of the Mogul rule are to be found. I must now conclude with love to all at home & hoping you receive monthly the Delhi mail and Summary. Farewell

Yr affect. Brother

Daniel G. Robinson

9

Daniel George Robinson to his sister

Camp Nr. Noorpore Sepr 27th [18]46

My dear Sister

We are still encamped on the same ground as my last have [*sic* half] dozen letters have been dated from so that I cannot please your ears or rather eyes with eloquent descriptions of new beauties of scenery. This last month has as usual been an exceedingly unhealthy one to us taking us as a party altho' I personally thank God have enjoyed excellent health considering of my company out of 97 sepoys at this moment 60 are in hospital. Our chief Abbott the Commissioner also is ill but Young & I have escaped with merely a touch for one day the complaint being intermittent fever vulgarly called ague. The rains however being nearly over we hope to have them all well in a fortnight. There have been no deaths & the illness seldom lasts more than 8 or 10 days at a time. I lay our good health entirely to the great exercise we take & precautions in dress &c to say nothing of having an excellent house of its kind over our heads. I have only two syces (grooms) to my three horses & they both being ill they cannot exercise my horses so that I generally manage somehow or other to ride two every day some little distance and back. My newest fellow the prettiest of the lot does not at all understand his work yet so that I have had to build some hedges adjoining the house & teach him to jump them & ditches without trepidation & it is surprising how well he is getting on but he makes a sad fuss about ditches which generally

103

intersect my work to a very great extent. However I hope & think he'll yet be something more than first rate. A horse for my present work must fear nothing be able [to] walk on the back of a knife & stand without moving a muscle to allow to me to take angles off his back & when they do the latter properly they become truly invaluable.

Perhaps when I next write I shall be on the road to Cashmere but it is still in my opinion very doubtful. Goolab Sing⁶² of Jummoo⁶³ to whom we give over the territory of Cashmere can't hold his own at present there & if he be again thrashed of course we shall go and help him & has [*sic* as] that will have to be done pretty sharply I shall of course be senior officer of Sappers in this spot & command them & if in loss it turns out something like the Kangra business I may still have an opportunity of distinguishing myself before I settle down quietly which I think it very probable after I return from my wanderings in this part of the country to the plains of Hindostan where one cannot live in tents without suffering in one's health. I have not received any letters from you this six weeks so that I cannot tell you any thing in answer to any letters you may have <u>meant</u> to have written. Being hard up for any more news than you will find in the overland Mercury I must now conclude with hopes that you have enjoyed your country trip & got a little more active & are in good spirits & with kind love to you & Jack farewell.

Yr affect. Brother

Daniel G. Robinson

10

Daniel George Robinson to his sister

6th December [1846] Camp So[ ]pore⁶⁴

My dear Sister

The 6th of December being your birthday and I having also received another letter from you to day I'll write you a long letter with out abusing you much especially as your last letter is a little more charitable than the former. I also send you a little hair to

Dear Miss
  You wanted pictures & you've got 'em
(Letter 10)

stick in your ring in case you have not put in my friends which would do just as well. If you are a regular trump you must be the Queen or a small Jack and if so I win since I must be the King and consequently a greater score [than] you therefore praise not thyself again. I am glad to hear Agnes is going to be married and hope she will then turn steady. As to my writing to her first it was absurd. Smith is certainly common and John Smith horridly so but only think of Higgin or Stiggins or any other such cognomen. Smith would be paradise compared to it. You seem to think seven fowls a very serious undertaking for a single gentleman's consumption. My friend certainly has a wonderful appetite & not content with that is the most troublesome fellow to came [*sic* cater] for it was ever my misfortune to close with he is so fond of the tit bits. If you and Mrs Milford mean to pay me a visit I am afraid you must be a little mad as no English lady was ever in this part of the world & I'll answer that an Englishman has never been into these immediate villages & how you would find your way without palankeen bearers I don't know as I do not think you would ride 10 miles on a ghoont[65] twice in a week. I think you had better stay where you are until some young lady having fallen desperately in love with me & I having a very respectable fortune may wish you to escort her to Calcutta where having been hailed for one week and disgusted with the natives for another I have no doubt you will wish to return to England immediately. I have now been some little time in India & have a decent notion of the language and customs of the natives and I should now be very sorry to throw up my present appointment & return to England on 400 a year altho' a much larger sum. I love the roving independent life I lead. I get any thing done by mentioning it I have no troubles about small accounts & I don't miss the want of society at all, at all. I get up before day light & as soon as I have washed and dressed am in the saddle. At 9 o'clock in the evening I have eaten my dinner smoked a cheroot and in all probability am asleep in bed or going to. Sundays are generally days of rest comparatively speaking at least I never shoot or do any work beyond perhaps marching 8 or 10 miles. Sometimes when I have time I sketch a little but I seldom can find that [*sic* the] time. Today I received one letter yrs being the first for the last month not that others were not written but somehow or other they never come near me & this is the only nuisance I have to complain of. Since my separation from the commissioner[66] letters seem to go here there & every where but the right place. I am much obliged to you for your kind offers with regard to the Miss E[dlmann]'s but you must neither commit yourself nor me. From some little things you have mentioned occasionally I should fancy Mr E[dlmann] a very queer character. I should like to hear more of him & I think you might venture a sketch so as to give me a good idea not only of the man but of your powers of description. I think I once heard a queer scheme about an old castle in Germany & feudal times &c quite romantic in conception but perfectly absurd in practise and if that be true I think [little of] your chance of any of them staying with you for fear of their learning any of the sad practices of society dancing &c. I have just been interrupted by a visit from about 20 big & little wigs who after talking to [me] very gravely for the last half hour have driven all my beautiful thoughts out of my head. However I'll try and go on again. As to Mr E[dlmann] letting his daughter visit in such bad company I think it very improbable as even our good father no doubt a very respectable man was never admitted to the honor of dining with them. As to your visiting them it is quite another thing and I think quite practicable & tho' I give you a carte blanche as to some things you must not subject yourself to a defeat by committing either yourself or me but be guided by circumstances. I dou[b]t more than one half of what you say about Charly's threat of leaving the Navy. You merely state something about some such fact but do not mention any thing of the contents of his letter. I am very anxious indeed that he should quickly return to England or I am afraid he may be entirely ruined by a few years more riotous life away from his friends & true advisers. That he of his own free will should leave the Navy is I think highly improbable all I fear is that he may be obliged to do so. If of his own free will he does leave he can of course expect nothing more from our Father not even his present allowance & how he is to support himself I cannot tell. I don't think he can either. I fancy I shall see Henry Hyde[67] in a few days he is bringing

'Evening costume to receive visitors'

Camp Sepore 20th

My dear Sister
Our tents &c. [sic: from] your affec^te Br.

D.G. Robinson
(not from life)

(Letter 10)

up the relieving Company which he will have to make over to me and he then returns with my old company to Meerut. I shall be sorry to change as I know my old company so well. They are old veterans. My new company is composed of new recruits who will require a steady breaking in. I don't know whether he expects to hold my appointment if so I fear he will be disappointed.

I think I have forgotten now three times now being thrice. I have written & forgot to mention a telescope I want the best that can be got under £10 decently portable without stand or any thing of that kind but with leather cylinder & end covers & a strap to the same for the shoulders. A large field & great power for seeing great distances if the two can be combined & if no the greatest power with the largest field combinable with the same.

I think I have now performed my promise and written a pretty long letter.

[Not signed]

I have sent to you some hair of my own

11

Daniel George Robinson to his sister

Camp Ramgurh[68]
Jany 5th 1846 [*sic* 1847]

My dear Sister

I am going to write to you now not because I think you deserve it considering the manner in which you wasted a full half sheet of paper in writing half a dozen lines of next door to nonsense but because I have filled the sheets of our good father's letter & I want to tell him some of the wanderings of Daniel Robinson Esq & as I can thus <u>kill</u> two birds with one stone I have let you have the honor as I could not deny you the profit namely the power of reading the aforesaid Generals letter. You will therefore I hope appreciate in a proper manner the honor conferred. Christmas day has passed away as all other Christmas days have done and had it not been for the usual presents of sweetmeats &c, the noise of the buglers & other martial customs by which the natives shew their respect for the sahib's <u>birra</u> din (great day) I should hardly have know that it was Xmas. My companion Young heretic that he is could not help getting ill and the result was that I [had a] quiet dinner all to my self. Not that the dinner was a bad one. I had shot a pair of wild ducks beautiful fish capital soup for the principle excellent mutton & a filling pudding & one bottle of champ[agne] that he carefully kept back for the last six weeks. This Xmas was spent in a house. It [has] a small room with a double verandah [which] might be called so in the city of Jummoo. On the road to Jummoo just as I had returned from a capital run after something of the wolf species that had got up on the road I was met by a detachment sent from

109

Jummoo by Rajah Rumbeer Sing, Goolab Sing's eldest son.[69] They rode with us into Jummoo and escorted us to the house which the Maharajah[70] had built for Capt. Nicholson[71] and after seeing as much after our comfort as they as natives could, they took their leave, first requesting to know when we would visit the Rajah. I said that I could go that day but that I would call the next day at 12 o'clock. The same evening, just as we had sat down to dinner, the gentleman with the the [*sic*] green dress & green & yellow spindle shanks something thinner than my wrist whose duty it was to attend on all Englishmen visiting Goolab Sing's capital made his appearance with a present of 225 rupees for me & sweetmeats & provisions for us all. He also gave me to understand that it would be highly inconvenient to the Rajah to receive us at 12 o'clock but that if we would go early in the morning it would be better. Of course we concurred in his opinion. Having eaten 8 mutton chops, 4 eggs, sundry sweetmeats, 4 oranges & a few chauppattis &c I feel in a fit condition to continue my episode. What do you think of my notion of a breakfast. Like Capt. Clutterbuck it is necessary to lay in store kana[72] for the whole day as you may & you may not get your dinner after a ride of 20 coss.[73]

Breakfast been [*sic* being] finished I will now proceed sending on the traps to find us in dinner in the evening when we canter over to Kaine[74] about 11 coss. Well the next morning I found myself in uniform at 8 o'clock in the morning much to my astonishment I hardly knew myself I looked so spruce not that I went in full dress I merely put on a plain shell jacket & white trowsers not neglecting the sword which shows the gentleman, always amongst natives who on visits of ceremony never neglect their sword and shield. On going to the palace we first looked at the guns which were in a shed near the gate of the palace. The[y] were very fair guns considering but not of very heavy calibre, brass of course iron being rarely seen in this country at least in native states. We then went to the Sheesh Muhul, or receiving room, and after having been left seated alone for a few minutes the rajah made his appearance. On entering the room he took of[f] his shoes the same as we do hats he shook hands with us & motioned us to sit down. Of course being my first time of visiting I was not exactly up to the etiquette of the occasion altho I perfectly understood receiving people according to their rank. However, after a few questions we got into an animated conversation about things in general the country of Cashmere &c amongst other things of his shooting preserves which he invited me to shoot over. I asked him his mode of hunting he said that he generally took up his station near some part of the wood and some hundred beaters drive the game towards him & as he always has five or six guns loaded the number of hares, pigs & deer slaughtered were considerable. I explained to him that our custom of hunting was in this country vulgarly called "pig sticking" was by riding swift horses and spearing them explaining how necessary it was to be very active or that the boar in his charge would rip up your horse. He did not at all seem to admire such sport. We then took our leave. Next morning I went up to the top of the range of hills on which Jummoo stands to see what kinds of observations might be got from them & on returning to breakfast was told that a gentleman of this parish vulgarly called Runbeer Sing[75] meant to call upon us as soon as we had breakfasted. The gentleman made his appearance and had the forethought to send a couple of chairs of which we had not a super abundance. I had had a guard of honor drawn up to receive him. On arriving at the gate of the court yard he dismounted and walked in leaving his shoes at the entrance of the 2nd verandah. He of course was anxious to know something about the foundry & I shewed him the rough map I had made of it. He then looked at the theodolite & compass & understanding just as much about such useful things as you lady ignoramuses would have was of course much edified. He then began talking of guns &c and I asked him how it was that he had such a taste for war[like] affairs. He said that when his eldest brother, who was killed with Heerah Sing[76] on the Lahore anarchical outbreaks,[77] was alive his brother (the heir apparent) attended to the affairs of the country i.e. civil affairs & that he therefore attended to military affairs & that his fancy for such things still remained. He told me also that he had just raised 2 companies of Sappers & Miners who had pleased Colonel Lawrence the Poll. Agent[78] much in the passes to Cashmere. He then wished to see the arms and equipments of our sappers & miners & their tools. The tools he thought too heavy to be carried on the march & shewed me his designs which were very clever but much too light in my opinion for sappers. In part his men were pioneers. He admired our carbines & swords but wondered why they were only sharpened at the point. I explained to him that if they were sharp at the sides the discipline of the men would be destroyed and that instead of charging steadily with the point they would always cut. He then made some shrewd remarks about his being a hill country & consequently unadapted for combined movements & that it was therefore desirable to make every man able to fight independently. He then shewed me his own guns & seemed to prefer shooting with them to our English ones because they carried further. They were all made in Jummoo the trade of which he takes great care to support & it to[o] seemed to me that for this reason he used these guns the designs about the locks were some of them very clever. On my companion who had been ill for some time attempting to shoulder one of his long matchlocks he found he was not strong enough. The Rajah then took it up and shouldered it as easy as possible. He was certainly a powerful young man for a native of his rank who are generally very debauched. He is only 19 in my opinion polite & very clever. When I asked him why he had not brought his younger brother[79] he said that he was with his schoolmaster & informed me what he was learning & what it was intended he should learn. After a long talk he went away & sent me back one of his matchlocks which I admired, as a present, & I sent him my six barrelled revolving pistol which they tell me he admires immensely & always carries in his heart. His matchlock was not worth half the pistol but is a great curiosity having got the signet of his uncle engraved on it. This latter was that celebrated Commander in Chief of Runjeet Sing[80] and one of the celebrated brothers mentioned in a dozen tales in the Punjab. I have seen now several of the great characters of the Punjab and had a good opportunity of studying them. Some I found to be intelligent & pleasant in their conversations, others imoderate & coarse [ ] vain stupid & proud only of [their] lineage which of course [means] they never receive poor Europeans.

You[r] threat of sending me some jams I hope you will not carry out. Just fancy paying the carriage of jams for 1200 miles of inland conveyance in addition to the sea carriage so that your jams could cost about 30 or 40 shillings the pot. Much obliged to you but would rather not. The evening before leaving Jummoo the Rajah sent us the usual present of Rooksutana.[81] Mine consisted of 9 magnificent Cashmere shawls, some silks & fine linen. Of course I refused them although tempted to accept them. But I should have to paid [sic pay] Govt about £100 for the pair of shawls & I therefore thought would not treat you to such a vanity. Capt Abbott our chief & the Boundary Commissioner is an intimate friend of Mrs. H. Hardinge but I am not aware that he is considered well here.

Kind love to Jack, Father & self & all the Uncles, Aunts &c you may correspond with. I hope Uncle William[82] is well. I have not written to him for want of time but shall soon. Knap Jonas not having answered my letters I do not consider him my debtor. I hope Aunt Jonas is better.[83]

Yr affect. Brother

Daniel G. Robinson

[P.S.] With regard to Mary Miller I have written once or twice. Send her my kind love and tell her that her letters pleased me much & I entreat a continuance of them merely omitting the nonsense. From what I saw of the life of a Midshipman & the manners of the mates on board Greene's ships[84] I am afraid Freddy Miller[85] will not be much improved by a voyage to India. I think something better might have been found for him. I suppose you are not aware that I am going to be married. It is a secret & only known to a very limited few. I shall not describe the young lady for fear you might be able to recognise the portrait. One thing I'll tell you and that is that she is not in India & has never been there.

You admit that you love scandal, that you love scolding & every woman's curiosity is insatiable so I have merely found you food for the latter the most amiable. With regard to your album & the sketches wanted I am going to turn stingy also. First because I am fourteen hundred miles from Calcutta & next that I have no time to copy those few out for myself because I remember you committing some petty larceny & stealing all the good sketches I made in England but I shall be happy to sell you them. Bye the Bye ask Father to send me some black sable brushes in a bottle, 9 large, 6 small & 4 small red sables 6 pieces of India rubber, 1 cake of burnt sienna & some <u>constant</u> white & a new very thick ivory protractor & half a section of very thin Tone in [a] pot.

12

Daniel George Robinson to his sister[86]

My dear Sister
Another of your disgraceful scraps of paper has found its way into our good father's letter. I wonder he admits such light articles & that you are not ashamed to write such short notes. Next time I receive one so short I'll write you an Anglo-Indian chit which none of you shall understand without the aid of some Indian friend as an interpreter such as my dear Sister your last chit was a most cutcha[87] affair and not at all d[ ] so a ghania.[88] I am much obliged for your little news and shall be glad of more & as to changing my mind that is a privilege that only belongs to ladies delightfully shewn by Agnes in her late affair de coeur.

I think it is quite as probable that Mrs Hughes treated her husband [as] shamefully ill as he [did] her. She was extremely light headed, vain and extravagant & I should think very likely to drive a grave old Major Genl mad. I don't know much of her but the little I saw of her struck me that such was the case.

I hope you enjoyed yourself at Pencraig Court.[89] The scenery of the Wye is more quietly beautiful than hereabouts, but you have not the snow clad mountains retiring one behind another with the red rough dreary looking mountains below & below them again beautifully wooded hills with here and there a village or white palace of one of the Sikh Sirdars. If you want water you must look up the bed of the Ravee or some one of the fine rivers and see it wind amongst immense rocks with a bed half a mile wide. The

Wye is a quieter sweeter kind of scenery & I am not sure which I like most. I now lead a life entirely solitary. Sometimes I & the commissioner meet and we entertain each other and are very friendly but this is seldom above once a month and were it not for the climate and the scenery I think I should soon wish to be back in cantonments with a comfortable house in the hot weather. Sometimes I breakfast at six in the morning & dine at ten at night; sometimes I breakfast at four and get no dinner. I therefore follow Capt. Culpepper's advice & eat whilst I can heartily. What do you think of three or four mutton chops and an equal quantity of eggs for a breakfast, or how should you like to sleep in an open shed with nothing but a military cloak as covering with a sharp frost falling. These are some of the pleasures I have to endure, but they are light compared to getting out of a warm comfortable bed in the middle of the night to observe fires lighted as signals for observing. This latter is really cold work & one which disgusts me much. Then also many other privations such as being unable to procure servants, clothes and other necessaries all of which can be easily obtained in cantonments. Water and tea have been my only beverages for a long time, brandy being to[o] valuable to be expended in drink & to add to my sorrows my cheroots have been long expended. I have now written much more than you deserve & with kind love to all friends.

your too affectionate Brother
Daniel G. Robinson

13

Daniel George Robinson to his father

Camp via Lahore Nr. Wuzerabad[90] on the Chenab
Feby 22nd 1847
My dear Father
The contents of your letter were on the whole not new to me as you had always given me to understand how matters stood and would be arranged and of course I always saw and appreciated the justice of your views. I am as you say well enough provided

115

for, Jack is as well and perhaps better but Charly will always have up hill work of it & though I could easily spare funds for the support of Ninetta I could not and would never consent to find her a home in this country which is so entirely unsuited to her energetic habits. I have seen but very few ladies in this country who ever manifested the least energy but how many have I seen who spent the heat of the day & the mornings in sleep and taking a ride in a comfortable carriage in the cool of the evening [and] called it exercise. Such a country would never suit Ninetta's habits and would necessarily be injurious to her health. Still though I willingly give up all claims or even wishes for personal property there are a few family relics I think I am entitled to viz your minerals, manuscripts & a few things of that kind also my grandfathers portrait & I think I have several times desired that a portrait of yourself might be painted. You know how both yourself and all your children regret that we have not a portrait of our dear mother's who was torn from us when we were so young as to have hardly any recollection of us [*sic* her]. Think then how much more valuable a portrait of yourself would be after the many years of labour and sacrifice bestowed upon us and of companionship upon me. I would request you to purchase one out of the £150 I shall send you home as a birth day gift on my coming of age did I not think that you have at present more urgent use for the money. There is also one more thing I claim as the only soldier in the family and that is your medals. I am indeed delighted to hear that you are all to have the peninsula medals.[91] Action of tolerable severity is never fought now a days without a medal being given for the same & yet I have seen no hardships during the campaign equal to what I have experienced since. I don't think that excepting in the first actions we ever went all day without food or slept the whole night without tents. Things are managed more comfortably than that when the heads of departments have to move. Some little baggage was lost & some of us always slept on the ground in our clothes but the number was limited and they always had a tent over their heads. Since in my long marches I have often gone without dinner till twelve o'clock at night & slept wrapped up in my cloak in a native's tent in which Knap Jonas would not keep his cows in the winter for fear of their catching cold. For the peninsula it was different. Happy was the man who ever had a tent or a good dinner. I do not mean to say that I am now in luxury. Beer and wine have long been strangers to my table and I live a life of almost solitude. The commissioner and I meet occasionally perhaps once a fortnight otherwise I have no companion but my own thoughts & so much work than [*sic* that] I get no rest during the day. The hot weather is however now rapidly drawing on and then I mean to take care of myself during the heat of the day & shall work only in the morning and evening out of doors. My health is excellent and I love the life I lead. Solitude occasionally is in my opinion an excellent thing for a weak mind. One can then thoroughly examine himself and feel more drawn towards God than at any time when he may in society, especially that of India where churches are known only in the largest and old stations. Evil society corrupts good manners & in no society of young men is conversation entirely free from something gross. Solitude by removing this temptation must therefore be good for the mind & soul too unless the man be of a morbid disposition. Let him have plenty of work & he cannot then well turn morbid.

In England during the vacations, those times of a schoolboy's happiness, you know that I always led an almost solitary life during the day. This perhaps is the reason why I now never feel lonely. Another thing is that my means are so simple that I have enough for small follies and to spare & I feel content because I carry out any little plans without being obliged to consider whether I could afford it. I have just had a new tent made at Futtehgurh[92] & now on its way. This tent will cost me 500 rupees before I get it, a terrible hole in a subaltern's pay, but I don't consider it any inconvenience because it is necessary for my health which I consider beyond all things in this country. Contentment is a great thing and I believe I enjoy it thoroughly excepting luxuries I have every thing that I want. My clothes certainly are of the coarsest and rudest finish but I care little for such vanities provided they are only clean. Natives love dress and gold embroidery to an extent that makes the opposite extreme approach very near to our idea of a quaker's simplicity. When they bring things for a sale I always laugh at the appearance and tell them to make strong & good things instead. Here we are curiosities and natives come from far and wide to see us. The commissioner, who wastes a good deal of money by giving it to children and beggars, is known every where as they very soon find their way like vultures to get some of the pickings. I am held in tolerably [high] respect but they declare that I am very severe because I punish the sepoys for any extortion they commit and abuse themselves [*sic* them] if they give me false information. I am now writing this by candlelight to enable you to get some news from me but as daylight is breaking I must give you an essay on Indian villainy at some further period.

I hope Ireland is getting on better and is now more quiet. Why don't some of the Tipperary gentry shoot O'Connell as their greatest pest instead of some of their good landlords.

You are all well I trust & happy. Ninetta I hope admired her valuable present. I remember the beautiful piece of opal but I never fancied you would be so good as to spoil your collection to make jewels. From Charles I hope accounts have been received. There is much in his letter which I admire, a good deal of fine feeling and straightforward speech and I feel confirmed that the [*sic*] his warm tender feelings will bring him back to the right course the moment he thinks better of it. His temper is most unruly & can in my opinion be only checked by a residence in England of some months & in my opinion Cousin Charles' society would be better than all others. God bless you all.

Yr affect. son
Daniel G. Robinson

London May 1st 1847

It is my earnest desire that the wishes of my son Daniel George herein expressed should be conformed to by his sister and brothers as far as possible.[93]

Daniel Robinson

14

Daniel George Robinson to his sister

Camp Fort Nungle[94]
March 21st 1847

My dear Sister

I have just received your letter in company with the pamphlets &
Millington's book. I admire some of your notions but that you
desire my praise for writing such a long letter certainly nothing
beyond the common. Next you coolly ask for a drawing. I have
hardly time to make any sketches. I therefore consider them
valuable & if you choose to offer a good price I have no objection
to sell them but as to a gift it is quite out of the question not to be
thought of for the hundredth part of one half minute. I had some
thoughts of sending you a prospectus of my intended publication
of views in the northern Punjaub with a portrait of the author of
the size you mention done on thick paste board but as I should
have had to pay some 8 or 10 rupees for the postage in this part of
the world I thought you were not worth the trouble of such an
expensive joke & that after all it would not come out of your
pocket. You know the price at which you may earn some thing for
your album & when I hear that you have done what I asked you I
shall think [of] sending you some drawings. The drawing of this
place would not be very bad. The Jhelum rushing over the rocks
from the mountains into the plains with the fort of Nungle on a
precipice about 200 feet high over hanging it backed by successive
ranges of mountains & until last of all the snowy range peers above
all.

I have exceedingly hard work just now in order to avoid having
over much work during the hot weather & am rather surprised at
finding myself writing to you, but as you might go to the expense
of mourning did I not, I write merely to let you know that I am
alive & if you don't receive this write & tell me. I suppose Mary
Miller is with you. Give my <u>love</u> to her & tell her I have very good
opinions of her sometimes which between you & I & the bed post
is more than I ever had of you. I wish you were in this country
climbing the goat paths. I think you would get rid of the cholic for

a minute & get a little more sensible & reasonable. Joking apart I wish your letters wrote more from the feelings & less from facts. Nor do I who consider myself above such vanities care for dances, balls & all such humbug. I want you to write your feelings, what you think not what you do, then your letters will be much more interesting. The only news I care at all about you never tell me of.

If you want to acquire habits of thinking just lead a strictly solitary life for a month or two without any European to speak to. It is an excellent schooling & one I much admire. One then becomes thrown on ones own resources & without books so resources must be thought & thinking can do no harm as it never falls on bad subjects of itself. I shall be very loth to return to the stiff forms of civilized life so called I much prefer my present life. I dress as I like I do as I like & nobody dares to critisise me. How very different it is in the miscalled civilization of society w[h]ere every body is the slave of his neighbour's opinion. If people took it into their heads that the polka was indecent nobody claiming the rights of gentility would venture to dance it & so it is with every thing else only in a lesser extent a certain rule is laid down for the handling of one's fork another for the dressing of the hair, the cut of the trousers &c ad absurdium infinitum.[95]

I have no patience with such follies. As if the breadth of the toe of one's shoe could put one any nearer heaven, which I look upon as the only great object to be obtained in this life – in my opinion – at least all other thoughts ought to be made subservient to it as far as the weakness of our natures will admit of it. I think that mixed society has a tendency to destroy all grave thoughts of this or any other kind & this is one of the objections I have to it. I like a limited silent society & am well contented with the partial companionship of Capt Abbott & my colleague Young. The latter [*sic* former] I see about once a fortnight, the latter I have not seen these three months but we correspond constantly. This letter has as you see had a drenching, but I cannot afford time to write you another. Since I commenced this I have received your letter of the 20th of Jany. You call yours a prosy letter. It is the first sensible letter I have received from you.

I hate the follies and the absurdities of fashionable life where every body seems anxious to appear what they are not instead of what they are. That there should have been gaiety this year follows as a matter of course because there is more distress. It is the way of the world & like a man who tries to drown his grief & sorrows in drinking. It makes me quite melancholy to read such dreadful news of the famines & distress at home & all I care is to hope that it is for the best. That Ireland needed purging there is no doubt & it may do good. That you shall not suffer I hope to prevent. I sent home duplicates for £140 a day or two since to our good Father of which the first bill for £125 went some time since through Allen Duffel & Co[96] & [I] now send the other for £15 direct. Mary Miller is now with you I suppose. Give my love to her & tell her I would write had I leisure but with the immense amount of work I now get through I cannot find time. I ride on average 20 miles a day, no trifle at this season of the year. I have escaped this morning from a dreadful attempt a poney of mine tried to drown me. I am obliged to ride him occasionally in the hills as my other horse could never stand the double work & my mare I use to carry baggage. He twice tumbled down with me 12 & 18 feet respectively & I allways fear his going along the edges of precipices. To day in coming down the Jhelum with me in a small boat where there was just room for him (the only good thing he can do is to jump in and out of boats). The river here confined as it is with rocks rushes with great rapidity & at every bend there are rapids & whirlpools. We got through the first two of these pretty well but at the third the boat lad who was holding his head & who had probably never held a horse before in his life let him step over the seats where he liked until he got up towards the bow of the boat. Another man tried to get him to retrace his steps but fancy a horse walking backwards over the seats. Well first he went on one side & then on the other & the boat nearly overturning at each step he had [sic at] last put his hind legs over board & I thought we were upset. I immediately ordered them to push him overboard & let him take his chance but meanwhile he somehow or other managed to get into the boat again. I then took him into my own care & we arrived safely at our destination. My other horse is invaluable to me. He climbs up & down the rocks like a goat & I am quite sure I could ride him up & down any steps or stairs in your house at home. Moreover he is never tired & carries me the last mile of thirty as well as the first, & I generally ride fast.

When I say I hate the vanity of the fashionable world I do not mean to say I should dislike to dine at parties again or go to balls but I dislike the direct of fashion. I call it a tissue of lies indirect. I have no doubt I shall be an unpolished ill dressed being when I again join in these follies but I doubt if I shall be half so happy as I am now with only my own resources to depend upon. Bread, butter, beef, mutton I have not seen since we left Nurpore. Vegetables we get once a week so that even as you used to say I am an epicurean. I manage to rough it pretty well. I generally say nothing about dinner but if I give it any order it is always any thing. As long as I can get out it is pretty well but what I hate beyond everything is when it rains & blows for two or three days together deluging you with dust every thing damp & the walls of the tent soaked through. Such weather is real misery. That Jack says he is very busy is a small excuse for his never writing to his affect. brother. It is a duty he owes to his seniors & if I were at home I should strongly impress the sentiment on his mind. With best love

Your affec. Br.

Daniel G. Robinson

15

Daniel George Robinson to his sister

Manikeejala tôp[97] April 20th 1847

Nr. Rawul Pindee[98]

My dear Sister

I write this from one of the celebrated tôps supposed to be prior to the time that Alexr the great invaded India or as he is called in this country Sultan Secundra. I spent last evening in seeing what information I could obtain but excepting its being a huge mound built of very large wrought stones there is no beauty in it. Ventura[99] opened this one by means of blasting. They found a few

88

coins, some lead and in a small box something they know not what. At least my knowledge of Persian is so very slight that I could not understand the whole of the story. On the box there was a gold plate by the description of which it appears that the top must have been built at least 4000 years ago. They are to be found along the whole line of Alexander's conquests.

In this country there is a very little tradition to be got at excepting from Brahmins & moulvees, the priests of the Hindoo & Mahomedan creeds respectively, & their traditions resolve every thing into either the acts of Brahma or Mahommed as may be most convenient. The Mahommedans are however the most rational of the two but their creed is of a nature to make them of a savage disposition. Women instead of being companions are men's instruments of pleasure bought & sold for so much & treated much worse than their horses. A few certainly do rule the roost & when that happens they do it right properly. Seven wifes is the limit of a good Mahomedan but if he is rich there is no great sin in having fifty more. Because then he can afford to support his male children the female are not of much consequence unless they are pretty & then they are good articles of merchandize & sell at a high price. A man's stock of pretty daughters is valuable in proportion to the number of them & should he be blessed with 8 or 10 he may consider himself a rich man. What a nice law this would be for England, would it not? I should have no objection. Would you?

They tell me one of my sowars who I had sent with a letter has been murdered about 5 miles from here. I don't not [sic] quite believe it but I have sent for evidence. He was one of Goolab Sing's & I take it that is his offence. They are always very civil to us Europeans but I do not mean to trust them.

The weather is now hot enough to cook one's dinner without a fire. What an excellent opportunity for economy if fuel were at all expensive. I am now inured to it & whilst I remain in doors do not suffer any inconvenience. I now take things easier & do not march more [than] 10 to 16 miles a day & chat [sic start] always in the evening starting about an hour before sunset. I then get at my work by sunrise the next morning so as to avoid being sunned more than I can help. I therefore now enjoy good health. You would be astonished on what a little I live. Principally chauppatties, jam & vegetables when I can get them. Love to all.

Yr affect. brother

Daniel G. Robinson

16

Daniel George Robinson to his sister

Camp Nr. Rawul Pindee
April 27th 1847

My dear Sister

I have received your very improper & extraordinary epistle of the 20th of Febry. As to your being the eldest & that giving you any claims to command it is a gross error & were you only here you would be daily be [*sic*] convinced of that fact & of your little worth. You might sell for ten rupees the price of an ordinary wife, and you might meet with a husband who would not thrash you more than once a day until you learned to make his chauppatties properly. Here & very properly women are looked upon as helps to men and are not treated much better than their horses or cows. Indeed a mussalman (& a very well educated man) told me yesterday that it was a very wicked thing to love, and that marriage should never be contracted between any two persons who had seen each other and altho' I don't quite agree with him & I do partially I don't mean to love you any more to see how the experiment acts. If you come out to India for a husband as I cannot provide you with a white one you now know what is to be expected from a black one. I am sorry you could not appreciate the hair I sent you. It would have done as well as any other, but you are curious animals & have many odd notions that first enumerated amongst them. You seem to have taken a greater liking also to raking a little in the country. [It] is well enough in its way & I believe picnics do a world of good but that nightly dancing in hot crowded rooms is the hot bed of half the consumptions of which ladies die of in England. Follow my example. I am always up by an hour before day light and generally in bed one hour after dark or about 8 o'clock. I ride generally about 18 to 20 miles a day sometimes nearly double that excepting on Sundays when I seldom go out at all & if so not more than two or three miles at the utmost. In England the same quantity of exercise on foot would be a fair equivalent & if you would only walk one half the distance daily I'll answer for it you will keep your strength even in London.

The weather is now pretty hot and has been very so, but if the atmosphere only remains clear I hope to complete the work of this season in another fortnight or three weeks. Indeed the rains commence on the 1st of June and finished or unfinished I must shut up shop then. Most probably my next letter will be dated from Attock of [sic or] some where close to it. It is not more than 50 miles & a two days journey from here but I have to go first to one part & then to another part of the country visiting my various stations for money. I had heard that Rawul Pindee was a very considerable city and was much disappointed to find it a very small & dirty affair, much smaller than any of those on the other side of the Jhelum and yet it is the only place of any importance between the Jhelum & the Indus and on the high road between Caulbul[100] & Hindostan and on one of the roads to Cashmere. Property out of the city is certainly not very safe, the mountains being only 6 or 8 miles distant and filled with a lawless race like the highlanders of former days. They are sturdy, honest in their way, brave & [not] brooking any thing like command or being kept in order. They want to have us as their rulers & declare that if [sic in] that case they will remain quiet, but that they won't have Goolab Sing at any price and they are quite right too & I think that it is a great act of oppression in us to <u>sell</u> a whole country to an oppressor who beyond the purchasing has no claim on these lands of which the people hate him so cordially & are of a different race and religion and who were so oppressed by him when he was governor of this country in Runjeet Sing's time. The Sikhs are sufficiently oppressive but their rule is a paradise compared with Goolab's. His avarice overcomes every other good or bad quality & he has some of the former and the consequence is that he is hoarding up money at the expence of his kingdom for no earthly purpose. His eldest son[101] and heir apparent is said to be an idiot and totally incapable of public business neither beloved nor feared. From the little I saw of him I thought him intelligent but little respected by those about him & much less sensual than most young asiatic princes are. Whether Goolab Sing or his family are much governed by Brahmin priests I have never heard but I have noticed that in all his newly possessed large towns & cities he has built a Hindu temple. Perhaps he thinks that this will cover his multitude of sins. His vizier[102] and other principal high officers seem generally speaking to be men of low origin who hope to raise themselves & the wind[103] at the expense of such districts as they may be put over and right well they fleece the poor ryots[104] and as Goolab takes all that he knows they can spare & these jackals fleece the greater part of the remnant the condition of his subjects is wretched in the extreme. I do not think that our rule is a good one for the natives under us, on account of the misdeeds of the natives understrappers but it is better than that of these countries. A native is always afraid to complain to the sahib for fear of being beaten or murdered by him of whom he complains or else he cannot afford to tip the door keepers of whom there are numbers always about a judges kutcherry.[105]

What my prospects after the rains are likely to be I cannot say. Most probably we shall spend another year in a similar duty only in the mountains & if not I shall then bid adieu to the sappers & take some other appointment less pleasant but certainly more comfortable and less expensive as far as carriage & tentage goes. Perhaps the canals. If I cannot get on the survey that is the branch I mean to apply for. That scamp Jack has never written to me once, he ought to be ashamed of himself. I suppose he is now grown pretty tall. Love to all friends. I have not written to any aunts or uncles for several mails but perhaps I shall soon find time. Enclosed is a letter for Mary.[106]

Yr affect. Brother
Daniel G. Robinson

P.S. What instrument do you like best, the chrich settabah or what.[107]

I have just received your letter of the 9th of March. Thanks for the congratulations.[108] I am glad the telescope is en route. Altho rather late in the day considering that the season's work is all but finished.[109] Love to all.

29th

17

Daniel George Robinson to his sister

Wuserabad Augt. 21st 1847

My dear Sister

I have positively at last received a letter without any <u>galee</u>[110] in it & allow me to congratulate you on your improvement in niput adable.[111] However I will not bully you by making my letter unintelligible to any but an Anglo Indian.

I am very glad Charles has passed & hope he will turn steady.[112] I have quite made up my mind that if he will not turn steady I will not give a particle of assistance until he be tamed. Indeed so great are my fears for his prospects that I should be delighted to hear of his getting into some such difficulties as will open his eyes to the folly of attempting to kick against the pricks. Should he after being promoted to Lieutenant get into any of these scrapes he will be smashed to a moral certainty & then his prospects will be ruined forever. I believe him to have a most excellent heart & good principles but to require taming. He seems not to comprehend the meaning of discipline & obedience. Indeed I do not think these words are in his vocabulary. However this is all between you & I and your favourite bed post – that receptacle of so many secrets. If it could only speak what tales it might tell.

I hope when you went to Chishelhurst [*sic*] you went & saw the Edlemann's. I had a long kind letter from Miss Agassiz the other day. They seem to have a beautiful place to live in.

The mail is in but my letters if there be any have not yet arrived. I therefore do not know whether you have given me news of my friend Adine,[113] but if not I shall be much disappointed. You seem to think 10 miles far. I ride that every evening for exercise between sunset and dark & when I want to go any distance I lay my horses in stages & gallop over in a very short time. I rode the other day 60 miles in the night of which the 1st 20 were entirely through water & took me 8 hours, I was much fatigued & wet through & through. I am now thank God relieved from the tramels of society. I was quite disgusted when at Lahore to hear the unkind things <u>everyone</u> had to say of his neighbour <u>behind his back</u>. In the jungles we have but few acquaintances & those only existing in correspondence but they are very true. My new assistant has been sometime at Lahore sick. When he will rejoin me I know not, but I want his assistance much as altho' I work hard all day I see no chance of my work being finished before the time appointed when I shall have to take charge of the new survey & receive my extra pay. I ought now to get rich, but I am afraid that to save money is contrary to the laws of my kismut. Not that I am extravagant, my expenses never exceeding 400 rupees a month but there are so many ways of getting rid of money & I consider it my duty considering that we pay no tithes to subscribe largely to charities &c at least to the amount of £50 a year which I do not but are [*sic* am] always meaning to do. I am sorry to hear that the Irish potatoe crop is failing again. I hope this will not turn out true. I really forget the names of my old friends the Bruyères[114] but I am well acquainted with their features. I never thought the strong so[ur]puss who used to squeeze my fingers so cruelly would be pretty, but the youngest had nice black hair & eyes. I am glad they are all well for they are a family that I greatly respect. I hope all the Jersey folks also are well. I want to write to them but I really can find time to write to no one excepting you & father. I hope you feel the compliment. Excepting my garden & house all the surrounding country is under water so that I am a close prisoner. It rained fearfully last night & blue great thunders & small lightnings. I shot a tortoise this morning about 2 feet in diameter with my rifle at 100 yards & right through the head. It did not kill him so I sent a man across the rivulet to throw him on his back & he had 4 balls in him before he died. Two right through the head.

The tortoise can bite tremendously & will cut a rope in two like a knife. I have now finished my scribble & with kind love to all at home adieu.

Yr affec. Brother
D.G. Robinson

N.B. Wrote the Governor this mail enclosing draft.[115]

18

Daniel George Robinson to his father

September 8th [1847]

My dear Governor

Rather than let the mail pass without letting you know that I'm alive I scribble a few lines altho' my mind is so occupied at present with other duties that I can hardly find time for scribbling. I meant to have to [*sic*] written to Charles by this mail also but one excuse must answer for both. I am again in tents & find my health all the better for it. Of news I have none. The Sikhs seemed to treat the imprisonment of their Ranee as a matter of course or rather as if they could not help themselves. Their is no feeling of gallantry or commiseration for women in an Asiatic's heart & had not Mehtab Kumar[116] by good luck caught Runjeet Sing's attention she would in all probability have married a common horseman & had a good thick stick laid over her shoulders when the chaupatties were not properly baked à la Alfred the Great.

How go the Irish concerns. Well it is to be hoped. It is quite disheartening to read of this continued famine year after year. That benefit may accrue from it is just possible but I should be much surprised if the Irish have such industry to cultivate other crops which require more labour than potatoes. I wish I could help you with the waste land society.[117] That it ought to persevere I feel convinced. Undoubtedly there will be much loss just a[t] present but if they break the thing up now they will lose the whole of the capital invested without the least chance of a return. Our rains are now pretty well over & I shall soon commence work up in Hasarah but at present I am overwhelmed with work which ought to be finished by the 1st of October but which in all probability will not be these 3 months. So with kind love to Ninetta [and] Jack. Salve et omnes qui musso lavebant.[118]

believe me yr. affec. Son

D.G. Robinson

19

Daniel George Robinson to his father

Jelalpore[119] Oct 27th 1847

My dear Father,

Since I wrote to you the enclosed scribble I have received yours from Ireland. Your picture is a dreary one indeed but we must hope for the best and would to God that it laid in our power to remove it. I wish to write at length now but I really cannot find time. We are now in the Salt Range which stretches from the Jhelum to the Indus and I am making diligent enquiries for mineral wealth which I feel assured must extensively exist in these regions, coal especially, but at present my search has been fruitless. Salt exists in great quantities, also sulphur [and] alumen but I cannot hear anything of coal. Indeed in the absence of fossils it is almost impossible to distinguish between the old & new red sandstone formations.

I wish to assist me in this you would get for me a chemical test box & small blow pipe, and with it send me some brown buttons for a shooting coat. The chemical test box to come out overland. Kind love to Ninetta & all at home.

Yr. affect. Son

D.G. Robinson

Ninetta disgraces "long" by applying it to her letters. When next you make me up a parcel send me well packed in tin

10 sheet[s] largest drawing paper

1   pr alberts dividing compasses

    pair screw & point compasses

1   "   "   pencil spring compass with regulating screw
1   "   "   pen   d[itt]o   "   "
24 sheets smaller drawing paper
Indian ink & pencils

20

Daniel George Robinson to his father

Camp Pindee Saybeawala[120]
Novr. 7th 1847

My dear Father

Altho' desperately tired & it is late at night I hasten to scribble a few lines in hopes of not missing this mail but I am now so much out of the way of Post office communication that I have my doubts. Since I wrote last I have travelled through part of the Salt Range which extends about 120 miles on either side of the Indus. I was very anxious to travel through this country as I felt sure coal must exist in or near that formation & it was also a new country. I found the coal[121] & had an excellent opportunity of studying the geological formations & tracing them through their various series also of seeing a new country & people the knowledge of the language, manners & customs of whom lends a helping hand in my great object political employment.

I have also made a pretty good geographical map of the whole of it which will be very useful to me when I have to carry my trigonometrical survey over it. I expect to be in Hasara by the end of next week & then my really arduous duties commence. The mountains are very lofty, much detached & the winter most bitterly cold so the Jany & Decr will be anything but delectable to the inhabitants of tents. I am trying to construct a portable fire place but doubt whether I shall be able to succeed. I am now hard at work also collecting old coins & have now ventured to take old Persian such as those of Nadir Shah, Mahmood of Ghuznee, Shah Jehan, Akboor &c in addition to those coined by the descendants of the colonists left by Alexr the great & if I only go on as well as I am going now my collection will be very valuable & conjoined with your minerals & curiosities will make a valuable cabinet.[122]

I hope you have long ere this returned safe from your Irish trip & that your fears of the potatoe disease have not been realised. Ninetta I doubt not expects a letter but I have not time to write to her or Knott.[123] I wish her however many happy returns of her birthday. D[itt]o D[itt]o of yours & a merry merry Xmas &c. all trifles which I am so disused to that I had almost forgotten them. Do not [be] surprised if you do not now hear from me so regularly as formerly but I am afraid I shall have some difficulty. I am now 60 miles from the nearest post town but I carry this in my Port[manteau] 24 miles of the road tomorrow [morning]. Bye & bye I shall be much further removed. Good bye & god bless you all.

Yr. affec. Son
D.G. Robinson

[P.S.] I don't know whether I told you that the sappers have been altered to 5 companies of Sappers & 7 companies of pioneers [with the] pioneers to be officered from the Infantry in all probability. In consequence of this my company may be recalled. I shall however remain with 400 [rupees] staff [pay]. Still it will be a loss of 100 rupees a month to me.[124]

21

Daniel George Robinson to his father

Camp Nr. Attock
Decr. 4th 1847

My dear Father

A week's steady rain in tents do[es] not much tend to make a letter very lively but notwithstanding the infliction I am on the whole well, happy & hard at work. I have been vainly attempting for some time past to construct a fire place but I am sorry to say my efforts at present have been of no avail. I am sorry that exchange is now so low that it would be folly to send home money & I regret more so that my funds are at present at so low an ebb as to prevent my doing so for some little time to come. But in about March when exchange may I think be expected to rise again I dare say I shall without inconvenience be able to send you another hundred pounds. I have lost my company of Sappers since I last wrote, but as it saves me much trouble and I could not do my duties towards both it & the survey thoroughly at the same time on the whole I am rather glad than otherwise. I shall now have a guard of Sikh infantry & cavalry who are much more rough & ready that [*sic* than] our spoiled, overfed & overpetted Jacks especially amongst the snows & frosts of these mountains.

I have been thinking seriously whether it would be worth while to speculate in exchanges. The rise & fall seems to be extremely regular. In March & April about 1.10 to 1.11½ & in August to November 1.9 to 1.10. By sending home at good rates & receiving back at low rates I think a good interest might be got on money but as I can allways get six per cent in India I think I would prefer the safer & slower to the more rapid & uncertain. If I did speculate in that manner I should leave it entirely in Allan's hands. Bye the bye I have paid them your account & thanked for the pains they took.

Saunders & May & Co have failed owing to Reid Irving & Co.[125] Their liabilities are only 1 lakh & their assets five lakhs on Reid Irving & Co so that I think they may yet recover.

I bought some of your wine from them at Co[mpany] Rs 18-0-0. The corks had been so destroyed that the wine was not drinkable. I did not think it necessary to tell you this unpleasant circumstance before but I now consider it only just to Miss F[ry] of M & Co to tell you so.[126] The compass has arrived, so have the brushes. All are <u>first rate</u>. It is a pity that the compass was not graduated to 360 nor do I see the use of the two spare tops, but the instrument itself is uncommonly good & the brushes are very fair & have arrived just in the nick of time d[itt]o the India rubber. The heavier portions of the package will arrive hereafter. I forget now what were the immensity of items I required on my anticipated return to civilization, but if you should not have procured any of the following if I have funds to meet the emergency & you yourself be not hard up kindly procure & dispatch them.

One pair double barrelled pistols. Barrels over one another to fit close to the side with a catch spring for the belt. Length of barrel about six inches (not more). Bore about 36 or 30 to the pound. Easy trigger. Low half cocks & stops. Inclined to the saw handle.

2 colors   (½ cake carmine
              (1   "   crimson lake
              (1   "   neutral tint

3   (test box, blow pipes &c for a mineralogist not to
          (exceed £5 cost. An expensive article not required.

4   (pair of boiling thermometers & a spare thermometer not
          (intended for boiling in apparatus.

It is now so late that unless you have already obtained the theodolite I am afraid it would arrive too late to be of any use, so don't send it if not already sent.

5   A beam compass with vernier & scale. Something first rate.
          3 pairs sheets.
          2 dozens shirts.
          2   "   white socks.

The epaulettes & sword knot were stolen by some thieves between Lahore & Wuzerabad but the Engineer papers & some instruments that were in company arrived safe. I have demanded & expect to receive from the Lahore durbar their value. You ask me to select something for a present.[127] Chesterfield[128] says that you should never send as a present what you have been commissioned to purchase. I shall however break through this admirable advice & if you will allow of it I will consider the telescope as your present & shall pocket whatever dibs I may get from the durbar. Possibly Ninetta may object to this arrangement. If she feels insulted she had better work a pair of slippers or a nice velvet cap to keep my head warm in doors in the cold weather & send it me with a respectable epistle as a present. The saddle has also at last arrived. A very nice article &

the drill will serve for next my present fit out of white trowsers having long been considered disreputable. I don't think the flannel good for much. The Engineer papers are laid on the table for perusal but I regret to say the day is not named. Of India and its politics I have little to say. All is as quiet as it is in England & the Punjab [is] under the best possible rule. The people get justice & not law. Native perjury is so prevalent & the cunning is so great that when English law gets introduced into our provinces, frauds generally remain undetected or when detected unpunishable.

The wholesome practice of flogging has also been discontinued in the army & the consequence is that three men have lately been shot for striking their superior officers – a crime which is unhappily fearfully common. Of this you will no doubt have seen much in the papers.[129] I will write to Mr. Brown as you wish but it is impossible I can be of any use to him at this distance.[130] I keep up very little intercourse with my friends in Hindostan almost from necessity. I have written a few words to Knott to congratulate him on his accession of honors & the troubles of a wife & the little etceteras.[131] D[itt]o. D[itt]o. something short to Ninetta on the birthday. Love to Jack. Month by month I purpose to write to him & to my uncles & other friends but really cannot find the time. God bless you all.

Yr affect. Son
D.G. Robinson

22

Daniel George Robinson to his sister

Decr. 4th/[18]47

My dear Ninetta
This being <u>the</u> birth day altho' very busy I scribble a few lines to wish you many happy returns of the day, the complements of the season & some improvement in the art of lexicography. You should study letters. You seem to consider that the inventory of the number of oysters or the pots of porter you may have

consumed in one given a [*sic*] week or the pottles of strawberries you have picked in a certain garden [is important]. Such letters are incorrect, not to say disreputable. Try and write from the feelings instead of from memory of the palate. What care I for reviews in Hyde Park or palaces in Westmoreland. If you could write politics or essays on political (not domestic) economy they might be readable but as you can['t] why don't you give me some account of my friends, yourself & the characters appertaining thereto. Of such things as these I can judge even at this distance. Mary Miller can when she likes write a much more respectable letter.

We have got it really cold and I should not be surprised if some day I was fairly blocked in by snow for a day or two. Winter has set in unusually severe and much snow has already fallen on many of the mountains not more than 10 or 14 miles from here & as [we are] in tents we cannot exclude the air without excluding the light. Also I shall not anticipate much pleasure from experiencing any of these freezings but I dare say it will do something towards setting me up again, not that I see much necessity for it as I never enjoyed better health even in Europe. I have got another addition to my family in the shape of a spaniel dog & a nice colt I bought the other day. The latter is rather mischievously inclined but about 18 months hence will I think make a nice riding horse. Horses are cheap in this country as my first purchase will be getting unserviceable about 2 years hence from hard work and age. I think that it is not impossible I may if I see another nice colt buy him also.

Of myself I have little to say. I am not married yet nor engaged to be nor do I think it is likely I shall be just yet & this seems the only item of any importance to you ladies I shall not say much more on myself.

I am glad Sarah Miller is at last to know the cares & duties of the marriage state & should I ever meet her doubt not to see her a most staid & respectable matron.[132]

Yr. affect. Broth.

D.G. Robinson

23

Daniel George Robinson to his father

Shumsherabad[133] Hasara
Decr 31st [18]47

My dear Father

Owing to press of business I was unable to scribble a few lines last mail & now it is so cold that I can hardly hold my pen. We have ice half an inch think every morning but the heat of the day is so great as to thaw it before twelve o'clock. This rapid change in the climate must be prejudicial to health but that cannot be helped. My Hindustanis all want to return to their own country but as I have a tolerably dispotic power out of our own provinces I do not mean to let them. I am glad that the £37.10.0 arrived so opportunely & wish it were more. Exchange is fearfully low just now but if it will only rise a trifle I will send home more money as soon as I can. If you can only borrow money on my security do so & I promise you a hundred pounds on my next birth day.

My expenses are perhaps now unnecessarily heavy. I have 6 horses in my stable. One a colt unrideable but if he lives he will pay me cent per cent on his expenditure. I have also one or two screws who I could sell for a mere nothing & who doing their work I still keep. Whenever I make a ride of 50 or 60 miles in these short days which I always do at a gallop these horses are necessary so that I hardly wish to part with them but I mean to load traps on three of them when not used for riding. I have also been spending a good deal of money in antiquarian pursuits & my collection of the coins of the successors of Alexander in the east is now pretty valuable but as I possess singularly good opportunities for collecting & as I can allways sell my cabinet at three times its cost to me I mean still to collect.

I have stated these circumstances because otherwise you might think I am improvident considering the large allowances I receive for my standing in the service. I manage still to save a good deal of money & shall no doubt be able to send you £100 on the 8th of March next.

I spent Xmas day at Peshawur where we assembled five

Europeans & had a quiet sedate dinner returning the next day but one stopping the Sunday. The Peshawur country is curious, the inhabitants are genuine Affghans & it is tilled & irrigated in a peculiar way much resembling the Affghan principle.

I met with uncommon civility from every village through which I passed & they seem to consider the European as a great Godsend to them after the Sikhs. The whole of this part of the country west of the Jhelum may now be said to be under English rule. The Sikhs only receive the produce & furnish the means of keeping it in order. The consequence is that instead of the country being plundered for revenue, a fixed revenue is levied from each village & when a village does not pay up its revenue it is burnt to the country [*sic* ground]. The Eusoofsaies have also the pleasure of having a most indefatigable young officer over them who will make a 60 miles night march on any turbulent village much to their astonishment & chastise them. They are consequently in much better order than they ever were before. So much was I pleased with my short ride through their country that I mean to survey the whole of it next year collecting old farthings and antiquities at the same time with which it abounds. The numbers of old topes is really surprising but the place which abounds with them most is the valley of Swat which unfortunately is filled with bigoted mussalmen & is not under our rule. But if they continue to afford the same casi belli which they have been doing lately in all probability their country will be invaded soon & then I expect a rich haul on the ancients. I was close under the Khyber Pass the other day & was surprised at i[t]s affording so much trouble to our people. If the attacking army only consist of Europeans accustomed to the hills I cannot understand why the Khyberrees should not soon be driven to a stand still in the narrow belt of mountains which separates Peshawur from Jelalabad.[134] There is said to be a scarcity of water in their hills but one of my servants who is a Kyberree declares that there is plenty. The Kyberrees are now fighting amongst themselves & the consequence is that the pass [is] entirely closed against all merchants much to their own loss.

Day by day the Sikhs seem to be more pleased with the general state of affairs but they are disgusted with the vanity of our sepoys declaring that it was by their valor the Sikhs were thrashed. Of our Europeans they have a high opinion & declare them to be children of the devil & that nothing but main force can drive them back but as for the <u>poorbeeas</u> (Eastern[er]s) only take away their European officers & see what a licking we will give them. Taking it all and all the Punjab was never in so flourishing a condition & the best thing that ever happened for it was when it invaded the English frontier. I now understand that I am likely to remain in the Punjaub until little Maharajah Dhuleep Sing[135] becomes of age about 6 or 7 years hence. If so I shall quietly pass the time here & at the end of it come home on the new furlough regulations. However I cannot be certain because all the Engineers & Artillery that they are able to lay hands on they are remanding to their corps. It stands to reason that Engineer officers must be the most talented body in the service & consequently more fitted to hold those appointments which require most ability. The consequence is that within the last few years a great many political appointments have been given to young Engineer officers & such is the lack of officers in the scientific corps that I fancy that Hon[oura]ble John[136] will be obliged to give us soon another Citation. I am now getting on fast in the corps & hope still to save [*sic* have] the brevet [of] Capt.

I fancy Courtneay[137] who is coming out as Lord Dalhousie's[138] private secretary must be a friend of Lord Devon's[139] if not a nephew. I do not think I want any letter of introduction to him but it might be useful. If Lord Dalhousie only does as much for the country as Lord Hardinge has done we shall do well enough but every new governor general seems to plunge the country into a war. When Miss Eden (Lord Auckland's sister) was Govr. Genl.[140] we had the Caubul business & had there been only a young soldier instead of an old woman at the head of affairs all would have [been] well & at this moment Caubul would have been in our possession.

I should not be surprised if I had the pleasure of marching to Caubul or Bokhara yet before I died & I should not at all dislike the fun. I have now scribbled my scribble without one word of home affairs. I am glad you visited my old friends the Agassiz the other day. They are a family which I much admire from their good principles. Susanne I thought a very fine lassy without much brains & who if put to it might cross her spouse if necessary. I shall not tell you now who is my favourite but she is I hope as good as human nature can be. In England you thought me irreligious & tolerably wild but though not far wrong I have always had an inclination toward religion & I can assure you I never saw a Christian service attended with more apparent zeal than it was by five young men on Xmas day & the Sunday after at Peshawur the other day. I find that the society of young men in the army generally contaminates but that where there is knowledge & understanding religion is generally carried far and the characters are more formed & steady.

I was much amused on reading over the inventory of things you are sending me to see another cloth[es] brush & a shaving brush neither of which I ever use. I have either two or three cloth[es] brushes already & my clothes are not of the description to require much brushing not being English broad cloths but the manufactures of the country. Shaving is an unnecessary punishment self inflicted for unknown sins as my conscience does not afflict me I shall leave the moustachios to take care of themselves till the society of the civilized obliges me to undergo daily penitence.

I shall give you a commission soon to purchase some English clothing for me. I want shirts, shooting coats, great coat &c [ ] but I shall not send in an indent until March remittance is ready. The 1st instalment of costs 400-0-0 is already banked.

Should Knott's wedding not have taken place yet or I should not be too late now for the fair, give him some little present from me not to exceed £10-0-0 for which I must go tick.

I also want a light strong silver pencil case for myself with hard leads one of Mordans[141] and with a ring wherewith to fixt it to the neck. God bless you all.

Yr. affect. Son
D.G. Robinson

12th Jany.

24

Daniel George Robinson to his father

Camp Rajoreea[142] Hazara
Feby. 8th 1848

My dear Father

As I cannot expect to hear from you without writing to you in return I now make the attempt of scribbling a few lines notwithstanding it is so cold I can hardly hold my pen. I have managed to push so far but altho we are only [a] little more than 3000 feet above the sea the cold & the snow are so rapidly destroying the camels that I am obliged to beat a retreat & to go back into a lower & warmer locality where I can work with more convenience and effect. The change of temperature is rapid & great. In the night it is far below freezing point – how low I cannot say as I am much too lazy to get up and look, but the heat in the day ranges from 60° to 70°. Of sport there is abundance & I generally manage to get something dur[ing] the first hour or two after daylight, either hares or partridges, which helps to break the monot[on]y of our fowl feeding. I have also got into a district of wild beasts. I shot my first hyaena not long since. Wild boars are numerous, so are bears, tigers & leopards but as I have something else to do than to look after them & no one can shew me their exact position I do [not] feel disposed to go on a wild beast chase.

This is taking it all & all by no means a pretty country – mountains & valleys with gushing streams & horrid precipices make a romantic picture. But I prefer to see the hills well clad with woods & shrubbery & such they tell me I shall find in the interior. In the hot weather I hope & expect to be in the higher mountains which if my health required it would be almost as good a reservation as a trip to England. Indeed I shall be sorry when I am obliged to leave the mountains & commence surveying in the plains. I was never stronger nor more healthy in my life & I find that nothing but this wandering rambling life without cares or the want of the one thing needful keeps me in good health & spirits. Altho by no means a cynic I feel no desire to dive deeper into society. Whenever I do fall in with an Englishman for a few days in

the jungles we have a jollification so long as we are together &
when we separate things move on in their accustomed course. As
all officers employed in the jungles must have talents or tact to
recommend them, their society is far more pleasing than scandal,
quarreling, backbiting & other bad &cs so prevalent in stations
amongst people who have nothing else to do or think of.

They tell me that the higher parts of these hills are curious &
beautiful. If so I expect to have rich treats in sketching & had I but
more leisure in shooting whenever good shooting & consequently
uncultivated ground exists [although] it is a sure sign that
misgovernment has existed. This is a great pity & does much to
destroy the pleasure of it. I usually walk 14 or 15 miles every day
over the rocks & stones with which this country is covered to keep
my legs in practise for mountain climbing. But I would far sooner
walk 20 or 30 miles along a good road. Of mineral wealth I have
found nothing excepting some inferior coal. I hope however
amongst these slates to find lead & possibly copper wherever a
barren surface exists, & it does exist here. Mineral wealth is most
likely to occur beneath the surface but the difficulty is to find
where it crops out. I am anxiously expecting the test box I wrote
for some time since, thermometers I have got.[143] I exchanged two
coins which cost me about two pence for them. The coins were
worth 25 rupees a piece but I hope to collect duplicates of them.
My collection increases rapidly in bulk & value & should I ever
sell, it will give me a rich profit. I hope however to cover the
expenses of the duplicates. I have one coin of 256 B.C. as fresh &
much more beautiful than a half crown of yesterday, indeed it is
wonderful how these coins have been preserved. They do not
range through a very large series but are beautiful beyond
conception as works of as works of [sic] art only. I collected some
pieces of sculpture from an ancient tomb on the West bank of the
Indus in the Eusoofsaie country which were really very beautiful;
far more so than any artist in India can now turn out.

There is no fear of my trusting any money in houses of agency.
With my usual providence I have saved nothing since I have been
in India & I am not quite sure yet where the 1000 rupees I have to
send you in March is to come from, but I suppose it will turn up

somehow. Ninetta is no doubt enjoying herself on the continent, I hope profitably. Charly I am glad to hear such good accounts of. Jack is my loadstar to whom I look for everything good, bright & glorious & I am or at least I hope you think so

Yr. affect. Son

D.G. Robinson

25

Daniel George Robinson to his father

Camp Kooree Hasara

Feby. 23rd [18]48

My dear Governor

So long as the tent continues standing I will attempt to write my usual scrawl, but as it is blowing a hurricaine you must not be surprised at any rather sudden stoppage. Enclosed I send you Allan Duffel & Co's account. You will see I have paid over to them 93 rupees to close your acct. I have also sent them 200 rupees to remit to you in payment of the stores you have sent me. This is all I can scrape together just at present. Indeed I have come in for my share of misfortune lately in consequence of my having been placed at the disposal of the Resident at Lahore for employment in the Punjaub. I am no longer a mily servant & the mily Pay master will not give me my pay of 256 a month, neither will the civil department untill it is ordered in the usual manner. I am therefore obliged to live on my mere staff salary of 400 rupees a month which merely suffices to cover my current expenses. I used to live on less but my position now obliges me to keep a moonshee or persian secretary to conduct all my native correspondence, also a larger establishment & travelling in the hills with half the comforts of the plains is twice the expense. I do not think I shall therefore be able to send the promised remittance of £100 for a few months to come. I have now due to me on various accounts 1200 rupees which must be paid to me during the ensuing three months so that you [must] not feel uneasy. Misfortunes never come singly. The same post that I received the pay master's letter refusing to send

143

my pay I heard that the gems of my collection of ancient coins for which I had refused 600 rupees had been stolen from the residency. I cared more for their loss than I should have for the money as many of the coins were very beautiful & rare and a few I believe previously unknown. I am much grieved to hear to [*sic* of] the sad amount of sickness & mortality at present raging in England. I am very thankful so few of the deaths are amongst my own personal friends & relations. India has been very healthy during the last year, but I know so few people out of the Punjaub and the country & people of the Punjaub are so entirely different from those of Hindostan proper that I feel as if [I] hardly knew any thing of the latter country & often wonder when I shall return to it.

I have now well fixed in it & I think have a chance of making an opening into the political department hereafter. Young my clown I am sorry to say has been thrown out of the coach & is now doomed to practice on bricks and mortar, repairing old walls, cleaning out drains, making indifferent roads & other paltry work such as a respectable builder would refuse to have anything to do with. However there is but little choice, one must have money & something to do to keep out of debt & live comfortably & happily in this country. In the hot weather one is generally confined to the house from half an hour after sunrise to an hour before sunset & without employment how can one fill the time unless it be by resorting to billiards, moping, cards, drinking & other similarly respectable amusements. In the cold weather, if the station is a good one, time is filled with races, steeple chases, hunting & shooting & occasionally picknics if the lasses muster strong enough. This is better, but not in my opinion fit employment for men. The women spend much of their time in making & repeating scandal & so disgusted was I with the backbiting I heard from all the ladies during my short stay in Lahore that I was only too glad to escape to the jungles.

I saw a good deal of the Tremenheere's during my short stay in Lahore.[144] There is no hospitality or warmth of friendship in England to be compared with that of India. As an officer of the same corps I was of course free of the house. He is a very nice fellow & has a nice wife but the lady though a good housewife &

manager is not gifted with such good brains as I should like my wife to have. I should not exactly like to have a Mrs. Dr. Mary Somerville[145] to called [*sic*] me "stupid" – God forbid – but let my wife be able to give advice & counsel on subjects of importance.

We have had fearful weather for the last two months. Foul has equally divided the time with the fair weather the consequence is that altho I labour hard to push on the survey my progress is but slow. Moreover, such is the dread that the natives have of the inhabitants of this country that I can get no native surveyors or assistants to join me. I find that the British name is so much respected for its justice & the people have derived so much benefit by our stopping any oppression on the part of the Sikhs that I am allways with [*sic* well] received with the outward shew of hospitality & pleasure, if not the real, wherever I go. Next year I expect I shall be obliged to survey the Eusoofsaie country. The inhabitants are all Affghans, thieves, & paying but half homage to the Sikhs their rulers. When I go amongst them I shall in all probability require a stronger guard & shall not be at all sorry for the pistols I begged you to send me, not that I think they will ever be of any use but there is a great deal in the appearance of being well armed. I now never ride without my dagger & my pistols & a orderly horseman carries the double gun, another the rifle, another powder & shot & another telescope & compass. The telescope & compass you sent me from England are the most beautiful I have ever seen. In my saddle bags I generally have a book or two, a small bag of tea, clean clothes & a soda water bottle of brandy with a silver tumbler attached. Should I be separated from my camp for a day or two I am thus set up in a way.

Ninetta is of course enjoying herself on the continent. I hope the trip will not only improve her constitution but her mind also. You should call upon her for a diary of what she sees, thinks &c the same as I am called upon for. I am obliged to give my opinion of the country, its roads & the resources for military movements, also my opinion of its political state & the feelings of the people. Should my opinions turn out correct & the information I give [be] useful it may hereafter be the means of putting me into the political department.

As the rain insists on finding its way through the roof of the tent I shall make a clean bolt for bed so good night. God bless you my dear father.

Yr. affect. Son
D.G. Robinson

[P.S.] Sir Frederic Currie is coming immediately to Lahore in the place of Colonel Lawrence for one year. He is a real beast but will have so little to do with me that I do not think he can turn me out especially as he has no young Engineers for nephews or relations.[146]

26

Daniel George Robinson to his father

Camp Hasara
March 14th 1848

My dear Father

When mily. officers draw their pay & allowances from the civil instead of the Mily. Dept. they are considered to be employed under the foreign department & the officers are no longer under the orders of the Com in Chief but under the Govr. Genl. I am not a political yet, but in process of time hope to be so. I am at present only a surveyor with nominally large means, & a heavy expenditure. I am entitled to C[ompany] Rs 650 a month but only draw 400, it not being as yet determined whether I shall receive the odd 250 a month from the [*sic*] our own or from the Sikh treasury.

Of all the articles which I am most anxious to receive are the double barrelled pistols. My own are too heavy & clumsy & they constantly miss fire. In this country it is necessary to travel allways armed. On the other side of the river they are Affghans & the fanatics constantly make attempts on the lives of those in authority over them. Edwardes[147] the Pol. Offr. in charge of Bunnoo, Tank & Dhera Ishmael Khan[148] has had his life twice attempted within the last month. On one occasion the sentry at the door had his head nearly severed from the body with a stroke of the assassin's sword. On the other occasion he saw the man making for his door & had just time to reach the head to his bed, draw a pistol from under the pillow & shoot him as he came in. I shall go into the Eusoofsaie country in a few days. They are Affghans but are rather better than those of Bannu [and] Tank. Probably next year they may sent [*sic* send] me to Bunnoo. I think you had better therefore if you have not already despatched the pistols send them out overland. I sent you £20 through Allan's people some little time since. I will send more as soon as I can get my first dues. At present I am very hard up, also extremely busy.

I am afraid in this Ultima Thule[149] of British India I shall be of little use in recommending your agency. I possess about half a dozen intimate friends in the country, all young, all employed in the jungles & none with the slightest prospect of going home, however I will do what I can.

You speak of the <u>comforts</u> of the foreign department. I have just sat down to breakfast & huge iron bowls supply the place of dishes, a silver mug which gets most confoundedly hot the place of a tea cup & one knife & fork, 2 small plates & two Britannia metal spoons, all carried in my saddle bags, supply the rest of the furniture. However I have no doubt after 20 miles ride I shall enjoy my breakfast & I am only to[o] thankful to get anything to grumble for want of better. Indeed I find that all who rough it in the jungles instead of idling away or killing time in cantonments are more contented, happy, healthy & I think better better [*sic*] men than the more polished & luxurious brethren of cantonments. My vanity does not consist in furniture, a good table & all those luxuries which people keep for shew. I prefer good serviceable horses, guns, tents, instruments & my greatest vanity is old coins. I must now go to work.

20th March

I have just heard from Allan's people that they have sent you £20-0-0 at 1–8¼. This is at a ruinous exchange & I could have remitted through the N.W.B. at one penny higher.[150] You will therefore be able to send me the pistols by the overland route. I have heard that I need not commence regularly on Peshawur until after the rains. It is now late at night & I have a good deal of work to complete before morng so I will send this off in its present state. Kind love to all.

Yr. affect. Son
D.G. Robinson

[P.S.] Pistols – double barrelled – <u>over & under</u> – 5 inch barrells. Bore 30 to 36. Stop cocks, easy triggers, belt springs, saw handled with receptacle for caps or a cartridge in them, a case complete & 2,000 caps to accompany them. Also 3 pair of nipples for my guns to be of cast finish, strong, serviceable weapons & not to[o] heavy which you could shoot with.

27

Daniel George Robinson to his father

Camp Hurreekisherguhr[151]
April 4th 1848

My dear Father

I am now going to occupy a few moments of the evening. to scribble to you as I am too lazy to work any more. The silver spectacles & glasses last sent arrived to day. They are very nice. From the constant use of an eye glass for one eye I cannot see with the specs at all but I suppose I shall get used to them by degrees. Sir Robert Campbell[152] will come into the direction again for a certainty after the expiry of his one or two years of exit & if by that time I have not made myself a <u>pucka</u> political I shall not at all object to his good offices. Things go on pretty steadily. One day I am in the snow on the mountains & three or four days afterwards probably baking with the thermometer in tents at 90° in the plains at the foot of the said mountains. I hardly know which I prefer – the climbing of the precipitous peaks is so awfully fatiguing that I think it amply compensates for the advantage of a better climate. Next rains I am happy to say I have a prospect of vegetating in Cashmere.

As you are aware I have been for some time collecting coins.

148

Could you sell my duplicates for me if I sent them home. They fetch a higher value in England than in India, but they must be sold through the professional coin sellers who are very careful to only purchase those which they are certain cannot by any possibility have been forged. If you can sell them I will consign to you £50 or 60 of old coins. Many of them are exceedingly rare & are I believe at present unknown in England. In this country some of my coins will fetch 100 to 200 rupees (silver) & 1 to 25 rupees copper cash. I buy them at about double their weight but am obliged to destroy many copper coins as useless & not worth keeping. I certainly destroy 30 copper coins for every one I keep.

I am glad Jack goes on so well. I have written him a line by this mail. Charles has all the bases of a splendid officer but unfortunately he has not been sufficiently strictly disciplined to make his temper & general conduct subservient to his better principles.

Of news I can give you none. It would not afford you much amusement to narrate the names of the principal robbers of this part of the world & with them I have principally to deal. Aladdin fell amongst 40 thieves. I have the satisfaction of being amongst 40,000 respectable cut throats. They however fear us so much that they are not likely to break out again for some time. They are fickle & faithless but hospitable & not particularly treacherous, at least to individuals. I have read your paper on the Irish waste lands with much pleasure. I can hardly appreciate your designs. In India every thing is done in such a half & half manner that your your [*sic*] recommendations immediately struck me as magnificent. We call a common enclosure 60 feet square & built of sand or loose stones a fort. In this country there is not one which could stand for five minutes against a six pounder.

I have always thought Knott a most excellent man & I can assure no you nothing ever gave me greater pleasure than your taking him into partnership. It is unfortunate that no funds are now forthcoming. I could remit you £60 by the next mail but it is an enormous sacrifice to risk at 1/8 instead of 1/10 or 2/- which it ought to be at this season of the year. I shall therefore wait a little unless you be hard pressed. God bless you all.

Yr. affect. Son

D.G. Robinson

28

Daniel George Robinson to John Harding Robinson

Hasara
April 6th [18]48

My dear Brother

I have received yours of the — & congratulate you on the improvement in your handwriting & style. Neglect <u>no kind</u> of study let it be what it may. I am as yet very young in the world but there is not a thing that I have read that does not become useful so much so that my leisure hours are generally devoted to some kind of study instead of light reading. Without a knowledge of mathematics I not only could not carry on these surveys but I could not even calculate for the construction of a tent.

Of classics & historical knowledge I feel a great want. I understand enough for the purposes of general society but this is not sufficient. It is necessary to be a good classic[ist] to understand the <u>exact</u> meaning of many words of our language & it is from the elegant writers of the ancients that we derive the power of good & classical diction.

I am also glad to hear that you are learning to fence &c. All athletic excercises are good. To ride, walk, swim & fence are useful as well as agreeable amusements & afford a pleasant & pure relaxation after the hours of business.

I am glad you enjoyed yourself in Jersey. Cousin Charles is a rare example of goodness. I know no one for whom I have more love & respect. You cannot do better than take him for your model. Of gaieties & all those sort of things I have not partaken these 3 years. I have therefore lost all taste for them, but my delight is reading in doors & riding & shooting out of doors. The first is pleasing to the mind, the latter conducive to the health. I in conclusion must acknowledge that I am proud to hear such a good character of you. God bless you.

Yr affect. Brother
D.G. Robinson

29

Daniel George Robinson to his father

Camp Oosman Khatir[153]
April 15th 1848

My dear Father

I am sorry to intrude upon the time I generally devote to my proper business in order to scribble to you a few lines. It must therefore be my excuse for being brief. I have just received your two notes of the 19th and 23rd of Feby with Knott's of the 24th. The latter is deposited for the present in the unanswered drawer of my writing box. I am exceedingly vexed at your being so pressed for money on my account. Some months since I might have remitted 20 or 30 pounds to you at 1/10 and denied myself the collection of my coins to cover the expense. At present Govt & the Lahore Durbar are fighting for who shall give me my pay or rather certain portions of it & meanwhile I am made a victim & go without any. I however fall back on my staff salary which is ample for my own purposes & as this business of the pay must soon be settled I shall get it all in a lump of 1200 or more rupees & I hope then exchange will be rather better. I shall send you home some coins for sale through Allan's people immediately. I shall give you a list with the market values here. In England they will be more valuable, but coin collectors & sellers are very cautious in buying coins from people little known & there may be difficulties in disposing of them. However, I myself have collected them all from the places they were found & they have never yet been into Hindostan. There are some professional coin dealers who know their value. Should they be loth to take them I will try & get introduced to some old Indian collectors now residing in England & who have rather a higher opinion of the honesty of our Indian officers that [*sic* than] the cautious inhabitants of Cockaigne.[154] I can send you £30 or £40 in duplicate coins which I want to sell & I think this will be [a] better arrangement than waiting until the dispute about my pay is over & remitting at the ruinous exchange of 1/8.

Allan's people have lost very heavily indeed in various ways. They have also unfortunately taken 4 shares of the Union bank[155] as security for a debt of Sir Thomas Fenton's.[156] This was done by

Mr. Duffell without the knowledge of the other partners. They therefore become liable for the debts of the Union bank & will in all probability be bled. I rather suspect I am rather more in their debt than they in mine. It cannot however be a matter of more than 50 rupees either way. I sold a horse & sent you £20 through them a short time since. I hope you have received it by this time.

I send you the letter you received concerning the Hampshire property of Vernons Hill.[157] I had almost forgotten its name.

I am glad Ninetta has been enjoying herself. I hope the trip will improve both her body & mind.[158] I would not have all women blue stockings because an unamiable blue is unbearable, but reading books that require thinking improves the mind & banish[es] all trifling notions and vanities. Love to Jack. His answered letter stares me in the face but my heart is as strong as these mountains just at present & altho' I wish to write him rather a more loving epistle than my last I cannot find time.

I am in excellent health & have as much energy & physical strength as ever notwithstanding the thermometer stands at 95° in tents for the greater part of the day. God bless you my dear Father.

Yr. affect. Son
D.G. Robinson

[P.S.] On reading over the letter I am to write I find that two witnesses are required as Ram Narain Das or Ajoodhea Pinshand won't do.[159] The letter must go without for I have no English or other European neighbours within 30 or 40 miles.

30

Daniel George Robinson to his father

Hurkishurgurh,[160] Husara
May 7th 1848

My dear Father

It is so long since I wrote to you that I am afraid I may have missed a mail. I am also sorry to say I did not receive any letter from you by the last mail, probably you did not write. The European news was of course startling, but it has since been quite drowned to us selfish beings by the prospect of disturbances in this country. Poor Vans Agnew & Anderson[161] have been treacherously murdered at Mooltan[162] & the danger is that it is merely the commencement of a general outbreak & we all are anxious to have either the Colonel or his brother John Lawrence[163] back as Resident as they from their energy, knowledge of the people & soldierlike qualities are admirably well adapted to take care of such a country.

For ourselves here I have no fears. We are as it were the parties who keep the peace between the Sikh troops & the mountaineers of this well known turbulent district. I have also a few of my own sappers who would enable us to hold out the bastion we occupy for some hours, so that should the Sikhs attempt to attack us there would be ample time for the Hasara people to come to the rescue & should the district rise in insurrection we are in a good position to subdue it with the troops at our command. Nevertheless I should be glad to hear that on some excuse or other all European officers employed in the district entirely peopled by Sikhs & who are furnished with Sikh soldiers as an escort were recalled into Lahore. Should there be a general shindy throughout the Punjaub I should immediately become Capt Abbott's assistant in the political department & thus the opening I so much court would be afforded me. Perhaps I write too strongly & the whole affair may be settled in a few months but with a civilian who is no soldier but merely a good secretary at the head of affairs one's ardour is considerably damped.

We were all afraid that the result of the late revolution in France would have been a universal war all over Europe. That an extensive warfare will soon be carried on there is but little doubt, but if Great Britain is wise she will keep out of it herself & merely eat up the tails after the Kilkenny cats have done fighting, but with Lord Palmerston this is hardly to be expected.[164]

The overland summary of course gives you all the necessary intelligence of this country so that I will not attempt to say any thing about the Mooltan business. At Peshawur & in this country the two places which afford most anxiety to Lahore all is quite quiet. The various chiefs declare they hate the Sikhs, but they will do whatever we wish them. They certainly shew much outward respect & love for us. I only hope that the professions may remain sincere. There is much cause for complaint of [*sic* on] both sides. Formerly the Sikhs oppressed & did much injury to the country & on the other side the people are very fickle.

We have still comparatively cool weather but the climate of the Punjaub is wonderfully superior to that of Hindostan & Calcutta in particular. The stations are much sought after by our troops, but I don't think our Govt would like to hold the country. It would be long before it could settle down & the extra expense required for its keep & to keep in order the frontier tribes alone would swallow up all the revenues. As a barrier with a strong Govt able to control its troops the Punjaub was invaluable to us & it will certainly be a great misfortune if we are obliged to take it into our own hands as the establishments attached to the troops of native powers are always much smaller than in our service & consequently the difference of expenditure nearly treble. The matter of pay still remains unsettled, but as soon as I can get some money I will remit. At present I am as poor as a church mouse. I hope you are free from the ungentlemanly inconvenience of a want of money. What annual premium should I have to pay were I to ensure my life for £1,000 per annum in the Mutual.[165] Kind love to all.

Yr. affect. Son
D.G. Robinson

31

Daniel George Robinson to his father

Camp Hurripoor[166]
May 25th [18]48

My dear Father

To my great regret last mail brought no letters from you. I hope you are not one of the sufferers from the anarchy & confusion which now reigns all over the continent. Our little row goes on unchecked. The deportation of the Ranee[167] from Lahore to

Benares & the hanging of two of the principals found tampering with our troops has for the present checked any immediate commotion. Still one can hardly expect the Sikh troops will remain quiet for five months. We have I am happy to say removed from Hasara city to a delightful glen in the mountains within a couple of hours [ride of] that city but by its elevation much cooler and healthier. There are also they say tigers, leopards, wild pigs & wild goats in the neighbourhood & we promise ourselves some sport. Our position here is in my poor opinion a good political one sufficiently distant to be safe from any sudden emeute & sufficiently near to be able to come down on the rebellious point in a few hours with an overwhelming force of the armed population of the country. There is a prevalent notion that Goolab Sing whom we put in possession of Cashmere & a very large portion of hill country is intriguing against us. The Sikhs owe him a heavy grudge for the tricks he played them in the late campaign thereby despoiling them of a large portion of the Punjaub for his own benefit & he is anxious to remove that enmity by apparent assistance. He would also be glad to see us a little further removed from his territories in which we have rather too much influence for so avaricious & cruel a ruler. But it can hardly be supposed that he the cleverest intriguer, the shrewdest villain & most far sighted politician in the Punjaub if not in India would ever make an open rupture with us however much he might strive to subvert our power by underhand proceedings. I believe that a mere proclamation that we meant to oust him & take possession of his country would cause all the four hill chiefs to arm & rise in our favor, against them his half starved & unpaid troops would not stand for a moment. This chance of his intriguing will however in all probability prevent my making a trip to Cashmere this rains as it had been intended I should do. This is a pity but still perhaps the year after if I live I shall be able to accomplish it.

From other parts of India I can give you no information. The Delhi summary is a good & generally a very true informant especially on military subjects.

I can understand how it is that all the German monarchs

behaved with such pusilanimity.[168] It seems to me that the petitions should have only been listened to after the mob had dispersed. For the future the lowest class will consider themselves the most powerful & until a pitched battle takes place between the middle classes (which I hope will be represented by the national guards) & this rabble I do not see how anything like stability of Government can ever exist. It is true the rabble can make a very good defence from behind barriers, but let the troops first destroy or remove as much provisions as possible then march outside the city & blockade it & I think the rabble would soon be forced to terms from starvation. They could never stand the result of a battle on the open plains. Ninetta is I hope ere this safe in England if there be no immediate personal danger to her on the continent. Revolutionary ideas of modesty & propriety are seldom of the best & purest. What have you done with Charles. I quite agree with you that it is desirable to have him home but when home you <u>must</u> keep him there for a twelve months at least. Nothing but <u>your</u> own example & remonstrances will ever be able to check his extravagant propensities & loose opinions & principles. I would even insist on his working in your counting house for his subsistence or else keep him with Cousin Charles in Jersey. The former would in all probability be the more successful mode but more bitter than the latter. With his warm heart it would be almost impossible not to love & admire Cousin Charles & by so doing now to be imperceptibly led to follow his good example. Still he might easily fall into bad company in Jersey. I would also keep Johnny[169] out of the influence of his example & advise keeping them as much separate as possible. This is severe discipline, but I allways find immediate severity mildest in the end. I check the growing evil at once & I generally find that my sepoys soon become attached to me more so than if I were to punish often & leniently.

Give my kind love to Knott & all at home. It is my intention to write to Knott & my brothers & sister whenever I have time. God bless you my dear Father.

Yr. affec. Son
D.G. Robinson

32

Daniel George Robinson to his sister

Camp in Jurrôl,[170] Hasara, Punjaub
June 4th 1848

My dear Sister

It is [a] long time since I have written to, or heard from, you. Partly owing to the gadding propensities which induced you to go a wandering on the continent & which rendered the chance of my hearing from or writing to you very remote & secondly because I have been too busy to write to any one to whom I was not immediately necessitated to write. Our Mooltan business goes on quietly enough. A general opinion seems to prevail every where that we are running great risks by our procrastination & we all pray for the speedy return of our late Resident, a man of energy & spirit, to replace the old woman at present at the head of the affairs of the Punjaub. Still matters have mended since last mail & we now know where we can & where we cannot look for assistance & good faith.

Our Father writes that it was [his] intention to take you to call on the Edlemann's on your return from the continent. I hope he has done so & that you remembered me kindly to them all & especially to Adine. The governor is evidently aware & approves of my weakness in that corner & if you have not given my love & all the other little paraphanalia & do not send me a full true & particular account of the visit you shan't have a cashmere shawl "that's all." This Mooltan business & the extreme probability of Goolab Sing being engaged in some intrigue again prevents my visiting Cashmere as I intended to have done this summer & should I be [in] this neighbourhood next year I suppose something will interfere to prevent it. However be that as it may should I ever go & you not send me a proper account of your visit to Bexley I shall not present you with a Cashmere shawl.

We are now living in the hills. The weather is hot in tents but the climate is very fine, almost as good as that of England but much drier and purer. Our space is however very limited, there is no going a mile from home without some difficult climbing. It is very pleasant to go down hill if it were not for the returning up again. The tops of these slate hills are very barren & wanting in the picturesque, but at the bottoms of the valleys there are some lovely nooks & corners. But as I said before there is no pleasure in a return climb of 2,000 feet ascent on a hot summer's morning or evening with the thermometer at 120° in the sun so that we never go down & as we cannot get much higher upon this ridge we are content to wander round & round our small encampment forever. Were it not for the generally excited state of the country I do not think I should remain in such a fixed position long but continue my wanderings in more beautiful & lofty mountains. However I must not repine but rather think myself lucky in being so well situated as I am. How did you enjoy your trip on the continent. I hope it has improved both your body & mind. Habits of thought & reasoning on the causes of all results cannot fail to be of mental improvement. I find from being so much thrown on my own resources & to think of matters of importance I already begin to get an old head on the young shoulders at least I am told so. It is now three years since I commenced my wanderings & I have now got such a taste for tents & change of scenes & people that I do not think I could exist 4 months in one station but should die of sheer ennui.

June 26th Sherwan[171]

At last I have got a few minutes to finish this scribbilarium. The weather seems to get warmer every day & notwithstanding our exalted situation I have the thermometer as high as 100° in my tent sometimes still the cool air of the mountains (after the scorching heat of the plains) in the morning is very comforting & bracing. I have received your letter & am delighted to hear you were so pleased with your Italian trip. Enjoy your visit to the galleries of old masters & the inspection of the antiquities. At present I have a little mania for the latter & take much trouble in collecting old coins & seals, copying & translating inscriptions &c. I shall seal this & the Governor's letter with the obv. & rev. of a seal pressed from a coin 1600 years old. I hope you will feel sufficiently awed. We have just heard of Moolraj having been completely defeated in an action which lasted from 9 a.m. till 4 p.m. & in which he lost all his guns.[172] It is by no means unlikely this may close the whole business & Moolraj will be given over to us by his present friends. If so I shall perhaps be able to go to Cashmere this year. I certainly hope so, for this may be my last opportunity of visiting the valley. I do not wish to make a hasty visit but on the contrary to spend some little time in a careful examination. Having now scribbled my scrawl I will conclude, with most affect. love to all at home, Jack to have a double share, & believe me

your loving brother

D.G. Robinson

33

Daniel George Robinson to his father

Sherwan June 26th 1848

My dear Father

Having missed another mail I have determined such few spare moments as I can find every day to scribbling a few lines in hopes of making up something for transmission by each mail. I know how vexed I always am if by any accident no letters reach me by each mail & I can therefore understand your disappointment at not receiving expected letters.

We heard yesterday the news of Moolraj having been completely defeated by the combined forces of Bhawul Khan[173] & the raw Pathan levies of Edwardes the political in charge of Bunnoo, Tank & the Derajat, namely all the country on the right banks of the Indus between the river & the mountains & extending from Kohat to Scinde, peopled by wild half tamed tribes & a station for about 5000 Sikhs & 12 or 20 guns. When poor Agnew & Anderson were first wounded they wrote to him as the nearest British officer for assistance & he immediately pushed across the Indus to their assistance & on the second march towards Mooltan he heard of their murder. He then set to work to oust the rebel Moolraj's governors & take possession of the Doab of the Indus & Chenab rivers. After a short time the rebel Moolraj sent 4500 men & 4 guns against him & Edwardes intercepted a letter shewing that the six Sikh regiments had corrupted his off[ice]rs to desert to Moolraj for 12,000 rupees & to take Edwardes's head with them for 12,000 more. Here was Edwardes then in a pretty fix. He could not run had he wished so he called a council of war & overruled the kind offers of his officers who declared that they were staunch, brave troops & objected on Mily. grounds to hazarding his 1500 men & two guns against Moolraj's 4500 men & 4 guns. He then retreated across the river & commenced raising Pathans (mussalmans) for soldiers. In this manner he severely checked the enemy at Leeiah[174] in a smart affair of piquets thrashed the force at Dheyrah Ghasee Khan[175] & from being obliged to act on the defensive he actually gained the initiative drove Moolraj's force across the river Indus & gained possession of all the boats (70) on the river, & this with only raw levies his own Sikh troops being all placed in such positions that they could do no mischief whatever. At last he crossed over, joined Bhawul Khan's advancing force & thrashed Moolraj in an action that lasted from 9 a.m. till 4 p.m. & in which he took all his guns.[176] Meanwhile our new resident Sir Fredc. Currie, Bart, who was made a baronet for heaven only knows what reason sits quietly at Lahore, asserts his right to do as he pleases, neglects the repeated advice of all his numerous assistants & neither assists Edwardes nor takes means for his safety, thinks it too hot for our troops to move on Mooltan & thus leaves the whole die to rest on the head [and] health of one noble fellow & the murders of two Englishmen to be revenged by our allies. I only wonder at our allies not deserting us. Is it not disgraceful to have our battles fought for us by allies? Are we not soldiers? & yet soldiers must not fight in the hot weather, their health must suffer & such trash as this is offered as an excuse for one doing nothing from May till October. Nothing but extraordinary good fortune has assisted the Resident. He h[as] shewn himself as unfeeling as he is incapable & if the truth only finds its way to Head quarters and England I hope he will meet with his reward. He confesses that he is aware that the whole Sikh army is ripe to turn upon us. He sees that many men from distant regiments have deserted & one regiment near Mooltan had instead of fighting gainst, joined Moolraj & yet his plan of assisting Edwardes is to send converging columns of Sikhs (known traitors) on his flanks. Should Edwardes fall sick there was no British officer to take command, I believe one is now sent, & there was not even one of the steamers of the Indus flotilla placed at his disposal.[177] So much for a civilian, a secretary, placed as head of the affairs of a country whose chief stumbling block is their mutinous army & their warlike neighbours & this idiot being a civilian gets more than double the allowances Col Lawrence received. As a secretary, being a good man of business he was in his proper place & acquitted himself well. Edwardes is a young man of 28, very talented & first became known as the writer of the letters from Brahminee bull to his loving cousin John Bull. Perhaps you may have seen them formerly.[178] I expect if he lives he will rise to high honor.

I don't know when I shall be able to send home £100 I hear nothing of my [debtors] but a good deal from my creditors who dun me without a mercy. I am living very closely to satisfy the latter & have sent down to Lahore one of my horses, my large tent & (500) five hundred rupees worth of coins for sale. With this I expect to save Rs 150 one hundred a[nd] fifty a month from my staff [pay] for the next three months making about Rs 1,500 fifteen hundred in all. Govt will also purchase the theodolite from me as also my prismatic compass so that I expect independent of pay to be able to scrape together two thousand rupees in all before the ensuing three months are over. This will enable me to pay all my debts & I hope to send you £100 & when I get my arrears of pay another fifteen hundred rupees I hope to send another £100-0-0 but you see I am entirely at the mercy of the fates & must trust to providence for a sale for my property. I want particularly a new eyepiece of very high magnifying power for the Dollands glass you sent me out last year.[179] I believe they call it (Huygensian).[180] I require it to put on at night for the purpose of examining the stars & planets. I also want a piece of dark glass to fit the same telescope. Dolland will perfectly understand what is wanted.

I hope you have news from Charly. That he should be punished for his folly is only right & proper, but that the whole fruits of seven years service should be lost & at this time particularly without the greatest efforts being made to put him into another ship is I think most lamentable & ruinous.[181] I would give everything I possess rather than it should so happen. With all his faults Charles has a noble heart & intellect & the misfortune is that he should ever have been in bad company or gone to the South American station. After the warmth of feeling & hospitality of Indian society I have no doubt I should feel chilled by the distance & want of sincerity of English manners & am not therefore at all surprised at Charles not feeling so comfortable in England as in South America. On a Mediterranean station amongst the French or Spanish or Germans he would meet with stiffness & formality & might soon perhaps find out that England after all is not the worst place in the world. I am delighted with Jack's conduct & hope he will continue to improve daily in wisdom & virtue. A good moral education, good society & a proper respect for religion & the Queen cannot fail to push a boy in his situation rapidly up the hill.

How does the partnership progress. I fear much that the convulsions of Europe must at present considerably injure your business. However I hope for the best & doubt not but that with God's help you will prosper & be happy. It is not wor[l]dly wealth that makes a man happy, it is a contented mind & cheerful disposition conjoined to sufficient means to prevent the shoe pinching.

I have cut wine & all luxuries. My table expenses do not exceed 30 rupees a month for myself & companion & with the fine air & pleasant life notwithstanding the heat I lead a pleasant life.

I am exceedingly sorry for Mrs & Mr Kerr. I hope that they may soon recover from their present distress. Had the house failed their distress would have been infinitely greater, but as it is altho fallen in wealth they are more respected & will I hope soon be as large & as influential a house as ever. Pray remember me most kindly to them when you see them & say how sorry I feel for them. I am afraid I am but a Jobs comforter so dare not attempt to write. God bless you all.

Yr. affect. son

D.G. Robinson

P.S. The Telescope eye-pieces to come out overland to Allan Duffel & Co. Shew the seal to Ninetta.

34

Daniel George Robinson to his father

Sherwan Hasara July 12th/[18]48

My dear Father

A week since I received the packages containing the theodolite &c. I am unwilling to offer remarks, but as I may require other instruments I will tell you the faults which exist in those just received. In the first place the upper plate carrying the vernier does not move truely on the divided plate. This is owing to the spindles not moving truly one within the [other]. It is however quite possible that the instrument may have got a shock in the voyage out. The next nuisance is the limb being divided to 180° & to 180° again instead of to 360° all round, an inconceivable nuisance. Lastly the telescope wants power. I shall try & sell it to the Lahore durbar & get what I can for it. Formerly I was supplied with a very inferior Govt. instrument, now I have four or five excellent ones. The shoulder straps are for infantry. Engineers in India always wear trophy shoulder scales the same as the horse artillery.[182] They must be sold also. Paper, Caps, instruments &c are all excellent. The box containing the whips, ball & socket has not yet reached me. I have traced it half way up country & hope it will turn up someday. I have a notion that it went to Hosheapore[183] instead [of] to to [sic] Hasara. If so I shall soon recover it. I have just received your letter of the 18th May. I am glad the things are starting altho' I fear that I shall be out of the land of primitive rocks & mountains ere the apparatus will arrive however they will

163

assist me in my studies. The pistols I wanted were rather too heavy than too light. [With] a holster pistol one can afford to have some weight but when a double barrelled pistol has to be carried in one's belt it cannot be too light. A mere pea is quite large enough for close quarters, the only time one ever needs a pistol in this country. I find even those single barrelled tools I brought out from England with me quite heavy enough when climbing up 2,000 or 3,000 feet of steep ascent with the thermometer about 100 added to which is the weight of a minute dagger, cartridge box &c however I will not condemn until I see them. I merely give these hints that you may know what is required for India. I should recommend a six inch barrel, bore about 50 to the lb, under & over, good locks with stops & the strap spring fixed with three screws thus. In the same way guns should always be double barrelled & not of greater than 18 bore. Above this size they do not carry ball well. I fire ball from my double barrel quite as often as shot. When I get rich I have a great notion of indenting on you for a rifle, double barrelled, bore about 36, not very long & two grooved made by a good maker & with first rate locks. I am not quite sure but that I should like the bore even smaller, however this is an idea at present hardly in posse much less in esse. I am doing all I can to raise the wind to send you home a good round sum of money but what between the paymaster & the expense for books necessary for me to study languages I save but little out of four hundred rupees a month. My actual expenditure is not above 250 but there are numerous charges incidental to my position which eats up a large portion of my income. I have sent a number of things down to Lahore for sale in hopes of raising the wind. My large tent, some coins, a horse & the theodolite will now follow it. These I hope will raise about 1200 rupees to which I may add 500 from my pay so as to enable me to send home altogether £150 possibly more. At present I am rich but cannot put my hand on the money. I cannot sell the property I wish to dispose of, nor can I get my pay from the paymaster. However as I get money I shall send it by instalments down to Allans to be remitted to you. His house has fared better than any of the other Calcutta houses. My friends the Cadogans have I believe lost much money. I feel much for Mr Kerr & should write to him but I feel my unfitness to write letters of consolation. I know I am too much of a philosopher to make other than a Job's comforter.

I hope that Charles really is on board the Thetis.[184] I was exceedingly uneasy about him & was afraid that he had seriously or entirely ruined his prospects for life. When will experience ever teach him to be more careful & more inclined to suit his own views & inclinations to those of his superiors. The South American republican notions that have taken possession of his brain unless speedily eradicated will allways keep him in hot water & trouble.

Our Mooltan shindy progresses quietly. We have shewn much want of spirit by refusing to take the field in the hot weather & leaving the whole brunt of the business to a lieutenant of eight years in the country who has raised his own army of mussalman & thrashed the Sikhs in two actions. Edwardes with his undisciplined troops has now got Moolraj blockaded in his fort & has two European officers, a doctor & two of the little river steamers sent to join him.[185] A siege train has been ordered to get ready & a brigade of our troops are to go down to help in the siege. Butt [sic] strange to say altho' it is now three months since our unfortunate officers were murdered, the Ferozepore authorities say that it will take 20 days ere the train will be ready. Really this is a disgraceful state of things, the blessed effect of having a civilian at the head of affairs a man who made an excellent secretary but without the energy & knowledge of military affairs necessary to all Residents & especially to him of Lahore. The Caubul business arose from just the same cause. The result of Sir Fredc. Currie's coming to Lahore is the attempt to shove all civilians into the Residency & to shove down the Mily. assistants from which cause probably arose the murders of our countrymen & the loss of much character. I am sick of such imbecility.

July 14th

I did for my rifle this morning in firing at a deer. The nipple blew out. As this is the fourth or fifth time that this has occurred I begin to think the lock must be pretty well done for. There is certainly no one in this country who can cut a new screw for me. I therefore think more seriously of getting a double [barrelled] rifle some day. At present as I said before I am too poor, still be on the look out for me.

I am in excellent health & spirits. The fine mountain air & exercise every morning keeps me wonderfully well, moreover I have a gentlemanly lad for an assistant & Capt Abbott for another companion so that comparatively speaking we have something like society & that a merry one. Of course there are no ladies not [*sic* nor] do I regret their absence & their frivolities. Fancy not being allowed to run about in one's shirt sleeves, no braces, nor heeled heavy shoes & a hat with a turban twisted on it to say nothing of the amount of time that must be necessarily spent in small talk. Nor [*sic* not] that I object to ladies society – by no means when one has plenty of leisure & no roughings. I work from early dawn till dark & generally fall asleep in my chair after dinner. My assistant[186] snores with his head on the table & the worthy Capt.[187] nods & nods till at last he trots off to bed. We were [for] some time at a loss what to do with the shaving brush & I am by no means sure that we have even yet found out any really useful office for it.

A note yesterday received from Mrs Cadogan states that they were immediately going home to England. I suppose to assist in winding up the affairs of Alexander's house.[188] I believe that Bagshaw's house[189] have lost much money but are (at least I hope so) not in a desperate way by any means. If you see them you will find Mr Cadogan a most excellent shrewd man & Mrs Cadogan a most excellent hearted unostentatious good wife. I am sure you will like them much for themself setting aside their kindness to me during my stay stay [*sic*] with them. I find [I] have filled these sheets so with every wish for your health, wealth, happiness an[d] all other blessings earthly & heavenly farewell.

Yr. affec. Son
D.G. Robinson

35

Daniel George Robinson to John Harding Robinson

Hasara July 18[th 1848]

My dear Jack

Altho' not often honoured with a note from your worship I just scribble a few lines to let you know how we be & to try & induce you to scribble to me monthly. I am glad to hear you are getting on so well. Read, read, read everything carefully. Every species of information is of use sooner or later & if you will only prosecute your studies with zeal during youth I expect someday to see you amongst the famed men of your country. Above all things avoid bad company, it is truly the root of all evil. In good company all our good intentions prosper. I am glad to hear that you get a little riding & other such manly amusements. It is now quite a treat to me to get the fine mountain air & am [*sic* the] opportunity or more properly speaking the obligation of walking. I generally have my gun with me of a morning & often get a shot at a wild boar, a wolf or a deer. The smaller game being left in peace until the end of next month when I purpose to wage war against them also. During the day I attend to my own proper duties not neglecting two hours a day devoted to study & so one day telleth another in the most regular manner during the rainy season during which I am always stationary. I shall lose the post if I do not now conclude so believe me my dear Jack with every wish for your health, fame & happiness.

Yr affec Brother

D.G. Robinson

36

Daniel George Robinson to his father

Shirwan July 31st 1848

My dear Father

I just scribble a few lines by this mail to let you know that up to this time all is well. We have a report to day that Edwardes has had another victory over Moolraj but it requires confirmation.[190] I am also happy to say that a small force & siege train are on their way down & no doubt soon after their arrival the fort will be taken & every thing will again be quiet & then we shall [be] forced to sit on a fresh shell until it shall be ripe enough for another explosion for altho' there is no doubt that the whole of the Sikh lower classes & many if not all the Sirdars hope for the prosperity of Moolraj & his cause still I do not think we shall find sufficient judicial evidence to encriminate them & on the whole our name has rather suffered than gained by the present outbreak.

I sent down Rs 250 two [hundred and] fifty the other day to Mess. Allan, Duffel & Co to be followed in a day or two by another two hundred & I begged them to send you a bill at sight for £25-0-0 twenty five which I hope to follow up next month with a similar sum & so on every two months until I can bring up the long arrears due to you. I have recovered a large portion of my arrears of pay but I have still very heavy retrenchments to be recovered & due to me & I have not yet succeeded in selling my property which I sent down to Lahore for sale. When all these things are put together I have no doubt I shall be pretty rich again. Exchange is at present seriously low. I hope it will soon rise again altho' there is but little chance of its so doing. I think I told you that Bagshaw & Co have dissolved partnership & that Mr Cadogan & his wife have gone home to England. I hope you will some day meet them as they are very superior people as far as warm hearts & sticking friendship goes. I have not heard anything of the reason why this partnership is dissolved but I suspect it is a good deal connected with the break up of Fletcher Allexander & Co.[191] I have written a short letter by this mail to Mr. Kerr but I much fear that I am a very Job's comforter. I hope long ere this you have heard from Charles & that he is again going on smoothly. I fear much for him & much wish that you could get him & keep him at home for a year. It might have a great effect in taming him. Jack I trust is well & flourishing, Ninetta happy & not more in love than usual. You as should be.

Yr affec Son

D.G. Robinson

[P.S.] I hope you have stated the Huygensian eye piece for my telescope <u>overland</u>.

37

Daniel George Robinson to his father

Sherwan Hasara July [*sic* August] 8th [18]48[194]

My dear Father

In case you should be alarmed at the news that will reach you by the coming mail of the insurrection of the Hasera troops, the murder of Coll. Canora[195] &c a man in the Sikh service who was massacred whilst trying to do his duty in the most gallant manner, I just write this few lines in great haste & not a little out of temper to assure you that I am well & hope soon with the help of these mountaineers & the help of Providence to serve out these mutinous & treacherous troops. I need hardly say that this is the last letter which is likely to reach you for some little time.

From yr. affect. Son

D.G. Robinson

38

Daniel George Robinson to his father

Margulli,[196] Augt. 20th [18]48

My dear Father

I just write a few hurried lines in hopes of saving the mail. Thanks to our excellent energetic & soldierlike Resident the Mooltan business is not yet settled & we have another rebellion of Sikh troops here. We were prepared for it & altho' they thought from the apathy we displayed in the Mooltan business that they would be supported by a larger portion of the Sikh population the Resident's assistants are rather more energetic than he is & we have already got rather the upper hand. Abbott the Poll. agent is looking to the force at Hurripore the capital of Hasara 3 regiments & 7 guns with a strong fort & a fortified town to support either flank – a very strong position. Nicholson another assistant guards the lower passes into Hasara & has possession of Attock which prevents the Peshawur force offering any assistance & your humble servant has got half a regiment to the rear & a regiment & a half, four guns & 200 cavalry in front to look after. Our armies being composed entirely of the armed peasantry, so that I am doing a bit of the general under difficulties & of the political. I keep two Persian writers at work all day writing orders & drafting letters, trying to separate the mussalman portion from the Sikh portion of the Sikh army & I trust I have succeeded in inducing the whole of the artillery including their commander, a large portion of the cavalry & several of the infantry to desert. I expect they will desert to me to morrow. As you may suppose I have very hard work & have nightly little rest & what with the truants, the bickerings lurking between the various chiefs & other troubles I am pretty well tired out. However you shall have a full true & particular account some day or other.

I am rejoiced to hear of Charles' promotion.[197] I trust he will turn steady. With love to all.

Yr affec Son
D.G. Robinson

P.S. This was written during dinner time so you may suppose the amount of work I have.

39

Daniel George Robinson to his father

Camp Nara Sepr 15th 1848

My dear Father

I have received your letter of the 18th July with much pleasure & am glad that affairs are now no worse than they were. I remitted to you some time since £25 at a most ruinous exchange & have prepared to send you more but at present our letters are so often seized on the road & so seldom reach us that I dare not send money by post. You have from time to time heard from me of the excellent high minded pateristic warm hearted Resident we now enjoy over us at Lahore who left that gallant fellow Edwardes to beat the rebel Moolraj with his own talents & the troops raised on his own responsibility assisted by two trust worthy regiments & 10 guns with Bhawul Khan's force of 12,000 men & 10 guns & who instead of sending him assistance in the shape of British troops sent three converging columns of Sikh rebels to join Moolraj on the first opportunity but whom Edwardes carefully kept 150 miles away from him. Well owing to the delay in sending troops to Mooltan who ought to have gone early in the month of May the Resident was forced to send them in the much more unhealthy season of July & instead of having only one rebellion to crush we have had another broke out here & half the Sikh force at Peshawur is in rebellion, open or concealed being in a strong country & amongst a mussalman population who hate the Sikhs & were cruelly oppressed by them until we arrived in the country. The moment Sirdar Chutter Sing[198] (whose daughter is married to the little Maharajah Dhuleep Sing) murdered Coll. Canora [and] broke into open rebellion we issued purwanahs[199] calling on the country to rise & commenced levying irregular levies the consequence of which was that we cut off 2 regiments from the main body & actually got the upper hand & Chutter S[ing] was considering whether he should take poison or fly across the mountains to Cashmere & take refuge with Goolab Sing. [In] this state of things the Resident instead of sending us up [a] British force to crush the rebellion sends up the Sirdar's most intimate friend & colleague in the government of this province to separate the army from the rebellious Sirdar. This new ally Sirdar Jhundur Sing having nothing to lose persuaded the rebel to continue & so pacified the army that instead of remaining divided into two parts one of which was anxious to join us they all determined to follow the Sirdar thro' thick & thin & by prolonging the negotiations & various arts of treachery he gained time for the rebels so that another regiment, 4 guns & 400 irregulars joined his camp without being opposed on the road.[200] Sirdar Chutter Sing had thus in camp 4 Regts. [of] regular infantry, 13 guns, 300 cavalry & 400 irregular infantry opposed to Capt. Abbott & Lieut Nicholson who had 1000 & 2000 men respectively hardly any cavalry & no guns.[201] They were obliged to retire into the mountains. Meanwhile I with about 800 men was keeping in check 2 regt infy. 4 guns & 300 cavalry in the upper part of Hazara my force increasing daily both in numbers & spirits & we making up the roads making breastworks & making everything as tight as possible. When Chutter Sing wanted to relieve them Nicholson however was too quick for him & marching 30 or 40 miles in the sun arrived before him at Dumtour[202] a stronging [sic] pass between Hasara & Pukli where I was. Abbott joined him the next day but they could not unite their forces as there were two roads to be defended passing on either side of a high mountain. Nicholson's irregulars were convinced that they could not hold their own & the worst was that the moment the Sikhs advanced they fled without firing a shot & I found myself between two fires. Had no action have taken place I would have held my ground & fought them both but as it was half of my wavering troops took fright at Abbot's & Nicholson's defeat & said we could not fight. I therefore disbanded my levies & started off by a bye road across the mountains for Nara in Hasara where I now am & the two Sikh forces having united are now winding their way back again to this place.[203] We are in a very strong position where we now are but against bribes & treachery no one can be safe & I should not be surprised if we are again obliged to f[ight]t as to expect any assistance from Sir Fredc. Currie Resident at Lahore is out of the question. As it is we have kept in check a rebel army of 4500 men with 18 guns, 600 cavalry & 400 irregulars with the most obstinate irregulars of half that number, men who like the Spaniards always want to do every thing tomorrow[204] & without exception the worst behaved soldiers I ever saw. Had it not been so I should have been much distressed by our defeats but as it is I only laugh at it as very good fun.

I believe that a very considerable force is now assembling at Lahore, probably far larger than the necessity requires & meanwhile we lose time. I start this evening on another expedition northwards to try & stir up the people again & raise anew my levies. We have hard work often spending 30 hours in the saddle without rest, but without troops who will obey orders & not run away we can do but little. However it is a very jolly life & my health & spirits are excellent. Of course there is a stoppage to all my other work & I hope I shall not lose by the opening into public notice thus afforded me. I have not time to scribble more just now so shall terminate with kind love to you all. Pray send my congratulations to Charles on his promotion. I would write if I had time but I have not a minute.

Yr. affec. Son
D.G. Robinson

40

Daniel George Robinson to his father

Oct 10th 1848 Mansera[205]
Upper Hasara

My dear Father

I hope you received my two last letters as also another £25 I desired my agents to send you making in all £50 fifty. £35 more will start some day. At present our dâks are shut & an occasional messenger arrives with our letters at Lahore. I think I told you how we were humbugged or rather how the Resident at Lahore contrary to the advice of all his assistants was humbugged by the Lahore durbar & how Chutter Sing thus gaining time released the different portions of his rebel army who we held in quod.

It is just a month since this last skrimmage I can't call a fight took place & Chutter Sing is still at large & no force has even yet marched from Lahore to the assistance of the mussalman population who rose in arms & joined us altho it is now 3 months since Col Canora was murdered & what is more the commander in chief swears that not a man shall march to our assistance until Mooltan is taken.[206] I suppose when by the exertions of his brave army he shall have fought & won some 8 or 10 more battles occasioned by the fellow & want of energy amongst our rulers he will be made a Viscount or an Earl. In three months under Lord Hardinge the last campaign was fought, the Punjaub conquered & we had returned to our own country. Six months since two of our British representatives were murdered in cold blood by a rebellious governor of a small province & up to this moment the siege of his stronghold & seat of Govt has not progressed one inch.

In May last a much cooler & healthier month our two officers were murdered. Sir Fredc. Currie (a cold hearted unfeeling civilian an excellent secretary but never before a political) hesitated whether he should send troops or not & referred the case to the commander in chief who declared that it was <u>too hot</u> to move troops. <u>All</u> Sir F. Currie's assistants, officers of long standing in political employ, men who had long been in the Punjaub from the commencement of our dealings with them & who knew the Sikhs well & the feelings of the troops to us urged & remonstrated against this inactivity again & again declaring that unless the rebellion was crushed at once the whole country would soon revolt.[207] Mr John Laurence who from time to time had officiated as Resident & a brother of Sir Henry Laurence's wrote in the same strain but all to no purpose. Owing to the energy, talent & unswerving exertions of Sir F. Currie's assistants & the fidelity of the Hindostanni regiments & a few of the chiefs the intended outbreak in other parts of the country was put off for three months in which time Lieut H. Edwardes, who had been attacked by the rebel Moolraj & was to have [been] betrayed by his Sikh troops had gradually turned the tables & from acting on the defensive had driven Moolraj under the walls of Mooltan. When there, seeing it was impossible to delay matters any longer two brigades & a weak train of siege artillery was sent down to attack the fort & city, the former one of the strongest in India. Instead of Sir John Littler[208] a fine gallant officer, Genl Whish[209] an old woman on service but a smart officer on parade now commands the Punjaub division & went in command. Major Jarbett,[210] an officer who when on promotion he was transferred to the foot artillery, publicly declared he would never do a days duty until he was replaced in the Horse artillery & <u>of course</u> he was immediately, commands the artillery. Brigadier Hervey[211] supposed to be the worst officer we have commands one of the two brigades. Major Napier,[212] individually a very brave man but wanting in dash & so amiable that he always gives in to the advice of others is Ch[ief] Engineer. & now that, in consequence of Rajah Shere Sing & the Sikh troops with him deserting to the enemy a third brigade is sent the command is given to Brigr Eckford,[213] a dreadfully slow thick headed tho' gallant soldier who thinks that the only road to heaven is to read the bible day & night & never to appear happy & I suppose the siege which was raised will now be resumed.

The first parallel was opened (1) <u>one mile</u>!! from the city!! At this rate when will the fort be taken and any force march to our assistance. The force under Edwardes was proved sufficient to defeat Moolraj & drive him under the walls of Mooltan & with the addition of two brigades of our regular troops I don't think the siege should have been raised however necessary the reinforcements might have been. And there is no doubt that instead of troops being sent to assist the Mooltan force, troops should have been sent to crush the rebel Chuttur Sing who roams the country at large & plunders all those who have assisted us. Two brigades would have done the thing handsomely one would have been enough with a double complement of guns. C[hutter] S[ing] has no stronghold to retire into, he roams the country like a caged tiger. He cannot cross the Indus, we have seized all the boats & have possession of Attock for which same reason the Peshawur force cannot join him. He dare not go to Lahore or Mooltan as in either case he would fall into the hands of superior forces. His only hope is to bribe the garrison of Attock & this he is trying to do. His whole force amounts to not more than 4000 Regulars, 3000 irregulars & 18 guns whilst we can bring 5000 irregulars into the field to help our troops when they arrive. It seems to me very like a breach of faith first to call on a people to rise & check our enemies until our troops can arrive to our assistance & when after checking that enemy & the enemy gets the upper hand no troops march to their assistance but lay idle at Lahore whilst our poor friends & their families are plundered & their houses & crops destroyed & this is to last until the old women who open first parallels at <u>a miles</u> distance can take Mooltan. I hope the British Press will handle this subject as it deserves to be. If you give the Times any hint be anonymous.

A month since I was doing a bit of the general against the Sikhs who were encamped under this fort. I now find myself a kind of deputy governor of Upper Hasara as also collector & magistrate for the time being. I wonder what I shall turn to next. I will say this for my kingdom that there is scarcely a more lawless, litigous, lying, uncertain set of scoundrels I have ever met day by day. I hold my court of justice & every case brought before [me] is one of litigation. We are not troubled with lawyers or wills in this country & the cases are consequently very quickly settled 8 or 10 per diem. So you think this would satisfy the Lord Chancellor & the law community of England. I think I have now scribbled enough for today.

11th Oct./[18]48

You will no doubt hear that Maharaja Goolab S[ingh] is deeply implicated in this rebellion. If he is at the bottom of it he is much too cunning ever to let it appear & altho the Sikh soldiery used to brag that he had prepared every thing & would assist them I doubt if it can be proved against him & he certainly has refused them any assistance but has helped us with money & some guns which arrived yesterday. I dare say the old gentleman will plead his innocence & his devotion to our Govt but one thing is certain that he is & always was at the bottom of every bedevillment which has taken place in this country since Runjeet Sing's death & has with extraordinary tact kept aloof during the struggles to come in for the lions share afterwards.

Give my best love to all at home. I am excellent in health & spirits. I possess three books here one on Physic one on Hindostani & a Persian grammar, also a prayer book & map of this part of Aelia.[214] You can therefore understand that my reading is profitable, my recreation is generally two or three hours shooting in the morning when sometimes we slaughter "the beast" as they call pigs in this country. Of course pork is forbidden at my table as well as Beef the one because Mussalmans despise the eaters of it & my [*sic*] I would not order my cook a mussalman to dress any thing for me he considered unclean & the latter is a forbidden food in the Sikh Dominions where the cow is worshipped. I hope this will find all well in soul & body. God bless you.

Yr. affec. Son
D.G. Robinson

41

Daniel George Robinson to his father

Camp Nawashuhr[215] Pukli
Octr 31st [18]48

My dear Father

In troublous times like the present I write often firstly because there are very great probabilities of many of the letters not reaching & secondly because all sorts of reports are constantly flying about & a line from the living gives them all the lie. Since I last wrote the whole of the Sikh force at Peshawur has mutinied and have been joined by the Nujeeb regiments (Mussulmans & hindoos).[216] The Governor, old Goolab Sing Provindra[217] and his son were exceedingly averse to the mutiny, the former was siesed by the mutineers but the latter with Sooltan Mahmood K[han] Dooranie[218] fled with our officers Major Lawrence[219] & Lieut Bowie[220] towards Kohat. The mutineers have got seven boats that were on the Goondie R[iver] (the Caubul) so that they will not have much difficulty in crossing the Indus. United with Chuttur Sing they will not have more than 10,000 regulars & perhaps the same number of irregulars with a good proportion of cavalry & 40 guns. Chuttur Sing swears he will rout us out before he goes to Lahore. If our adherents remain in tolerably good heart I hope we shall pay them out well. Abbott has 300 or 400 more good mountaineers & a couple of mountain guns. His position is one of immense strength & if the Sikhs attack it & there is no treachery they will probably again get the worst of it. It is a place which has often been attacked & never taken by the Sikhs excepting once when Runjeet Sing came against it with 80,000 men & having invited the chiefs to a conference he seized their persons & kept them as a [*sic*] hostages until his people arrived on the top of the mountain where he built a fort & having thus got possession of this stronghold he blew two of the chiefs from the mouths of guns. This is merely one of the many specimens of Sikh treachery. In those days its defenders seldom exceeded 2000 men whereas Abbott must have 3000 men with him in addition to the inhabitants of the place. The seven boats ought never to have been left on the Caubul R[iver]. I wrote two or three times about them but Lawrence having possession of the guns & relying on the Nujeeb regiments thought it unnecessary to seize these boats & thus to destroy all communication between the left & right bank of the Goondi. Attock is well garrisoned & supplied with 13 guns & 2000 men [so] there is no danger save against treachery. This outbreak took place on the 6th of Aug[us]t very nearly 3 months since & no British force has yet marched. All this is owing to Sir Fredc. Currie a man who was made a Bart for his political talents & services!!! A man who takes the advice of his writers & the Sikh Durbar in preference to the warnings of his assistants. In March last I wrote to both Abbott & the Resident that the Sikh sepoys openly spoke of massacring all the British officers & [excited] our troops in the latter end of May. Agnew & Anderson were murdered at that time but various circumstances prevented the rest of the conspiracy being at that time carried out. The moment it broke out instead of sending troops they sent one of the principal conspirators by which act a whole month was lost & from being on the offensive C[huttur] S[ingh] by his bribes threw us on the defensive in which state we have remained for the last two months.

In health I am excellent & also in spirits, tho' in the midst of such troubles I am not in the least excited & go out shooting every morning as if nothing was the matter. The only thing is that being in the minority I find it not a little difficult to induce the Zemindars to pay up the revenue. No tailor ever had to dun a gent in the way I have to do but I back my duns with 10 or 12 sepoys who live at the Zemindars expense until he pays up. I have got some stuffed birds – the chicore & black partridge. The former a larger bird than our partridge beautifully marked & something in colour similar to the turtle dove. The latter has a black breast with white spots & darker plumage than our partridge [and] it [is] also much larger but not so large as the chicore. If I have an opportunity I mean to send them to Knap Jonas to put in to his game cases of preserved birds.

I am afraid I shall have to procure some new shaving irons since I lost my penknife. Having no further use for my razors I have used them for cutting pencils & mending pens, but <u>when</u> the British Army comes I suppose I must conform to custom & shave regularly, a Nuisance I am not at all accustomed to. In this country they judge of a mans sagacity by the length of his beard but they generally shave the crowns of their heads. I to please them let my beard & moustaches grow & to please myself leave my hair alone unless it becomes troublesomely long when I cut it off evenly all round. I am sure the first respectable barber who cuts my hair will observe that some bungler was last at [it] – no artiste – Sir I think your hair was last cut in the country.

Novr 14th/[18]48

Since I last wrote our affairs have not mended. One good thing is however certain; a strong British force is advancing [and] this puts our people who were desponding into good spirits again. Chuttur Sing is *wasting time in besieging* Attock without treachery & can never take that fort. I for my part being out of the reach of a surprise from the enemy am not in the least decomposed but go on with my work as if nothing was the matter. My subjects are not anxious to pay up the revenue but I am now forcing them to do so. They are also more ready to settle their disputes by a reference to their swords than to my court.

Chuttur Sing's son Tejah Sing went to Cashmere not many days since to solicit assistance for his father from Maharajah Goolab S[ingh] but that wily chief flatly refused it. Chuttur Sing was formerly the tool of G[oolab] S[ingh] in the murder of Peshorah Sing, a son of the old line. He was always looked upon as the son or brother of Goolab Sing & if Goolab would assist anyone it would be the Ateriwala family namely Chuttur S[ingh] or his sons & nephews.

Our affairs are getting very rotten. Most of the chiefs, our adherents, are either tired of this warfare without plunder or else *seduced* by the *liberal offers* of Chuttur Sing are ready *to betray us.* However, Abbott is extremely vigilant & has some about him devoted to his cause. I am in perfect safety & should our force not delay its progress unnecessarily there is no fear for Abbott or our other people. *Major Lawrence tho' nominally a guest is in reality a prisoner* at Kohat with his *wife & Lieut Bowie* of the artillery.

Should our affairs progress fairly I have no fears for their safety but in case of anything like a reverse or a check there is *no saying what may become of them.* Further, this [is] in the Greek character because Chuttur Sing has taken my clerk, a Bengalee who writes & reads English, prisoner & he reads all our letters which fall in to his hands.

Please now conclude with kind love to all at home.

Yr affect Son
D.G. Robinson

42

Daniel George Robinson to his father

Gurhi[221] n[ea]r Mosuffurabad[222]
Novr 21st/[18]48

My dear Father

I just send you a few lines to let you know we are as yet all right. I am now in the confines of Cashmere where I am come to receive some treasure kindly sent by Maharajah Goolab Sing. Our force is apparently asleep somewhere near the Chenab or Jhelum. They will probably advance in a month or two. God only knows the reason of all this absurd delay. Every day to us is of importance & yet we go dilly dallying as if we had the game entirely in our own hands. Dost Mahomed Khan of *Caubul has joined* Chuttur Sing & he is *waiting for him and his army at Peshawur* this is the is the [*sic*] latest news. *Our political officers are prisoners but are well treated –* perhaps the same may soon be *our fate.* I am *going across* the *mountains in a day or two to join some of Goolab's troops* whom I hope to persuade *to act in concert with our people.* I am glad to learn that the bill for £25.0.0 was remitted to you safely by Allan's people making £50 in all. I will endeavour to remit another £50 as soon as affairs are more settled. God bless you all.

Yr. affect. son
D.G. Robinson

43

Daniel George Robinson to his father

Camp Mosuffurabad on the Jhelum
Novr 27th 1848

My dear Father

I received your letter of the 7th Octr just as I had narrowly escaped a serious fall which would in all probability have diddled me my ghoont in descending the Doob pass jambed one of his fore feet in a cleft of rock & pitched on his head. I jammed the spurs into his flanks manfully & he made such an effort that he drew the shoe clean off his foot, altho' it had been put on the day before & recovered himself. He is the heaviest ugliest looking beast of a poney I think I ever saw but perfectly wonderful for sagacity & sure footedness. I am now on the direct road to Cashmere. I go writing [*sic* riding] two marches of it & then turn off by Aureh[223] & Poonch[224] to Meerpore hoping from the latter point to join our dreadfully slow army which for the last four months has been for the last four months [*sic*] preparing to crush a rebellion which we almost without resources have kept pretty much in check. Had Lord Hardinge or Lord Ellenborough[225] been in the country the Mooltan business would have been at once settled or at any rate Chuttur Sing would not have remained for <u>four</u> months unmolested within 150 miles of Lahore in the neighbourhood of which we had 25,000 men. A single brigade could have crushed the whole business at the end of the first month but by delay the rebels are now encreased fourfold or nearer sevenfold & 3 of our officers are their prisoners. Fortunately we have one of Chuttur Sing's sons in our possession so that there is no fear of another repetition of the Mooltan tragedy. These three officers were placed in the most exposed & difficult position of [*sic* in] the Punjaub in the midst of a Sikh force of 6000 men & 30 guns without a single man of ours for escort. By extraordinary tact & courage Major Laurence kept these Sikhs to their duty for 2½ months whilst a mutinous Sikh army was within 50 miles of him. At last won over by the promises of Chuttur Sing & surprised at no British army advancing Sooltan Mahomed Khan Dooranee &

the other Mussulman portion of the Peshawur force joined secretly Chuttur Sing. Laurence & Bowie had gone to bathe in some house in the city. Bowie was the first to come out when he was immediately pursued by a regiment of Sikh dragoons. His fleet Arab & a couple of broad ditches baffled his pursuers & he got to the Residency in safety. Laurence managed to get from house to house & some how home unobserved. That night they fled Kohât (the Nujeeb of [sic or] Mussulman regiment having agreed to join the Sikhs) at the urgent invitation of Sooltan Mahomed K[han] arrived there they were treated as guests but placed under surveillance. Peir Mahomed K[han], Sooltan Mahomed K[han]'s brother had been placed by Laurence in charge of the boats on the Goondi or Caubul river, 12 in number (I had recommended that they should be placed in the fort of Attock). He made them over to Chuttur Sing who by their aid was enabled to cross the Indus & moved to Peshawur there by extraordinary promises he persuaded Sooltan Mahomed K[han] to give up his prisoners to him. Chuttur Sing & the Barrukzaie Sirdars went out to meet them with nuzzurs (presents from an inferior to a superior) & fired a salute. They are treated pretty well but are under the most painful restraint [of] a sentry being in their tent. Mrs Laurence the Drs wife & too [sic two] little Laurences are with them.[226] The siege of Attock continues. Lieut. Herbert[227] with a rabble garrison & 11 guns are inside. At present the Sikhs have been able to make no impression on the walls whereas the fire of the garrison has been very severe & the loss of the besiegers in guns elephants & men considerable. If the garrison remains true all will go well but our people do not understand why our army does not advance & there is no placing much reliance on them longer. They have been so often defeated by the Sikhs and so cruelly treated that they are completely cowed, altho the Sikhs cannot take Attock we could take it in 10 days but they understand nothing of the science of sapping & attack.

About the 8th of this month one of the best officers in the Queen's service Brigadier Cureton[228] arrived within one march of Ramnuggur[229] on the Chenab with 6 regiments of Cavalry two of which were H.M., 1 H.M. infy, 3 N.I. & 24 or 30 guns. Opposed to them was Chuttur Sing's son Shere Sing with 10 guns & 6000 or say 10,000 rabble. Cureton was for immediately smashing him but he received orders from <u>bate 'em pound 'em</u> i.e. Lord Gough[230] one of the <u>least</u> scientific officers of H[er] M[ajesty's] S[ervice] not to attack him until he Lord Gough should arrive i.e. 14 or 15 days later. In India people are governed by appearances & appearances are that we are afraid & so people think. The fact being that Gough was afraid than [*sic* that] any one else should have the honor of bating & pounding the Saikhs as he calls them. Had Cureton attacked Shere Sing who was only 1 march from him he could have pushed across the Jhelum & through the difficult passes into Potwar & Chuttur Sing could never have attacked Attock. Cureton's force 6500 picked men & 24 guns was fully a match for the Sikh army of 10,000 men & 40 guns & <u>we</u> could have brought from Hasara into the field 15,000 or 20,000 good irregulars to act on the rebels flanks & rear. However the C in C seems determined to have a good fight of it so gives the enemy lots of time & has assembled a most overwhelming army for the purpose. When Cureton arrived near Ramnuggur Shere Sing was in his front with not more than 10,000 rabble the mutineers from Bunnoo were separated from him by 4 or 5 marches. Chuttur Sing with the main body of his forces was 12 marches in his rear – why was he not allowed to attack? His force was a light one & he might have smashed the troops opposed to him in detail without the slightest fear of not succeeding. A single brigade at Mooltan has in these late occasions attacked Moolrajs force of 8000 men & defeated them without loss to themselves. There are few better troops in the Punjaub than Moolrajs carefully drilled & appointed & with tatters round their sides they fight with desperation but they cannot stand before the bayonet. I recollect a long time since reading in the United Service Journal a long dissertation about the superiority of the sword over the bayonet. The Indian sword or tulwar is so sharp that I generally mend my pencils with one when out surveying, but in every instance of the bayonet against the tulwar the bayonet has been successful. On the march to Caubul two British soldiers having got drunk lost their way. They were attacked by a large number of Khyberrees but they so handled their bayonets that they defeated the whole posse. As my informant says they turned over 9 of them in the same way as one turns over straw with a pitch fork.

Doputta[231] [November] 29th [1848] morning

My dear Father

The above being written when I was more than half asleep I am afraid you will have some difficulty. A very long tedious march brought me to this place last night & I am now waiting for the sun to warm a little before I cross the Cashmere branch of the Jhelum River. The men & baggage cross by a kind of suspension bridge called in this country a <u>kude</u> [?]. It consists of three ropes, two for the hands & one for the feet. At ever[y] 20 feet a forked branch serves to keep altogether. It is a ticklish affair & trying to the nerves of the unaccustomed. It is something like the accompanying rough sketch. In this country the ropes are made of leather but I hear higher in the mountains they are made of birch twigs & the ropes are so thick that the hand cannot fairly grasp them. The horses swim for it a rope is tied to their heads & they are swept across <u>somehow</u>. The river being fresh from the snow is dreadfully cold & I am therefore waiting for the sun that they may soon dry again. I must now make haste thro' the passes or I shall be caught by the snow in the passes. It does not close them but renders the passage a terrible business to our Hindustani servants who cannot stand the cold at all. The least frost completely paralyses them. I have 4 or perhaps 6 long double marches before me of as rough roads as one could wish <u>not</u> to go over after the road improves & descends to the plains of the Punjaub. I cannot take my horsemen with me. They have only got so far the best part of the road with great difficulty.

I am glad that the £25 arrived so opportunely. I trust the last I sent will not be so much required. I will send more by the first opportunity but at present I am so cut off from the world & the pay master that I cannot make the necessary arrangements. However as soon as I join the army I trust that I shall be able to send you another £50 & soon after 50£ worth of Bact[r]ian coins for sale in London. I shall in all probability take electrotype copies

'. . . trying to the nerves of the unaccustomed.' Robinson's rough sketch of a suspension bridge.
(Letter 43)

of my own choice collections which will answer my purpose, the study of them, as well as the more valuable originals which I shall then sell for I suppose about £200 two hundred & I must however wait for leisure time.

I really cannot understand Charles. At one time he was so affectionate so careful & so considerate that with a lieutenants pay he would never have required to draw on you. It is possible that he requires a little money for his outfit but after that on board ship he ought not to have many expenses. I live very nearly on my bare pay, if not within in [*sic* it] without touching the staff allowance of 400 rupees per mensem which I spend almost entirely on the appointment. Take from me the survey & I should not spend more than 240 rupees a month even in this expensive country. Wine & beer now cost me nothing, neither do European stores or clothes for the very simple reason that I cannot [buy] them. I therefore lead I trust a godly [existence] a temperate & sober life. I get one meal per diem about 7 p.m. when making forced marches & two when halting one about 10 or 11 a.m. & the other at 7 a.m. [*sic* p.m.] In stations it is the custom to eat three meat meals per diem & I think this is the reason why there is so much sickness. I am sorry to hear that there is the probability of the Asiatic cholera visiting England. I do not know what the doctors say to my remedy which is 20 grains of calomel followed by laudanum & hot brandy water, feet in hot water & hot wet clothes to the stomach. The patient if he <u>feels inclined</u> may drink as much soda water as he likes. Tamarind sherbert very often greatly alleviates the reaching. These are sharp remedies but in this country the patient is generally carried off in 6 hours.

I shall not write more now tomorrow or the next day. I trust I shall be able to send a few lines to Ninitta when you will learn any further news. God bless you.

Yr. affec. Son
D.G. Robinson

44

Daniel George Robinson to his sister

Camp on the Budusta or Cashmere R[iver]
Novr. 29th 1848

My dear Sister
I have received your letter with Agnes appenditure thereto. The first English letter I have received for some time. I am glad you are so well & so well pleased. I do not think Sarah is likely to see Harry at Bombay this trip as I hope his regiment will be ordered up to Mooltan where he may have an opportunity of distinguishing himself & [he] is sure to see service at any rate. I am glad that Lewis Browne as you call him is such a nice fellow & [I] shall be glad to make his acquaintance the first opportunity. I am now on the direct road to Cashmere. I do not visit it but turn off at Ooreh[232] two marches on this side of it where the road from Jhelum joins that from Hazera. I run down by it to some point wherever I can join our slow sleepy army which I hope to pilot up to Hasera or to Chuttur Sing. If not quick I am afraid I shall be too

late. I have twelve marches to make & am in danger of being detained by snow in the passes which if it happens will completely prostrate my Hindustanis. This is a very wild country the river runs in a narrow valley between precipices two or three hundred feet high from which again spring mountains several thousand in altitude. The scenery is nothing. The river runs tolerably straight but winds sufficiently to prevent one seeing more than a few hundred yards of its length at once & the high mountains which rise from either side are too destitute of wood to make them pleasing to the sight. The road is all but impassable to horses. My moonshee's (Persian writer) horse fell over a precipice to day & was killed. My poney also got a fall. I was on him & was just going to jump off his back when he recovered himself. The path is extremely narrow & much choked with the thorns which overhang it. I am now so much accustomed to the mountains that my head never swims however bad the road may be & I now ascend 2,000 or 3,000 feet without inconvenience. Not the kind of hills one finds in England more like the ascent to the dome of St Pauls steps all the way some times not larger than the palm of one's hand & very slippery. The suspension bridges also are curious affairs consisting of only three ropes, one for the feet & two for the hands connected at about every 20 feet by the forked branches of trees. The one I crossed to day was between 150 & 200 feet in span. I first started with my shoes but found the foot rope so slippery that I returned took off my shoes & then crossed without trouble. The cattle have to swim for it & a dreadfully cold bath they must have had as the water is fresh from the snow & little less cold than ice.

I am now pretty well tired of knocking about in this Barbary. I do not see a European above once in three months & then only for a few hours at a time. For the last three years I have roughed it considerably & I would not now mind settling down quietly for a few months. I seldom get more than one meal a day & that late at night when I am marching & when tolerably stationary I generally get one about 12 at noon & the other about 7 at night consisting almost always of fowl, fowl sometimes with & sometimes without vegetables. This is sometimes altered for game of which when tolerably at leisure I shoot a goodly quantity. The day before

'. . . a greenish black river flowing over rocks . . .'
(Letter 44)

yesterday I dined breakfasted & lunched all at once on stewed hare, grilled wild duck & roasted partridges no sauce & no vegetables no bread no butter no wine no beer & no tomakoo as they call it in this country. The inhabitants on this side of the Jhelum are very different from those in Hazara on the other side. They are dirty miserable wretches perfectly unacquainted with washing cleanliness honesty truth or any other of those virtuous accomplishments. I should think they were poorer also but the price of provisions is one third of that of Hazara which is generally considered cheap. Of scenery there is none. At one's feet rolls angrily along a greenish black river flowing over rocks & dashing against its precipitous sides on either side rise to an immense height barren steep mountains & there is no extent to the river. I send you a sketch of the country which I trust will edify you.

[the remainder of this letter is no longer extant]

45

Daniel George Robinson to his father

> Camp between Ramnuggur on the Chenab
> & Jelalpore on the Jhelum
> Decr. 12th 1848

My dear Father

Some tremendous marching which did not quite kill my cattle brought me in here on the night of the 10th & my baggage I am happy to say came up last night. Coming from where I did I was well received by the principal people in camp & dined last night with the Commander in Chief who is a very kind hearted old man, without many brains & much altered since I saw him three years since looking very old, very seedy & it seemed to me that his mind is apt to wander at times. I am now going back to Ramnuggur to assume charge of the political agency there for a few days during the absence of the Chief Assistant Resident to Lahore.[233] These I look upon as a step in the right road & if I can only get time to read will in all probability fix me as a political. I am not in my own opinion yet fit for & would prefer a little training as a second fiddle first, however the opportunity ought not to be lost & therefore I shall make the most of it. After a not very creditable business near Ramnuggur on the 20th ulto. in which no one seems to have been exactly in command & every body to have given orders the force marched to Wuzerabad & crossed by the ford there. They were opposed & altho' not mounting to more than 7,000 men defeated the enemy i.e. turned their right flank & silenced their fire but did not advance or follow them up when they retreated because they had strict orders not to engage. For the same reason we are now to make a flank movement to our right!! i.e. a retreat on to the Chenab because the Govr. Genl. at a great distance has strictly forbidden any advance beyond that river until he arrives. It seems the fashion now a days for the Govr. Genl. be [he] a military man or not to control the movements of the army when a daily encreasing enemy is in the field. In consequence of these instructions, repeated instructions I should say, the whole of the Punjaub is now in rebellion & the opposing army in our immediate front has more than trebled in numbers & guns & now we are to retire on the Chenab until their whole force is concentrated. I have said as much as I could say & Nicholson the only other political who knows the country has said as much as he could say but the advance is not to be heard of & we both wish we were back in our old places with our raw but moveable levies & at partizan warfare at which we annoyed the Sikhs much more than they did. As it is considered above a British Army to molest them or their foraging parties in any petty manner nothing but at [*sic* a] charge at the horns is considered proper. I do not myself see any mily. objection for our taking up a position on the Chenab & awaiting the fall of Mooltan but the moral effect will be very very bad & will only add to the difficulties already sufficiently aggravated by our absurd hesitation & delay in the attack of Mooltan. I will not now write more. I have received with great pleasure yours of Octr. the 7th & am glad the remittance was so acceptable. I will endeavour to remit some more in a few days when I shall be more settled & see more about me. At present I require a little rest & a little refit. Kind love to all at home.

Yr affec. Son
Daniel G. Robinson

46

Daniel George Robinson to his father

Camp Janekachuk[234]
Jany. 2nd 1848 [*sic* 1849]

My dear Father

Altho' a day too late for the safety of catching the mail I write a few hurried lines to let you know that all is well. I think I wrote to tell you of my safe arrival in camp & of the state of affairs in general. Dost Mah[omme]d Khan of Caubul has seized Peshawur & proved a treaty with Chuttur S[ingh] an infidel & worshipper of idols & called upon all mussalmans to rise to a religious war upon us who are of the book i.e. we both believe in Christ & the old testament. His call is not however much responded to & another extraordinary fact is that none of these commands carry his seal merely those of his son & grandson.

I continue to act in political employ & hope to hear soon that I am appointed a permanent assistant. If Mr Staple's friend chose he could easily turn the balance in my favor. I forget the gentleman's name but I think it is Sir — Campbell.[235] We remain much in statu quo, nor do I think that there is any immediate prospect of an advance. Our force is ridiculously small. We have only 15000 men here & to keep up our communication with Lahore whereas Shere S[ingh] has 40,000 & his father 10,000 or 12,000 more without the Dost's assistance of 10,000 or 12,000 more & 18 guns. We are obliged to hold Lahore with 5,000 men. Govindgurh,[236] Jullundhur,[237] Ferozepore & the whole reserves at Loodheanah[238] are not more than 12,000 men however when Mooltan falls we shall have 15,000 more men available of which 5,000 are European Infy. We have only 4 regiments of European Infy here.[239] Last campaign we were terribly in want of cavy. After we cross the Jhelum we shall get into such difficult country that cavalry will be but of little use & we shall want more Infy. However I have no doubt that we shall conquer in the long run. We have plenty of artillery I am happy to say & what we cannot command in England Field batteries of 18 pounders & 8[in] howitzers drawn by two elephants each.[240] A most effective weapon for long ranges such as crossing rivers &c. Our expenditure however is enormous £5,000 to £10,000 per diem additional & after the business is over we must either increase our army & annex the Punjaub or withdraw from it for ever which we cannot do without disgrace.

We learned by express last night that the suburbs of Mooltan had been stormed & taken with hardly any loss. 4 columns of 2000 each & each headed by a European Regt attacked them.[241] This is rather better than the last absurd proceeding of opening the first parallel at one mile distance from the city. However I plainly see that until they make Major Napier or me Govr. Genl. & Comr. in Ch. things will never go on properly. I don't think I have much chance & the first named gentleman certainly does not deserve it considering his scurrilous conduct to our honorable masters & I think if all those gentlemen who cheered him at Cheltenham were cashiered it would be a wholesome example & of much benefit in the way of promotion to the rising generation.

Wishing you all a merry Xmas & a happy new year & kind love to all.

Believe me now

Yr affec. Son
D.G. Robinson

47

Daniel George Robinson to his father

Hormuck March 12th/[18]49

My dear Father

The Sikhs have given up all their guns & zumbourucks & are now dispersing to their homes first publicly laying down their arms. Such Sirdars as formerly possessed jagheers are to have a sufficient subsistence granted them to enable them to live in tolerable comfort & the sipahis are to [be] allowed to return to their homes without molestation. Now that Goolab Sing's army is of no further use they will return to their own country & my connexion with them ceases. The Dooranees only remain to be polished off as fast as they can. Attock will not I think be defended. From experience the Dooranees have an exceedingly great objection to being caught by us within four walls without the means of escape. They will however in all probability defend the passage of the Indus, a very difficult operation in the face of an enemy. I do not think that I shall remain in political employment. I shall return to my survey duties & perhaps when the maps are completed & I can pass the Hindustani & Persian examinations I may get put permanently into this employment. Abbott I think would like to have me for an assistant but he himself I imagine is at this time in no very good odour with the Government. He is so great an alarmist & views every thing in so black a light & [so] that his reputation in all quarters is not of the best. Your letter of the 19th of Jany reached me this morning. I was much pleased with the contents & trust that Charley following out his good intentions will yet do well. I do not myself approve of Foreign service if it can be avoided. I regret that Jack is not so studious as you could wish but this is just the turning time in his age when his conduct will be regulated entirely by the society he keeps which renders it necessary that his mind should be most carefully regulated with good principles. To avoid bad associates poisoning it with bad. I consider 16 to 21 as the most dangerous time for the soul & mind in a man's life. Your mentioning Mr Kerr as being in London has freed my mind of a good deal of anxiety as I saw the death of a Mr Charles Kerr mentioned in the Calcutta papers and it struck me that he might have come out to India to wind up his business. I will not write more now as I may lose the Dak (post). I see Harry Miller who is with this army pretty constantly i.e. whenever I am with this camp. I fancy a large portion of the Bombay force including his regiment will be stationed at Peshawur with the Bengalees in all about 8,000 men. Annexation is not yet settled on. It remains with the home Govt. I see no other way for us to indemnify ourselves for our expenses & at the same [time] to keep the country quiet. We should require no larger force to hold the country than w[oul]d be requisite to protect our frontier against the Sikhs.

With kind love to all.

Yr. affec. Son
D.G. Robinson

48

Daniel George Robinson to his father

Peshawur March 27th 1849

My dear Father[242]

It was with exceeding vexation & disgust that I saw extracts from two of my strictly private letters to you <u>dated</u> from <u>Hazareh</u> in October re-published in the Indian papers from some English journal.[243] I know not whether this paper be edited by your friend or not, at any rate he can be no friend of mine, who for the sake of some trifle has done his best to ruin me by making patent to the world my private opinions of the public functionaries connected with the Punjaub & my immediate superior officers. I feel however quite sure that you are too wise to have consented to his copying the letters & I am encouraged in this hope by observing abridgements & mistatements. At all times I have the greatest possible objection to my private letters & opinions being made patent to the world, as I consider that I am not authorized to thus censure the acts & opinions of my superiors, it being both irregular & to my mind very much like insubordination. But [what] was the use of suppressing my name when the letter was dated & evidently written from Hazara & there was only Abbott [and] myself covenanted officers in that district with my assistant & a corpl. of sappers. There was mighty little doubt in the eyes of the offended functionaries as to who wrote the said letters & I feel quite sure that a bar is now being placed against my ever getting into political employ. I request that in future that without my express sanction you will not shew any of my letters to Editors of papers & if there be any abstract news you may wish to communicate that you will according to your discretion make it known by word of mouth.

We arrived here on the 22nd. I believe I wrote you that I had taken political charge of Maharaja Goolab Sing's army & pushed them across the Jhelum & over the mountains on to the right rear of the Sikh army or rather its remnant. I know not whether it was this that caused them to abandon the defence of the Bukra pass[244] or not but they did so precipitately & by following them up sharp we so pushed them that they soon were glad to make terms & gave up the prisoners. The terms, considering that they were called rebels were in my opinion much too easy. The prisoners were first given up & terms granted afterwards. The murders at the [com]mencement of the outbreak were forgotten. The guns about fifty odd in number were given up. The soldiers publicly laid down their arms & received a rupee each to find their way to their homes with & all Sirdars, officers & jagheerdars were promised a sufficient subsistence to allow them to live in comfort. They were also not to be ejected from the Punjaub, neither was any property which they might possess at the time of the surrender to be confiscated, nor were they to be called to account for the revenues of the country they had seized & disbursed on their soldiery.

I do not think that we shall annex, Sir H. Laurence being decidedly against it & yet it is the only way in which I see how we can repay ourselves for the enormous expenses of the war & prevent ourselves from being again subjected to its expenses, however the idea seems to be to employ a subsidiary force. After two or three days of hard work & riding I rejoined the camp at Hussun Abdal[245] just as it was on the point of being struck with the view of marching on Attock. This by a forced march of (47) forty seven miles we completely succeeded in, so completely indeed that the Dooranees were only able to burn two or three of the boats & to cut the bridge adrift so that we were enabled to save fourteen of the boats. During the next day the boatmen made a rough bridge with them which I superintended & assisted in & by night the troops were crossing over. Had the Engineers made the bridge it might have been better but it would at least have taken three days & as it was the troops merely got their rest after the forced march & the next day we went thro the Gidha Gulli pass[246] to Akora. Next day to Nowsherah[247] 14 miles & the same night into Peshawur 24 miles which we secured uninjured but all the cantonments, the Residency & the fort of Jumrood[248] had been burnt. The Dooranees also had got thro the Khyber Pass unmolested by the Khyberrees who had been promised a lakh of rupees to shut it against them. These long marches have distinctly proved what I have often tried to convince the Com[mande]r in Ch[ief] that our armies can make as long marches as any native armies & that those marches can exceed 20 miles. Had he remained with us we should not have got the boats on the Indus, Peshawur would have been sacked & destroyed & we should not have been on the Indus by this time. In fact had the pursuit been properly followed up at first viz by moving up a portion of the infantry to support the pursuing cavalry & artillery, who should have bivouacked where they were instead of returning 12 or 14 miles into camp to be gone over again the next day, we should have secured every gun they had in the action &

the sixty boats they had at Jelum which they were just burning when our advanced cavalry arrived on the opposite bank of the river having crossed over the 7 guns which escaped a few hours before. We thus lost 24 hours in the pursuit & five days in the passage of the Jelum. I looked after the action every where for the C in C during the pursuit to recommend to him that the infy. might be moved up but could not find him & just as I was about to return to camp I dismounted to get a drink of water when my horse shook himself & one of my pistols out of the holsters which went off & shot him in the shoulder. To my great sorrow he had cost me 950 rupees & was worth 1600 & was a great pet of mine. In fact the only good horse I possessed. I was thus obliged to tramp home & arrived much too late to effect any thing. In fact before I had been home an hour the horse artillery & cavalry had returned. I return to complete my survey in Hazara in a few days. My prospects of political employ having now totally vanished.

Yr. affec. Son
D.G. Robinson

[P.S.] A strong division remains at Peshawur a Regt. at Attock, a division or strong brigade at Rawul Pindi, a brigade at Jelum & a strong division at Wuzerabad in addition to the usual force at Lahore & the garrison in Govindgurh of Amritsir & the troops at Ferozepore, Jullundhur, Umballah[249] &c.

49

Daniel George Robinson to Edward Thomas

My dear Sir[251]

Having come here dâk I am unable to give you a complete list but it is something like the following. The coins are with Mr. G.A. Knott 4 St Mildred's Court Poultry, London. There [sic] are all duplicates of my collection with the exception of the Mahn. Hindoo and Sapanian coins –

a silver drachmas of Cucratedes [?] helmeted
copper coins Do
Merrander 10 or 12 silver and ten or twelve copper of the common
types –
Antimachus 2 silver Dms
Philoxenus – copper coins
Lysias –   "   "
Antiatkidas – silver Dms 10 or 12 copper coins –
Himoens & Kadphins – 28 fair and indifft. copper coins –
Kadaphis – two or three copper Moas – 1 (4 Dm) Silver – very
scarce 3 copper coins
Vonones. Some silver & copper Gondophenas dynasty 20 of
different copper types
Soter megus (nameless) 8 or 10 good copper
Spalygis & Spalagramus two or three copper –
Agas – Several tetradrachms and drachms
silver Tetra Dm of Hippastiatus and a great many copper coins of
different types.
Several early Hindus & their silver & copper coins –
Some later thick metal coins
a gold Kadphisus & several copper Indo Scythian and many silver
gold & copper Sapanian, Mohommedan, & Hindoo coins

This is all I can remember of them at present. As I miss it from
my own collection I am afraid that I have sent a very curious coin
with Pali on <u>both</u> sides.

I call all the small silver drachmas and those you term the size
tetradrachms without reference to the actual weights

Yours sinc
D.G. Robinson

Mussoorie
23rd Augt 1852

[P.S.] The collection is richest in the Scythian than in the earlier
Bactrians

BL Add Mss 39,997 f.21.

197

50²⁵²

Daniel George Robinson to James Henry Greathead

Mysore, India
June 17th 1860

My dear Cousin²⁵³

I have long been thinking of entering into correspondence with you, but I am a bad correspondent at all times and rarely write to anybody unless it be a matter of duty, or as in the present instance because I want something. My sister Ninita Agassiz writes me that you have left your wife and bairns²⁵⁴ in England and returned to the Cape for a few months only, so I write to ask you to send me a small quantity of delicious Cape wines I have lately tasted, ridiculously cheap and only requiring to be more known to be much appreciated in India. I refer to Pontac and Stein wines,²⁵⁵ the latter I think very superior. I believe these wines are exported to India in tubs, and will not keep long. I should therefore wish to have the smallest type of cask, which is, I fancy the quarter cask, or not more than one dozen of each if in the bottle.

I also want to know something about the facilities for getting Cape horses. I have an old pet which I rode in the Punjaub Campaign 1848–49, and who is still in first rate working order. He cost I believe about £100 at the Cape. This would make the cost about £140 before he came into my hands, and that would be rather more than as a married man I can now afford. At the same time I like him so much that I feel inclined to replenish my stable from the same quarter. I think there is nothing like a first class Arab, but a 15 hand Arab to carry 14 stone across country can hardly be got for less than £150 to £300. I believe you can land a very useful specimen of the Cape horse for about £70. The style of horse suited for my work is a three quarter bred powerfully made horse, pretty quick with his feet, good shoulder, strong and pretty fast. Is such a style of horse now easily procurable at the Cape? If so at what price, and in your absence how could I procure him – or rather three or four of them for I would club together with two or three other men to get them over.

So much for shop, I am sending my wife and three bairns (we have just lost one) home this cold weather.²⁵⁶ She will leave them with my sister Ninita (from whom I have great accounts of you) and then return to me; and I hope if all goes smoothly to go myself in five or at the most six, years for furlough, and to retire at the end of that time as lieut-colonel. By then our Uncle Harding will have returned to England again, and we shall not be many then.[257] I don't know what has become of Frank[258] – whether he is still alive or not, – but even with him we only number 10 cousins in all from 17 children.

I had got this far when in came English letters. I am sorry to hear from Knott that you had just lost the flower of your flock (Arthur).[259] It is a dreadful shock, that loss of the first child. But then again one cannot help remembering how much better it is for them – that they are free from sin and misery and that their election is sure.

I shall send this through my agent S. Ferguson Esq., 17 Clive Street, Calcutta.[260] Your answer should be addressed to me at Dalhousie, N.W. Province, which will be tolerably central for my tour during the winter. Draw on me through Ferguson for any expenses for the Pontac and Stein wines.

Your ever affectionate cousin,

D.G. Robinson

51[261]

Daniel George Robinson to Cecil Beadon

Calcutta 27-7-65

My dear Mr Beadon[262]

If Col. Bruce[263] can put up the wires and posts in a serviceable manner, which will require care, I shall be grateful to him for the assistance rendered, but unfortunately this alone will not restore telegraphic communication. Two cables will be required for the Teesta and Omlah rivers these cannot be made under two or three months and without them communication will have to be maintained by one of the methods proposed by Major Murray[264] in the accompanying note and here the shoe pinches for our supply of signallers is so limited that to furnish even two extra officers would be inconvenient.

Yours very truly

D.G. Robinson

Add Mss 43,990 f.228.

Appendix 1

The pay and allowances of Engineer subalterns

(a) *In garrison or cantonment.*

2nd Lt	Lt	Description
(Rupees)		
60	70	Pay
45	60	Half batta
12	24	Gratuity
50	50	Tent allowance
25	30	House rent if only in receipt of ½ batta & not provided with quarters
—	—	Horse allowance
192	234	

(b) *In the field.*

2nd Lt	Lt	Description
(Rupees)		
60	70	Pay
90	120	Full batta
12	24	Gratuity
50	50	Tent allowance
—	—	Horse allowance
212	264	

Horse allowance could only be drawn by an officer below field rank if he was commanding a Corps of Infantry.

The East-India Register and Army List for 1845, Allen, p. 32.

Appendix 2

Lieutenant Robinson's memoir on the map of Hazara

Copy

Report upon the Military Survey of Hazara surveyed under the Superintendence of Lieut D.G. Robinson Engineers in 1847–48–49, and connected with the Great Trigonometrical Survey partially by Mr. Carty[1] Sub Assistant G.T. Survey in 1852 and finished by Lieut. D.G. Robinson Engrs. in 1853 addressed to Colonel A.S. Waugh Engineers, Surveyor General of India and Superintendent G.T. Survey of India.[2]

Camp Paswai Decr. 1st 1855

Sir,

By G.O.G.G. of the 12 of August 1847 I was placed under the orders of the Resident of Lahore for the purpose of making a Military Survey of Hazara which had just been transferred from the dominions of Maharaja Goolab Sing to that of the Lahore Durbar.

2. The Governor General (Lord Hardinge) sanctioned the Survey, and the Entertainment of the following Establishment, the expense of which was defrayed by the Lahore Durbar.

1 Superintending Engineer Officer on a Staff Salary of Cos.Rs	400
1 European assistant	250
1 do do	150
3 Native Surveyors at 60/.	180
50 Khalashies @ 6/.[3]	300
Total Cos Rupees	1280

3. My instructions were simply to Entertain this Establishment from the 1st October (1847) & to take the field without delay. On the principles on which the Survey was to be conducted, and of the Extent of detail and accuracy required, as also of the scale no mention was made, neither did I receive any instructions from Colonel Napier, when I was placed under his orders, by his appointment as Durbar Civil Engineer, a few months later.

4. I also received from the Resident at Lahore the following instruments

1 (8") Theodolite by Gilbert
(a very inferior Instrument with two Verniers and the Telescope immoveably fixed to the body of the Instrument thus rendering change of face and collimation by any of the simpler methods impossible).

1 (5") Theodolite by Troughton & Simms, Everest's Pattern
(This Instrument issued from the Magazine had a large dent in divided azimuth Circle, as large as a four anna piece).

3 Excellent Prismatic Compasses
2 Large Sextants without artificial Horizons
1 Perambulator – Madras Pattern
3 Common Measuring Chains

From Colonel Napier I afterwards received a 4 inch Theodolite by Troughton & Simms (Everest's Pattern) which he procured from the Magnetic Observatory at Simla (a very superior Instrument for its size). I also received upon my indent from Calcutta

2 Artificial Horizons
3 Telescopes by Jones
2 Standard Steel Chains

I moreover procured from England at my own Expense a 6 inch Theodolite with 2 Telescopes by Jones, and a very fair instrument. I was induced to send for this instrument in consequence of the great demand for Instruments at that time, rendering it impossible to get any good [ones] from the Magazines. This completed my instrumental equipment.

5. Of these Instruments the standard steel chains did not arrive till long after I had measured my base, and the 6 inch Theodolite and artificial Horizons only in time to fall into the hands of the Dooranees who plundered our baggage, and all the Instruments, except one 4 inch Theodolite, two telescopes, and two Prismatic Compasses in February 1849.

6. The selection was not made by me & in many respects was very faulty. Firstly the only instrument that could be depended upon was the 4 inch Theodolite, a very good instrument for its size, but

of necessity deficient in telescopic power and nicety of graduation. Secondly, Perambulators and Chains were actually useless in a mountainous country, and lastly the Sextants were but of little use in triangulation and none at all for astronomical purposes without artificial Horizons and a nautical Almanac.

7. The Establishment sanctioned was ample but not procurable. In the time of the Sikh Dominion, Hazara was always disturbed more or less, and was as much dreaded as the Khyber Pass; and as 2 new Revenue Surveys were started at the same time (one in the Cis Sutlej States and one in the Jullundhur Doab) who offered the same Salaries to natives, I never received a single application for an appointment from a Native Surveyor, in answer to my long continued advertisements. I was training a Moonshee & 2 European N.C.O. of the Sappers and Miners who were getting on fairly, and might have eventually been of some assistance, when the Campaign of 1848/49 broke out and put a stop to our operations. Before they were resumed, on the conclusion of the Campaign, the Moonshee had deserted to the Enemy. Serjeant Denton[4] had been drowned on service in the Indus and Corporal Cartly [*sic*] had been made a prisoner of the Sikhs at Attock. The only survivor was too ill, and had no wish to return to Hazara. Colonel Napier therefore provided for him otherwise.

8. When the Survey was first started, the Resident at Lahore sent me two European Assistants. The Senior Assistant Mr. W. Lloyd was a young man of great education and talent from the Civil Engineers College at Putney. Had he remained with me, I doubt not but that he would have been of great assistance to me, but after drawing a month and a half's salary, and just as we were about to commence field work he received the offer of an appointment in Bengal on considerably higher Emoluments & resigned his appointment under me. My junior assistant Mr. J. Ingram was deficient in Mathematical knowledge & knew nothing of drawing. I had therefore a great deal to teach him, and it was some time before he became useful. Latterly he gave me much assistance in computing and surveying the plains, but he was never able to master the difficulties of sketching hilly ground. On the

conclusion of this survey he was presented with a Commission in the 1st Bengal Fusiliers for his Gallantry in Hazara, and now holds a high Staff appointment on the Dacca & Aracan road. Besides these two Gentlemen W.J. Leeson was for a short time posted to the Survey, he was uneducated & utterly unprincipled. He remained with me for four months during which he did no work whatever. He was then at my request eventually removed from the Survey and finally ejected from the Punjab.[5]

9. Having entertained several men as Klassies, and Messrs. Lloyd & Ingram having joined me, we marched from Wuzeerabad on the 20th of October for Hazara, via Dingee, Jelalpoor, Pind Dadun Khan, and Chakowal to Hasan Abdal. As we marched we made route surveys of the country right and left of the road. They were of necessity very limited, but were the only maps that could be depended upon, when that country became the seat of war in 1848/49. From Hasan Abdal we marched to the level plain of Chuch to measure a Base-line. For the ends of the Base I selected 2 Mounds 5.15 miles apart, the N End near the large town of Huzroo, the S.W. near Shamshabad, the direction being thus nearly parallel to that measured for the G.T. Survey in 1853/54. As the Standard Steel chains had not yet arrived, and there seemed to be no chance of their arriving for many months, I was obliged to use common Gunter's chains, & 2 ten feet deal rods compared with a 2 foot Gunter's brass scale. I measured my Base in this wise. The Ends of the Base being marked by 2 straight poles, the bottoms of which were charred & sunk 4 feet deep into the mounds. Around these poles as centres, I built 2 conical frustrum of stones & mud six feet in diameter at top, and six feet high. These were my Trigl. stations. I then drove in Stakes in a perfectly straight line between the 2 Stations, forty or fifty yards apart, as it was not easy to measure accurately up the mounds. I took a stake about half a mile from each station to mark the end of my measured Base. The straight line between these two stakes was then carefully levelled and beaten with rammers. I then stretched a long line along the Stakes, and stretched the chain upon the line. to maintain an even strain upon the line I made up a machine like the accompanying sketch.

10. Instead of the common measuring Arrow, I used strong iron pins 15 inches long 1 Wide & exactly ¼ inch in thickness. These were well driven home. The chains were nominally 60 feet long of 60 links, 1 foot each, the base thus measured gave the following result.

		ch	ft
1st measurement		296	15
2nd	"	296	28
	Mean	296	21.5
	=	17781.5 feet	

and corrected by by [*sic*] 3.9 inches per chain, the Excess of the chain above 60 feet & .021 feet per Chain for the iron piece, the result became 17871.8. I then measure with the rods

the results were	17890.35
	17789.3
	17890.0
	17890.25
Mean	17890.23
Correction – 1/20 per rod)	7.45
defect of a rod from 10 feet)	
	17882.78

I took a mean of the two, 17877 as a correct measure of my measured Base. This base was then prolonged by means of triangulation, on both sides of the Base, to obtain the true value of the Base.

11. This occupied us until the beginning of January, after which I commenced triangulating. I took 30 [degrees] as the limit of symmetry for my triangles, as instead of working by the modern and more Scientific System of quadrilaterals & polygons, I established Stations on Peaks & prominent Knoles 5 to 25 miles apart, and from these Stations observed to every other Station visible. I consequently obtained several values for each side, but as the probabilities of error were not equal my taking a mean of these values was an erroneous proceeding. My stations were marked similarly to the ends of my Base & when the piles of Stones were white washed, they were distinctly visible in clear weather at a

distance of 25 miles. Until I observed from a Station the pole in the Centre remained Standing, it was then cast down, and the instrument placed immediately over the Centre of the Pole. The common sides measured with the 8 inch Theodolite agreed within 1 foot per mile, but with [the] 4 inch Theodolite the discrepancy was nearly 2 feet.

12. In the beginning of May 1848 Messrs Agnew and Anderson were murdered at Mooltan, and all the Officers on detached duty were called into Military Stations. We, amongst them were ordered to join Major J. Abbott (Assistant to the Resident) at Huripoor, and from that time until the conclusion of 1849, we were employed on other, and Military duties; – the Salaries of the Establishment for this period ought therefore to be debited to the Political Department.

13. When I discontinued Surveying in May 1848, I had done but a small part of the triangulation, and sketching of Eastern Hazara, and when I returned in April 1849 I was ordered by Colonel Napier to do all that I could before the commencement of the hot Weather, and then I was to return to Lahore and the Survey party was to be broken up. These instructions compelled me to hurry over the work in a less accurate & detailed manner, than I wished to do, and being extremely anxious to complete Hazara if possible, I remained in the field throughout the rainy season, when I marched into Lahore. Consequently on the severe exposure I had endured, I was shortly after attacked with Rheumatism which confined me to my bed from 18 November to the middle of February, and consequent on this sickness could not complete the map until the end of May 1850, when it was at once sent to the Board of Administration at Lahore. They kept it for nearly a twelve month, and it was then sent to the Dy. Surveyor General at Calcutta who sent it back to me again last year that I might recompile it on the wish, and in connection with the triangulation of the Gt. T. Survey of India.

14. This may be said to be the history of the first Edition of the Hazara Map and it now remains to show in what respects the revised map now submitted differs from the original.

1stly Since the time of the original survey i.e. 1848–1849, a large portion of the Mountains inhabited by the Dhoonds & Suttees and all the low hilly country to the South of them has been transferred from Hazara to Rawul Pindee; consequent on this change these mountains have been surveyed with great fidelity by the Topographical Survey Party, employed on the Jheelum & Rawul Pindee Districts under my charge. Such portions of the Rawul Pindee District as appear on the revised Map have therefore been compiled from the records of the Rawul Pindee & Jheelum Survey and as the General Maps of this portion of the District are now nearly completed & being accurate & on the one inch scale, much more Valuable. A great deal of what appeared upon the old map has been purposely omitted.

2ndly The South Eastern portion of Hazara in the old map was compiled from many sketches made since the triangulation was being laid out. It was my intention to have sketched in this ground more accurately & in regular order when the triangulation should have sufficiently advanced but the very short time to which I was limited prevented my doing so. However as you had ordered a revision of the Map, I took advantage of Mr. Sub Assist. Dyer's[6] being employed in the Neighbourhood to save that portion of the District resurveyed. Mr Dyer appears to have done this work very creditably.

15. 3rdly Time and circumstance did not admit of my visiting the wild country Kugham in 1848–49. Since then that valley is much quieter & Lt Peter Lumsden[7] Dy Asst. Qr [Master] Genl. was last year able to make a recconnaisance up to the head of the Valley and from the summit of the Mountains overlooking Chelas he obtained a view of the Country over the Indus beyond Chelas & which no European had ever before seen. As this recconnaisance was based on data furnished from my Office I have had no difficulty in incorporating all this additional & valuable information in the revised map.

16.   Lastly. The want of proper instruments for Astronomical Observations and the divergence of the Plumb line caused by mountain attraction prevented my making Observations for Latitudes & Longitudes. The original map was therefore deficient in these most important points & being based on a different unit of measurement from the G.T. Survey of India could not be incorporated into the Atlas for India. The revised map has none of these defects, it has been projected on the basis of the G.T. Survey of India & to connect with it five triangles were observed by Mr. Assistant Carty and myself with a 12 inch Theodolite which originating in the G.T. Survey side Kagriana to Gandgarh, enhanced all the most important of my old Stations in the Southern portion of Hazara. Thus the revised map is complete in these essential points and as the results from the triangulation with the 12 inch Theodolite appears fair, the errors are very limited and are those of detail rather than extension.

17. The details have been copied from the original Map.

18. Appended is a Statement [Appendix A] showing the expenses incurred by the late Durbar at Lahore for the Survey to have been Cos.Rs 18553.14.3 being at the rate of Cos.Rs 2.7.0 per square mile.

I have for

Sd. D.G. Robinson Lt Engrs
In charge Topograpl. Survey
Bengal Establishment No. 1

Appendix A

Month	Year	Super-intendents Staff Salary			European Assistants Salary			Native Establish-ment			Contingent expenses			Total			Remarks
		R	A	P	R	A	P	R	A	P	R	A	P	R	A	P	
August	1847							55	13	.				55	13	.	Klassis training
September								149	15	.				149	15	.	
October		400	.	.	400	.	.	249	7	.				1049	7	.	
November		400	.	.	266	10	8	230	12	10				897	7	6	
December		400	.	.	150	.	.	234	.	.				784	.	.	
January	1848	400	.	.	300	.	.	376	7	.				1026	7	.	
February		400	.	.	300	.	.	252	.	.				982	.	.	
March		400	.	.	300	.	.	280	8	.				980	8	.	
April		400	.	.	300	.	.	268	.	.				968	.	.	
May		400	.	.	171	14	4	286	.	.				857	14	4	
June		400	.	.	190	.	.	236	.	.				826	.	.	
July																	
August																	
September																	
October																	
November		. . . .												6550	.	9	
December																	
January	1849																
February																	
March																	
April		400	.	.	170	.	.	104	4	2				674	4	2	
May		400	.	.	290	.	.	111	14	.				801	14	.	
June		400	.	.	290	.	.	106	.	.				796	.	.	
July		400	.	.	250	.	.	84	.	.				734	.	.	
August		400	.	.	250	.	.	84	.	.				734	.	.	
September		400	.	.	250	.	.	84	.	.				734	.	.	Finished the
October		400	.	.	250	.	.							650	.	.	field work &
November		400	.	.	250	.	.				200	7	.	850	7	.	discharged the
December		400	.	.	250	.	.							650	.	.	the establish-
January	1850	400	.	.	250	.	.							650	.	.	ment
February		400	.	.	250	.	.							650	.	.	
March		400	.	.	250	.	.							650	.	.	
April		400	.	.	250	.	.				160	.	.	810	.	.	
May		400	.	.				191	13	3				591	13	3	
														6558	.	9	Area surveyed 7500 square miles

$$R \quad A \quad P$$
$$18553 \quad 14 \quad 3 \quad \text{at 2 7 . per square mile}$$

Time 1 Year 11 Months Deduct amount from July to March when the whole party was employed on other duties

Total Expenses of Survey

Sd. D.G. Robinson Lt. Engrs.
In charge Topographical Survey
Bengal Establishment No. 1

True Copy
A. Scott Waugh Lt. Colonel
Surveyor General of India

Appendix 3

Lieutenant Robinson's claim for compensation for property lost during the Second Sikh War

Fort William, Foreign Department.
Claims of Lieutenant D.G. Robinson, of the Engineers, and of all who served under him, in the Huzara Survey, to special compensation for losses sustained during the outbreak in the Punjab.

Extract Fort William, Foreign Consultation, dated the 18th January 1850 (Duplicate) No.375.
From Major H.P. Burn Dy. Secy. to the Board of Administration[8]
To   Sir H.M. Elliot, KCB, Secy. to the Govt of India[9]
      With the Govr. Genl.
D/Lahore, 13th Decr. 1849

Sir,
By direction of the Board of Administration I have the honor to transmit for submission to the Most Noble the Governor General, copies of a Correspondence with Major J. Abbott, Depy Commissioner in Hazara, as marginally noted*, regarding claims to compensation for losses of Baggage taken by the enemy in the last Campaign, preferred by Lieutenant D.G. Robinson, of the Engineers, the men of the Sappers and Miners, who served under him in Hazara, and Government Servants and other Camp followers attached to the Hazara Agency, amounting in the aggregate to Cos Rs 2,798.
2d These claims the Board submit for the favourable consideration of Government, and would recommend that they be treated as special claims, the situation and employment of the parties being

---

* From Depy. Commr. Hazara to Dy. Secy. Board of Administration of 19th Augt. 1849, No.73, with Contgt. Bill and Vouchers.
  From Dy. Secy. Board of Administration to Dy. Commr. Hazara of 31st Augt. 1849 No.815.
  From Supt. Hazara Survey to Dy. Secy. Bd. of Admn. of 19th Novr. 1849 No.73 with a valuation Statt.

altogether different from those of the Regimental Officer or Soldiers, taking the field, with the prospect of a Campaign before him, lightly equipped with such necessaries only as could be replaced for the sum fixed by Regulation as a compensation for all losses that might be suffered in the course of active service.

3d Lieutenant Robinson and his party were situated in the heart of the Punjab when the war broke out, employed on a duty requiring a most expensive outfit both as regards efficiency and comfort than could be required for troops taking the field who have the opportunity of leaving all heavy Baggage behind them in a place of safety. Under the circumstances the Board trust that the claims now submitted will meet with the most favourable consideration that Government can bestow on them.

I have &c

S of H.P. Burn, Major

Depy Secy

Lahore
13th Decr. 1849

Documents alluded to in the above

(Duplicate)

No.73

From Captain James Abbott Depy. Commsr. Hazara
To Major H.P. Burn Depy. Secy. Board of Administration Lahore
D/Huzara, Augt. 19th 1849

Sir,

I have the honor to forward, for the approval and sanction of the Board of Administration a statement of Baggage of Officers, Men and Camp followers, plundered by the enemy, during the late rebellion at Hurripoor and Srikote, Huzara, and the estates of many of the plunderers to a large amount, are now the property of the Government. I humbly hope it will please the Board to recommend the claims of zealous and faithful servants to the favourable consideration of the Right Honorable the Governor General of India.

2d I have not included a statement of my own losses, because I have to regret the loss of some Government Instruments committed to my care and plundered at the same time.

I have &c
S of J. Abbott
Dy. Commsr.

(True Copy)
S of H.P. Burn
Depy. Secy.

(Duplicate)

Statement of the Property of Government Servants and other Camp followers of the Huzara Agency plundered by the Sikh and Dooranee Armies in the late rebellion.

Huzara, 1st August 1849

Names		Value of Property plundered
		Cos Rs As Ps
Mohur Sing	Chuprassee	35 8 .
Kunhaie	do	14 4 .
Bundur	do	13 8 .
Esrie	do	17 8 .
Saywah	do	4 4 .
Dowlut	do	5 12 .
Encha	do	3 5 .
Bhowany	do	6 . .
Sohun Lall	Moonshee	16 2 .
Shadi Mistree	Body Guard	14 13 .
Hecra	Govt. Muleteer	4 4 .
Goo Gar	Syce	5 8 .
Kurm Ha hi	Syce	2 4 .
Phomany	Dhobee	15 12 .
Seetul	Bearer	9 . .
Edad	Bhisty	4 4 .

Grand Total, Cos Rs one hundred and seventy two   172   .   .

I do hereby certify that the above to the best of my knowledge and belief, after the fullest and most particular enquiry is a faithfull statement of the losses sustained by the above Camp followers from the enemy.

S of J. Abbott
Dy. Commsr.

CC   (True Copy)
S of J. Abbott   S of H.P. Burn
Dy. Commr.   Dy. Secy
Huzara

(Duplicate)

The Honorable Company   Dr

Camp Huzara, 25th April 1849

To Compensation for Baggage, personal property, &c looted from me by the Sikh & Dooranee from Hurrypoor during the outbreak of 1848/49	500 . .
Do Do Do Do from Srikote by the Dooranees	650 . .
Do Do for professional Books & Instruments Do Do Do Do from Srikote	700 . .
Total Cos Rs	1900 . .

Recd. Payt.
S of D.G. Robinson, Lt. Engrs.
Supt. Huzara Survey

I do hereby certify upon honor, that I have unavoidably lost Property of not less than the above set forth in the above Bill, at the hands of the Sikhs and Dooranees, and in consequence of my professional employment in the Country.

S of D.G. Robinson, Lt. Engrs.
Supt. Huzara Survey

(True Copy)
S of H.P. Burn
Depy. Secy.

(Duplicate)
Contingent Bill

For losses sustained from the Sikh and Dooranee armies by Officers, Soldiers and Camp followers, in Huzara in the execution of their duty.

The Honble. Company		Dr
Names or designations of losers	*Values of Property lost*	

Lieut D.G. Robinson	550	.	.
Engrs. Supt. Huzara	650	.	.
Survey	700	.	.
Corporal Carty, Sappers on duty with the Survey			
Huzara subsequently at Attock	112	4	.
Sapper Detachment on duty with the Survey			
1 Havdr 2 Naiks & 13 Sappers	613	12	.
Shadi Govt. Mistry	14	3	.
8 Govt. Chuprassies	100	1	.
Sohun Lall, Moonshee	16	2	.
Servants, Camp followers	41	.	.

Grand Total Cos Rs two thousand
Seven hundred and ninety eight 2798 . .

Nature of Property	*By Whom Plundered*	
Baggage	Chutter S at Hurripoor	
Do	Dooranee Army at Srikote	
Professional Books, Instruments &c	Do	Do
Clothes, Books, Baggage		
Do		
Do		

I do hereby Certify that the above is to the best of my knowledge and belief after full and particular enquiry a true statement of losses in Baggage sustained by the parties above specified, from the Sikh and Dooranies Armies, during the late rebellion.

S of J. Abbott   EE
Dy. Commsr.   Recd. Payt.
                                            S of J. Abbott
                                            Dy. Commsr. Huzara

                                            (True Copy)
                                            S of H.P. Burn
                                            Dy. Secy.

(Duplicate)
Lieutenant Robinson, Engineers, &c

Sir,

I respectfully submit these few lines, to your consideration the following, being a list of the articles taken away from me by the enemy during my Imprisonment in the Sikh Camp, after the siege of Attock in which I was engaged.

	Rupees &c		
Cash	60	.	.
One Box	3	.	.
Cooking Utensils	8	.	.
Three Flannel Jackets and			
3 ditto Drawers (new) one Rupee each	6	.	.
Two pair of new Shoes	4	.	.
Three Waistcoats	3	.	.
Regimental blue cloth Cap	4	.	.
Do one pair of Trowsers	3	.	.
Two pair of canvas Trowsers	2	.	.
Looking Glass and Towels	2	.	.
Brushes and Hair Combs	2	.	.
One Mathematical author viz Bonny Castle's Algebra	2	4	.
Two Shirts	2	.	.
One Turban	2	.	.
Bed Clothes	8	.	.
Stockings	1	.	.
Total	112	4	.

(True Copy)   S of Corporal Patrick Carty
S of H.P. Burn   3d Co. Sappers & Miners
Depy. Secy.   Huzara Survey

(Duplicate)

Memo: Value of Property belonging to sepoys of Sappers and Pioneers which fell into the hands of the Sikhs and Dooranees, when they plundered Hurripoor and Srikote, as per accompanying Persian valuation Statement.

Camp Mahuzul, July 10th 1849

No	Rank and Name	Remarks	Value of articles lost
1	Havildar Sewdeen Sing	Vide accompanying	44 8 .
	Naik Chopye	Persian Statement	20 14 .
2	" Purnhain	for value of	22 4 .
	Sepoy Kundeo	articles lost	38 4 .
	" Doorgah		25 4 .
	" Jeaun		41 7 .
	" Adjudheea Misr		34 5 .
5	" Bussaon Sing		49 12 .
	" Sunkesh Sing		42 2 .
	" Narain Misr		52 13 .
	" Sheik Nehal		32 7 .
	" Rajjubehi		29 7 .
10	" Bunsee		46 2 .
	" Aman Sing		39 3 .
	" Doorgah Misr		38 3 .
13	" Mehtab Sing		56 13 .

613 12 .

S of D.G. Robinson
Supt. Huzara Survey

(True Copy)
S of H.P. Burn
Depy. Secy.

(Duplicate)
(Copy)
No.815

From Major H.P. Burn Depy. Secy. Board of Administration for
the affairs of the Punjab
To   Major J. Abbott Deputy Commissioner Huzara
D/Lahore, 31st August 1849

Mily. Dept.

Sir,
I have the honor to acknowledge the receipt of your letter No.73,
of the 19th Instant, with a Bill for Company's Rupees 2,798, on
account of compensation for loss of Baggage sustained during the
late war by parties serving in Huzara.

2d In reply, I am desired by the Board to call your attention to
the Regulations on the subject of Compensation for the loss of
Baggage and Camp Equipage when on duty in the field, in
which you will find the rates of compensation allowed to parties
for the total loss of their Baggage, to be below the sums drawn
by you. A Subaltern of Engineers being allowed for total loss of
Baggage Rupees 910, Corporals of Sappers and Miners Rs 24-7-
10, and Soldiers of the Native Army one month's pay and full
batta.

3d Compensation is allowed to officers of Engineers for loss of
Professional Instruments at rates which are specified. A statement
of the Instruments lost is requested with the Bill.

4th You are requested to submit a Bill for your own losses which
shall be transmitted to Govt with those of your fellow sufferers.

I have &c
S of H.P. Burn
Depy. Secy.

Lahore
31st August 1849 }

(True Copy)
S of H.P. Burn, Major
Depy. Secy.

(Duplicate)
No.73

From Lieut D.G. Robinson, Engineers, Supt. Huzara Survey
To   Major H.P. Burn Deputy Secretary to the Board of
       Administration
D/Lahore 19th Novr 1849

Sir,

I have the honor to acknowledge the receipt of a copy of your letter
No.815, dated 31st August 1849, addressed to Major J. Abbott,
Deputy Commissioner, Huzara, and forwarded by him for my
information and guidance.

2d In reply, I have the honor to request that you will lay the
following Statement before the Board of Administration for their
further consideration.

3d The composition and employment of the establishment of the
Huzara Survey was Civil, and the way in which their losses were
incurred was entirely dissimilar to that of Troops employed in
military operations in the field. The establishment (myself
included) was paid by the late Durbar, employed for the Durbar,
placed civilly under the orders of the Resident at Lahore and
afforded guards, and other protection by the Durbar. The
property lost was partly plundered by the Durbar Troops, under
whose protection it was placed, and partly owing to their
defection. Under these circumstances I consider that we are as
much entitled to compensation from the Durbar or their
successors, as Lieut. Col. G. Lawrence and the other Political
Assistants.

4th For myself particularly I also urge that I was throughout the
whole Campaign acting by order of Sir F. Currie, as a Political
Assistant, and in that capacity specially entitled to
compensation the same as the other Political Assistants who
were sufferers.

5th The two Serjeants and 12 Sappers were sent up to join in
the Establishment of the Huzara Survey in consequence of the
impossibility of procuring sufficient Native Surveyors, and if
compensation is to be granted only according to the Military

Pay and Audit Regulations the uncovenanted portion will receive nothing, and the Serjeants who were acting in a Civil capacity will not receive compensation for one third of their losses.

With reference to para: 3 I have the honor to submit the accompanying valuation Statement of private Professional Books and Instruments lost.

I have &c

S of D.G. Robinson Lt Engrs

Supt. Huzara Survey

late Actg. Asst. to Resdt. at Lahore

Valuation Statement of private professional Books and Instruments belonging to Lieut D.G. Robinson, Engineers, Supt. Huzara Survey, and late Acting Assistant to the Resident of Lahore lost by him in Huzara, owing to the defection of the Durbar Troops in Augt. 1848.

1	6 Theodolites by Jones, with two Telescopes, &c complete, cost £42 . . in England and arrived in Huzara in July 1848 (examining do £2 . . freight, Banghy here, Insurance &c not included	500	. .
1	4½ Sextant (Mathematical prize at Addiscombe)	150	. .
	Spare Glasses, silver rings, Prismatic needle, and spare tops for Prismatic Compasses	20	. .
	Professional Books, Drawing Paper &c	150	. .
	Total Cos Rs Eight Hundred and Twenty)	820	. .
	Total Cos Rs)		

Estimate amount in Bill formerly forwarded Cos Rs 700 . .

S of D.G. Robinson, Lt. Engrs.

Supt. Huzara Survey

(True Copy)

S of H.P. Burn

Depy. Secy.

Ordered that the following letter be written to the Board in reply.
(Copy)
No. 15 of 1850
From The Secretary to the Govt. of India with the Govr. Genl.
To The Board of Administration for the affairs of the Punjab.
D/Camp Mooltan, 1st January 1850
For. Dept.

Sirs,
I have the honor to acknowledge the receipt of your Deputy
Secretary's letter dated 13th ultimo, No.375, submitting copy of a
Correspondence with the Deputy Commissioner in Huzara,
regarding the claims preferred by Lieutenant Robinson and all who
served under him in the Huzara Survey, to compensation for losses
sustained by them at the hands of the enemy during the late outbreak.
2d With regard to your recommendation that this should be
considered as a special case (the charges made being above the
prescribed rates of indemnification) the Governor General directs
me to refer you to the stringent rule enforced by the Honble
Court's despatch of 3d October last, No.34, by which His
Lordship is precluded from granting any thing more than what
the claimants are entitled to under Military Regulations.
3d Whenever there are special grounds to urge, they can be stated
in a Memorial to the Court, but the Governor General has no
powers to relax the rule.

I have &c
S of H.M. Elliot
Secy. to the Govt. of India
With the Govr. Genl.

Camp Mooltan ⎱
1st Jany. 1850 ⎰

(True Copy)
S of E.C. Bayley[10]
Under Secy to the Govt. of India
With the Govr. Genl.

IOL F/4/2397 enclosure 129,060.

Extract Foreign Letter from Fort William dated the 7th of March no.2 of 1850.

Para 99 Contingent Bills of the office of the agent to the Governor General with the late army of the Punjaub, from Decr 1848 to April 1849, amounting in the aggregate to Rs 24,275 as also Bills from Lieuts Lake and Robinson for expenses incurred by them during the time they were exclusively under the Agent's orders, amounting to Rs 970.12.4, were sanctioned by the Governor General.

1849   Cons 7th July 121 to 123
        Cons 29th Sept 149 to 151
        List no.92

IOL F/4/2362 enclosure 125,382; IOL E/4/212; IOL E/4/806 p. 581; IOL Z/F/4/12.

Fort William Foreign Department The 17th August 1850.

To The Honourable the Court of Directors of the East India Company.

119 The Board submitted a Correspondence with the Deputy Commissioners in Huzara, regarding certain claims preferred by Lieut D.G. Robinson of the Engineers, and of all who served under him in the Huzara Survey, to compensation for losses sustained by them at the hands of the Enemy during the out-break in the Punjab; and recommended that this should be considered as a special case, the charges made being above the prescribed rates of indemnification.

120 In reply, the Board was referred to the stringent rule enforced by your Honble Court's despatch of 3rd October last, No.34, by which the Government is precluded from granting any thing more than what the claimants may be entitled to under Military Regulations. The Board was further informed that whenever there were special grounds to urge, they could be stated in a Memorial to your Court but that the Governor General had no power to relax the rule.

IOL E/4/215; IOL E/4/808 p. 985; IOL F/4/2397 enclosure 129,060.

Military Department No.8 of 1851 2nd April replying to various letters transferred to Military Dept.

119 & 120 Huzara Claims of Lieut. D.G. Robinson, of the Engineers, and others on account of losses during the late outbreak, to be decided under the Military Regulations. Applications for special consideration not admissable under Court's orders.

IOL E/4/809 pp. 75–6.

23rd June 1852 No.22

65 Agreeably to Court's instructions, compensation to the extent of Rs 845 has been granted to Lieutenant Robinson, Superintendent of the Huzara Survey for losses sustained during the insurrection in the Punjab.

IOL E/4/815 p. 1605.

Appendix 4

Daniel George Robinson's subsequent career

Robinson unfortunately failed in his ambition of joining the political service following the close of the Second Sikh War and instead returned to the Hazara Survey in April 1849. The first task he faced was the preparation of his accounts and finishing the necessary fieldwork. This was followed by completing the map, which he did at Lahore between November 1849 and the end of May 1850. The map was subsequently revised in 1854/5 (IOL X/1737/1/1–4) before being published (IOL X/1737/2/1–4). The details of the survey will be found in his report comprising Appendix 2 above (IOL X/1738).

As related in the letters, Robinson's first experience of topographical work was the Jammu Boundary Survey which he undertook between April 1846 and September 1847. The final revision and preparation of the maps was undertaken in 1850–1, whilst work on the Hazara Survey was being completed, on a scale of 4":1 mile (IOL X/1800).

Robinson joined the Great Trigonometrical Survey in July 1850 as First Assistant in the Topographical Branch, when he had completed his work in Hazara. He spent the next nine years working on the Jhelum and Rawalpindi District Survey under the superintendence of Lt-Col Sir Andrew Scott Waugh, the Surveyor-General of India and Superintendent of the Great Trigonometrical Survey. This was completed in 1861 in a scale of 1":4 miles (IOL X/1759/1), but was also prepared in eight parts comprising twenty-eight separate sheets in the larger scale of 1":1 mile (IOL X/1760/1 to IOL X/1767/1); these maps were also published at between six and twelve shillings per part.

The only copy of the report Robinson wrote on the Jhelum and Rawalpindi District Survey, and the Chart of Triangulation, appears to be in the Survey Correspondence held by the National Archives of India at Dehra Dun, having been transferred there from London in 1924. However, details of the work conducted may also be found in the published annual reports of the Topographical Survey of India, though for the Jhelum and

Rawalpindi District Survey only that for the three years ending 1858/9 could be traced (IOL V/24/4307). His work on the survey meant that Robinson did not participate in the Mutiny campaigns of 1857/8 with the exception of supervising the repulse of an attack on the hill station of Murree on 1 September 1857.

Robinson was promoted to Captain on 21 November 1856 and subsequently officiated as Superintendent of the Great Trigonometrical Survey between November 1863 and March 1865. His report on the 1863–4 year may be found in IOL X/39/5. This was followed by promotion to Deputy Surveyor General and officiating Superintendent of the Revenue Surveys in April 1865 – responsibilities which he held for only three months before being appointed officiating Director General of the Telegraph Department, a post in which he was confirmed the following October.

It is the period of his service with the Telegraph Department for which the majority of documentary material has survived relating to Robinson's career. Regular dispatches were sent by the Government of India to the India Office in London on all matters concerning administration and policy. Those relating to the Telegraph Department are to be found in IOL L/PWD/3/133–143 for the years 1864/5–1877. These dispatches are essentially 'covering letters' which summarise and refer to other letters and memoranda sent to the Government of India by subordinate departments and interested parties. The enclosures, which are numbered in sequence by department, are contained in IOL L/PWD/3/114–122 (for the years 1860/6–1877) and include numerous reports and other material from Robinson. These relate to the minutiae of departmental administration (such as recruitment criteria, personnel matters, the ordering of equipment and storage of sensitive apparatus) to overall policy decisions including obligations under international telegraph conventions, the development of the telegraph network, internal departmental organisation and discussions with railway and other companies.

Robinson spent much of his tenure as Director General of Telegraphs on business in Europe, attending the international telegraph conferences at Berne and Rome (in 1871/2) or St. Petersburg (1875). Negotiations with the directors of Indian railway companies based in London, the recruitment of suitable personnel and discussions with equipment manufacturers also took up much of Robinson's time when at home. These duties resulted in a considerable volume of correspondence from Robinson to the India Office and their draft replies to him, all of which may be found in IOL L/PWD/2/207–208 and IOL L/PWD/2/212–217 (for 1866/7 and 1871/6 respectively). Copies of the final versions of letters from the India Office to Robinson are in IOL PWD/2/197–199 (for 1863/8–1876/9).

A general overview of the work of the Telegraph Department may be obtained from the published reports which, for the period of Robinson's service, are contained in IOL V/24/4284, 4285 and 4286. Those for the years 1862/3–1865/6, 1867/8–1870/1 and 1873/4 were written by Robinson, with others being prepared by his deputies during his absences from India. They are useful as an initial starting point for determining the principal issues affecting the Department and the policies adopted.

Robinson's health was eventually broken by long service in India and so he obtained leave to return to England but died at sea on the P & O steamer *Travancore* on 27 July 1877 aged fifty-one. He was buried during the passage through the Red Sea.

Appendix 5

Gazetteer

Each entry in the gazetteer consists of three elements. The first of these is the place name which is as spelt on the 1" Survey of India map series compiled in the 1920's and 1930's. These spellings will be those most familiar to students of British involvement in India. In cases where the place does not appear on the Survey of India maps, the spelling used by Thornton is substituted and the name placed in inverted commas.

The second element of each entry comprises the description of the place mentioned. These descriptions have been taken from any of the three works by Thornton or the work by Watson (see bibliography) and have been placed in inverted commas. In many cases, Thornton's description is significantly longer than can be accommodated in this appendix, meaning that extracts have been made; full references have been given at the end of each entry should the reader wish to have more detail by consulting the original work (it should be noted, however, that the 1854 volumes by Thornton do not contain page numbers). Thornton's nineteenth century spellings of place names have been retained, however.

The last element comprises the longitude and latitude of the places mentioned. These have mostly been taken from the 1993 edition of the Times Atlas (see bibliography), but in the case of some villages and smaller settlements which do not appear in that publication, the longitude and latitude has been taken from the 1" Survey of India map series. In the minority of cases where a place does not appear in either of these sources, the longitudes and latitudes used by Thornton have been used, or when these are absent, they have been derived from the Indian Atlas map series, and enclosed in inverted commas. It should be noted that these nineteenth century data are inaccurate by several minutes.

Agra – 'A celebrated city, the principal place of the British district of the same name, and of the pergunnah or subdivision of Huzoor Tuhseel, is situate on the right bank of the Jumna. The city boasts of numerous large structures, memorials of the resources and magnificence of the sovereigns of the Timurian dynasty of Hindostan.' (Thornton 1854 Vol. 1). 27.09N 78.00E.

Akora – 'The chief town of a small district of the same name belonging to the Khuttuks, is situate on the south or right bank of the Kabool river, about ten miles above its confluence with the Indus at Attock. At the commencement of the present century, it was a considerable and prosperous town, with a great mosque and a handsome bazaar, built of stone; but has been nearly laid in ruins by the Sikhs.' (Thornton 1844, 1, p. 49). 34.00N 72.05E.

Allahabad – 'A British district under the lieut.-gov. of the N.W. Provinces, named from its principle place. The town is situate on the south east extremity of the Doab, on the tongue of land formed by the confluence of the Ganges and Jumna rivers. A strong fort is bounded on two sides by these rivers. It is situated 128 miles south east of Lucknow and 391 miles south east of Delhi.' (Thornton 1857 pp. 21–4). 25.72N 81.50E.

Ambala – 'Lies on the route from Kurnoul to Loodiana, 55 miles north of the former, 69 south-east of the latter. It is a large walled town, situate in a level and highly-cultivated country, well supplied with water, and capable of furnishing abundant supplies. The houses are built of burnt brick, but the streets are in general so narrow as scarcely to admit the passage of an elephant.' (Thornton 1857 p. 999). 30.19N 76.49E.

Amritsar – 'A walled city of the Punjab, is situate nearly half-way between the rivers Beas and Ravee. It is a place of pilgrimage for the Sikhs. Amritsar is a very populous and extensive place. The streets are narrow, but the houses in general are tolerably lofty and built of burnt brick. The most striking object at Amritsar is the huge fortress Govindghur, built by Runjeet Singh in 1809, ostensibly to protect the pilgrims, but in reality to overawe their vast and dangerous assemblage.' (Thornton 1857 p. 33). 31.35N 74.56E.

Araul – A village about 1 mile from the west bank of the River Ganges and approximately 38 miles north-west of Cawnpore. 26.66N 80.02E.

Attock – 'A fort and small town in the Punjab, on the left or east bank of the Indus, 942 miles from the sea, and close below the place where it receives the water of the Kabool River, and first becomes navigable. The fort was built in 1581 by Emperor Akbar but though strongly built of stone on the high and steep bank of the river it could offer no resistance to regular attack being commanded by neighbouring heights. Its form is that of a parallelogram; it is 800 yards long and 400 wide.' (Thornton 1857 p. 48). 33.52N 72.20E.

Bakrala – 'In the Punjab, a small town on the route from Attock to Rotas, is situate on the banks of the Kasee, which here winds its way through frightful defiles.' (Thornton 1844, 1, p. 66). 33.05N 73.25E.

Bannu – 'A fertile plain south-west of the Salt Range in eastern Afghanistan.' (Thornton 1844, 1, p. 74). 33.00N 70.40E.

Benares – 'The principal place of the British district of the same name, is situate on the left bank of the Ganges. Access is obtained to the water of the ghats or flights of broad steps. They extend nearly along the whole length of the river's bank in the city, though in some places interrupted by temples reaching down to the water's edge. The town is situated 421 miles north west from Calcutta and 74 miles east of Allahabad.' (Thornton 1857 pp. 89–91). 25.20N 83.00E.

Bhimbar – 'In the Punjab, a town on the route from Lahore to Kashmir, through the Baramula Pass. It is situate on a small stream, which falls into the Chenaub, from which river the town is distant about forty miles.' (Thornton 1844, 1, p. 108). 33.00N 74.55E.

Bokhara – Is located in Uzbekistan approximately 145 miles west of Samarkand and some 160 miles north-west of the northern frontier of Afghanistan. 39.47N 64.26E.

Bombay – 'The principal place of the presidency of the same name. The island on which the city is situate, extends from north-east to south-west eight miles, with an average breadth of three, and landlocks the harbour lying between it and the mainland, protecting it from the violence of the Arabian Sea.' (Thornton 1854 Vol. 1). 18.56N 72.51E.

Calcutta – 'The principal place of the presidency of Bengal, and the metropolis of British India. It is situate on the left bank of the river Hoogly, a branch of the Ganges, regarded by Hindoos as the continuation of the sacred stream, and is distant by the river's course about a hundred miles from the sea. Its extent along the river-bank from north to south is about four miles and a half, and its breadth from thence to the Circular Road measures about a mile and a half; the entire site, which comprises an area of nearly eight square miles, being inclosed between the river and the line of the old intrenchment known as the Mahratta Ditch.' (Thornton 1854 Vol. 1). 22.30N 88.20E.

Cawnpore – 'The principal place of the district of the same name, is situate in the pergunnah or subdivision of Jaujmau. The site is on the right bank of the Ganges. The commerce at the ghat or landing-place is busy and important, the Ganges being navigable downward to the sea, a distance of above 1,000 miles, and upwards to Sukertal, a distance of 300.' (Thornton 1857 pp. 189–191). 26.27N 80.14E.

'Chuk Janoo Khan' – Is located 10 miles north-west of Ramnagar. '32.25N 73.50E.'

Colgong – 'In the British district of Bhagulpore, presidency of Bengal, a town on the right bank of the Ganges, on the route from Berhampore to Dinapore, 130 miles N.W. of the former, 163 E. of the latter. It has a small bazaar and a fort, now in a ruinous state. Abreast of it, in the river, are the insulated masses, consisting of huge blocks of rocks, having their crevices and rifts filled with stunted trees, and fifty or sixty feet above the water.' (Thornton 1854 Vol. 2). 25.15N 87.15E.

Delhi – 'A celebrated city, the principal place of the British district of the same name, under the lieutenant-governorship of the North-Western Provinces. The site of the present city is a low rocky range, about a mile from the right bank of the Jumna, and on an offset of that river, which leaves the main stream five miles above the town, and rejoins it two miles below. The approach from the south-east, or the direction of Agra, is very striking, from the inumerable ruinous monuments of former prosperity and grandeur.' (Thornton 1854 Vol. 2). 28.04N 77.14E.

Dera Ghazi Khan – 'Is a large, populous, and commercial place, situate in a low alluvial tract, four miles from the right or west bank of the Indus, and contains numerous ruins of mosques, and of extensive and well-constructed residences of the former Durani governors and officers.' (Thornton 1844, 1, pp. 162–3). 30.05N 70.44E.

Dera Ismail Khan – 'In Afghanistan, a considerable town of the Derajat, built a short distance from the right or west bank of the Indus, to replace the former town, which, having been situate only a hundred yards from the river, was, a few years ago, swept away by it so completely that not a vestige was left. The town is well laid out, but is ill built of unburnt brick, and in general has an air of desolation, though in spring there is much business it being then crowded by the Afghans of the Lohani tribe, who purchase great quantities of goods to transport by their caravans for the supply of Afghanistan and Central Asia.' (Thornton 1844, 1, pp. 163–4). 31.51N 70.56E.

Dhamtaur – 'Valley extending from lat 34 5'–34 10' and long 72 45'–73 15'.' (Thornton 1844, 1, p. 175). The town of the same name is at 34.05N 73.15E.

Dopatta – Is located on the River Jhelum approximately 15 miles west of Abbottabad. 34.10N 73.35E.

Fatehgarh – 'The British military cantonment of Futtygurh is three miles east of the town [Furruckabad], and on the right bank of the Ganges. It lies twenty miles to the right of the great north-western route from Calcutta to Delhi, by the new line, and distant N.W. from the former 660 miles, S.E. from the latter 160, N.W. from Lucknow 95, E. from Agra 90.' (Thornton 1854 Vol. 2). 27.22N 79.38E.

Ferozepore – 'The principal place of the pergunnah of the same name, in the British district of Goorgaon, lieut.-gov. of the N.W. Provinces, on the route from Delhi to Alwar, and 74 miles S. of the former.' (Thornton 1857 pp. 308–9). 30.55N 74.38E.

Garhi Habibullah – 'An important village on the Abbottabad – Kashmir road, 19 miles from Mansehra and 12 from Domel. It is situated on the left bank of the Kunhar, which the road here crosses by a suspension bridge.' (Watson p. 232). 34.20N 73.20E.

Gidha Gulli – 'In Afghanistan, in the province of Peshawur, is a pass between Peshawur and Attock, and has received its name, the Jackal's Pass, or Neck, from its being so extremely narrow, that the natives, in exaggeration, say that a jackal only can make its way through it. The defile is not more than ten or twelve feet wide, and is bounded on each side by rather high and rugged hills. Though much frequented, it does not appear to be regarded as important in a military point of view, probably from the facility with which it can be turned. It is five miles west of Attock.' (Thornton 1844, 1, p. 190). 33.50N 72.05E.

Govindgarh – 'In the Baree Doab division of the Punjab, a fortress, built in 1809, by Runjeet Singh, avowedly for the purpose of protecting the pilgrims resorting to Amritsar, but in reality to overawe the dangerous assemblage. Since its occupation by the British, measures have been taken for adding to its security.' (Thornton 1857 p. 356). 31.35N 74.56E.

Haripur – 'Situated on the River Dor on the great route by the Dub Pass into Cashmere. It was founded in 1822 by Sardar Hari Singh and was at this time the headquarters of Hazara District before being superseded by Abbottabad.' (Thornton 1844, 1, p. 228). 34.00N 73.01E.

'Harkishangarh' – Was a formidable fort half a mile to the east of the town of Haripur. As with the town, the fort was built by Sardar Hari Singh. (Watson, p. 233). 34.00N 73.01E.

Hassan Abdal – 'In the Punjab, so called from containing the tomb of a reputed Mahometan saint of that name. It is situate in a delightful valley, watered by numerous springs, which gush from among the rocks.' (Thornton 1854 Vol. 2). 33.49N 72.48E.

Hormuck – 'A small town in the Punjab, on the road made by the Mogul emperors from Rotas to Attock. It is situate in a very difficult country, abounding in intricate, deep, and narrow defiles.' (Thornton 1844, 1, p. 250). '33.45N 72.51E.'

Hoshiarpur – 'In the Punjab, a small town near the southern base of the Himalaya mountains, and on the route from Lahore to Nadaun.' (Thornton 1844, 1, p. 251). 31.30N 75.59E.

Jalalabad – 'Situated nearly a mile from the south bank of the river of Kabool and five miles below the confluence of the Soorkh

Rood. Jelalabad is wretchedly built of unburnt bricks, and has little either of manufactures or trade, though advantageously situated on the main road from the Punjab to Kabool. The place owes its importance to the fact of its being the residence of the governor of the fertile province of which it is the chief town.' (Thornton 1844, 1, p. 260). 34.26N 70.82E.

Jalalpur – 'Is a town in the Punjab situated on the right or western bank of the River Jhelum in a valley extending from that river to the eastern edge of the Salt Range.' (Thornton 1857, pp. 438–9). 32.35N 73.20E.

Jammu – 'A considerable town in the north of the Punjab, and among the mountains forming the southern range of the Himalaya, is situate on a small river. The town and palace are built on the right or western bank of the river; on the east is the fort, elevated about 150 feet above the stream.' (Thornton 1857 p. 435). 32.43N 74.54E.

Jamrud – 'A fort and small village, the former now in ruins, the latter scarcely traceable, in the province of Peshawur, 10 miles or according to some 14 miles, west of the city of that name, and a short distance from the eastern entrance into the Khyber Pass.' (Thornton 1857 p. 469). 34.01N 71.82E.

Jarl – Is situated approximately 10 miles north-west of Haripur and 12 miles west of Abbottabad. 34.05N 73.00E.

Jindrai – Is situated close to the road between Pathankote and Kashmir, some 5 miles north of the former place and 2 miles south of the River Ravi. 32.20N 75.40E.

Jullundur – 'A considerable town near the right bank of the Sutlej. It is situate in a tract of great richness, amidst flourishing orchards of mangoes and other trees. The vast number of large and finely built mausoleums which are around, bear evidence of its former greatness.' (Thornton 1857 p. 466). 31.18N 75.40E.

Kabul – 'Capital of the province of the same name. Situated on the Kaboul river immediately above its confluence with that of Logurh. The immediate vicinity of the town is highly picturesque, well watered, and fertile.' (Thornton 1844, 1, pp. 307–15). 34.31N 69.12E.

Kangra – 'In the north-east of the Punjab, among the mountains in the lower ranges to the south of the Himalaya, in an extensive hill fort situated on the top of an eminence, about 150 feet above the Ban Gunga, near its confluence with the Beas. The eminence is about three miles in circuit, bounded for the most part by precipices nearly perpendicular, and, in places of less declivity, rendered inaccessible by masonry and ramparts.' (Thornton 1857 p. 481). 32.04N 76.16E.

Karachi – 'Is a seaport of Sinde, near the north-western extremity of the coast of that country. It is situate near the base of the southern extremity of the Pubb or Brahooic Mountains, on a level space intervening between them and the sea, and is the only seaport in Sinde for vessels drawing more than ten feet of water.' (Thornton 1857 pp. 545–7). 24.51N 67.02E.

Khanor – Is situated half a mile south of the Jammu boundary and fifteen miles east of Sialkot. 32.30N 75.00E.

Kohat – 'Situated in the hilly tract north of the Salt Range in an extremely fertile valley of the same name.' (Thornton 1857 p. 509). 33.37N 71.30E.

'Kooree' – A region of Hazara situated approximately 10 miles north-east of Hazro, or 27 miles north-east of Attock, on the south side of the River Indus. '34.00N 72.45E.'

Kotla – 'In the Baree Doab division of the Punjab is a town situated on the right bank of one of the branches of the River Beas, 124 miles east-north-east of the town of Lahore.' (Thornton 1857 p. 528). 31.43N 77.16E.

Lahore – 'A large city in the Punjab, is situate about a mile east of the Ravee river. Runjeet Singh built a wall twenty-five feet high around the town and surrounded this with a ditch and a line of works, the whole extending for seven miles. The streets of Lahore, which are very narrow, contain numbers of lofty but gloomy houses, inclosed within extensive but dead walls.' (Thornton 1857 pp. 555–6). 31.34N 74.22E.

Leiah – 'In the Punjab, an important commercial town, situate on a small branch of the Indus, about three miles east of the main stream. It is a place of great business, not only in direct but in transit trade, as it lies on the main road from Hindostan to the west by the Kaheree ferry, and is, besides, the mart for the abundant and rich produce of the surrounding fertile country.' (Thornton 1844, 2, pp. 22–3). 30.59N 70.58E.

Lucknow – 'The capital of the kingdom of Oude, is situate on the right or south-west side of the Goomtee, which is navigable upwards for many miles above the town, and downwards through its whole course to its confluence with the Ganges.' (Thornton 1854 Vol. 3). 26.50N 80.54E.

Ludhiana – 'The chief town of the Sirhind district. It is an ill-built town without a wall, but having a fort on the north side, situate on the bluff rising over the nullah. It was built about 1808, but is of no great strength. Situate on one of the great routes from Delhi to the Punjaub, has long been an important place from a military point of view.' (Thornton 1857 pp. 565–6). 30.56N 75.52E.

Madras – 'The seat of the presidency bearing that name, and the principal place of the territory subjected thereto, as also of the district of Madras. The city is on the Coramandel coast, or the western shore of the Bay of Bengal, to the beach of which its buildings extend.' (Thornton 1854 Vol. 3). 13.05N 80.18E.

Mankiala – 'General Ventura, a European officer in Sikh service, sank a perpendicular shaft in the centre of the platform on the summit and at various depths found repositories one below the other.' (Thornton 1844, 2, pp. 36–8). 33.25N 73.10E.

Mansehra – 'Lies on the Abbottabad – Kashmir road, 16 miles north of the former place.' (Watson pp. 238–9). 34.23N 73.18E.

Margala – Situated approximately 35 miles south-east of Attock on the road between Rawalpindi and Attock. The height of the pass is 1,831 feet. 33.40N 72.50E.

Meerut – 'Principle place of the British district, and also of the pergunnah of the same name, under the lieut.-gov. of the N.W. Provinces, is situate nearly in the middle of the district, being distant twenty five miles from the Ganges on the east, and thirty from the Jumna on the west. The military cantonments are two miles to the north of the town.' (Thornton 1857 pp. 611–12). 29.00N 77.42E.

Mirpur – 'A town in the native state of Cashmere, 92 miles S.W. from Sirinagur, and 113 miles N. from Lahore.' (Thornton 1854 Vol. 3). 33.32N 73.56E.

Mirzapur – 'Within the limits of the lieut.-gov. of the N.W. Provinces, a British district named after its principal place. Situated on the right bank of the the Ganges. Its appearance to those passing it by water is imposing, from its great extent, numerous mosques and Hindoo temples, excellent houses of Europeans, and handsome ghats or flights of stairs leading to the water's edge. Situated 61 miles east of Allahabad and 27 miles south-west of Benares.' (Thornton 1857 pp. 618–21). 25.09N 82.34E.

Multan – 'Situated 3 miles east of the River Chenab. It is the third largest city in the Punjab after Lahore and Amritsar.' (Thornton 1857 pp. 627–8). 30.10N 71.36E.

Mussoorie – 'On the northern frontier of the Dehra Doon, towards Gurhwal, is a sanatory station, established by the British to suspend, relieve, or remove the consequences prejudicial to health from the sultry climate of Hindoostan.' (Thornton 1854 Vol. 3). 30.26N 78.04E.

Muzaffarabad – 'Situated at the confluence of the Jhelum and Kishengunga rivers. A small town but in a commanding position at the entrance of the Baramula Pass leading into Cashmere.' (Thornton 1844, 2, pp. 44–5). 34.23N 73.34E.

Nangal Dunna Singh – 'In the Punjab, a village on the route from Amritsar to Vuzeerabad, and forty-five miles south-east of the latter place.' (Thornton 1844, 2, p. 82). 31.55N 74.20E.

Nara – 'A small village lying on the edge of the Haripur plain at the base of the Gandgar range, some 8 miles north-west of Haripur. The position of the village was important in former times, as it commanded the most practicable route to Sirikot and the heart of the Gandgar hills.' (Watson p. 240). 34.00N 72.50E.

Naushahra – 'In Afghanistan, a town in the Peshawur territory, situate on the banks of the Kabool river, eighteen miles north-west of Attock. Here, in 1823, the Afghans were utterly routed by the Sikhs, commanded by Runjeet Singh. The Sikhs have a fort here, built for them under the direction of General Avitabile. It has four bastions and a double row of loopholes.' (Thornton 1844, 2, p. 79). 34.00N 72.00E.

Nawashahr – Is located 5 miles east of Abbottabad. 34.13N 73.20E.

Nurpur – 'In the north-east of the Punjab, among the lower and southern mountains of the Himalaya range, a town of considerable importance, as being on the route from Hindostan to Kashmir.' (Thornton 1844, 2, p. 83). 32.18N 75.56E.

Pallavaram – 'A town in the British district of Chingleput, presidency of Madras, 11 miles south-west of Madras.' (Thornton 1857 p. 747). 12.56N 80.11E.

Pathankot – 'In the north-east of the Punjab, and in the southern range of the Himalaya, fourteen miles north-west of Nurpur, and on the route to Kashmir. The fort has a fine appearance, is built substantially of brick, has a ditch and glacis, and being situate on level ground, is not commanded in any direction; it consequently admits of an obstinate defence. A lofty citadel in the interior rises above the ramparts.' (Thornton 1844, 2, p. 96). 32.16N 75.43E.

Peshawar – 'The capital of the province of the same name, is situate about eighteen miles east of the eastern extremity of the Khyber Pass. The Sikhs built a fort here after defeating the Afghans at the battle of Noushera in 1823.' (Thornton 1857 pp. 764–5). 34.01N 71.40E.

Potwar – An area of the Punjab between the Rivers Jhelum and Indus, south of Rawalpindi. 33.50N 73.00E.

Pukli – 'In the north of the Punjab, a small tract east of the Indus, it is very fertile. Runjeet Singh obtained possession of it about twenty years ago, by expelling the Mahometan chief, Poyndu Khan, who took refuge in the island of Chuttoorbye, in the Indus.' (Thornton 1854 Vol. 4). 'Lat 34.15–34.30 long 72.50–73.15.'

Punch – 'A small town on the south slope of the mountains bounding Cashmere on the south. Situated at the foot of the Punch Pass on the banks of the Punch River which discharges into the Chenab. Two of the most frequented routes from the Punjab to Cashmere meet here and proceed north through the Baramula Pass.' (Thornton 1857 p. 788). 33.46N 74.08E.

Rajmahal Hills – 'In Bengal are lower than 2000' in elevation but are the most important range in the Santal Parganas District. The town of Rajmahal is in the British district of Bhaugulpore, lieut.-gov. of Bengal, a town situate on the right bank of the Ganges. The general aspect of the town is ruinous and dismal, as it is now a collection of wretched houses or huts, dispersed amongst twelve market-places, situate at considerable and inconvenient distances from each other.' (Thornton 1857 pp. 813–14). 25.03N 87.49E.

Rajoia – 'A large village on the left bank of the Dor, south of the Sarban hill, and about 10 miles from Abbottabad. It is the centre of the stony plain which forms the eastern continuation of the Haripur tract.' (Watson p. 243). 34.00N 73.10E.

Ramgarh – Is located approximately 24 miles east of Sialkot and 17 miles south of Jammu. 32.30N 74.55E.

Ramnagar – 'In the Punjab, a walled town close to the left or east bank of the Chenaub, stands on a spacious plain, where, during the reign of Runjeet Singh, the Sikh troops frequently mustered for campaigns to the westward.' (Thornton 1857 p. 822). 32.20N 73.51E.

Rawalpindi – 'In the Punjab, between the Indus and the Jhelum. It is a large populous town, consisting of mud houses with flat roofs.' (Thornton 1857 p. 830). 33.40N 73.08E.

Shamsabad – 'In the Punjab, a small town near the left bank of the Indus, and a few miles east of Attock. It is situate in a fertile and well-cultivated plain, and is built on an artificial mound.' (Thornton 1844, 2, p. 198). 33.50N 72.25E.

Sherwan Khurd – 'Is located on a ridge 5,000' high 17 miles to the west of Abbottabad. Major Abbott had a bungalow located nearby where he used to spend the hot weather.' (Watson pp. 244–5). 34.10N 73.00E.

Simla – 'A British station in the lower or more southern part of the Himalayas, between the rivers Sutlej and Giree, celebrated as a retreat for those seeking renovation of health, or relief from the oppressive heat of the plains of Hindostan. It is situate on the route from Soobathoo to Kotgurh, 22 miles N.E. of the former post.' (Thornton 1854 Vol. 4). 31.07N 77.09E.

Sind – 'An extensive and important province of Western India, so called probably from the river Sinde or Indus. It is 360 miles long, from north to south, 270 miles in its greatest breadth,

from east to west, and contains a surface of 52,120 square miles.'
(Thornton 1854 Vol. 4). '23.37–28.32N 66.43–71.03E.'

Tank – Is situated to the west of the River Indus, close to the
Afghan border. 32.14N 70.29E.

Urie – Is located on the south bank of the River Jhelum. 34.05N
74.03E.

Usman Khattar – Is located approximately 16 miles S.W. of
Haripur and 34 miles E. of Attock. 33.45N 72.50E.

Wazirabad – 'A town in the Punjab, is situate about three miles
from the left or eastern bank of the Chenaub, here half a mile
broad. The country immediately about it is exceedingly fertile,
and the view of the Himalaya probably the most extensive and
magnificent anywhere. It is one of the handsomest towns in
India; General Avitabile, a European officer in the service of
Runjeet Singh, having caused it to be rebuilt in the European
style, with wide streets and a handsome and commodious bazar.
Runjeet Singh made here a pleasure-ground, and palace of
singular construction, and covered outside with rude full-length
figures of the ten Gurus, or spiritual leaders of the Sikhs,
painted in fresco.' (Thornton 1857 p. 1009). 32.23N 74.10E.

Notes

Full publication details of works cited in the Notes are given in the Bibliography. Unless stated otherwise, the place of publication is London.

Notes to Introduction

1 Information on the career of Daniel George Robinson is contained in Oriental and India Office Library and Records, London, (hereafter IOL) L/MIL/9/197 pp. 663–9; IOL L/MIL/10/78 pp. 232–3; IOL L/MIL/10/84 pp. 104–5; Stephen, L. & Lee, S. (eds.) (1885–1901) *Dictionary of National Biography* (hereafter *DNB*), Vol. 17 pp. 6–7.

2 Parliamentary Papers (1849) *Papers relating to the Punjab 1847–1849. Presented to both Houses of Parliament by command of Her Majesty. May 1849*, pp. 542, 601.

3 The information for this brief summary of the Second Sikh War has been taken from: Punjab Government Journals and diaries of Captain J. Abbott 1846–1849. In *Journals and diaries of the Assistants to the Agent, Governor-General North-West Frontier and Resident at Lahore 1846–1849*, pp. 200–65; Mahajan, J. *Annexation of the Punjab. A historical revision*, revised edition, 1990, pp. 55–85; Singh, B.S. *The Jammu fox. A biography of Maharaja Gulab Singh of Kashmir*, 1974, pp. 131–2, 139–42.

Notes to Letters

1 The suggested date of 25 April 1845 for this letter is based on internal evidence. DGR sailed to India on board the *Tartar*, a ship of 481 dwt built at Blackwall in 1840 and owned by Green & Co. The firm was owned by Frederick William Green and operated from 1 St Michael's Alley, Cornhill. Cadet Papers IOL L/MIL/9/197 pp. 663–9; *Lloyds Register of British and Foreign Shipping 1842*; *The Post Office London Directory for 1844*, p. 707.

2 DGR's elder sister was Maria de Guadaloupe Anna Antonia Robinson (1824–1901) whose Spanish name was given to her on account of her being the first English child to be born in Mexico. She was known to members of the family as Ninetta.

3 This letter is no longer extant.

4 Bonito (probably *Sarda sarda* or Atlantic bonito) is a large mackerel-like fish. Albacore (*Thynnus germo*) is a large species of fish allied to a tunny.

5 Colonel and Mrs Milford, and their daughter Agnes, were friends and neighbours of DGR's maternal uncle and aunt, the Hardings, and lived at Laugharne, 9 miles south-west of Carmarthen.

6 Pallavaram is 11 miles from Madras. The 2nd and 41st Madras Native Infantry were stationed there in 1845. *The East-India Register and Directory for 1845*, 2nd edition, pp. 53, 92.

7 In the absence of the Adjutant-General (Lieutenant-Colonel Robert Alexander of the 40th Madras Native Infantry) the Acting Adjutant-General was Charles Alfred Browne (1803–1866) 15th Madras Native Infantry. Ensign 1821, Lieutenant 1824, Captain 1830, Major 1843, Lieutenant-Colonel 1850, Colonel 1854, Major-General 1862. His office was located in Arsenal Street, Fort St George, Madras. *The Madras Almanac and Compendium of Intelligence for 1845*, p. 229; *National Army Museum, Hodson Index* (hereafter cited as *Hodson Index*).

8 This letter was probably written in June or July 1845 from Calcutta.

9 John Ward Harding (1804–95) was formerly a Captain in the 14th Madras Native Infantry and retired in 1837. He married Eliza Greathead (DGR's aunt) at Camberwell in 1832. At the date of this letter, the couple were living at Laugharne in South Wales where two of their seven children died in 1845, those being Harriet Blanche in March and Albert in April. *Hodson Index*.

10 The birthday of Queen Victoria was celebrated on 24 May.

11 John Harding Robinson (1833–90) was DGR's youngest brother.

12 Mary Shield and her ?sister Kate appear to have been either friends or relatives of the Hardings.

13 Thomas Charles Cadogan was a partner in the firm of Turner, Cadogan & Co, merchants and agents, of 10 Clive Street, Calcutta. He lived in Church Lane, Calcutta. *The Bengal and Agra Directory & Annual Register for 1845*, pp. 350, 369, 445.

14 Charles Kerr lived at 51 Great Ormonde Street, Bloomsbury, London. He had recommended DGR to Henry Alexander, one of the Directors of the Honourable East India Company, who nominated him for a Cadetship. IOL L/MIL/9/197 Cadet Papers.

15 Peons – servants or footmen. Yule, H. & Burnell, A.C. *Hobson Jobson*, pp. 696–7.

16 Saunders, May, Fordyce & Co, merchants and agents, of No. 4 Lyon's Range, Calcutta. The partners were Richard Saunders and the heirs of George May and Arthur Dingwall Fordyce. *The Bengal and Agra Directory & Annual Register for 1845*, p. 329.

17 Araul.

18 George Simson Laurenson (1803–56) Bengal Artillery. 2nd Lieutenant 1819, Lieutenant 1821, Captain 1835, Major 1845, awarded the CB 1846, Lieutenant-Colonel 1849, Brevet Colonel 1854. *Hodson Index*.

19 Meerut was the Headquarters of the Bengal Sappers & Miners between

1845–7 and 1852–4. Sandes, E.W.C., (1948) *The Indian Sappers and Miners*, p. 163.

20 John Laughton (1811–1861) Bengal Engineers. 2nd Lieutenant 1828, Lieutenant 1839, Captain 1846, Major 1857, Lieutenant-Colonel 1858, Colonel 1861. He served as the Executive Engineer, Allahabad Division, 1844–8. *Hodson Index*.

21 Samuel Charles Woodcock (1824–1922) Bengal Artillery. 2nd Lieutenant 1841, Lieutenant 1844, Captain 1855, Lieutenant-Colonel 1862, Brevet Colonel 1867, Hon Major-General 1872. He was serving with the 3rd Battery in 1845. Like DGR he was educated at the Royal Naval School, Camberwell. *Hodson Index*.

22 Ghaut – a flight of steps leading to a river. Yule & Burnell, *op cit*, pp. 369–70.

23 Mirzapur.

24 Colgong.

25 See Appendix 1 for details of pay and allowances.

26 Alexander Taylor (1826–1912) Bengal Engineers. 2nd Lieutenant 1843, Lieutenant 1847, Captain 1857, Major 1858, Lieutenant-Colonel 1858, awarded the CB 1858, Colonel 1864, Major-General 1874 (antedated to 1868), Lieutenant-General 1877, awarded the KCB 1877, General 1878, awarded the GCB 1889. *Hodson Index*. Alexander Taylor was a close friend of DGR's and a Godfather to his son, Charles Taylor Robinson. Letters written by Alexander Taylor to DGR during the Indian Mutiny are held at the National Army Museum, London, 7605–21.

27 Henry Hardinge (1785–1856) served in the Peninsular War and at Waterloo. He was Secretary at War (1818–30, 1841–4), and Irish Secretary (1830, 1834–5) before serving as Governor-General in India (1844–8). His Indian service is most remembered for the First Sikh War, but he also achieved much in promoting various civil projects concerning irrigation, education and railway communications. After leaving India he served as Master General of the Ordnance (1852) and subsequently as Commander in Chief (1852–6). He died a Field Marshal. Buckland, C.E. *Dictionary of Indian Biography*, p. 189.

28 Jindrai.

29 Pathankot.

30 This is rather inaccurate, since Jindrai is situated at lat 32.20 N long 75.40 E.

31 The Miller family lived at Epsom and were cousins of the Robinsons. The children, who were all contemporaries of DGR, were Henry (Harry), Frederick, Kate, Mary, Sarah and Anne. Mary did go to India and married Henry de Tessier of the Bengal Artillery on 17 January 1854, in Calcutta. She was in Delhi at the outbreak of the Mutiny in 1857. Sattin, A. (ed) *An Englishwoman in India. The Memoirs of Harriet Tytler 1828–1858*, p. 117.

32 The word *Kerri* means the tent of a soldier or merchant from Afghanistan. Whitworth, G.C. *An Anglo-Indian Dictionary*, (1885), p. 157.

33 Nurpur.

34 This was the 56th Bengal Native Infantry, which arrived at Nurpur in 1846. *The East India Register and Army List for 1847*, p. 146.

35 Bhimbar.

36 Peshawar.

37 This word does not appear to be either in Urdu or Hindustani and is therefore unidentified.

38 Nazar – a present or offering made by an inferior on his presentation to a superior. Whitworth, *op cit*, p. 225.

39 Jagheer – a hereditary assignment of land and of its rent and annuity. Jagheerdar – the holder of a jagheer. Yule & Burnell, *op cit*, pp. 446–7.

40 The battle of Sobraon was fought on 10 February 1846 between Sir Hugh Gough and the Sikhs under Tej Singh and Lall Singh. The action resulted in defeat for the Sikhs and was the last battle of the First Sikh War.

41 Amritsar.

42 Henry Newdick Miller (1826–87) 1st Bombay European Fusiliers. 2nd Lieutenant 1842, Lieutenant 1846, Captain 1856, Major 1862, Lieutenant-Colonel 1868, Colonel 1873, Hon Major-General. He was a cousin and close friend of DGR and was also educated at the Royal Naval School, Camberwell. *Hodson Index*.

43 Karachi.

44 The 1st Bombay European Fusiliers embarked at Bombay on 24 December 1845 and arrived at Karachi in January 1846. The unit marched on 30 January for Sukkur in order to join a force under Sir Charles Napier, but after the close of the First Sikh War it returned to Karachi on 30 March. Anon *Historical Records of the 103rd Royal Bombay Fusiliers*, p. 66.

45 Nurpur. According to Abbott's journal, this camp was two miles from the fort in that town. *Abbott's Journal*, p. 22.

46 This letter is no longer extant.

47 The Sikh commandant of Kangra refused to surrender his fort according to the terms of the Treaty of Lahore, so a small force and siege train were sent against him. There was no road to transport the guns over, but one was built in a week by the 4th and 5th Companies commanded by Lieutenants H. Drummond and J.H. Dyas assisted by working parties from the artillery and gangs of native labourers. The garrison surrendered on ?29 May 1846 when they saw the siege train. After this, one company was always stationed at Kangra. Sandes, *op cit*, p. 178.

48 Amritsar.

49 Henry & Thomas Peat, saddlers to Her Majesty's cavalry, harness makers, etc., 167 Piccadilly. *The Post Office London Directory for 1846*, p. 910.

50 Daniel O'Connell (1775–1847). An Irish barrister elected MP for County Clare in 1823. He campaigned vigorously against the governance of Ireland through the Act of Union, but his influence lessened in the 1830's due to his support for the Whigs and still further during the 1840's as he appeared too

cautious in comparison to the more extreme Young Ireland Party. He had campaigned from February 1846 onwards for a committee to relieve the distress in Ireland caused by the famine and at the same time urged for the defeat in the Commons of a coercion bill for the repression of disorder in certain Irish counties. The bill was defeated, largely through the opposition of Disraeli. Palmer, A.W. *A Dictionary of Modern History 1789–1945*, pp. 241, 338, 357–8.

51 Ralph Young (1825–97) Bengal Engineers. 2nd Lieutenant 1844, Lieutenant 1850, Captain 1858, Lieutenant-Colonel 1867, Colonel 1875, Hon Major-General 1877. His father was John Adolphus Young, a solicitor of St Mildred's Court, London, where DGR's father also had an office. *Hodson Index*.

52 Miss Agassiz was probably a sister of Robert Agassiz who married DGR's sister Ninetta in 1849. Miss Agassiz may be the Susanne mentioned in Letter 23.

53 Annie Jessie Bruyères (?–1863) married DGR's cousin Charles Daniel Palmer Robinson in 1843. The couple lived in Jersey before moving to Alderney in 1849 when Charles was appointed curate.

54 Charles Francis Robinson (1828–51) DGR's younger brother, was at this time serving as a Midshipman on board HMS *Talbot* on the South American station.

55 John Harding Robinson had commenced working as a Committee Clerk in the House of Lords on 23 June 1845.

56 The Edlmann family actually lived at Chislehurst, which is adjacent to Bromley.

57 Jenkin Jones (1826–?) Bombay Engineers. 2nd Lieutenant 1844, Lieutenant 1848, Captain 1856, Lieutenant-Colonel 1863, Colonel 1871, Major-General 1878. DGR's younger brother served under Jones' father between 1839–42 when the latter commanded HMS *Curacoa* on the South American station. *Hodson Index*.

58 James Henry Burke (1816–82) Bombay Engineers. 2nd Lieutenant 1834, Lieutenant 1845, Captain 1854, Lieutenant-Colonel 1860, Colonel 1863, Major-General 1864. He was Executive Engineer at Mhow from 27 Nov 1844. DGR's father knew Burke's father through his work with the Irish Waste Land Society. *Hodson Index*.

59 'Death steps' were the means by which officers gained promotion by filling the vacancies created by their seniors who had died.

60 Sind had been conquered in 1843 by a force predominantly drawn from the Bombay Army. It was administered by the Government of Bengal until handed over to Bombay in 1846.

61 Mussoorie.

62 Gulab Singh (1792–1857) rose to prominence from humble origins through his ability on the battlefield. Ranjit Singh made him Raja of Jammu in 1820, and despite his geographical isolation from the centre of the Sikh kingdom

at Lahore, Gulab managed to increase his influence and survive the upheavals that resulted in the deaths of many of the leading figures in the Punjab. Gupta, H.R. *Panjab on the Eve of the First Sikh War*, (1956), pp. 100–1; Singh, *op cit*, pp. 3–21.

63 Jammu.

64 It has not been possible to identify the spelling of this place from the original letter, nor is there any obvious site on the maps in either the Indian Atlas or 1" Survey of India series. It is probable, however, that DGR was either on the direct road between Pathankot and Jammu or else surveying the boundary to the west of the former place.

65 Goont – a kind of pony of the northern Himalayas, strong but clumsy. Yule & Burnell, *op cit*, p. 387.

66 The Commissioner for Hazara, James Abbott (1807–96) Bengal Artillery. 2nd Lieutenant 1823, served at Bhurtpore 1825–6, Lieutenant 1827, Army of the Indus 1838–9, Captain 1841, Commissioner for Hazara 1845–53, commanded a column in the Black Mountain expedition 1852, Major 1854, Lieutenant-Colonel 1857, Colonel 1861, Major-General 1866, Lieutenant-General 1877, General 1877. Awarded the CB 1873, KCB 1894. Buckland, *op cit*, 1–2; *Hodson Index*.

67 Henry Hyde (1824–87) Bengal Engineers. 2nd Lieutenant 1844, Lieutenant 1850, Captain 1858, Lieutenant-Colonel 1866, Colonel 1875, Hon Major-General 1878. His father, Henry Woodcock Hyde, was Curate of Camberwell where the Robinson family lived. Like DGR, he attended the crammer run by Stoton & Mayor at Wimbledon. *Hodson Index*.

68 Ramgarh. The date of this letter is clearly January 1847 since this matches with DGR's movements at that time. A year earlier he was either at Meerut or with the army operating against the Sikhs.

69 Ranbir Singh was Gulab Singh's eldest son after the deaths of his elder brothers Udham in 1840 and Sohan in 1844. He had been adopted by Suchet Singh, Gulab's childless younger brother, so that his father could lay hands on Suchet's territory and property which occurred after Suchet's death in March 1844 at the hands of his nephew, Prime Minister Hira Singh. Ranbir became Maharajah in 1856 when Gulab Singh abdicated in favour of his son. Gupta, *op cit*, pp. 100–1; Singh, *op cit*, pp. 3–21, 61, 179.

70 Gulab Singh.

71 John Nicholson (1822–57) 27th Bengal Native Infantry. Ensign 1839, Lieutenant 1842, Captain 1848, Brevet Major 1849, Brevet Lieutenant-Colonel 1854, Brigadier-General 1857. *Hodson Index*.

72 Kana – food?

73 Coss or Kos – a unit of distance equivalent to about two miles. Whitworth, *op cit*, p. 171; Yule & Burnell, *op cit*, pp. 261–2.

74 Khanor. The identification with Kaine is based on the fact that it is situated only half a mile from the Jammu boundary which DGR was surveying at the time and it would have been on his route to Wazirabad from Jammu via

Ramgarh. Capt. Abbott visited DGR and Lieutenant Young in the vicinity of Sialkot on 11 January 1847 only five days after the two surveyors passed through Khanor, which is only fifteen miles distant. *Abbott's Journal*, p. 35.

75 Ranbir Singh. See note 69 above.

76 Hira Singh was the son of Dhian Singh, the Prime Minister of the Punjab until his death in 1843. Hira Singh became Prime Minister on the death of his father, and thus became the most powerful individual in the Sikh kingdom, since the head of state, Maharajah Dalip Sing, was then aged six. Hira Singh was murdered on 21 December 1844. Gupta, *op cit*, pp. 60–70.

77 This refers to the periods of anarchy which existed in the Sikh kingdom following the death of Maharajah Ranjit Singh in June 1839, and the consequent ending of strong central control. Ranbir Singh's eldest brother was Udham Singh who was killed on 5 November 1840 after being crushed by falling masonry from an archway. The death (as well as that of the heir apparent, Nau Nihal Singh) was attributed at the time to the Prime Minister, Dhian Singh, though was almost certainly an accident. Udham Singh was not related to the family of Ranjit Singh and DGR has confused the identities of the two casualties. Gupta, *op cit*, pp. 32–5, 52–3.

78 Henry Montgomery Lawrence (1806–57) Bengal Artillery. 2nd Lieutenant 1825, Captain 1840, awarded the KCB 1848, Major 1850, ADC to the Queen and Brevet Colonel 1854, Lieutenant-Colonel 1856, Brigadier-General 1857. He was appointed Agent in the Punjab in 1846 and Resident at Lahore the following year. As President of the Board of Administration (1849–53) he was responsible for the Punjab following its annexation. He died of wounds received during the siege of the Lucknow Residency, on 2 July 1857. Buckland, *op cit*, p. 246; *Hodson Index*.

79 This may well refer to either Jamait or Chiman Singh, Ranbir's younger brothers.

80 This is probably Suchet Singh who never actually held that office but was the uncle (and adopted father) of Ranbir Singh.

81 Rukhsat – the act of closing an interview or the leaving or dismissal of a guest. The host gives the guest a garland of flowers on his departure, or, as in this case, some other present. Whitworth, *op cit*, p. 270.

82 William Greathead (1799–1867) was the younger brother of DGR's mother.

83 Jonas – Sarah Jonas was the sister-in-law of DGR's grandmother. William Knapp Jonas, who lived at Bishop's Waltham in Hampshire, was her son and therefore a cousin of DGR's father.

84 The *Tartar*, on which DGR sailed to India, was owned by Frederick William Green of Green & Co. which operated from 1 St Michael's Alley, Cornhill. *The Post Office London Directory for 1844*, p. 707.

85 Frederick Francis Miller (1832–?) joined the Royal Navy as a Clerk in 1854 and was promoted to Assistant Paymaster in 1855. Although he behaved courageously during the siege of Sebastopol his general conduct was not

good and he left the Navy in 1859; PRO, London ADM 11/46; ADM 13/79; ADM 196/11; *Steel's Navy List*.

86 This letter has been placed somewhat tentatively in the sequence; however, it is clear from internal evidence that DGR was surveying the Jammu boundary in the vicinity of the River Ravi which would fit with his movements at this period.

87 Kachchá – unfinished, rough, a person deficient in skill or experience. Whitworth, *op cit*, pp. 74, 142.

88 It has not been possible to translate this phrase which appears to be in a language other than Urdu or Hindustani.

89 The village of Pencraig lies in the Wye Valley some six miles north-east of Monmouth. The Robinsons had relations or friends living there.

90 Wazirabad.

91 The Military General Service Medal was authorised by a General Order dated 1 June 1848, but there may have been advanced reports in the press prior to this date. DGR's father was not entitled to the medal, since he did not serve in the British Army and was not present at any of the actions for which bars were awarded. The medals he did receive were all Spanish, as follows: Order of Isabella the Catholic (Chevalier), Medal for Bagur and Palamos 1810, Cross for Tarragona 1811 and the Medal for the First Army 1811.

92 Fatehgarh.

93 This did not in fact happen, as according to the terms of Daniel Robinson's will dated 18 August 1848, the medals were left to each of his children and the minerals to John Harding Robinson. DGR did receive his Grandfather's portrait and his Father's manuscripts.

94 Nangal Dunna Singh.

95 To endless absurdity (Latin).

96 Allan, Deffell & Co, merchants and agents, of 140 Clive Street, Calcutta. The partners were John Allan, John Deffell and John Hutcheson Fergusson. *The Bengal and Agra Directory and Annual Register for 1845*, p. 327.

97 Mankiala.

98 Rawalpindi.

99 Jean Baptiste Ventura (?–1858) was of Italian origin and served in Napoleon's army in Spain and Italy. He was subsequently made a General by Maharajah Ranjit Singh and assumed responsibility for training the Sikh infantry. Lord Ellenborough secured a dialogue with him from early 1843, and thus had regular news of the Lahore political scene. He retired from the Sikh service in 1843 and settled in Paris. Bruce, G. *Six Battles for India*, p. 48; Buckland, *op cit*, pp. 435–6; Colyer, W.J. 'The Maharajah Ranjit Singh and his foreign officers' in *Royal United Service Institution Journal* 99 pp. 90–4 (1954); Gupta, *op cit*, p. 97; Majumdar, *op cit*, p. 261.

100 Kabul.

101 Ranbir Singh. See the letter dated 5 January 1847.

102 Gulab Singh's vizier was Roop Chand. *Abbott's Journal*, p. 36.

103 Wind – i.e. money.

104 Ryots – farmers. Yule & Burnell, *op cit*, p. 777.

105 Kutcherry or Kachahri – court house. Whitworth, *op cit*, p. 142.

106 This letter is no longer extant.

107 It has not been possible to translate this phrase which appears to be in a language other than Urdu or Hindustani.

108 DGR would have been aged twenty-one on 8 March 1847.

109 The telescope was requested in the letter dated 6 December 1846, which reached England in March 1847.

110 Galee – swear word (Hindustani).

111 Unidentified. This does not appear to be either an Urdu or a Hindustani phrase.

112 Charles Robinson was appointed Lieutenant on 28 June 1848. This refers to the examination which all Midshipmen had to pass as a prerequisite for promotion.

113 Adine Edlmann.

114 The Bruyères family lived on Jersey.

115 This letter is no longer extant.

116 Mahtab Kumar was the second wife of Ranjit Singh and mother of Sher Singh.

117 The Irish Waste Land Improvement Society was established in 1837 with Daniel Robinson as a founder member. At this time, its offices were at No. 5 St Mildreds Court, Poultry, London. It was a charitable organisation aiming to help the Irish diversify their crops by growing corn on marginal lands, which was of considerable help during the subsequent potato blight. *Post Office London Directory for 1843*, p. 386.

118 This Latin sentence is incorrect as written.

119 Jalalpur.

120 This place does not appear on either the India Atlas map series or the 1" Survey of India maps; it has therefore been impossible to identify, though the name suggests that it was in the vicinity of Rawalpindi.

121 The entry in Abbott's journal for 10 April 1848 states: 'The salt mines have been worked time out of mind, but I believe Lieutenant Daniel Robinson of Engineers was the first to bring to the notice of Government the existence of a coal mine in this neighbourhood [Pind Dadun Khan]. It had been some time known to the natives, but fuel is there abundant and the coal is ill-adapted to their primitive cookery; so that it is quite disregarded by them. The coal, considering that only the superficial strata have yet been opened, offers very fair promise, and its proximity to the Jelum will render it a valuable mine.' *Abbott's Journal*, p. 140.

122 *Nadir Shah* (1687–1747) of Persia invaded India in 1738 and crossed the Indus at Attock. He defeated the Moghul army sent from Delhi and subsequently occupied that city in 1739 massacring many thousands of its inhabitants.

Mahmud of Ghuznee (967–1030) invaded India many times from his kingdom in Afghanistan. He is regarded as one of the greatest champions of Islam by Muslim historians, due to his many campaigns to spread the faith.

Shah Jahan (1593–1666), although an active soldier in his youth, left military operations to his sons once he became Moghul emperor in 1627, occupying himself with his love of art and architecture. He was ousted by his son Aurangzeb in 1658 and imprisoned in the Red Fort at Delhi.

Akbar Shah (1542–1605) was the grandfather of Shah Jehan. He extended the Moghul empire through marriage and conquest but is also remembered for many architectural achievements. Beale, T.W., *An Oriental Biographical Dictionary*, pp. 46, 233–4, 288, 363–4.

123 DGR's father, Daniel Robinson, had a partnership with George Alexander Knott as wine importers and East India agents. *Post Office London Directory for 1849*, p. 488.

124 A General Order of the Commander-in-Chief of 30.9.1847 laid down that the establishment would change from ten companies of sappers to three companies of sappers and seven companies of pioneers. All companies were of 100 men. The sappers were to be the most highly skilled men and were officered by Engineers, whilst the Pioneers represented second line units and were officered from the infantry. This organisation lasted until March 1851 when the Pioneer Companies reverted to Sappers, Sandes, *op cit*, p. 163.

125 Reid, Irving & Co., East India Agents, 16 Token House Yard, London. *The Bengal and Agra Directory and Annual Register for 1847*, p. 6.

126 The identification of Miss Fry has been made on the basis of entries in the cashbook of Daniel Robinson in the possession of the editor. M & Co is unidentified.

127 This probably refers to DGR's twenty-first birthday which was on 8 March 1847.

128 Philip Dormer Stanhope, 4th Earl of Chesterfield (1694–1773), statesman and diplomatist chiefly remembered for his 'Letters' to his son. *DNB* Vol. 18 pp. 911–24.

129 DGR refers to the execution of three soldiers of the Meerut garrison. They were 3919 Gunner Richard Riley, 1st Troop 2nd Brigade Bengal Horse Artillery, executed on 20 October 1847 for striking a Medical Officer; 786 Private William Henry Fulcher Palmer, 9th Queen's Royal Lancers, executed on 23 October 1847 for throwing his cap at (i.e. striking) his Commanding Officer; 2398 Private Thomas Jardine, H.M.'s 32nd Foot, executed on ?27 October 1847 for striking Sergeant Thomas Bush. The executions fuelled a debate concerning punishments in the Army. *Delhi Gazette* 24.11.1847, *Supplement to the Delhi Gazette* 23 & 27.10.1847.

130 This implies that Lewis Brown went to India. A Mr Brown, gentleman, was listed as a steerage passenger on the *Minerva*, Capt. J. Greg, which sailed from Portsmouth and arrived at Calcutta in October. Other passengers

included a Mr Robinson, gentleman, and Miss Robinson. *The Bengal and Agra Directory and Annual Register for 1847*, pp. 490–1.

131 i.e. babies.

132 Sarah Miller married Lewis Brown at the Parish Church, Epsom, on 15 August 1848. This letter probably refers to the announcement of the engagement.

133 Shamsabad.

134 Jalalabad.

135 Dalip Singh (1838–93) was the son of Ranjit Singh and Rani Jindan. He was proclaimed Maharajah in September 1843 on the death of his elder brother, Sher Singh, but his mother acted as regent during his minority. Following the British annexation of the Punjab in 1849, Dalip Singh was granted a pension of £50,000 a year and exiled from the Punjab. Gupta, *op cit*, p. 63; Majumdar, *op cit*, pp. 290–1.

136 John Company – the Honourable East India Company. Yule & Burnell, *op cit*, p. 462.

137 Francis Foljambe Courtenay was appointed Private Secretary to Lord Dalhousie on 13 January 1848. He was a personal friend of Dalhousie and a barrister by profession. *The East India Register and Army List for 1849*, p. 42; Government of India *List of the Private Secretaries to the Governor General and Viceroys from 1774 to 1908 with Biographical Sketches*, pp. 45–6.

138 James Andrew Broun-Ramsey, 10th Earl of Dalhousie (1812–56) succeeded Lord Hardinge as Governor-General in January 1848. Dalhousie's period of office was characterised by an unusual degree of military activity, including the Second Sikh War (1848–9) and the Second Burma War (1852–3), meaning that by the end of his tenure the British dominions were over a third larger than before. However, Dalhousie established the Public Works Department and greatly improved communications as a result of the railway and telegraph systems, in addition to his social and educational reforms. Buckland, *op cit*, pp. 106–7.

139 William Courtenay, 10th Earl of Devon (1777–1859) was the son of the Right Reverend Henry Reginald, Bishop of Exeter, and succeeded his cousin, who died unmarried, in 1835. He was closely associated with the Irish Waste Land Improvement Society. *Debrett's Peerage, Baronetage, Knightage, and Companionage 1902*, p. 264.

140 Hon Emily Eden (1797–1869) was sister of Lord Auckland, whom she accompanied during his term as Governor General (1836–42). She published several works, amongst which were *Portraits of the People and Princes of India* (1844) and *Up the Country* (1866). Two volumes of her *Letters from India* were published by her niece in 1872. Buckland, *op cit*, p. 131.

141 Mordan (Sampson) & Co of 22 City Road & 50 Cheapside, London, *The Post Office London Directory 1843*, p. 698.

142 Rajoia.

143 DGR requested the chemical test box in the letter dated 4 December 1847, which reached England on 20 February 1848.

144 George Borlase Tremenheere (1809–96) Bengal Engineers. 2nd Lieutenant 1825, Lieutenant 1827, Captain 1839, Major 1848, Lieutenant-Colonel 1854, Colonel 1856, Hon Major-General 1856. At the time DGR stayed with him he was Superintending Engineer of the Punjab Circle, holding the appointment from 1847 to 1854. In 1844 he married Sarah Swaine Lumsden (née Hough), the daughter of an American clergyman. Her first husband, Captain John Lumsden of the Bengal Army, had been killed in 1841 when a crocodile bit off his leg as he was bathing. *Hodson Index*.

145 Mary Somerville (1780–1872) was perhaps the most brilliant female intellectual of her generation. She wrote several books on scientific subjects including *The Connection of Physical Sciences* (1834) and *Physical Geography* (1848). She lived most of her life after 1838 in Italy and died in Naples. *DNB* Vol. 18 pp. 662–3.

146 Frederick Currie (1799–1875) Indian Civil Service. Foreign Secretary to the Government of India 1842–7 during which time he drew up the treaty of peace after the First Sikh War. Made a Baronet in January 1847 and succeeded Sir Henry Lawrence as Resident at Lahore in 1848. He retired in 1853. Buckland, *op cit*, p. 104.

147 Herbert Edwardes (1819–68) 1st Bengal European Fusiliers. Ensign 1840, Lieutenant 1843, Captain 1850, Major 1850, Lieutenant-Colonel 1853, Colonel 1860, Major-General 1868. Served as ADC to Sir Hugh Gough during the First Sikh War and spent the remainder of his career on the North-West Frontier. It was largely due to his efforts that the fortress of Multan was captured in January 1849. *Hodson Index*.

148 Dera Ismail Khan.

149 Ultima Thule was the ancient Latin name of a country six days sailing north of Britain, supposed to be the most northerly region in the world.

150 The North Western Bank of India was based at Meerut but had branches at Bombay, Lahore, Calcutta and Mussooree. It had been established as the Mussoorie Bank in 1841. *The Bengal and Agra Directory and Annual Register for 1849*, pp. 322–3.

151 Harkishangarh.

152 Robert Campbell (1771–1858) spent twenty years as a merchant in Madras before becoming a director of the HEIC in 1817. He was created a Baronet in 1832. *Hodson Index*.

153 Usman Khattar.

154 Cockaigne – London.

155 Union Bank, Tank Square, Calcutta. Established in 1829. John Allan became a director in 1844. *The Bengal and Agra Directory and Annual Register for 1845*, p. 318.

156 A Thomas J. Fenton lived at 2 Goswell Road, London, in 1847 but had moved by 1848. *The Post Office London Directory for 1847*, p. 1565.

157 Vernons Hill House is located south west of Bishops Waltham, Hampshire.

158 Ninetta was travelling on the Continent as part of her education between 27 November 1847–19 April 1848, according to the cashbook of Daniel Robinson in the possession of Mrs B.R. Thomas. This turned out to be during a period of great political unrest on the Continent, referred to in the next letters.

159 Dewan Adjoodhia Pershaud of Jammu. *Abbott's Journal*, p. 3.

160 Harkishangarh.

161 Patrick Alexander Vans Agnew (1822–48) Indian Civil Service. He served as Assistant to the Superintendent of the Cis-Sutlej States before undertaking political work in Kashmir, followed by an appointment as an assistant to the Resident at Lahore. Buckland, *op cit*, p. 7.

162 Multan.

163 John Laird Mair Lawrence (1811–79) Bengal Civil Service. Served as Assistant and then District Officer at Delhi (1830–8, 1843–6). Hardinge made him Commissioner of the Trans-Sutlej Jalandhar Doab in 1846, when he acted as Resident at Lahore. After the annexation of the Punjab in 1849 he was appointed to the Board of Administration. His strong hold of the Punjab prevented unrest there in 1857 and his despatch of the 'moveable column' greatly aided military operations in northern India. Buckland, *op cit*, pp. 246–7.

164 DGR is referring to the unrest which broke out in Paris between 22–24 February 1848 as a result of King Louis Philippe's refusal to extend the franchise. Palmer, *op cit*, p. 233.

165 The Mutual Life Assurance Society was established in 1834 and based at 37 Old Jewry. Daniel Robinson, DGR's father, had been a director since 1836. *The Post Office London Directory for 1836*, p. 708.

166 Haripur.

167 Rani Jindan was deported from the Punjab in May 1848 on the orders of Sir Frederick Currie. She had been implicated in a plot against the Sikh regime and had laid plans for subverting the Company's sepoys. Cook, H.C.B. *The Sikh Wars: the British Army in the Punjab 1845–1849*, pp. 118–19.

168 Social disorder troubled the governments of Italy (from February) and Austria, Hungary and various German states from March onwards. Palmer, *op cit*, p. 233. Ninetta witnessed disturbances in Naples.

169 DGR's youngest brother John Harding Robinson, usually referred to as 'Jack' in these letters.

170 Jarl.

171 Sherwan Khurd.

172 This refers to the action at Kineyree which was fought on 18 June between Herbert Edwardes with approximately 11,500 men and six guns and Rung Ram with 8,000–10,000 Multanis and ten guns. The battle commenced shortly after 7 a.m. and was over by 4.30 p.m., with the retreat of the Multani force and the capture of all but two of their guns. Edwardes, H.B. *A Year on the Punjab Frontier in 1848–49*, Vol. 2, pp. 380–400.

173 Nawab Bhawal Khan of Bhawalpore (a province located south of the River Sutlej) commanded a column of Daudpatras or 'Sons of David' numbering some 8,500 men which commenced co-operating with Edwardes' forces in May 1848. Edwardes, *op cit*, pp. 244–97.

174 Leiah.

175 Dera Ghazi Khan.

176 Dera Ghazi Khan was occupied by Moolraj's allies in early May 1848. The action at Leia was fought on 16 May 1848 between a picquet of Pathan levies recently raised by Edwardes and the advanced party of Moolraj's troops. The Pathans beat off the rebels without loss and pursued them for several miles. Edwardes, *op cit*, 2, pp. 217–19, 221–3.

177 This refers to Lieutenant Edward Lake, Bengal Engineers, who was appointed by Sir Frederick Currie to act as Political Officer to Bhawal Khan's force on 9 June, but in practice became the commander of this column. He had previously been Acting Deputy Commissioner in Jullundur. Edwardes, *op cit*, 2, pp. 325–9.

178 Edwardes wrote a series of pieces which were published in the *Delhi Gazette* in 1847 entitled 'Brahmini Bull's letters in India to his cousin John Bull in England' criticising the military and political system.

179 DGR requested the telescope in the letter dated 6 December 1846. George Dollond, 59 St Paul's Churchyard. *The Post Office London Directory for 1848*, p. 1401.

180 A negative eyepiece of an optical instrument invented by Huygens, consisting of two plan-convex lenses, with their plane sides towards the eye.

181 Charles Robinson was serving as a Mate on board HMS *Thetis* at this time. His insubordination had been officially reported in November 1847 and again in February 1848. Despite this, he was promoted to Lieutenant in June, but subsequently jumped ship and was dismissed the service on 15 December. PRO ADM 196/37 p. 1160.

182 The Bengal Horse Artillery wore shoulder scales on their shell jackets between 1841 and 1851. Infantry officers, on the other hand, had shoulder straps with a gold plaited cord on the shell jacket. Carman, W.Y. *Indian Army Uniforms under the British from the 18th century to 1947. Artillery Engineers and Infantry*, (1969), pp. 4–5, 105.

183 Hoshiarpur.

184 Charles Francis Robinson served on board HMS *Thetis* as a Midshipman until 28 June 1848 when he was promoted to Lieutenant and joined HMS *Hibernia*. PRO ADM 196/6.

185 These were Lieutenant Edward Lake who joined Edwardes on 28 June, Mr G. Quin, a second clerk at the Lahore Residency, who arrived about a week before, Lieutenant Harry Lumsden who joined on 5 July and Mr Hugo James, a volunteer, who arrived at about the same time. Dr Cole arrived from Lahore in mid July as a result of an accident by which Edwardes shot himself through the right hand with a pistol on 3 July. The river steamers

were commanded by Captain Christopher and Mr McLawrin. Edwardes, *op cit*, 1, pp. 313–15; 2, pp. 421–2, 461–3, 502, 504–5.

186 DGR's assistant at this time was James Scott Ingram (1829–c.67) 1st European Bengal Fusiliers. Ensign 1849, Lieutenant 1854, Captain 1861 (in the Army) 1863 (in the Regiment). Ingram was given a commission for the good work he did as an Assistant Surveyor under Major Abbott. IOL MSS EUR F 171/25; *Hodson Index*.

187 Captain James Abbott.

188 This probably refers to the partnership of Fletcher, Alexander & Co.

189 Bagshawe & Co., British merchants and agents, No. 1 Church Lane, Calcutta. The partners were William Clode Braddon, Thomas Charles Cadogan and James Church. *The Bengal & Agra Directory and Annual Register for 1847*, p. 330.

190 Edwardes fought Mulraj at Saddoosam on 1 July in a battle which resulted in the Sikhs being driven into the fortress of Multan. A further engagement was fought two days later. Edwardes, *op cit*, Vol. 2, pp. 442–54.

191 Fletcher, Alexander & Co., East India merchants and agents, 10 King's Arms Yard, Coleman Street, London. *The Bengal & Agra Directory & Annual Register for 1847*, p. 5.

192 Unidentified. There was no soldier of this name in any of the Company's Bengal or Bombay regiments. IOL L/MIL/10/123 Bengal registers of European soldiers in H.C. Service 1788–1839, names L–Z; IOL L/MIL/10/125 Ditto, 1840–1850, names L–Z. IOL L/MIL/12/110 Registers of Bombay Army European soldiers 1795–1839, names L–Z; IOL L/MIL/12/112 Ditto, 1840–1850, names L–Z.

193 John Evans was a servant living in London before he enlisted in the 1st Bombay European Regiment on 7 July 1840. He sailed to India on the ship *Sir Edward Paget* later that year and was subsequently transferred to the 2nd Bombay European Regiment where he was placed in No. 4 Company. He died at Aden on 3 November 1848 and was buried the following day by Assistant Chaplain George Percy Badger. His age in the muster books was given as 27 in 1848, which would have made his year of birth 1820 or 1821, but the burial register gave his age as 26 years and 4 months which would place his birth in July 1822. IOL L/MIL/12/111 Registers of Bombay Army European soldiers 1840–1850, names A–K; IOL L/MIL/12/179 Bombay Army muster rolls and casualty returns Sept. 1848; IOL N/3/22 Bombay burials 1848.

194 The date of this letter was actually August 1848, as revealed by the internal evidence (see note 19).

195 Colonel Canora was an American in Sikh service who commanded a troop of horse artillery. On 6 August 1848 he refused to deploy his guns for the defence of Haripur when Captain Abbott surrounded the town with locally raised levies. The Sikhs remonstrated with him, but on his continued refusal he was shot. Mahajan, *op cit*, pp. 80–1.

196 Margala.

197 Charles Francis Robinson was promoted to Lieutenant in the Royal Navy on 28 June 1848.

198 The background to these events has been outlined in the Introduction. Chattar Singh lost the battle of Gujerat on 21 February 1849 and surrendered to General Gilbert at Rawalpindi on 12 March. Mahajan, *op cit*, pp. 77–82; Singh, *op cit*, pp. 83, 139.

199 Purwanna – a grant or letter under a royal seal, or a letter of authority from an official to his subordinate. Yule & Burnell, *op cit*, p. 744.

200 Sirdar Jhunder Singh was sent by Sir Frederick Currie to negotiate with the Sikh troops in Hazara in order to return them to their allegiance. He was actually in sympathy with them and managed to gain sufficient time (whilst pretending to negotiate) for the Sikh force at Haripur to join up with that of Chattar Singh. *Abbott's Journal*, pp. 232–5.

201 Abbott states that Chattar Singh had 4 Sikh regiments, 400 irregulars and 8 guns. *Abbott's Journal*, p. 235.

202 Dhamtaur.

203 This is a fairly accurate description of the action fought by Abbott and Nicholson on 11 September in the Dhamtaur Pass. Their forces numbered 1,000–1,500 matchlockmen, 300 cavalry, but no guns, compared to the Sikhs' 4000 men, 10 guns and 40 zumbooras. This numerical difference ensured a Sikh victory, for which Abbott had been prepared by ordering Robinson to disband his levies and rejoin the main force; this he did on 12 September. *Abbott's Journal*, pp. 241–2.

204 DGR would have heard stories from his Father about Spanish customs during the Peninsular War.

205 Mansehra.

206 The Commander-in-Chief was General Lord Gough, who had been appointed on 11 August 1843. *The East India Register and Army List for 1848*, p. 3.

207 Sir Frederick Currie's assistants at this time were: Lieutenant-Colonel H.M. Lawrence (Resident at Lahore); A.H. Cocks (Chief Assistant); Major G.H. Macgregor and Captain G. St P. Lawrence (Principal Assistants); Lieutenant H.B. Edwardes (First Assistant); Lieutenant H.B. Lumsden and Lieutenant J. Nicholson (Assistants); Lieutenant R.G. Taylor, Mr P.S. Melvill and Lieutenant F.R. Pollock (Extra Assistants). *The Bengal & Agra Directory and Annual Register for 1848*, p. 75.

208 John Hunter Littler (1783–1856). Joined the 2/18th Bengal Native Infantry as Ensign 1800, Lieutenant 1800, Captain 1814, Major 1824, Lieutenant-Colonel 1828, Colonel 1834, Major-General 1841, Lieutenant-General 1851. Commanded at Ferozepore 1845 and later the 4th Division. Awarded the KCB 1844, GCB 1848. Deputy Governor of Bengal 1849–52. *Hodson Index*.

209 William Sampson Whish (1787–1853) Bengal Artillery. Lieutenant 1804,

Captain Lieutenant 1807, Captain 1815, Major 1824, Lieutenant-Colonel 1827, Colonel 1838, Major-General 1841, Lieutenant-General 1851. Commanded the Punjab Division at Lahore 1848 and subsequently the Multan Field Force. He later commanded the 1st Division. Awarded the KCB 1849. *Hodson Index.*

210 Hubert Garbett (1803–58) Bengal Artillery. 2nd Lieutenant 1819, Lieutenant 1822, Captain 1836, Major 1846, Lieutenant-Colonel 1851, Brevet Colonel 1854. Participated in the Second Sikh War commanding the artillery at Lahore February 1848, and throughout the siege of Multan. He also commanded the artillery of General Whish's division. *Hodson Index.*

211 Andrew Hervey (1790–1862) Joined the 4th Bengal Native Infantry as Ensign 1806, Lieutenant 1811, Captain 1824, Major 1832, Lieutenant-Colonel 1838, Colonel 1849, Major-General 1854, Lieutenant-General 1861. Commanded the 1st Infantry Brigade during the Second Sikh War. Awarded the CB 1849. *Hodson Index.*

212 Robert Cornelius Napier (1810–90) Bengal Engineers. 2nd Lieutenant 1861, Lieutenant 1827, Captain 1841, Major 1854, Lieutenant-Colonel 1856, Colonel 1861, Major-General 1861, Lieutenant-General 1867, General 1874, Field Marshal 1883. Served in both Sikh Wars and as Chief Engineer in the Punjab 1849–56. He later became Commander-in-Chief Bombay 1865–9 and Commander-in-Chief India 1870–6. Awarded the KCB 1858, GCSI 1867, GCB 1868. *Hodson Index.*

213 James Eckford (1786–1867). After service in the Royal Navy as a Midshipman he joined the 3rd Bengal Native Infantry as Ensign 1805, Lieutenant 1806, Captain 1823, Major 1831, Lieutenant-Colonel 1837, Colonel 1848, Major-General 1854, Lieutenant-General 1861. Commanded the 3rd Infantry Brigade in the Second Sikh War. Awarded the CB 1849. *Hodson Index.*

214 Aeolia – a district of Asia Minor anciently colonized by Greeks.

215 Nawashahr.

216 Najib – Mahommedan irregular infantry. Ranjit Singh had one regiment and the British government retained several as militia. Whitworth, *op cit*, p. 220.

217 Sardar Gulab Singh Pohuwindia was appointed Governor of Peshawar in May 1847 and was pro-British in outlook. His son was Colonel Alla Singh. Political diary of Major George St P. Lawrence, Principal Assistant to the Agent to the Governor-General, North-West Frontier, at Peshawur. In *Journals and diaries of the Assistants to the Agent, Governor-General North-West Frontier and Resident at Lahore 1846–1849*, pp. 349, 363.

218 Dost Muhammad Khan (1783–1863) was Amir of Afghanistan when he was deposed by the British who installed Shah Shuja on the throne. British influence in Afghanistan received a severe setback in the First Afghan War, as a result of which Dost Muhammad regained the throne and ruled 1842–63. He was promised the province of Peshawar if the Sikhs were successful in the Second Sikh War, and this secured his participation against the British. Mahajan, *op cit*, p. 84; Singh, *op cit*, p. 139.

219 George St Patrick Lawrence (1804–84) 2nd Bengal Light Cavalry. Cornet 1821, Lieutenant 1824, Captain 1844, Major 1860, Brevet Lieutenant-Colonel 1849, Brevet Colonel 1854, Major-General 1861, Hon Lieutenant-General 1867. Served in the First Afghan War before being appointed Assistant Political Agent at Peshawar in 1846. *Hodson Index.*

220 Charles Vincent Bowie (1824–98) Bengal Artillery. 2nd Lieutenant 1841, Lieutenant 1845, Captain 1856, Brevet Major 1856, Lieutenant-Colonel 1862, Brevet Colonel 1868, Hon Major-General 1872. Present during the attack on the Peshawur Residency by the Sikhs 1848. Taken prisoner by the Afghans and afterwards by the Sikhs for 4 1/2 months. *Hodson Index.*

221 Garhi Habibullah.

222 Muzaffarabad.

223 Urie.

224 Punch.

225 Edward Law, First Earl of Ellenborough (1790–1871) pursued a political career which commenced with his election to Parliament in 1813. He subsequently served as President of the Board of Control (1828–30, 1834–5, 1841, 1858) before being appointed Governor-General of India (1842–4). Although he aimed at pursuing a peaceful policy, his period of tenure included the end of the First Afghan War, the annexation of Sind and the First China War. He was recalled by the Court of Directors and was subsequently created an Earl in 1846. His favouritism for military officers made him unpopular with civilians during his Indian career. Buckland, *op cit*, pp. 134–5.

226 Major George Lawrence, Lieutenant Bowie and Dr Thompson were being held at Kohat.

227 Charles Herbert (1820–97) joined the 18th Bengal Native Infantry as Ensign 1841, Lieutenant 1845, Captain 1855, Major 1861, Lieutenant-Colonel 1867, Colonel 1872, Hon Major-General 1878. He served under the Resident at Lahore in 1848 and was responsible for the defence of Attock against Chutter Singh between November 1848 and January 1849. He subsequently served as Political Agent and then Consul General at Baghdad 1868–71.

228 Charles Robert Cureton (1789–1848) HM's 16th Lancers. Cornet 1814, Lieutenant 1816, Captain 1825, Major 1833, Lieutenant-Colonel 1839, Colonel 1846. He served at Bhurtpore (1825–6), in the First Afghan War (1839) and in the Gwalior campaign (1843) in which he commanded a cavalry brigade. He was killed at the battle of Ramnugger during the Second Sikh War whilst leading a cavalry brigade. Annand, A. McK. 'Brigadier-General C.R. Cureton, CB, ADC.' In *Journal of the Society for Army Historical Research* 47 (1969), pp. 157–60; Buckland, *op cit*, p. 103.

229 Ramnagar.

230 Hugh Gough (1779–1869) HM's 87th Foot. Ensign 1794, Lieutenant 1794,

Captain 1803, Major 1805, Lieutenant-Colonel 1809, Colonel 1819, Major-General 1830, Lieutenant-General 1841, General 1854, Field Marshal 1862. Commanded the Anglo-Indian forces in the First China War (1841–2) for which he was awarded the GCB and made a Baronet. He was appointed Commander-in-Chief India in 1843 and as such commanded the army in both Sikh Wars after which he was created a Viscount. He was awarded the KP in 1857 and the KCSI in 1861. Buckland, *op cit*, pp. 172–3; *Hart's Army List* 1869 p. 3.

231   Dopatta.

232   Urie.

233   Arthur Herbert Cocks was Chief Assistant to the Resident at Lahore, having been appointed on 26 December 1846. *The Bengal and Agra Directory and Annual Register for 1849*, p. 42.

234   There is no place of this name but DGR was probably encamped at Chuk Janoo Khan, which appears on the nineteenth century Indian Atlas map series but not on the twentieth century Survey of India maps.

235   This probably refers to Sir Robert Campbell. See Letter 27.

236   Govindgarh.

237   Jullundur.

238   Ludhiana.

239   These were HM's 24th, 29th and 61st Foot and the 2nd Bengal European Regiment. Fortescue, J.W. *A History of the British Army*, Vol. 12, pp. 433–4.

240   There were two heavy batteries commanded by Major Horsford. Each heavy battery was composed of four 18lb guns and two 8" howitzers. Fortescue, *op cit*, 12, p. 450.

241   Four columns attacked the fort. Two were each led by five companies of the 60th Foot and the other pair by three companies each of the 10th and 32nd Foot. Fortescue, *op cit*, 12, p. 444.

242   Unknown to DGR, his Father had died earlier in March and his sister had moved to a different address.

243   Substantial extracts from DGR's letters dated 10 and 31 October 1848 (letters 40 and 41), were published in *The Delhi Gazette* of Wednesday 14 March 1849 p. 166. These letters criticised Sir Frederick Currie and the senior officers commanding the troops sent against Multan. It may be noted that DGR's brother Charles had access to these letters, as he was at home after being dismissed the service.

244   Bakrala.

245   Hassan Abdal.

246   This does not appear on the 1" Survey of India map series.

247   Naushahra.

248   Jamrud.

249   Ambala.

250   This addressed was owned by William Drew, baker. *The Post Office Directory for 1851*, p. 175.

251 Edward Thomas (1813–86) was a noted Indian antiquary. He joined the Bengal Civil Service in 1832, but his career was plagued by illness which caused him to turn down the post of Foreign Secretary to the Government of India in 1852. He retired five years later and devoted the rest of his life to academic pursuits, in particular the study of Bactrian, Indo-Scythic and Sassanian coins. He published 'Coins of the Kings of Ghazni' (1847), and 'Initial Coinage of Bengal' (1884) amongst other works. *DNB* Vol. 19, pp. 658–9.

252 Copy of a letter in the possession of Dr David Greathead. The original is no longer extant.

253 This letter was addressed to James Henry Greathead (1819–64).

254 James Henry Greathead was married to Julia Wright and had had ten children by this date.

255 Pontac – unidentified; Stein – a generic name for any South African medium dry white wine.

256 DGR married Jane Amelia Graham at Mussoorie on 9 September 1851. They had four children by this date of whom the youngest, Florence Mary, died in 1860.

257 John Ward Harding. The family moved from Laugharne to Taunton by 1847 and from there to Switzerland by 1851.

258 This may refer to Frank Greathead, James Henry Greathead's eldest paternal uncle, who would have been born before 1791.

259 Arthur Greathead was the eighth child of James Henry Greathead and died in 1860 aged four.

260 John Hutcheson Fergusson, merchant and agent, of 77 Clive Street, Calcutta. Residence 36-1 Park Street, Calcutta. His assistant was Charles Tovey who lived at 42 Mott's Lane, Calcutta. *The New Calcutta Directory for the Town of Calcutta for 1860*, Part viii p. 29, part ix pp. 211, 274.

261 The letter was written on Bengal United Service Club notepaper.

262 Cecil Beadon (1816–81) Bengal Civil Service. He arrived in India in 1836 and during his career held the posts of Secretary to the Government of Bengal, Home Secretary to the Government of India and Foreign Secretary. He was a member of the Governor-General's Council and his final appointment was as Lieutenant-Governor of Bengal, 1862–6. He was made a KCSI in 1866. *DNB* Vol. 1 pp. 1379–81.

263 Herbert Bruce (1826–66) 7th Bombay Native Infantry. Ensign 1842, Lieutenant 1844, Captain 1855, Brevet Major 1858, Brevet Lieutenant-Colonel 1859. He was awarded the CB in 1858. *Hodson Index*.

264 Robert Murray (1829–1889) Bengal Artillery. 2nd Lieutenant 1845, Lieutenant 1849, 2nd Captain 1858, Captain 1863, Bengal Staff Corps 1865, Major 1865, Lieutenant-Colonel 1871, Major-General 1886, CSI 1884. He was appointed Director of the Western Division of the Electric Telegraph Department on 22 January 1862. *Hodson Index*; *The Indian Army and Civil Service List*, January 1865. Allen. London. p. 78.

Notes to Appendices

1   Patrick Carty was a land surveyor from Galway. He enlisted into the Bengal Engineers at Limerick on 15 November 1845 for a term of unlimited service and proceeded to India on board the ship *Dartmouth* in 1847. He was promoted to Sergeant before being permitted to purchase his discharge in order to join his family in Ireland. He embarked on the ship *Coldstream* on 8 November 1851. IOL L/MIL/10/124 Bengal register of European soldiers in H.C. service 1840–1850, names A–K.

2   Andrew Scott Waugh (1810–78) Bengal Engineers. 2nd Lieutenant 1827, Lieutenant 1827, Captain 1844, Local Lieutenant-Colonel 1847, Lieutenant-Colonel 1857, Colonel 1861, Hon Major-General 1861. He joined the Great Trigonometrical Survey as a Sub-Assistant in 1832 and became Superintendent and Surveyor General of India in 1843. *Hodson Index*.

3   Khalashie or Khalasi – literally, a tent pitcher. Probably in this case meaning a servant or assistant. Whitworth, *op cit*, p. 158.

4   No Sergeant Denton could be found in any of the Bengal or Bombay Army registers of European soldiers. IOL L/MIL/10/122 Bengal Registers of European soldiers in H.C. Service 1788–1839, names A–K; IOL L/MIL/10/124 1840–1850 names A–K; IOL L/MIL/12/109 Registers of Bombay Army European soldiers 1795–1839, names A–K; IOL L/MIL/12/111 1840–1850 names A–K.

5   Leeson caused trouble amongst the local traders in January 1848 by 'taking their goods at his own arbitrary price.' He also committed irregularities over the hire of labour. Abbott's judgement was that Leeson would jeopardise the goodwill and respect rendered by the local population towards the survey party. *Abbott's Journal* pp. 123, 125.

6   Unidentified.

7   Peter Stark Lumsden (1829–1918) 60th Bengal Native Infantry. Ensign 1847, Lieutenant 1854, Captain 1861, Major in the Army 1861, Lieutenant-Colonel in the Army 1866, Major in the Regiment 1867, Brevet Colonel 1870, CSI 1870, Lieutenant-Colonel in the Regiment 1873, CB 1873, KCB 1879, Major-General 1881, GCB 1885. Like DGR, he was educated at Stoton & Mayor and subsequently at Addiscombe. *Hodson Index*.

8   Henry Pelham Burn (1807–82) 1st Bengal Native Infantry. Ensign 1824, Lieutenant 1825, Captain 1837, Major 1855, Lieutenant-Colonel 1859, Brevet Colonel 1855, Hon Major-General 1861. *Hodson Index*.

9   Henry Miers Elliot (1808–53) Bengal Civil Service. Served in the North Western Provinces before becoming Foreign Secretary to the Government of India in 1847. He accompanied Lord Hardinge and then Lord Dalhousie to the Punjab and negotiated the treaty with the Sikhs in 1849. Buckland, *op cit*, pp. 135–6.

10 Edward Clive Bayley (1821–84) Bengal Civil Service. Arrived in India in 1842 and served in the North Western Provinces and the Punjab before being appointed Under Secretary to the Foreign Department in 1849. Was subsequently Foreign Secretary to the Government of India for a brief period in 1861 and then Home Secretary 1862–72. Buckland, *op cit*, pp. 30–1.

Bibliography

(a) Unpublished sources

Oriental and India Office Library and Records, London

E/4/212	Letters received from India and Bengal,	Jan–Mar 1850
E/4/215	" " " " " "	Aug–Sep 1850
E/4/806 p. 581	Despatches to India and Bengal,	Sep–Oct 1850
E/4/808 p. 985	" " " " "	Feb–Mar 1851
E/4/809 pp. 75–6	" " " " "	Apr–May 1851
E/4/815 p. 1605	" " " " "	Apr–Jun 1852
F/4/2362	Board's Collections	1849–1850
F/4/2397	" " "	1850–1851
Z/F/4/12	Register of Board's Collections	1850–1851

L/MIL/9/197	Cadet Papers, 1840–1841	
L/MIL/10/78 pp. 232–3	Officers' service records, Bengal Army 1860–93	
L/MIL/10/84 pp. 104–5	" " " " " "	
L/MIL/10/122	Bengal Army European soldiers, 1788–1839,	A–K
L/MIL/10/123	" " " " " " "	L–Z
L/MIL/10/124	" " " " " " 1840–1850,	A–K
L/MIL/10/125	" " " " " " "	L–Z
L/MIL/12/109	Bombay Army European soldiers, 1795–1839,	A–K
L/MIL/12/110	" " " " " " "	L–Z
L/MIL/12/111	" " " " " " 1840–1850,	A–K
L/MIL/12/112	" " " " " " "	L–Z
L/MIL/12/179	Bombay Army muster rolls and casualty returns Sept. 1848	

MSS   Eur F 171/25 Abbott, J. Narrative of events in the Huzara District, Punjaub, during the struggle of the Sikhs for their liberty in AD 1849/50, 2 Vols.

N/3/22 Bombay burials 1848.

X/1737/1/1–4   Military map of Hazara, surveyed by Lieut. D.G. Robinson, Engineers, in 1848–9. Revised and adjusted under the directions of Lieut. Col. A.S. Waugh, Surveyor-General of India, on the basis of the Great Trigonometrical Survey of India in 1854–5.

X/1738   Report upon the military survey of Hazara by Lieut D.G. Robinson, 1847–49, and finished 1853.

X/1800 Survey of that part of the boundary between the British and Jamoo territories from the Ravi to the Jhilam, triangulated and surveyed by Lieut. D.G. Robinson, Engineers, and Messrs. H.B. Talbot, Joseph James, and J.P. Platts, Sub-assistants Great Trigonometrical Survey under the instructions of Lieut.-Col. A.S. Waugh, Engineers, Surveyor-General of India, 1850–51.

National Army Museum, London
Hodson Index

Public Record Office, London
ADM 11/46   Records of service for Assistant Paymasters.
ADM 13/79   Pursers' passing certificates.
ADM 196/6   Officers' records of service, 1843–75.
ADM 196/11 Paymasters' registers of service, 1852–61.
ADM 196/37 Officers' records of service, 1846–1867.

British Library, London
Add Mss 39,997 Letters to Gen. C.R. Fox 1837–1870 etc. f. 21.
Add Mss 43,990 Correspondence and papers of Lt-Col Herbert Bruce f. 228.

(b) Published sources – newspapers

Delhi Gazette
Supplements to the Delhi Gazette

(c) Published sources – maps and atlases

Indian Atlas map series. Scale 1/4": 1 mile.
Survey of India map series. Various editions. Scale 1":1 mile.
The Times Atlas of the World, Comprehensive Edition. Times Books. 1993.

(d) Published sources – books and periodicals

(all books published in London unless noted otherwise)

An Anglo-Indian Dictionary (Kegan Paul).
Annand, A. McK., 'Brigadier-General C.R. Cureton, C.B., A.D.C.' in *Journal of the Society for Army Historical Research*, 47, 1969.
Anon *Historical records of the 103rd Royal Bombay Fusiliers* (Swiss, Devonport, 1875?)

Beale, T.W., *An Oriental Biographical Dictionary* (Allen, 1894).

Bengal and Agra Directory & Annual Register (Samuel Smith & Co. Calcutta, 1845, 1847, 1849).

Bruce, G., *Six battles for India* (Arthur Baker, 1969).

Buckland, C.E., *Dictionary of Indian Biography* (Swan Sonnenschein, 1906).

Cambridge, Marquess of 'Notes on the Armies of India'. In *Journal of the Society for Army Historical Research* 47 pp. 65–156 (1969).

Carman, W.Y., *Indian Army Uniforms under the British from the 18th century to 1947. Artillery, Engineers and Infantry* (Morgan-Grampian, 1969).

Colyer, W.J., 'The Maharajah Ranjit Singh and his Foreign Officers', in *Royal United Service Institution Journal* 99 pp. 90–4 (1954).

Cook, H.C.B., *The Sikh Wars: the British Army in the Punjab 1845–1849* (Leo Cooper, 1975).

Cunningham, J.D., *A History of the Sikhs from the Origin of the Nation to the Battles of the Sutlej* (1849). Revised edition edited by H.L.O. Garrett and reprinted by Asian Educational Services, New Delhi, 1994.

Debrett's Peerage, Baronetage, Knightage, and Companionage 1902 (Dean & Son).

East-India Register and Directory. Volumes for 1844–1845.

East-India Register and Army List. Volumes for 1847–1849 (Allen & Co.).

Edwardes, H.B., *A Year on the Punjab Frontier in 1848–49*, 2 Vols, (Richard Bentley, 1851).

Fortescue, J.W., (1899–1930) *A History of the British Army*, 13 Vols. Vol. 12 (Macmillan, 1899–1930).

Government of India *List of the Private Secretaries to the Governors-General and Viceroys from 1774 to 1908 with biographical sketches* (Government Press, Calcutta, 1908).

Gupta, H.R., *Panjab on the Eve of the First Sikh War* (Panjab University, Chandigarh, 1956.) 2nd Revised edition 1975.

Hart's Army List 1869.

Hunter, W.W., (1881) *The Imperial Gazetteer of India*. 11 Vols. (Trübner, 1881).

Lawrence, J., *Lawrence of Lucknow*. (Hodder & Stoughton, 1990).

Lloyds Register of British and Foreign Shipping 1842, Lloyds.

Madras Almanac and Compendium of Intelligence for 1845. Edmund Marsden. Madras.

Mahajan, J., *Annexation of the Punjab: an Historical Revision*. Revised edition 1990 (Spantech, New Delhi, 1949).

Majumdar, R.C., 'The rise and fall of the Sikh kingdom.' In Majumdar, R.C. (ed.), *The History and Culture of the Indian People: British Paramountcy and Indian Renaissance* Part 1. (Bharatiya Vidya Bhawan, Bombay, 1963).

New Calcutta Directory for the town of Calcutta for 1860. (Thacker, Spink & Co. Calcutta).

Palmer, A.W., (1962) *A Dictionary of Modern History 1789–1945* (Penguin, 1962).

Parliamentary Papers *Papers relating to the Punjab 1847–1849. Presented to both Houses of Parliament by command of Her Majesty. May 1849.*

Phillimore, R.H., *Historical Records of the Survey of India*. 5 Vols. (Survey of India, Dehra Dun, 1945–65). Vol. 5.

Post Office London Directory for 1836 (Critchett).

Post Office London Directory (Kelly, 1843–1851).

Punjab Government, *Gazetteer of the Rawalpindi District 1883–4* (Civil and Military Gazette Press, Lahore, 1884).

Punjab Government, Journals and diaries of Captain J. Abbott 1846–1849. In *Journals and diaries of the Assistants to the Agent, Governor-General North-West Frontier and Resident at Lahore 1846–1849* (Pioneer Press, Allahabad, 1911).

— Political diary of Major George St P. Lawrence, Principal Assistant to the Agent to the Governor-General, North-West Frontier, at Peshawur. In *Journals and diaries of the Assistants to the Agent, Governor-General North-West Frontier and Resident at Lahore 1846–1849* (Pioneer Press, Allahabad, 1911).

Sandes, E.W.C., *The Indian Sappers and Miners* (The Institution of Royal Engineers, Chatham, 1948).

Sattin, A. (ed.) *An Englishwoman in India. The Memoirs of Harriet Tytler 1828–1858* (Oxford University Press, 1986).

Singh, B.S., *The Jammu fox: a biography of Maharaja Gulab Singh of Kashmir, 1792–1857* (Southern Illinois University Press, Carbondale & Edwardsville, 1974).

Steel's Navy List, 1854–1859.

Stephen, L. & Lee, S. (eds.), *Dictionary of National Biography*. 22 Vols. 1973 edition (OUP, Oxford, 1885–1901).

Thornton, E., (1844) *A gazetteer of the countries adjacent to India on the North-West including Sinde, Afghanistan, Beloochistan, the Punjab, and the neighbouring states*. 2 Vols. (Allen & Co., 1844).

— *A gazetteer of the territories under the government of the East-India Company and of the native states on the continent of India*. 4 Vols. (Allen & Co., 1854).

— *A gazetteer of the territories under the Government of the East-India Company, and of the native states on the continent of India*. (Allen & Co., 1857).

Watson, H.D., (1908) *Gazetteer of the Hazara district, 1907* (Chatto & Windus).

Whitworth, G.C., *An Anglo-Indian Dictionary* (Kegan Paul, 1885).

Yule, H. & Burnell, A.C., *Hobson Jobson* (Murray, 1903).

III
The Reverend George S. Duncan at GHQ, 1916–1918

Edited by
GERARD J. DeGROOT

Acknowledgements

This project would have been much more arduous and much less enjoyable without the help of my wife Sharon Roe who transcribed the Duncan diaries and, for me, brought the documents alive with her stories, over dinner, of what the Reverend had been doing that day. Duncan's handwriting is not as illegible as some, but he did have the annoying habit of writing in pencil which has, over the years, faded terribly. I am optimistic that Sharon will forgive me, someday, for the eye strain she suffered.

Both Sharon and I would like to thank Bob Smart, the archivist of the University of St Andrews Library for his tireless efforts in searching out the relevant Duncan material. My postgraduate student Alison Brown provided valuable help in chasing down the identities of the chaplains and other individuals mentioned in the text. Special thanks go to the Earl Haig and Dr Douglas Duncan for permission to quote from their respective father's papers and for commenting on the material. I have attempted to contact the holders of the copyright for the various letters to Duncan, but to no avail. If anyone's copyright has been inadvertently infringed, I hope that my sincere apologies will be accepted.

I am grateful for the research grants provided by the British Academy and the University of St Andrews. Finally, for help with the countless small tasks which arise in the editing of diaries and letters, I would like to extend my very sincere thanks to: Ian Beckett, Jane Dawson, Barry Doyle, Heather Hamill, Norman Macdougall, James Sheets, Steve Spackman, Alan Sykes, and Tony Upton.

Dr Gerard J. DeGroot
St Andrews, 1994

Abbreviations used in the Text

ADC	Aide-de-camp
Adv. GHQ	Advanced General Headquarters
AG	Adjutant-General
ASC	Army Signal Corps
Asst.	Assistant
BEF	British Expeditionary Force
Bp.	Bishop
Brig.	Brigadier
Capt.	Captain
CCS	Casualty Clearing Station
CGS	Chief of the General Staff
CIGS	Chief of the Imperial General Staff
CinC	Commander-in-Chief
C. of E.	Church of England
Co.	Company
Col.	Colonel
Con.	Conservative
Coy.	Company
Cpl.	Corporal
D.A.P.C.	Deputy Assistant Principal Chaplain
Div.	Division
DMI	Director of Military Intelligence
FM	Field Marshal
Gen.	General
GHQ	General Headquarters
GOC	General Officer Commanding
Hd.Qrs.	Headquarters
H.E.	High Explosive
H.L.I.	Highland Light Infantry
Hon.	Honorary, Honourable
H.Q.	Headquarters
Lib.	Liberal
Lieut., Lt.	Lieutenant

Maj.	Major
MP	Member of Parliament
MSS	manuscripts, manuscript collection
NLS	National Library of Scotland
QMG	Quartermaster–General
RA	Royal Artillery
RAMC	Royal Army Medical Corps
RC	Roman Catholic
RE	Royal Engineers
Rev.	Reverend
RS	Royal Scottish, Royal Scots
Rt. Rev.	Right Reverend
Sec.	Secretary
Sgt.	Sergeant
St.A.	University of St Andrews
U.P.	United Presbyterian
US	United States
YMCA	Young Men's Christian Association

Introduction

The Duncan diaries, which form the bulk of the following documents, provide a glimpse not just into the life of their author, the Reverend George Duncan, but also into that of Field Marshal Douglas Haig, the Commander-in-Chief of the British Expeditionary Force from 1915 to 1918. Duncan and Haig were together from March 1916 until the end of the war. The commander attended nearly every one of the padre's services and had Duncan as a guest at lunch nearly every Sunday. Though it would be inaccurate to describe the two men as intimates (a very rigid decorum and sense of hierarchy prevailed), nevertheless Duncan observed a side of Haig which perhaps no one else saw. An interesting symbiosis developed between the two men. Haig felt a spiritual hunger which became especially acute after he became Commander-in-Chief, and Duncan seems to have satisfied that hunger. Duncan in turn discovered a very special and important calling in serving Haig.

Duncan's diaries are also important for the glimpse they give of Haig's GHQ. Duncan was the true 'outsider as insider': a man with no military experience who was suddenly thrown into a community of staff officers who manned the control room of the British war machine. He dined and spoke with the most senior military and political figures of his day, from all the allied nations. His observations of this environment are uniquely revealing. At the same time, he often ventured outside the ramparts of Montreuil, where GHQ was located. He attended social clubs, church services and Casualty Clearing Stations near to the fighting front. He saw and heard of the effects of the war on junior officers and ordinary soldiers and was therefore closer to the 'real war' than was Haig. One often senses, in reading the diaries, that Duncan was torn between his devotion to Haig and his sensitivity to the sufferings of the common soldiers, whose spiritual needs would have seemed more immediate and profound.

The relationship with Duncan is perhaps not surprising given Haig's upbringing and his religious background. Born in Edinburgh in 1861, Haig was the youngest son of a stern, ill-tempered Fife whisky distiller who founded the firm which still bears his name.[1] As a boy, he was exhorted by his pious mother to seek God's guidance in any difficult predicament: 'you will be *wisely* directed and you may rest passive'.[2] But passivity did not imply complacency. In keeping with Calvinist strictures, Haig believed that hard work brought spiritual purification. The diligence inspired by his Presbyterianism and the self-belief which his doting mother encouraged undoubtedly contributed to his relatively swift rise in the Army. His religious faith at the same time transformed what might have been seen as coarse ambition into a Christian sense of purpose: to serve Britain to the best of one's ability was to serve God. As a young soldier, he saw action in the Sudan (1897–8) and in South Africa (1899–1902) where he was conspicuously disdainful of danger – a manifestation perhaps of his certainty that God had singled him out for a higher purpose.[3]

Religion made things simple for Haig: it provided life with order, meaning and justice, and left no room for self-doubt. The fact that he was near the top of the Army at the very time the Great War broke out seemed to him further proof of God's great plan. Haig's faith also brought sense to an incomprehensible war. As a cavalryman, he expected glorious charges but encountered instead stalemate, trenches and mud. Refusing to be unnerved, he drew solace from his favourite Bible passage, II Chronicles, (20: 15): 'Be not afraid nor dismayed by reason of this great multitude; for the battle is not yours, but God's.'

Haig's believe in divine direction did not prevent him from blaming the war's early misfortunes on the Commander-in-Chief of the BEF, Field Marshal Sir John French. When French's supposed incompetence became too much to bear, Haig campaigned hard for his removal and for his own promotion. In December 1915 he got his way when he was appointed Commander-in-Chief. Upon taking over, he noted a sense of relief among the GHQ staff: 'all seem to expect success as the result of my arrival, and somehow give me the idea that they think I am "meant to win" by some superior Power'.[4]

Shortly after assuming command, Haig attended a Church of Scotland service conducted by a 'most earnest young Scotch man, George Duncan'. He was profoundly impressed; 'one could have heard a pin drop during the service'.[5] Henceforward, according to Duncan, 'the half hour of worship' was 'not merely something Haig valued; it was apparently something which must not be missed'.[6] As the war progressed, Haig began 'to view in a more definitely religious light both the issues at stake . . . and the part which he himself was being called to play'.[7] He relied ever more on the 'fine manly sermons'[8] to provide sense to the carnage. Duncan became Haig's secret weapon, the chaplain who could, he claimed, 'make anyone fight!'[9]

George Simpson Duncan looked more like a young, suitably eccentric university professor than a potential Messiah. Born in 1884, he was the son of Alexander Duncan, a tailor's cutter from Forfar. He gained a first class honours in classics from Edinburgh University and then went on to graduate work in Cambridge, St Andrews, Marburg, Jena and Heidelburg. By 1914 he was a New Testament scholar of considerable renown within academic circles.[10] Angular, clumsy, and rather shy and soft-spoken, he was thirty-two years old when he arrived at GHQ, knowing 'next to nothing about Army life'.[11] Orphaned at an early age, he quite possibly found a father-figure in Haig, who he likened to 'an old Homeric hero'.[12] He gave Haig unquestioning loyalty which bordered on adoration. His services were noted more for their soft-spoken logic than for any fire or brimstone. Sermons inspired contemplation more than adoration; Duncan persuaded rather than exhorted. He was always more of an academic than a preacher. It was not a formula which inspired universal appeal, but it suited Haig perfectly.

Like a good chaplain, Duncan tailored his messages to suit the course of the war. But he also tailored them to suit Haig. On a Sunday in late February 1917, he noticed that 'the Chief looked much older than I have ever seen him before'. The padre consequently chose a subject 'relevant to him in the present situation'. Afterwards, Haig 'looked his old self, fresh and alert' and Duncan was rewarded with a 'very cordial and approving smile'.[13] But striking the right tone was not always easy. After a dejected Haig returned from a particularly difficult meeting with David Lloyd George, Duncan made the mistake of delivering a rather sombre sermon. He realised too late that 'perhaps what the Chief needs is something that is aglow with confident hope'.[14]

There is no doubt that Haig took what he wanted from Duncan's sermons. It is, for instance, difficult to believe that the padre, who had lost both of his parents, actually said (as Haig recorded) that 'We lament too much over death. We should regard it as a welcome change to another room.'[15] But both men nevertheless believed that the price of victory, no matter how steep, was ultimately worth paying. After a particularly disastrous action, Haig recorded that

Anything worth having has always to be paid for fully. In this war, our object is something very great: the future of the world depends on our success. So we must fully spend all we have, energy, life, money, everything, in fact, without counting the cost.[16]

As for the dead, their sacrifice was their reward. Duncan believed that 'a process of selection was going on by which the best were being picked out for some special service beyond the grave'. Those who survived the war, on the other hand, would be cleansed and purified by their experience. 'After the war none of us can be the same as before it!',[17] Haig wrote. Despite the enormous losses in men and money that Britain endured, he still thought that the experience would render the nation 'the greatest gainer, the whole empire would be welded together into one great whole, and imbued with a higher spirit'. By way of contrast, the United States, 'though more money had been amassed, would decline because of the spirit of luxury and extravagance which was being developed'.[18]

This glorious rebirth was of course dependent upon British victory, but of that Haig and Duncan had no doubts. The only uncertainty concerned the time required to defeat the Germans. After Duncan preached from St John's letter to the Christians at Smyrna, Haig concluded that

The contents of the letter might have been addressed to the British Army in France today. We must look forward to still harder times, to the necessity of redoubled efforts, but in the end all will be well.[19]

He remarked on how different was the attitude to that which was prevalent when the British began the war, when there was an expectation of being home by Christmas: 'Now we are beginning to learn our lessons, and to be sobered by hard experience and to be patient.'[20] But despite the fine words, Haig did not immediately accept the inevitability of a long struggle. His gargantuan self-assurance led him to believe that he would succeed with one great offensive in 1916. Forty thousand casualties on Day 1 of the Somme offensive did not destroy his confidence; he was still able to predict that 'in another fortnight, with divine help . . . some decisive results will be obtained'.[21] But God kept Haig waiting.

As victory seemed ever more elusive, Haig grew more circumspect. In a somewhat chastened mood, he told his wife, prior to the Messines attack of June 1917, that 'nothing is certain in war. Success lies in a higher Power than me'.[22] A modest victory followed and God was duly thanked. When, later in the year, Haig's high hopes were smothered in the deep mud of Passchendaele, he took solace in Duncan's promise that

'*At the right time* the Lord will bring about a great victory . . . we must be able to endure and not be impatient.'[23] Haig's faith was tested to the full in March 1918 when the German Army broke through the Allied lines and advanced as far as forty miles. '*Our* ways may not always be the ways chosen by the Divine Power', he concluded, but 'If one has full confidence that everything is being directed from above *on the right lines*, then there is no reason for fussing.'[24]

Confidence that the war was divinely directed absolved Haig from examining his methods of command. While French's failures had been human errors, Haig's were the will of God. 'Whether or not we are successful lies in the Power above', he explained to his wife. 'So I am easy in my mind and ready to do my best whatever happens.'[25] This meant that Haig, at least outwardly, refused to take credit for the successes which did come his way. 'It isn't me' he insisted when Duncan tried to congratulate him on a victory.[26] After the triumph at Arras in 1917, he wrote 'I know quite well that I am being used as a tool in the hands of the Divine Power and that my strength is not my own, so I am not at all conceited.'[27]

Late in 1918, Haig's faith was rewarded. The German Army, worn out by its own offensive, could not withstand Haig's counter-punch. An armistice quickly followed. The British people were initially grateful to Haig. 'But I scarcely feel that I deserve this gratitude,' he wrote rather sheepishly, 'for as the Old Testament says "the battle is not yours but God's" . . . I have only been the instrument to carry out the Almighty's intentions'.[28] His work done, he retired from the Army as soon as he could and spent the rest of his life working tirelessly for the British Legion, serving the soldiers who had fought under him. Unlike many of his contemporaries, he felt no need of self-justification when questions began to be raised about whether the massive casualties could have been avoided. His sudden death of a heart attack at the relatively young age of 67 might suggest a tormented soul existed beneath the surface serenity, but that is dangerous speculation.

As for Duncan, he succeeded to the Chair of Biblical Criticism at St Andrews in 1919, a post he had been offered during the war. He stayed in St Andrews for the rest of his career, eventually becoming Principal of St Mary's College in 1940 and Vice-Chancellor in 1952. He was Moderator of the General Assembly of the Church of Scotland in 1949. Though his diary reveals that he was deeply affected by the tragedy of the Great War, he never in any way blamed the losses on Haig, nor did he seem to worry that the deaths might have been in vain. He was bothered by the barrage of criticism levelled against Haig after the latter's death. This apparently motivated Duncan to write *Douglas Haig As I Knew Him*, in which he recalled his time at GHQ and eulogised Haig.[29] He died in April 1965, before the book was published.

What effect did Haig's religious beliefs and his relationship with Duncan have upon the fate of the British Army? Evidence suggests that at times Haig's tactical decisions were based on nothing more substantial than mere faith. For instance, on the eve of the Somme offensive, he wrote that 'The men are in splendid spirits . . . . The wire has never been so well cut, nor the Artillery preparation so thorough'.[30] But Haig could not have known his men's true feelings; the size of his army and his separation from the front precluded real intimacy. Trust in a benevolent God caused Haig to assume that his men felt as secure as he did. The same trust may have inspired the belief that the front had been well-prepared for the attack, when in fact it had not. Machine guns were not neutralised; wire remained uncut. Intelligence to this effect had been passed to Haig, but it was not believed by him. The problem with Haig's faith was that it could at times be blind.

In October 1916, Haig noted with profound interest Duncan's warning that 'We have all had . . . enough of good advice. What we wanted now was some help'. The padre told his congregation to 'Have patience, do your best and look above for help'.[31] Whilst it would be impossible to establish a causal link between Duncan's words and Haig's receptivity to advice, it is clear that suggestions from outside experts did not always find fertile ground at GHQ. Those who disagreed with Haig's methods found it difficult to maintain their opposition in the euphoria which pervaded his headquarters. In September 1917, the CIGS Sir William Robertson arrived at GHQ intent upon persuading Haig to adopt a change of strategy. The morning after his arrival, Haig noted that 'A night's reflection and Duncan's words of thanksgiving . . . seemed to have had a good effect' on Robertson, who appeared 'less pessimistic and seemed to realise that the German Army was in reduced circumstances'.[32]

To Haig, faith was at least as important as facts. When the War Office produced a report on the state of the German Army which was less optimistic than that provided by his own staff, he commented:

> I cannot think why the War Office Intelligence Department gives such a wrong picture of the situation except that General McDonough is a Roman Catholic and is (perhaps unconsciously)

influenced by information which reaches him from tainted (i.e. Catholic) sources.[33]

Confident of God's help, Haig never doubted that the British Army would eventually win. With the end predetermined, events along the way diminished in importance. If intelligence data was occasionally ignored, it was because the goodness of God was the most reliable indicator of the way the war would be resolved.

On a Sunday morning in February 1917, when the news from the front and from home was universally bleak, Haig listened to Duncan preach 'on the need for which all of us suffer of having nourishment for the spiritual side of life . . . We must really feel Christ in us, so that we are safe whatever happens'.[34] It would be easy to argue that the spiritual nourishment which Duncan provided led to a dangerous detachment from the real war. The belief that 'we are safe whatever happens' suggests that Haig's certainty in life everlasting may have caused him to be reckless with lives temporal. But to concentrate on the possible ill-effects of his deep religious conviction is to see but one side of the issue. The Great War was a ghastly, horrifying, utterly demoralising conflict. A commander with a vivid imagination and heightened sensitivity, a man who felt the utter tragedy of every death and who could sense the long-term impairment to society which so much destruction would cause, might not have had the strength to lead the British Army to victory. It is a sad fact that in order to win Britain needed Haig and Haig needed Duncan. Losses needed to be justified; victory had to seem worthwhile.

Note on Editorial Method

It was my original intention to include only the material from the Duncan collection in this edition. It occurred to me, however, that it would be useful to include selected excerpts from the Haig diaries and correspondence in which he refers to Duncan, to his sermons, or to religious matters. This, I think, provides an indication of what Haig sought from religious worship and the effect which it had upon him. It also provides very revealing evidence of how dependent upon Duncan he was, evidence which would not have been garnered from the diaries of the rather self-effacing Duncan.

The Duncan diaries are included here almost in their entirety. The reader might question why reference to seemingly trivial matters like the cost of food in the Scottish Churches Hut at Montreuil has been included, but it is my feeling that it provides detail to the life at GHQ which has heretofore been unavailable. It is unfortunate that there is no

Duncan diary for 1918. It is not clear whether he kept one; my guess is that he did not, though I have no idea why he would have decided to abandon his diary. He does not refer to a 1918 diary in his *Douglas Haig As I Knew Him*. I have included entries from the Haig diary and letters from the Duncan collection from 1918 and the immediate postwar period in order to give a sense of completion to the documents.

Documents are arranged chronologically. The dates at the beginning of each letter or diary entry are written as they are in the original. The text of the diaries and letters has been left as is, with idiosyncratic spelling, punctuation and grammar untouched. Short biographies of the major actors in this drama are included in the Biographical Notes. The identity of the lesser figures is given, where possible, in the endnotes. The reader will understand that it was not possible to identify every individual referred to in the diaries and correspondence.

I

1916

I

General Sir Douglas Haig to Lady Haig

27 December 1915

Everything is going very smoothly here, thanks. Indeed, I am astonished at the feeling of relief which is manifested at Sir J's departure.[1] On the other hand all seem to expect success as the result of my arrival, and somehow give me the idea that they think I am "meant to win" by some Superior Power. As you know, while doing my utmost, I feel one's best can go but a short way without help from above.

(Haig MSS, NLS, ACC. 3155, No. 143)

2

Haig Diary

Sunday, 2 January 1916

I attended the Scotch Church at 9:35 a.m. Service was held in a school up a stair. A most earnest young Scotch man, George Duncan, conducted the service. He told us that in our prayers we should be as natural as possible and tell the Almighty exactly what we feel we want. The nation is now learning to pray and that nothing can withstand the prayers of a great united people. The congregation was greatly impressed and one could have heard a pin drop during the service. So different to the coughing and restlessness which goes on in Church in peace time.

Sunday, 9 January 1916

I attended the Scotch Church at 9:30 a.m. The clergyman (George Duncan) is most earnest and impressive, quite after the old covenanting style. "Whatever your work is, he said, do it well, and have God always with you." He was well aware of the difficulties of praying in the barrack room, etc. that was not essential but constant communing with God for a regular period every day – when walking or when doing work. Such an habit gives one added strength. Pray without ceasing.

Thursday, 13th January 1916

The Rt. Rev. Bishop Gwynne (Deputy Chaplain General) also dined. I spoke to him regarding the importance of sending messages to all his clergy to preach about the great object of the war, viz, the freeing of mankind from German tyranny. Many are too narrow in their views. They must be enthusiasts to do any good.[2]

Saturday, 15 January 1916

I also called attention to the large number of clergymen who are now being sent out to join the army.[3] Army commanders must look to the efficiency of these as well as to any part of their commands. We must have large minded, sympathetic men as Parsons, who realise the great cause for which we are fighting. Men who can imbue their hearers with enthusiasm. Any clergyman who is not fit for his work must be sent home.

Wednesday, 16 February 1916

The following extract from a speech by the Emperor Baber to his troops on March 16th 1527 when fighting the Lord of Mewar, the great Rana Sanga, is curiously appropriate now! "The most High God has been propitious to us in such a crisis that if we fall in the field, we die the death of martyrs; if we survive, we rise victorious the avengers of the cause of God." This is the root matter of the present war.[4]

Sunday, 19 March 1916

I attended the Church of Scotland. Mr. Duncan officiated. "Remember your lives are not your own but purchased at a price." (Acts) "The Empire is living thanks to the gallant lives which have and are being expended in this war. After the war none of us can be the same as before it!"[5]

Haig MSS, NLS, ACC. 3155, No. 104, 105)

3

Duncan Diary

March 31st, 1916:
Montreuil-Sur-Mer

Another scene in the great drama. After six months of quiet happy work at St Omer I moved here today with GHQ. Sorry to leave St Omer – all the more as there are to be no definitely Scots units here (excepting the Scottish section of the Signals). I shall miss the Glasgow Highlanders dreadfully. But many of the old boys have moved on here and there is the further compensation that I'll have a definite job here – onerous though limited – and that I am to be in charge.[6]

Major Carey[7] (who is now the senior C of E Chaplain for GHQ) and I travelled by car from St Omer. After lunch at the Bellevue just outside the ramparts we motored up the steep incline through the imposing gateway in the wall into the old city. What of the city? As we approached it a mile or two away it seemed pathetically tiny after St Omer. Away in the distance the rolling sand dunes were distinctly ~~cheerful~~ stimulating and we felt a real thrill as we neared the ramparts and entered in state through the Boulogne Gate: but one had no sooner arrived in the town before one felt – "Yes: the place is all right, but it is too small." Found the Camp Commandant housed in a weird flat reached by a very-far-from-horizontal flight of winding wooden stairs. Learned he had bought it as a possible church for me – and the C. in C. – a wooden hut on the ramparts formerly an army canteen. He had bought it as he told everyone for 50 francs – "never bought a church so cheaply in my life". Whatever he thought of the suitability of his purchase for the object it was to serve, he certainly felt he had made a good financial deal.

After inspecting the wooden tabernacle – and the Theatre as a possible place for C. of E. services – we met a Y.M.C.A. Secy (Scott of Etaples) who was prospecting in the hope of getting permission to erect a Y.M.C.A. hut here. No time to lose there! Introduced by Scott to an English lady Mrs. Stevenson, wife of Mr. Macauley Stevenson, the landscape painter, who is resident here.

Duncan MSS, St.A. MS 37090/3/61

4

Haig Diary

Thursday, 30 March 1916

I saw three parsons of different persuasions standing together, – a Roman Catholic, a Wesleyan, and another; all most friendly! On the other hand, the clergy of the Church of England are squabbling terribly amongst themselves over High Church and Low Church methods.[8]

Haig MSS, NLS, ACC. 3155, No. 105

5

Duncan Diary

April 2nd:

Again a perfect morning. Had a walk up the hill behind the billet before breakfast. No service arranged for today. Busy rather, the same old task of arranging to have the Church ready for next Sunday. In the forenoon had a charming interview with Capt P in which this man absorbed in the task of tracing on a wall map the localities of reserve parks had leisure to listen to my business (re chairs for the church) and to unbosom his soul in a religious talk. "Why are there so many different professions of religion?" he asked respectfully: and then went on: "I'm afraid I am a fearful heretic" – and he told me how to marry the lady of his choice he had had to adopt a course long-foreseen viz. renounce the Church of Rome. "Yet one doesn't part easily with the faith of one's fathers."

A short informal service in the Y.M.C.A. Institute (outside the town) in the evening. The rush of the preceding two hours determined my text: "Let the lifting up of my hands be as the evening sacrifice." In the early evening first White, then Argent[9] (G.H.Q. Quartermaster) asked me with perfect unselfconsciousness: "What day of the week is this?" – and on my way to the service a minute or two before I met Argent, a Tommy of the R.E's smiled on me and said: "No Church for us next Sunday: 6 days shalt thee labour and on the seventh thou shalt work twice as hard as on the other days."

Duncan MSS, St.A. MS 37090/3/61

6

Haig Diary

Sunday, 9 April 1916

I attended the Church of Scotland Service at 9:30 a.m. in a hut in a citadel of Montreuil. The Rev. George Duncan said, he was very pleased to be here, and everything was going on well, and thanked me for having arranged that he should be with GHQ.

Sunday, 23 April 1916

I attended the Church of Scotland service at 9:30 a.m. the Rev. G. Duncan conducted and preached a good sermon. "We lament too much over death" he said. "We should regard it as a welcome change to another room."[10] Another point he brought out was that, though evil doers may seem to triumph for a period, you must rest assured and have full confidence, that the good will eventually gain the mastery and God's will be carried out.

Sunday, 7 May 1916

I attended Church of Scotland at Montreuil at 9:30 a.m. Mr. Duncan took as his text a verse in Hebrews "By faith Abraham went forth, and he knew not wither he went." He preached an excellent sermon. He alluded to the number of brave patriots who had come to France "by Faith" they had had "a call". They knew not whither they went, but whether they returned home again or not, the end would be satisfactory. They had done their duty and all was in the hands of the Lord. He alone could guide and direct us.

Sunday, 21 May 1916

We had quite a large party of clerics to lunch. The Archbishop of Canterbury,[11] and his Chaplain,[12] Bishop Gwynne (Deputy Chaplain General). The Principal Chaplain (Rev. Dr. Simms), Lord Cavan, and General Dobell[13] (from the Cameroons) also lunched.

The Archbishop was very pleased with all he had seen, and with the work the various Church of England chaplains are doing. The latter told him how much they have been helped in their work of late by all Commanders "so different to the old days" whatever that may mean. In reply to a question, I told the Archbishop that I had only two wishes to express, and I had already explained them to Bishop Gwynne and these are:

Firstly: that the Chaplains should preach to the troops about the objects of Great Britain in carrying on this war. We have no selfish motive, but are fighting for the good of humanity.

Secondly: The Chaplains of the Church of England must cease quarrelling amongst themselves. In the Field we cannot tolerate any narrow sectarian ideas. We must all be united whether we are clerics or ordinary troops. The Archbishop thought his people were very united now, but "possibly six months ago some were troublesome".

Haig MSS, NLS, ACC. 3155, No. 105, 106

THE REVD GEORGE S. DUNCAN AT GHQ, 1916

7

Duncan Diary

Sunday. May 28th, 1916:

Arrived back yesterday from leave. If leave was good it's better still to be back once more in this garden of God and at one's bit of work. A big congregation at this morning's service. Was introduced after the service by the C. in C. to Lord Esher, who accompanied him and who gave me a most hearty invitation repeated with emphasis to come to see him at his home in Callander.

After the evening service a Rolls Royce rolled up for me by appointment to take me out to the C. in C.'s for dinner. Sat next to the C. in C. on his left. The C. in C. raised the subject of the "auld alliance" between France and Scotland and the conversation showed that he had a sound grasp of history. He was very free in telling me about his Oxford work. He spoke of taking Quads there – but his degree was a pass one. His tutor at Brasenose was Walter Pater with whom he had many an unwelcome talk on Plato when he would much rather have been out hunting. But he was quite emphatic that his Oxford experience had been of immense service to him in his future career. "I have been at school all my life," he said, "and I found when I left Oxford that I thought for myself about things which other fellows were ready to take as gospel."[14] There followed a long discussion with my two neighbours on my left: Sir Philip Sassoon and Lieut. Haig,[15] brother of the C. in C., on oratory, the use of language, and other topics arising therefrom. Sassoon's conversation was brilliant. Possessed himself (as he confessed) of a powerful memory, he maintained that memory was a terrific snare and he tried to keep the exercise of his in abeyance. "In conversation some men use only their memory, others use their minds: – the former may be very interesting for a time but you cannot live with them." In conversation where subject after subject was raised and the talk went off at a tangent he saw the supreme test as to whether a man had personality. Immediately after dinner the C. in C. went off to work and I had a long talk with the A.G. and Lord Esher. Delightful freedom with conversation – Lord E's manner perfect. The A.G. (Fowke) big, burly, with clear eye, frank and honest. Both professed themselves unable to understand the Irishman. "I feel a lot down to his climate", said the A.G.: but both Lord Esher and I asked the natural question: "What about the West Highlander?" Lord Esher has unbounded admiration for the best type of Scot from the Western hills: while the A.G. who had fished and shot at Justinhaugh and neighbourhood had a profound respect for the men of Forfarshire, some of whom he had found just about to emigrate to Honolulu. Drove into town with the A.G. in his magnificent Rolls Royce with pennant flying!

Duncan MSS, St.A. MS 37090/3/61

8

Haig Diary

Sunday, 28th May 1916

I attended the Church of Scotland at 9:30 a.m. The Reverend Mr. Duncan spoke of the Great British Empire and our duties as citizens of it.

Haig MSS, NLS, ACC. 3155, No. 106

9

Duncan Diary

Tuesday. May 30th

In the afternoon I must needs have an after dinner stroll along the ramparts and I picked up a new acquaintance who, though he wore the M. Staff badge, turned out to be a Seaforth and a Scot who had been incapacitated through frostbitten feet and was now attached to the Staffordshire. He hailed from Bannockburn. I soon saw in him a man of fresh mind and strong character and evidently he found some affinity in me,[16] for after a bit he began to tell me in beautiful words that clothed some beautiful thoughts of his religious experiences. A rough fellow in his earlier days he had become a Christian in the trenches and now knew the joy and strength of the Christian life. It was sometime later when I asked whether he was a member of the Church at home that I discovered he could have none of these things. He was a staunch "Brother".

Travelled out to Sorrus in the evening and had a chat with some men in the Canteen there. One old soldier who wished me to know that he has been fasting often told me he had known more dinner lines than dinners.

Sunday. June 3rd:[17]

A less hearty service this morning than last Sunday – so at least I felt. The C. in C. and his personal staff the only officers present. Took a new hymn – "Be ye faithful unto death." Heard afterwards from Black that the Chief said he had liked the sermon – especially a reference to the changed temper of the British people today as compared with the earlier days of the war when there was much talk of steam rollers and crushing naval victories and everything being over by Xmas. A feeling of great tension in G.H.Q. – one might in some cases speak of it as depression – ever since news came yesterday afternoon of the Great Sea fight.[18] One felt the Chief looked less alert in body and mind today than usual. Generally he looks as if he carried his responsibility lightly and he hadn't a care in the world. But the burden is never absent and one knows how all sections of the staff here – and even the French – look to him and rely on him. Well may we pray for those to whom has been committed the leadership of our armies and our navies.

In the afternoon Montreuil had the excitement of a fire which broke out in a lingerie. The local firebrigade more funny than any comic opera. One remembers the officious civilians jostling through the crowd of would be helpers with two pails of water and employing the precious contents of one over the legs of a much aggrieved citizen. The fire which broke out about 4.45 had a natural effect on my church attendance in the evening. The congregation was small – and neither my batman (beadle) nor my organist turned up. I was anything but "in the spirit" for the service. At my evening services in June I am taking up some fundamental question of the X[ian] Faith. Tonight it was: "Is Jesus Christ the Son of God and Saviour of the World?"

Duncan MSS, St.A. MS 37090/3/61

10

Haig Diary

Sunday, 4 June 1916

I attended the Scotch Church at 9:30 a.m. Mr. Duncan took as his text a letter from St. John to the Christians at Smyrna. "Be ye faithful unto the end". "To you shall be given a crown of everlasting life." The contents of the letter might have been addressed to the British Army in France today. We must look forward to still harder times, to the necessity for redoubled efforts, but in the end all will be well. How different are our feelings today to those with which the British people and the men in the Army began the War. Then, many people prophesied a race to Berlin, with the Russian steam-roller, etc. Now we were beginning to learn our lesson, and to be sobered by hard experience and to be able to be patient. An excellent sermon.

Haig MSS, NLS, ACC. 3155, No. 106

11

Dr John Simms to George Duncan

4 June 1916

It is with feelings akin to dismay that I have learned you are a candidate for the Chair of Biblical Criticism in St. Andrew's University.[19] While I feel in duty bound to send on my good wishes for your success I must also say that I sincerely trust you may not be required to take up your [?lectures] till this grim struggle is ended. You have won your spurs by your faithful work among our soldiers in France. Should you be called away I dread to think of the great blank your departure would leave for I confess I do not know where to turn to find a man like minded to fill your shoes. You have exercised a powerful influence for good over our fighting men – and I am convinced that in the calmer regions of academic life the personal skill for good you would lay on all your students would be equally potent.

As for your mental fitness for the duties of the post you seek to gain, it would be presumption on my part to commend you. Many others with the right to express their opinions have put that important point beyond all dispute.[20]

Duncan MSS, St.A. MS 37090/3/76

12

Duncan Diary

Monday June 4th[21]

Carey and I met this morning for prayer. He "conducted". His prayer most beautiful, rich and fervent.

In the afternoon took Lieut. Margetson[22] of the Artists into Hesdin and had tea in the Artists Mess.[23] Dined with the C. in C., aides de camp and had a most enjoyable evening. Thompson, Straker,[24] [unintelligible], Black and myself formed the company. Owing to an epidemic of scarlet fever in their more regular village (Brimeux), the aides de camp have had to give up meantime their fine chateau and occupy a school (quite a nice place, it is) at Beaumen. Learned that Lieut Haig, whom I met at the C. in C.'s a week ago, is 59 – therefore older than his more illustrious brother – and that when a request had been made some time ago for men to act as transport officers he had offered his services and had arrived in France before the "Chief" knew of his movements. One hears many stories of men approaching three score years – and even over it – doing good work here.

More hopeful feeling today (and also yesterday evening) about the naval engagement. A disposition in some quarters to regard it as a victory or as a glorious episode worthy of the best traditions of the British navy – yet many find it difficult to shake off the "sunk" feeling which the first gloomy reports gave rise to.

Sunday. June 11th.

Following on the affair in the North Sea came the news some days ago of Kitchener's tragic death.[25] General regret esp. considering the manner in which he was cut off: yet his departure does not seem to be felt, as Bobs'[26] was, as a personal loss even as regards his loss to the nation it is felt his work was really done. Russians have begun to make great progress.[27]

Today is WhitSunday. The C. in C. is still in England,[28] but Col. Burn[29] was present at the morning service, as well as certain of the C. in C.'s personal staff. In the evening I spoke on "What does it mean to be a Christian?" Quite a fair congregation, including one "Artist" who hails from Govan Parish. Admitted three men to Communion today.

Tuesday. June 13th

Memorial Services for Lord Kitchener held today at noon in the Theatre. An interesting service – naturally considering the occasion and the nature of the congregation: but I cannot say I found it impressive. This due not a little to the poor appeal which "K" in death, as in life, made to the <u>heart</u> of his fellow countryman: and of further there was in the service little sense that his death sounded as an alarm call to the nation to go on with fixed determination and endurance, this again may have come from the fact that his death is not felt as a grave national loss. Bishop Gwynne, who knew "K" personally at Khartoum gave a short address – wonderfully guarded in its praise and with frequent acknowledgment of the less pleasing aspects of the dead man's character. I read the lesson from 1 Cor. 15.

Sunday. June 18th:

The anniversary of Waterloo. Is another Waterloo at hand for us? A vague expectation abroad that something big is going to happen soon, but no one knows anything definite. The secret is being well kept this time.

The preacher is not concerned with military details. But he ought to be able to read the signs of the times. Hence with the C. in C. present in the congregation today and with some sort of suspicion of the things that loom big before his mind and some in his outlook in the immediate future, I read at our morning service the great old world story of David's encounter with Goliath, then spoke on Samuel 17:45 and Zachariah 4:6: and after an act of intercession which I think was more than ordinarily real, we closed by singing Kipling's hymn "The earth is full of anger". As he shook hands before going out his eyes looked deep into mine. One was glad to see how fresh he looked today. (Joffre had a few hours conference with him yesterday afternoon: then left by car in the evening.)

About the usual size of congregation (20–30) at our evening service – including tonight a few old Jocks now doing sanitary work. Subject of address was: "Can God forgive Sins?"

Monday. June 19th:

Went by car in the afternoon to Etaples. The two magnificent huts erected by the Ch. of Scotland are now completed tho not yet in full use. At one of them I met the male workers (the 17 ladyworkers I did not see) Gardiner, Gibson, Christie, Bonalls and Caltanach. One heard with delight that at service after service (parades) on Sunday last one of these huts has been crowded out & I shd think it would easily hold 800.

Bearded Harry Miller in his mess: then with 3 young Aberdeen officers – who had just come out and were under orders to proceed up the line in the evening. I went down later to join him in his little manse where a fourth Aberdonian was making himself at home shaving in the corner of the microscopic apartment and evidently having a good frank chat with Miller all the time. We new-comers seated ourselves on the bed and we had a happy chat together, all of us having deeper feelings than we could put into words. Our friend of the shaving brush had already told Miller as I learned afterwards how much his stay at Etaples had meant for him: he was a keen Church worker at Aberdeen but army life and mess life had not been all that it might be for him: now he felt quite revived as with a draught of fine spring water and he was going up the line with the light once more gleaming in his eye. Another dear little fellow who has had less fortunate antecedents in the days of peace, sat clearly enjoying the conversation: new things seemed to be opening out before his eyes and he could not help breaking forth in words which very inaccurately described what he was really driving at: "Man, I didn't ken ministers could be so broad-minded." Then came the handshake, and the "God be with you" so variously expressed.

Next Miller and I set off to meet Pagan,[30] who is doing a few months work down there in training officers. On the way Tommies in Scots bonnets surged all round us like a sea and one could not but remember old Xerxes, upon a height as his hordes marched past and weeping as he asked himself where that mighty host would be so many years hence. Yet as we looked out on these crowds of brave honest loyal fellows, one felt that was no case for tears but rather for "Sursum Corda".[31]

Pagan we found in his tent like a venerable warrior of ancient Greece – or rather his firm set face supplies a view of old Imperial Rome. A hero indeed. Clearly duty is a very elemental thing for him. Once he has put his hand to the plough, all thought of turning back is ruled out. A few minutes passed and then we parted – Miller to give a lecture on The Way: I to get my car and to return to nothing in particular at G.H.Q: and Pagan – to his night operations.

After dinner I spent a very pleasant hour with brother officers in the Theatre where certain war films were being censored. Some extraordinarily good films – especially of mining operations.

Wednesday. June 21st:

Day spent with Mr. Stevenson and Mr. R. D. Gardiner from Etaples in purchasing all sorts of equipment for our proposed tea-bar in our Church Hut.

Thursday. June 22nd:

One can just hear these last days the distant – very very distant – report of big guns.[32] Doubtless something in the way of bombardment has begun. Much talk about an advanced G.H.Q. One <u>knows</u> in fact that such a place is ready and that the staff are moving up there quite soon. But <u>how</u> soon or where it is is not yet generally known.

On going out to breakfast this morning I met Col. Burn, the King's Messenger, now recovering from a nasty motor accident which marred for a time his exquisite features. He has a very gratifying report to give of the C. in C.'s appreciation of last Sunday's service. These things make one humble.

Called on Gen. Charteris at his office in the evening and he very kindly invited me to come along to dinner at his mess. An unusually big gathering as it chanced – many guests. Here especially was a Navy Officer, an expert on German shells, who had come over to confer with the military expert on the same subject (who was also present as a regular member of the mess) . . . . As Gen. Charteris' guest I had the place of honour at his right hand. I had a most interesting evening with him, first at dinner, then strolling round his most charming garden . . . and finishing up by a walk round the ramparts before he returned to his office. He is a sound man – to me exceedingly approachable and kindly. Before entering Woolwich (just after leaving Merchiston) he had spent some time at Gottingen where to fill up the time he devoted himself to the study of astronomy, and shortly afterwards he returned to Germany for a second visit. When war broke out he was a Captain: now he is a Brigadier General (aged 39) and he <u>was</u> (he cannot say that he is <u>now</u>) the youngest Brigadier in the British Army. A year or two before the war he returned from India – where he has spent: I think he said 12 years – to be Military Secy to Sir Douglas Haig at Aldershot; – both he and his Chief quietly preparing for the war which they saw staring them in the face; then he came out to France with Sir Douglas to do intelligence work with the First Army Corps and came to GHQ with him as Chief of the Intelligence Department. He tells me that he has 200 specialists engaged in Intelligence work – apart from the more ordinary Intelligence officers connected with the Brigade. Prof. Bragg and his son who conjointly won the last Nobel Prize are both on his staff. The latter out here, the former at home – doing sound ranging, i.e. locating heavy guns from the sound of their report.[33] We had also a good sound talk on modern education (he is no believer in education as merely training for a profession and is quite down on English public school education as compared with the best that holds sway – or used to hold sway in Scotland: the former he held is largely memory work and was not designed to prepare one to <u>think</u>). As we came round the ramparts we discussed the Church and its present opportunity. The Church of England, he felt, was in these days "cutting its own throat" – and he quoted a vicar friend of his (interesting as combining High Churchism with a great breadth of mind) – who had recently visited him out here – as being entirely of the same opinion. A great step towards remedy (he felt) would be Disestablishment still referring, of course, to the Church of England.

Duncan MSS, St.A. MS 37090/3/61

13

Haig to Lady Haig

22 June 1916, Thursday

I note what you wrote in Tuesday's letter that "for this coming offensive ask for God's help". Now you must know that <u>I feel</u> that every step in my plan has been taken with the Divine help and I ask daily for aid, not merely in making the plan, but in carrying it out, and this I hope I shall continue to do until the end of all things which concern me on earth.

I think it is the Divine help which gives me tranquillity of mind and enables me to carry on without feeling the strain of responsibility to be too excessive.

Anyhow you must realise that I <u>try</u> to do more than "do my best and trust in God" because the reasons I give above.

Haig MSS, NLS, ACC. 3155, No. 144

14

Haig Diary

Sunday, 25th June 1916

I attended the Church of Scotland. Mr. Duncan took as his text a verse from Chronicles "Yes, I will go in the power of the Almighty God". He pointed out that we must look upon God as ever present with us, and that His plans rule the Universe. Consequently, whatever we do, we must try and go with the Lord. We are merely tools in His Hands, used for a special purpose. And he quoted a saying of Abraham Lincoln's when asked if he was sure the Lord was with him. He replied that the important point was that "he should be on the side of the Lord". Mr. Duncan also told the story of how before the attack began, the Scots knelt down in prayer on the battlefields of Bannockburn in 1314. Altogether, it was a most inspiring sermon. I have arranged for Duncan during the forthcoming battle to be with Advanced Hd. Qrs. at Beauquesne. He is very pleased with the idea.

Haig MSS, NLS, ACC. 3155, No. 106

15

Alan Fletcher to George Duncan

June 26, 1916

The C in C asked me to tell you that if it is any convenience to you he hopes you will make use of our mess at advanced G.H.Q. till you get settled – I talked on phone yesterday to The Principal Chaplain and he said there would be no difficulty in your coming with us[34] so I hope we shall soon see you there –

Duncan MSS, St.A. 37090/3/64/2

16
Alan Fletcher to George Duncan

<u>June 28th, 1916</u>

It will give the C in C much pleasure if you will dine here Tomorrow <u>Thursday 29th</u> at 7.30 pm[35]

Duncan MSS, St.A. MS 37090/3/65

17
Haig to Lady Haig

Friday, 30 June 1916

I feel that everything possible for us to achieve success has been done.[36] But whether or not we are successful lies in the Power above. But <u>I do feel</u> that in my plans I have been helped by a Power that is not my own. So I am easy in my mind and ready to do my best whatever happens tomorrow.

Haig MSS, NLS, ACC. 3155, No. 144

18
Haig to Lady Haig

Thursday, 6 July 1916

Many thanks for all your kind words and for having such confidence in my decisions. I too feel confident and believe that strength is being given to me which will enable us to win. But it will be a hard struggle.[37]

Haig MSS, NLS, ACC. 3155, No. 144

19
Haig to Lady Haig

Saturday, 8 July 1916

In another fortnight, with Divine help, I hope some decisive results[38] may be obtained.

Meantime we must be patient and determined.

Haig MSS, NLS, ACC. 3155, No. 144

20

Haig Diary

Sunday, 9 July 1916

I attended church at Beauquesne at 9:30 a.m. One point made was that the difficulties of any problem depends very much on the way the individual regards it. But we must not be optimistic he said, simply by shutting our eyes to the truth, but, through confidence in God's help, believe that we can and will overcome whatever opposes us.

Sunday, 16 July 1916

I attended the Scottish church at 9:20 in Beauquesne. Mr. Duncan took as his text "The Kingdom of God is likened unto treasure hidden in a field" which in order to buy "a man sells all he possesses with joy". Anything worth having has always to be paid for fully. In this war our object is something very great. The future of the world depends upon our success. So we must fully spend all we have, energy, life, money, everything in fact, without counting the cost. Our objects cannot be obtained without the greatest sacrifice from each one of us.

Haig MSS, NLS, ACC. 3155, No. 107

21

Duncan Diary

Monday July 24th, 1916:

A month ago – on June 27th – I moved with the Advanced Section of General Head Quarters to Beauquesnes,[39] some 9 kilometres S.E. of Doullens. The great attack, after being postponed for 48 hours owing to very wet weather on the 28th June, was launched at 7.30 on Saturday morning, July 1st and a considerable part of the German first line was taken.[40] An attack at 3.30 am (summer time) on the 14th gained for us at a trifling expense the German second line between Bazentin and Longueval.[41] Since then the fight has been raging with great intensity and with varying fortunes. Bad

weather on the 18th and 19th as at other times before and after,
made reconnaissance work difficult and while causing a
postponement of our next attack gave the enemy time to man his
heavy artillery. By now he has collected against us a vast array of
heavy guns as well as reinforced his line by 20 divisions! And it
was the bringing up of <u>one</u> extra division at Neuve Chapelle and
two at Loos which enabled him on these earlier occasions to foil
our offensive![42] Query? Will he manage to foil this present
offensive? Whatever may well be said about our lighthearted
optimism <u>before</u> the attack was launched, there has been since July
1st no disposition at GHQ to take anything but a serious view of
the difficulties that must be overcome before we really get thru the
Boche line. In the last few days the general temper has been more
than ever solemn – though not by any means pessimistic. Since
Saturday we have been attacking the enemy's third line esp. round
Pozieres but apparently with no great success. The artillery
struggle today has been terrific. How full of fate these days are!

I called with Capt Robertson (ADC) – [Brian L. Robertson,[43]
son of Gen Wm R] – at Val Vion (C. in C.'s Chateau) after tea this
afternoon and saw the communiques: then walking home through
the field encountered the C. in C. with Col. Fletcher and Capt
Black coming back to the chateau on foot after their ride. How
sturdy and healthy the Chief looked as he strutted on with quick
pace and firm step – like some old Homeric hero. What sense of
self possession he imparts!

Sir Wm Robertson was here yesterday and today but I did not
see him. Today I saw Admiral Bacon, while yesterday I had in my
congregation Lord Northcliffe.[44] Shabbily arrayed in a brown suit,
an old cloth cap (held on his head as he came out of the motor)
and a most carelessly arranged collar and tie which at first looked
like a knotted handkerchief around his neck!

July 25th

Again the weather has been dull and hazy. We seem to have got ¾
of Pozieres: but as reconnaissance by aircraft in these dull days is
impossible and from our present position before Pozieres we can
not see over the ridge to watch the effect of our artillery fire – it

would be a great point if we could push on and get the Windmill (on the road beyond Pozieres) as an observation post. The Boche heavy guns are so active that we can do little until we knock them out and that again is exceedingly difficult indeed impossible without good aerial reconnaissance.

July 26th

I have spent more time than usual today among my parishioners. After breakfast I spent some time very pleasantly with the officers and some of the men of the "Wireless" and at 5 o'clock I joined the men there at their tea table. At 6.30 at the Church Hut – a Canteen as it is known on week days – I got a round-table discussion set agoing with a few fellows and soon we had quite a small crowd and the most interesting and lively debate. We started off with our French experiences – how, for instance, French ways compared with English. After a bit we got onto the subject of education. It was significant that among those who spoke, the general weight of opinion emphasised the importance of education and the desirability of the greater zeal on the part of parents and others to secure for children as sound education as possible (by keeping them longer at school, etc): while education which was merely an imparting of information, or was directed primarily to recurring utilitarian ends, was vigorously deprecated. The meeting broke up with the keen desire to have more such discussions.

The war news is still none too bright. It would seem that the attack made on Saturday morning was a failure and that the Glasgow Highlanders, while doing magnificently, suffered pathetic losses.

I am trying in these days to do some thinking on the great question of the life beyond the grave, on which I hope to speak on Sunday morning. A few days ago a young officer [George Black][45] said to me: "Padre, I wish ye would speak some morning on the subject of the future life" and then telling me of a great discussion he had had with some brother officers ("some of them atheists" as he said) and "speaking" seriously of the vital importance of the subject, he proceeded to discuss the matter with me at great length – until the call of work reluctantly took him off. Here is a matter which <u>does</u> grip men in these days. Last night a crowd of Artists Rifles after a Biblical Discussion in my billet said that, coming back on Thursday evening, they would like to consider with me this question of a future life, while at the close of our discussion in the Canteen tonight the men asked that <u>that</u> might be the subject of our second discussion here on Friday evening.

July 27th

Still a thick haze in the early hours this morning as in a spring morning. Later in the day the sun with difficulty asserted itself and though low visibility continued for long to prevail some reconnaissance work might well have been done in the evening. There is little tonight in the way of news. Yesterday it was announced that we had gained the whole of Pozieres.

Went to Puchevillers in the afternoon to see the 5th & 6th Royal Scots (the 5th RS= Queens Edinburgh[46]). I found them busy in preparation for moving on tomorrow to join the 32nd Division. To some of the more eager spirits (e.g. Capt. MacRae[47]) the prospect of a move-on after the weeks waiting in that orchard was distinctly invigorating: others (esp those who had been separated from the battalion in recent weeks, arriving back just in time for this move) felt their life since they left Edin. and went to Gallipoli has been one continual move, and they were none too keen to return to the rigours of the fighting line. I found Col. Wilson[48] (now returned from sick leave) more than kindly – as was also Major MacLagan[49] the 2nd in command, he feels himself rather superfluous now that the Col. has returned.

We had a most reverent discussion tonight in the billet regarding a future life. Davidson (the ASC private) joined in and was learned as ever . . . One man told us that the chief difficulty for him has been just to realise that in men there was a spirit as well as a body: once he had got clear on that matter he felt no difficulty in understanding that the death of the body need not involve at all the death of the spirit.

Duncan MSS, St.A. MS 37090/3/61

22
Duncan's Notes for a Discussion[50]

"Padre, will you speak to us sometime on the life to come?"
Arguments with brother officers – some atheists.
Importance of the subject – Relation of eternity to time.
Nature of life beyond. Souls all in a sense the same. But as they look on at life & see the working out of their actions in perspective, then retrospective & perspective view constitutes their heaven & their hell. St. Paul's joy: my sense of being a fool. So the consolation that comes to an erring fellow who has not had much of a chance in life. But what of looking forward? No looking forward – or action.
  Sense of rest.

Importance of subject in view of the bearing on present conduct.
  1) if there is, it behooves us to live well
  "   "   is not, it seems not to matter how we live?
  "   "   is, the sense of it, and make a fellow not merely good, but brave

The practical mans solution: the man in the Little Minister
  who thinks it is safest to go on the assumption that there is a life (live a decent life here)
  – if there is not, there's no harm done: & if there is, then he stands as it were a good chance

Arguments:)(a conviction

Supreme argument for: There is a God (the heaven & the earth declare that). Have we a part of the divine spirit in us? If so, we cannot die. Relation of death to sleep. Used by me as an argument why we shd be sure of a life beyond: but to my friend (arguing here as he said against his convictions) this was the great argument against. a) the spirit is perfectly inactive during sleep – for a time because the body is temporarily dead. Why shouldn't death mean that the spirit is now permanently inactive in that the body is permanently disposed of?

Duncan MSS, St.A. MS 37090/3/61

23
Duncan Diary

July 28th

A beauteous evening, calm and free. Over in the east the diapason of the guns goes on unceasing: but westward the tall trees stand out against a golden sky and reflect the beauty of His peace. It has been a day of much sunshine and heat – welcome both in itself and for the help it will give our attacking army. We are once again in possession of the whole of Longueval, and have got some useful gains beyond Pozieres.

At the Church Hut I had this evening a second discussion – this time regarding the Future Life. Considerable latitude was allowed as regards relevancy and irrelevancy. I tried during the first part of the talk to get men to realise that there was such a thing as a spirit in man. The second half of the discussion tended to develop into a duel between two men on the origin of evil – one believing in a power of evil, and fallen angels since God made all things good and he could not be the author of evil, the other preferring to speak of an evil tendency in us. One man, while believing that there was in each man during life a spirit which was part of the Divine Spirit imagined that at death that Spirit returned to God was merged in the Divine Spirit as part of an entity from which again a part would be taken to form the spirit of some new man.

After breakfast I went round this morning as usual to the Quarter Master's Office to look through the little handbags containing the more intimate belongings of men who had died during the last 24 hours. One was a young Lieut. A glance at some of his letters told me he was the son of a Welsh minister: and in one, possibly the last the boy had received from home, the father spoke of enclosing £s, "but I hope you will manage to repay it soon, for you know how it stands with us at home". Expressed joy at the boy's receiving a commission – he had been till then a private and hoped that he would see that everything was done for those who were under his care and responsibility, and asked him to keep account of his expenditures daily and to always set aside a little to fall back on. And on the envelope one saw how the boy had scribbled some last jottings of expenditure: 1.50 billet, 2f laundry, etc.

Duncan MSS, St.A. MS 37090/3/61

24
Haig Diary

Sunday, 17 September 1916

I attended Church of Scotland at 9:30 a.m. Mr. Duncan took as his text "The Lord is my refuge and my strength". He emphasised the mistake in sitting still in the belief that God is our refuge. We must all be up and doing since He is our strength. He preached a fine manly sermon, well suited for this time of battle.

Haig MSS, NLS, ACC. 3155, No. 108

25
Macaulay Stevenson to George Duncan[51]

Friday Morning
22nd September 1916

In the rush of our busiest time yesterday afternoon I scrawled you the line I sent on the outside of the packet of paper. Last night our new Padre – Rev. Bruce Nicol[52] (of Skelmorlie Parish – Firth of Clyde) came up, and he has promised to bring paper from Etaples on Sunday.

You will be interested to learn that your idea of material as well as spiritual sustenance and comfort for the boys has worked out well. We have done what we could to make it go – my wife and Jean, and I. It has taken our whole time since it was opened fully a month ago, and is so in demand that we are at times almost inconveniently crowded. "Our Celebrated Salmon Sandwiches" (at 2^d each) are the great "line". My wife makes them by splitting a $^1/_2$^{d} roll, buttering it, and putting in tinned salmon. Of these are sold 150 a day or more, besides bread and butter (we use 200 $^1/_2$^{d}

rolls daily) and biscuits and cake galore, washed down with tea, coffee or chocolate. We run all three all the time – all always freshly made. We don't make a troughful of anything. The men say it is the one bit of home they've seen since they came to France. We open at 7 a.m. to clean up, and serve early breakfasts – just odd ones for men going off for the day, etc. (just one or two or three per morning) from 8 a.m. – I come out in the morning and our cook's daughter and the orderly do the cleaning up. My wife comes along just before 10 and stays till 10 p.m. except for an hour off for our midday meal – 12 till 1. We have tried all sorts of ways, but it got on our cook's nerves our coming home for dinner irregularly after 9 p.m. and didn't suit our health (which is now excellent) so now we take supper here in the hut at 9 when the men clear out – have a read of the papers, and home to bed by 10.15 to 10.30.

We like doing our job immensely, and we believe the men like our efforts to please and comfort them.

We have covered all the tables with white wax cloth, and we have individual lamps, with lamp shades on them. When they are lit up in the darkening the place looks very cosy and inviting – in fact staff soldiers stand in the dark looking wistfully and interestedly in – evidently they would like something like this for themselves also.

General Simms and Mr Macalpine told us we were to try to make working expenses – i.e. price of coal, paraffin oil out of our modest profits, but not to "make money". We certainly are not making money though our till turnover is well over 100 francs a day . . . .

The piano you so kindly hired for the first month has been a great boon. It is very very much appreciated, and is played on by some very beautiful artists. Bless you!

These men clerking in the Ecole Militaire[53] are so thankful to get a light nourishing supper to carry them on (they work till 11 p.m. and even midnight) that in the evenings we are crowded with men wanting chocolate and salmon sandwiches. A little is done between 11 and midday – men doing fatigues in the town etc – Fire picket etc etc. At 1 there is a rush till 2 then a slackening off, then at 3 it begins again, by 3.30 it is full, and from 4 till 4.45 it is overflowing – Six of us are hard at it – almost dizzy – It would take 10 of these rushes to keep all going without being kept waiting!

It will be a great pleasure to you to know that our chaplain is a dear good fellow – quite different from you – but, like you, a man. and being a man he has the manly decency when offering his fellow human beings thoughts, to be clothes to their souls, to offer them clean fresh thoughts of his own making, instead of fobbing them off with reach me downs. I marvel sometimes what want of reverence people have for their souls. Some people who take a bath every day, or even twice a day and wouldn't think of second hand clothes, are nevertheless content to clothe what should be their nice clean souls in things so reach me downy [shabby, secondrate] that they have become lousy and verminous! as far as the soul is concerned! Give me the nice fresh thoughts of our Tommies, every time. Lyons has been withdrawn to do Church Army Canteen work (they are starting one at the Salle de Vendes). When he was here he used to tickle us! Desmond the painter, was in helping us, and Lyons said "Come on Tally ho! (comment allez vous!) – buck up old chap!" – then turning to us said, "He knows quite well what I mean, I'll soon teach him English!"

Duncan MSS, St.A. MS 37090/3/82

26

Haig Diary

Sunday, 24 September 1916

Mr. Duncan preached from "Prepare ye the way of the Lord" and said this Great War was accomplishing the preparation of the world for better living. It was ruthlessly sweeping away all shams, and in a larger sphere, was preparing what was done by John the Baptist centuries ago for the Jews and the coming of the Lord.

Haig MSS, NLS, ACC. 3155, No. 108

27

Alan Fletcher to George Duncan

Sept 28th, 1916

The C in C wishes me to tell you that Mr Poincaré the French President comes here on <u>Sunday next at 9.30</u> am –

Consequently will you postpone your service till 12' oclock & put out the necessary advisory –

Duncan MSS, St.A. MS 37090/3/66

28

Alan Fletcher to George Duncan

Sept. 30th, 1916

The French President has changed his mind again and is now coming here Monday morning so there is no necessity to change the Church hour –

Can this be stopped or have you issued orders to have the Church at 12 noon?

Anyhow if possible I think it more convenient if you could put back the Church to the original time 9.30 am

Duncan MSS, St.A. MS 37090/3/67

29

Haig Diary

Thursday, 5th October 1916

I entertained an American, Mr. Munsey,[54] the owner of Munsey's Magazine and several other American papers of good standing. He had recently been taking the waters at Vichy. I found him a most interesting man and extremely pro-Ally. In fact a thorough Englishman at heart. I was greatly struck with what he said about the results of the War. England would be the greatest gainer, the whole Empire would be welded together into one great whole, and embued with a higher spirit. On the other hand, the United States, though more money had been amassed, would decline because of the spirit of luxury and extravagance which was being developed.

Sunday, 5th November 1916

At 9:30 a.m. I attended Church of Scotland. Mr Duncan took as his text Hebrews Chap. 12. "Wherefore seeing that we are also compassed about with a great cloud of witnesses let us lay aside every weight and let us run with patience the race that is set before us looking unto Jesus." We have all had, he felt sure, enough of good advice. What we wanted now was some help. "Life was hard, but with God's help we must succeed, – and there was also the noble example of those who had gone before to encourage us. We must not grieve for the death of those who perished in the cause of their country and civilisation. They too were Saints. Have patience, do your best, and look above for HIS HELP." It was a fine address.

Haig MSS, NLS, ACC. 3155, No. 108, 109

30

Duncan Diary

Dec. 10th 1916[55]

Montreuil

Once more back in this dear old town. A disappointment after the high hopes with which we set off to undertake the advance in the end of June: but if a real advance was not to be possible during the month, it was better to come back here than remain at Beauquesnes. So I think most men feel except the Signallers who are none too keen on resuming their daily 3 mile tramp from their billet at Sorrus to their work at Montreuil.

On Sunday Nov. 17th just before the service the "Chief" suggested I might have a holiday as he himself was to be off from

305

Wednesday to the Monday following[56] (a short holiday for him and I hear since it was so thoroughly occupied with business that he did not even see Lady Haig!) As a result of this I took my fortnight leave: and after a good time in Edinburgh I returned on Thursday last to Montreuil. The greatest asset I have on returning is to find my little Church converted into the most "homey" Soldier's Club to be found in all France.[57]

The last few days have been for me one of those dry seasons of the soul that recur with pathetic frequency: hence there was a deplorable lack of spontaneity in my preparation for today's services and also (I am afraid) in the services themselves. In the morning I spoke as a prelude to the Christmas Gospel on the soul's <u>thirst</u> for God (Ps. 42: 1, 2). What a subject for a prophet whose own soul is parched! – yet not altogether inappropriate for did not the Psalmist know these dry seasons, too? The Chief was there as usual with Lord Esher, Col. Burn, Gen. Birch, Gen. Simms[58] and members of his personal staff. At the close he asked me in his usual kind way whether I had had a good leave and said he hoped I had found my people well.

In the evening I had a Home Night Service followed by Communion. It was strange when I arrived ¼ an hour before the time of service (6.30) to find the place still going strong as a Club Room with Refreshment Counter, Tables, etc. So is it again – less than ¼ of an hour <u>after</u> the service.

The place is so thorough a success as a Home for the men that I doubt if as a place of worship it loses much from this double function it seeks to serve. But he who seeks to find fun in it may easily find it. The altar of the Church becomes the counter of the shop – and Sgt. Follett facetiously asked yesterday for a cake from the altar, as preferable to one from the ordinary table that stood near by. At the service this morning I had on the raised dais, not far from the Communion table, a chest of drawers: and after the morning congregation had dispensed we discovered still pinned to the near edge of the curtain through which they would pass on their way to the door a notice saying "Buttered Rolls may be had in the Oven. 1d each. Please help Yourself" (One wonders if the

C. in C. saw it! – I think not) And one ought not to omit to record that in the course of the service there came from behind me – from the back kitchen where the French girls were cleaning up and preparing for the re-opening of the refreshment bar – the noise of a fallen utensil that rolled & rattled most irrelevantly [one thinks he meant "irreverently"] from the Church service point of view.

Monday. Dec. 11th

The Scottish Church Hut at Montreuil is the best thing of its kind in France. One has only to open the door and peep in to realise that here one has stumbled on a little bit of home. Especially is this so in the evening when once the little red-bordered curtains are drawn and the tiny lamps with their coloured shades adorn the tables. There is scarcely room such is the crowd to get a seat for one's cup of tea. Yet still the men throng in. Despite the crowd there is a sense of peacefulness about the place: as soon as one crosses the threshold one realises that all noise would be out of place here. Even the music of piano and of song is rarely heard – when it is, of course, it is welcome: but soon again the place reverts to its natural stillness. The men realise with great appreciation how much Mr. & Mrs. Stevenson have done for them: and a very spontaneous suggestion has come from some of them that this appreciation might find expression in a New Year's gift. It was particularly gratifying for me to find them following up this suggestion from one quarter that already another set of men had made a very distinct move in the matter and were organising a subscription.

Later in the afternoon the C of E. Chaplain Mr Plowden Wardlaw (a vicar in Cambridge) came to the Hut as he often does: and as in these winter evenings he and his congregation find the Theatre over cold, he would gladly, could he set a site and were all difficulties removable, have a hut erected alongside ours at C of E. expense, to be run on weekdays as a Club under the same management as ours and be on Sundays the C of E. place of worship. He seems a man ready and willing for cooperation: although he celebrated Holy Communion every morning, he is a Low as well as a High Churchman.

Dec. 12th

A day of rain and sleet. An officer just returned from Ypres says that up there the snow lies at least an inch deep: here rather it is water & slush. Despite the weather Wardlaw and I tramped all this afternoon to Sorrus and le Calotterie: at the latter a new town ("Geddesburg",[59] is arising – all huts – the home of the new Transport department[)]. Had a most interesting talk with Wardlaw, esp. on ecclesiastical matters. A <u>very</u> High Churchman, (he was for a time an R.C.), he is still by no means an extremist. He would like to see, though he knows it is impracticable – the High Church and Low Church party separately organised as two sections of one Church in communion with one another: the Low Church section might then unite with the Free Churchmen. He said he would welcome, on occasion, non-Anglicans to his Communion provided they came with proper spirit & with due preparation: but then would have them do so only on occasion as guests not regularly as ordinary communicants, because it is the regular communicants who create the genius & policy of the Church. I asked him whether he would be willing to receive the Communion from a Free Churchman. "Yes", he said: – because there was a symbolical as well as a sacramental aspect of the Supper: and he could quite well on such occasions take part with other believers in a reverent communication of our Lord's Passion.

I arrived back from this walk just in time to lecture at the Y.M.C.A. Hut on my German experiences.[60] I find in giving that lecture that men are peculiarly interested regarding the systematic education of the German mind from school days onward, in contempt and hate, and also in the mental woodenness which would make all human nature conform to some preconceived (& perhaps imaginary) type. One "Artist" told me that he had been at school at Hanover: and there in that town so frequented by many good representatives of sane English life he would be asked why he did not run about in "shorts", why he didn't haunt cafes and fling money about, etc.

Dec. 13th

Spent the forenoon indoors in initial preparation for Sunday. In the afternoon visited the Artists Officers at Ecuires while the evening was passed at the Hut chatting to men. An uneventful day. The newspapers tonight contain an official declaration from Germany that she has offered peace to the Allies.[61] So far as the British Army goes there will be, of course, not the slightest disposition to give ear to her proposals: and if the change of government means anything it means that the same mind rules our policy at home.[62] Preparations for the spring offensive are assumed to be going on apace. One indication is the reorganisation, on a huge scale, of the Transport Directorate: another is the presence in G.H.Q. yesterday of a number of silk-hatted Railway magnates from England: rumour speaks of thousands of tanks being got ready: and of our being back in Beauquesnes at no very distant date, say February.

Dec. 14th

The German offer of peace is an invitation for us to do now what we refused to do in August 1914 viz. recognise that might is right, and that when confronted with might, matters of principle are of no account. Of a truth present-day history is big with vital issues. Who shall interpret them? One feels that the Allies have enough honesty of purpose about them to do the right thing now as they did it at the outbreak following as it were the simple light of nature. But if our experiences in these momentous times are to take us deeper into the mystery of the Divine purposes, we cannot have a better interpreter than the sacred scriptures of the Jewish nation. I have spent a good part of today reading and reflecting on 2 Kings cc. 18, 19.

Campsie writes that he hears he has been recommended for the Military Cross for the work he did on Oct 19th. And I. Dow announces his engagement to Miss MacDonald. Verily the gods are not blind to man's deserts, and after the toil in the darkness they send reward with the morning light. Martial fame and a woman's love! One who has sought and sought in vain for the latter is not likely to find much delight in the praises of fame. "Oh talk not to me of a name great in story." But when in love he has found his heart's desire, he may well find a new zest in life and a compelling motive to do the things that achieve fame.

Dec. 15th

Encore beaucoup de pluie. Does it rain 3 days out of 4 in France in winter time?

One of today's trifling occurrences – a lengthy negotiation with Wardlaw regarding a combined announcement placard of Church Services, on which the printer had done our notice (in comparison with the C of E one) rather less than justice in the matter of type and space. But he and I ought surely to understand (should I say appreciate?) one another. I like him.

Dec. 16th

A day spent largely indoors. Παρασκευψ ο εστιν Προσαββατον.[63] At the Church Hut I found as usual Mr. Stevenson's brain full of ideas regarding the proposed extension: he hopes now to be able to give me a little permanent chapel. In the afternoon I accepted Miss Hawdon's invitation to an Exhibition of her Water Colours – she had some interesting paintings of Montreuil, which would make good souvenirs, but the best of them were already sold. The news of the very successful French offensive near Verdun is the best bit of military news we have had for a long time: and besides being in itself a "tonic" it may well be later as France's answer to the Berlin peace proposal.[64]

Dec. 17th

Sunday evening. At the morning service the C. in C. was not present (he has been away since Wednesday morning – in England on business, I believe) and he was prevented from returning last night as he was expected to do.[65] Heseltine[66] and Black were the only officers present and even the escort was much under strength, a section being up at Bailleul.

Had a good evening service. Forty to fifty men attend: and the singing is most hearty though marred for me by the raucous voice of an RAMC private who delights to sit in front and encourage the others by the volume of sound. I am coming to feel a unity of spirit with my evening congregation – as in the St Omer days a year ago. Tonight an hour or so before I left for the service I decided to scrap what I had thought of giving as an address and spoke simply but directly, by way of preparation for the Christmas Gospel on, "If there were no such thing as Christmas".

Dec 18th

Wardlaw's scheme of a placard with a notice of all the regular Church services (of all denominations) having matured itself he and I went round the various offices in the Ecole[67] this morning delivering a copy at each office. I doubt if this will result in any increased attendance of officers at Church: but I at least welcomed the opportunity this opened up of making the acquaintance of many whose names – whose faces even in some cases – were unknown to me. Most of them seem surprised at our visit and did not encourage us to stay – though, of course, in practically every case we were quite kindly received.

Tonight's Orders (from G.H.Q.) reproduce a Special Order of the Day by the C. in C. in which he seeks "to bring to the notice of the troops an incident which is illustrative of the spirit animating British women who are working with us for the Common Cause. One night recently a shell burst in a shop at a filling factory in which the great majority of the workers are women. In spite of the explosion the work was carried on without interruption though several women were killed and others seriously wounded.[68] The remainder displayed perfect coolness and discipline in dealing with the emergency. As the result of their gallant patriotic conduct the output of munitions was not seriously affected. The Commander in Chief feels sure that the Army will appreciate and be inspired by this splendid example of the loyalty and determination with which their comrades in the munition factories are helping towards victory."

As a sad contrast to this one read tonight in General Routine Orders of a 2nd Lieut. being tried and shot for desertion: he disappeared as his platoon was taking over duty in the front line trench and two days later was found a few miles behind. His name and regiment are given as in the case of an ordinary soldier: and one feels that news of this ~~cannot be concealed from the~~ will surely leak out at home causing untold grief to the man's own people and uncharitable feelings among their neighbours.[69]

Dec. 19th.

Snow has fallen today and is lying though not deep. Was present this evening with the Stevensons and Pte [?Thring], a good Artist who gives no end of help at the Hut at a Revue given by the Artists in the Theatre Royal – a most happy evening which for an hour or so made us quite forget the war – to some it was like going back to England for an evening. After it we had a sumptuous supper in the Church Hut as Mr and Mrs Stevenson's guests . . . In every truth a feast of reason and a flow of soul. Have just arrived back. 12.30 a.m.

Dec. 20th

Despite last night's festiveness I was awake in good time and ere I was out of bed had a visit from an RE Corporal to see about fitting up my billet (which I claim with good reason to be also my office) with Nissen stove. Yes: when you give orders for a thing to be done in the army, it's done.

Had a memorable ride all by my lonesome this afternoon. First towards le Calotterie where meeting by accident the Artists boys I am anxious to see. . . . Had dinner with these said Artists at Humbert. These good fellows are Cock, Crammer and Cole. They had another friend with them tonight new to me (Morris) and our good friend Wilson of the YMCA joined us at our meal. One expects these boys will soon get their long expected Commissions – and then? They have been doing fatigues at Calotterie for the 1st few weeks but this job over they return to Hesdin tomorrow. So it was good to be with them tonight reviving the brotherhood we had at Beauquesnes when they and some others came along and sat as Bible students at my feet in my billet there. A lovely evening as I walked out with them toward their camping ground. Through the frosty air came the sound of distant gunning and an occasional flash lit up the sky.

Dec. 21st

Visited le Calotterie this evening, where J. R. P. Sclater of Edin.
gave a lecture in the Y.M.C.A. Hut on "The Art of Being Fed
Up". He was obviously very tired – why do institutions work
their helpers so unmercifully? And the audience was neither
large nor over-cultured (some rotund faces of the Labour
Battalion glowed red in the front seats.) while from the counter
at the far end came a good deal of distracting chatter: so the
conditions weren't perfect. Of course he gave a splendid lecture:
. . . and the man's own heroic nature spoke so strongly towards
the end that anyone who came with the fed up feeling must have
gone away considerably reinvigorated. Much too was distinctly
entertaining – eg., his story of the man whose cup of tea was
unceremoniously seized by a chum to extinguish the fuse of a
fizzling shell – and who is still grousing over the lost tea! And
his reference to the earliest classical instance he knew of
grousing over rations viz the Israelites with their [?quails] and
their manna manna manna. But much of it was far too subtly
psychological – eg his excursion on Dante obviously prepared
for a more enlightened audience. Here, as in other
circumstances, one was tempted to feel of psychological
analysis: "However interesting it does not help much!" But as I
said, the fine manliness of the close on "the art of not being fed-
up" did really buck one up.

Dec. 22nd

"The time draws near the birth of Christ." And it evidences
itself in a quickened sense of brotherhood – lots of letters
are being written to friends long neglected and from the
outside world tokens of goodwill and friendship keep
coming in. It is men of goodwill who will best hear the
angels sing of "Glory to God, Peace on Earth". Spent a
good while today at the Hut. Had a long talk there with an
Oxford history student now an "Artist". [?Sturgeon] by
name – a fine Greek face, clear eye, strong jaw, frank
expression, who came out with the original battalion and is
still without a Commission.

Dec. 26th

Xmas is now passed. In addition to the regular Sunday services I had two services in the St. Andrews Church on Xmas morning at 9.30 and 11. and both on Sunday and on Xmas morning the C. in C.. was present at 9.30. He had been away in the 2nd Army area for a good part of last week. He looked well, and I got from him an uncommonly appreciative smile at the close of the Sunday morning service. Just as amid the tragedy of war men are prepared to see that the world needs such a Saviour as was born in Bethlehem, so also to the quickened moral conscience of the nation the shallow peace overtures of the Teuton swash-buckling bully served by contrast to reveal the deeper nature of the Peace which was proclaimed by the angels' song.

The day passed quietly. The Scottish Churches Huts entertained to tea all who cared to come: and good Mr. Stevenson and no more wouldn't have it but that the guests were entitled to white table-cloths for the occasion (despite protests from some of the men that the cloths would only too soon lose their whiteness): So Mrs. S. had to find the table cloths. In the evening I dined with C Coy.[70] of the Artists Rifles and spent from 9.20–11.30 at Ecuires where the officers had invited the Sergeants along to the Officers' Mess.

Dec. 27th

Have been in Sclater's company for a great part of the day. He came to Montreuil to lecture in the Y.M.C.A. Institute at St. Justin – his subject again being "The Art of being Fed-up": and I had begged John Buchan to take the chair. We went and had tea with Buchan in the Intelligence Mess. In the room in the Mess which he uses for an office – full of much material that the Germans would gladly have – Buchan told us he was trying his hand at putting Theocritus into Scots verse, and he showed us some other Scots verses (eg. Fisher Jamie) which he turns out, he says, on his long motor rides.[71]

The Intelligence Mess is always an interesting place. I met there yesterday with Buchan a naval officer whom I discovered this afternoon to be the American Naval Attaché. What was <u>he</u>

wanting? Charteris today was decent as ever. I gave him a puzzle which little Jean Dickson had given me for him (3 ribbons on a luggage-label: puzzle entwine them). He solved the puzzle with commendable alacrity (there's not much wrong with our Intelligence Department!): and was careful to get the little girl's address, that he might write and thank her. He was most interested in a cutting I showed him giving an American appreciation of D.H. (from Current Opinion) in which (inter alia) the Chief was described as "revelling in doctrinal sermons which are not at all brief": and he took it away with him to show to the Chief.

Dec. 29th

How goes it with Germany? & what are her intentions for future lines of action? Much speculation in these days. One is told that our authorities have now got unmistakeable evidence lacking until recently that she is in a thoroughly bad way internally. Food is scarce: oil is a great necessity and it is said that thanks largely to the energetic action of Col. Norton Griffiths (the founder of our Tunnelling Companies) who disappeared from this front and from England some time ago and turned up in Russia. The ore mines in Rumania were all destroyed. Letters found on German soldiers show great dissatisfaction with their officers who are safe in bomb proof shelters while the helpless soldiers are exposed to the ruthless fire of the British Artillery.[72] It is said the chances are even for Germany's violating the neutrality of Switzerland (what motive could she have in that unless the motive of the mad bull?): and again it is said that Holland will yet be involved.[73] Mr. Wilson seems to get little praise from any quarter for his name,[74] any more than does Germany for her peace proposals. Will there be war between Germany and America before long? Such are the speculations that are rife. Nobody knows. But meantime preparations go on apace here for the next offensive – Railway tanks would seem to be being constructed in great numbers.[75]

Dec. 31st

Sunday evening and New Year's Eve. This morning was the anniversary of Sir D.H.'s first appearance at our Church service.

On sentimental grounds – I was sorry he was not there today: I did not learn until turning up at Church that he had gone off yesterday. In our services today we celebrated the "Day of Prayer" as at home.[76]

A wet evening. So the old year goes out. That is no bad omen if tomorrow morning the sun shines. A quite distinct feeling about that Germany internally is in a bad way. The "sunk" feeling that followed the Rumanian collapse[77] and the Cabinet crisis has now given way to one of unmistakeable optimism. Even those who doubt if the war can be over within another year (& they seem many) do so because they feel now (at times more difficult to do a month or two ago) that it is now within our power to inflict on the Hun a thorough going defeat – only it will require time.

Duncan MSS, St.A. MS 37090/3/61

2
January to May 1917

31

Duncan Diary

January 1st, 1917

1917 began in a morning that was sombre but without any rigours in the way of storm or cold: and though the sky remained dull all day the evening was beautifully clear and mild. Such a day corresponds with the mood of our people. A cloud hangs over us but still the spirit is one of hope. I began by first footing Mr & Mrs Stevenson. Afternoon and evening were spent at the Hut where all who cared to come were entertained at the expense of the Principal Chaplain – or as we announced it – as the guests of General Simms. A most hearty time it was. As good Sergeant Spence from Aberdeen said as a hungry crowd fresh from the Cinema performance in the theatre surged round our refreshment counter, each man bedding his plate as he desired "If the Germans could see this, they would know whether they are blocading[1] us." We had hoped to make New Years day the occasion of a presentation to Mr & Mrs Stevenson but as the article has not yet arrived I invited myself to make an announcement and hand Mr Stevenson the balance of the subscription (60f) to be divided among the workers in the Hut. A scene of great enthusiasm as on the call of Mr Stevenson, the said workers were paraded. A most homely evening closed with 'Auld Lang Syne'. Mr S. insisting on singing all the verses – the final verses being practically a solo on his part helped out by the melody on the part of many others.

General satisfaction at the news that D.H. has been made a Field Marshal.[2] A vacancy in this "order" was created by Lord

Kitchener's death obviously to be filled by D.H. I heard it said tonight that our authorities were chary to promote him to a Field Marshal rank while Joffre was still a General: but Joffre's recent promotion to the rank of Marshal removed that obstacle.

January 7th

DH present at service this morning with the shoulder badge of a Field Marshal. A son of Lord Balfour of Burleigh[3] also present with Charteris. Had something of a chat with D.H. before the service. He evidently felt that today he arrived a few minutes before time and could therefore wait outside for a little. He is most precise in the matter of time. Generally he arrives punctually to the minute. On Xmas morning he was some 5 minutes late – "This is the first and only time we have ever been late" said Col. Fletcher then to me as he entered the Church: but as a matter of fact the Chief once apologised to me at Beauquesnes (he might have been two minutes late on that occasion) saying the car had been delayed en route. I had already heard confidentially that he was to go on leave tomorrow and he himself told me so as we chatted together – "I hope to cross tomorrow if General Nivelle[4] & the despatches allow me to get off": and he added that this was to be genuine leave – (I know that when he crossed in the end of November at the conclusion of the Somme battle he returned without having seen Lady Haig!) – though of course he would not be able to go far away from London – probably he wd go to Ascot or some such place. I was interested that he talked to me so freely of his movements – because some attempt was being made to keep his departure as secret as possible. But DH, though he likes quietness, is no lover of secrecy.[5]

At the evening service I gave the second of a series of addresses on the meaning & nature of Prayer – "The Naturalness of Prayer".

January 14th

D.H. and his staff being all away from G.H.Q. we had a very simple service this morning. In the evening I spoke on the question of Prayer in relation to Natural Law with very little preparation, and with much to upset one in the course of the service – men coming and going through the doorway, the absence of a regular pianist, etc. An officer came in late and sat down behind. At the close he told me he was a son of Principal Lindsay of Glasgow.[6] I was delighted to meet him. But I wasn't prepared for the full identification. A reference to Oxford made me say: "But it's not you who are at Balliol is it?" – "Yes". – "You're A.D.?" "Yes, I'm A.D.". And this philosopher is out to act in the Director of Labour's office! (He came out primarily for Intelligence work: but there was no real opening for him there).

Duncan MSS, St.A. MS 37090/3/61

32

Haig Diary

Sunday, 28th January 1917

At 9:30 I attended the Church of Scotland the Rev. George Duncan conducted the service and preached about St. Paul's conversion. "Except a man be born again, etc." He spoke of Paul and Rob. Burns "who can tell what wonderful genius lies in the infant's head" then in later life, we are literally born again in spirit. He closed with a reference to the change which must come over us all after the War, and of the new state which England must assume if she is to continue to progress in civilisation.

Sunday, 4th February 1917

I attended Church of Scotland at 9:30, Rev. Duncan conducted the service. "Except a man deny himself – and takes up his cross and follows me – he cannot enter into the Kingdom of God." Duncan preaches a fine manly Christianity always. We must daily ask Him for further "strength which is not our own" to enable us to win through, and to look beyond the present into the far distance of a life to come!

Sunday, 11th February 1917

I attended Church of Scotland at 9:30 Reverend Duncan conducted the service. His text was "I am the bread of life." He laid stress on the need for which all of us suffer of having nourishment for the spiritual side of life. We must feel that this life leads on naturally into the next – and we must feel that if we "go down into the valley of Death, I am there." We must really feel Christ in us, so that we are safe whatever happens.

Haig MSS, NLS, ACC. 3155, No. 110

33

Duncan Diary

Feb. 12th

What all has happened since my last entry? Firstly as to the "atmosphere" of the happenings – we have had a cold time of it with a spell of frost (unparalleled in recent years as regards both rigour & duration). After some attempts at cold snowy weather the frost began in earnest on January 22nd and has lasted for three weeks. A slight thaw set in on Saturday night and has developed in reality today. Meantime Germany has declared her programme of a ruthless submarine warfare on all shipping: and America having cut off all diplomatic communication with her we are waiting to see what Uncle Sam's next move is to be.[7] The Boche is being kept very restless all along the front especially on the Ancre: he evacuated Grandcourt some days ago and tonight's news is that we have made important progress south of Serre.[8] On Friday last leave was stopped: query <u>why</u> & for how long?

D.H. came back from his leave on January 23rd. He has been at church each Sunday since then – looking very fit and well. At a Communion Service yesterday morning Col. Burn acted as elder. He has been a stranger to these parts since early in December. I think until a fortnight or so ago when I met him about 8 am one morning on the ramparts. He told me had just come back from Russia. He was in Petrograd when Rasputin was murdered[9] (was, in fact, living quite near the spot). He had had a long interview with the Czar who had sent him away with a message of assurance to King George that England had no more faithful ally than Russia who would go on "jusqué au bout". The Col. admitted that travelling to Russia – & across it – was no joke in winter time and food on his long journey was often a difficulty: yet he carries his more than 60 years very well and he told me yesterday he enjoyed this cold weather "plenty of cold water outside and in is what I like". A.D. Lindsay is still at the D. of Labour's office here & attends Church most faithfully each Sunday Evening. Often he is the only officer there & it is good to see him take his seat unobtrusively in the centre of a crowd of Tommies. "Why don't you give us a Psalm?" he demanded of me on one occasion (my apology being that we had been using a copy of the Hymnary without Psalms). He likes coming to the service as a humble worshipper and he is a kindly critic of the sermon!

Last Sunday evening I conducted a service at the Upper Scottish Churches Hut at Etaples. There might be some 600 men there – a motley crowd: it was difficult to size them up so as to feel just in what spirit they had come together to the service: but the "atmosphere" of the service was determined for me as much as anything by the continual bombardment of coughing which (poor devils!) they kept on unwillingly from beginning to end. "If you walked thru the lines at night, sir, you would find it worse" they told me: and I am prepared to believe it: it can be no joke for them to sleep in tents in such weather as we have been having of late. Men who sleep in Nissen huts here have told me they quite frequently find their boots frozen fixedly to the ground in the morning: and Lindsay said he thought it was the limit when the water in his bath froze between the time the batman prepared the bath & the time he (Lindsay) got up – "not more than 10 minutes later!"

I lectured at Etaples on the Monday evening (after my Sunday service). I think of one Scots boy who, as soon as the lecture was over, while the crowd was on the move, sat still in his seat – pulled out a book. When I went over to speak to him I spotted "Environment" as heading one of the pages of his volume, and "Ah: the Scots philosopher".[10] I said to myself. It was disconcerting to my theory to find out on closer enquiry that the book was one of Ian Hay's.[11] The reader (while, by name, from Biggar) said he had been a mason's labourer before the war: but I drew from him that he knew Latin & French: then he spoke of having been at College in Glasgow. – I discovered that he had been at [unintelligible] studying with a view to the Civil Service. "What do you think of doing after the war?", I asked tentatively. "I never think of that, sir" he replied as I had expected him to do. "My folks were just writing me this week about that: but that may just have to lie over for the meantime". In the same hut, after the lecture was over, I came across many fellows sitting silently with set faces, clearly "up against things". I couldn't help speaking to two fellows whom I passed, sitting quite lost in their own thoughts. I asked them whether their thoughts were away ahead or whether they were back at home. At once they "came to" as it were and brightened into a smile: and one of them found words: "Yes, it sets you athinking, sir."

Feby 13th

There were no pastries to be brought back today from Boulogne for our Hut at G.H.Q. France now allows no cakes to be sold on two days a week (Tuesday & Wednesday). After the 25th I understand cakes are to be entirely disallowed so also are petit-pains (because of the finer flour employed for them): while to limit consumption no bread is to be sold until it is at least 12 hours old.

Feby. 17th

Saturday evening. My throat having croaked I have been ordered by Dr Johnson to have a day off tomorrow – so my mind is easy tonight.

Saw Hillaire Belloc[12] here yesterday. A more distinguished visitor was Gen. Nivelle for whom a guard of honour was on duty at Beaurepaire[13] yesterday afternoon and this morning. There seems some excitement in Parliament about this newspaper report of an Interview given by D.H. to some French journalists. One does not expect any public utterance of his to be justly subject to the charge of indiscretion![14]

France shows no great scarcity in the matter of food. Plenty of meat, etc. always appear on the table. I hear tonight that in the 3rd Army Area our men are now forbidden to buy bread <u>and</u> potatoes from the French civilians. Coal is still at a premium here. G.H.Q. seems "with difficulty" to be maintaining its requisite supply: but civilians here cannot get it. This has now been going on for more than a month. About New Year time there was also an oil famine, both for the military & for civilians.

Feby 18th

As I arranged yesterday, Hanson[15] from Etaples arrived by car this morning to do duty for me. As we were chatting away a few minutes before 9.30 Dr Simms said he wondered whether the Chief would come this morning – in fact he would be surprised if he did – for he had been away all day yesterday up the line with Gen. Nivelle: the party had left early in the morning (9 a.m. I think): twice Dr. Simms had passed the Chief's car up country: & Col. Fletcher had said the Chief would not be back until quite late. But I felt that if I knew the Chief that would not be sufficient reason to keep him away from church. And I was right. He appeared as usual looking keen & alive as ever. I had had a thin line of duck-boards laid down on the path leading up (by this time a pool of mud) to the Church-door: and it was comic that D.H., walking up from his car in conversation with Dr. Simms, should make the latter walk on the duck boards while he himself immaculately dressed in his brown topboots, walked abreast of him splashing unconcernedly through the mud, and entered Church with his boots well spattered. So, after the service was over the thick strong mud did not deter him from taking as usual the circuitous route by the Ramparts path to the Ecole.

Mr Stevenson told me the other day an interesting incident about the Chief. Mr Stevenson's brother in law Lieut. Garrett Fisher (16th H.L.I.: who in private life is on the staff of The Spectator & The Manchester Guardian) came up from Etaples a fortnight ago in time for the morning services: and he was introduced at the close by Mr. S. to D.H. "Where are you at present stationed?", asked the Chief. "I'm at Etaples, sir but I am longing to get back to my battalion." "Oh, but that will be all right." was the reply. Some hours later Lieut. Wood of the Camp Commandant Office came round to ask Mr. Stevenson particulars about his brother in law's name, etc., regiment, and present address, because by the C. in C.'s command an order had gone through the A.G. that the officer in question was to be posted to his battalion!

We made some very considerable progress yesterday both north and south of the Ancre.[16] Dr S. said that when up the line yesterday he heard that a big attack was to begin last night. That may have been a premature or exaggerated rumour: but certainly big things are on the near horizon. Leave is still in abeyance, and the most probable explanation is to be found in the quite huge number of men & guns that are being transported across from England these days. Again there has been no Boulogne boat (& so no letters & no English papers) yesterday or today & today at least (I cannot say about yesterday) no mail crossed from here to England. – This, too, no doubt, on account of the transport of troops & material.

I found our Printing Co. here today busily engaged in turning out – as they do, Lieut. Field told me, by the tens of thousands – bills printed in German with fine big type, etc. telling the Boche all the advantages enjoyed by the men who surrender to us (these bills are dropped among the Boches from our 'planes).

At an evening service tonight we had present Col. Malcolm,[17] of the London Scottish who had brought out the first battalion in 1914. – a fine keen face he has. I brought him to introduce him to Dr. Simms: and so a few of us had a talk together. Naturally we spoke of those awful & fateful days of 2½ years ago. "I told Lord Cavan", said Col. Malcolm "that I was asking such and such great arrangements for my reserves". "Reserves", he said, "every man you have will give you a thin enough line to hold the trenches."

Feby 25th

The Chief was at service as usual this morning. I watched him during the service & again as he shook hands before going: and I felt distinctly that he looked more aged. Never before have I had this impression. A Tommy who was present at the morning service, remarked to me this evening on this very matter, saying he thought the Chief looked aged today. Questions were raised in

Parliament a week ago about a very optimistic & self-confident interview which Sir D.H. was said to have given to some French journalists prophesying a breakthrough and a speedy end of the war, and he had been asked by the Government to explain the circumstances of the interview. My friend the Tommy thought the Parliamentary outcry shameful & was of opinion that this may possibly have worried the Chief. I am doubtful of that. I feel that he may at times feel the burden of his military responsibility almost too great to be borne – for the load is tremendous and he won't be satisfied unless the work is done as well as it <u>can</u> be done: but I do not think he will allow himself to be worried by what people say or think.[18] I spoke today on "If thy hand ensnare thee, hew it off", a Lenten sermon: but perhaps what the Chief needs rather is something that is aglow with confident hope.

As usual we had a very hearty service in the evening. Major Heseltine was present (this is the first time any of the C. in C.'s staff has been present in the evening), and he stayed for Communion. He was there with the Chief as usual this morning. One wonders <u>why</u> he was there this evening? Was it for the sake of the Communion Service? He told me as he left that he was going home on foot – & Brimeux where the Aides-de-Camp's chateau is, must be at least 6 Kilos out. He was the only officer present this evening.

I learnt from Major Heseltine tonight that we have been able to make very considerable advances on the Ancre Valley owing to the Boches evacuating certain positions – (viz. part of Serre, etc.) He seemed pleased about it. On the other hand I found our friend Evans at dinner quite reserved about the matter and disposed to say that time (say a day or two) would tell what the advantage was worth. It looked from his cryptic remarks that he suspected some deep laid Boche scheme.[19]

Rumours of a coming "stroke" are more current but are practically all of the vaguest description. My batman came to me the other morning on his return from breakfast & asked "Where is Kemmel, Sir?" & informed me that that was to be one of the advanced G.H.Q.s & that part of the "escort" had gone there.[20] (But Kemmel is under shell fire.) Today Evans was away on one of his rare secret missions up the line in a car: & that may be taken as a journey with a purpose. It may be taken too as "suspicious" that Major [unintelligible], G.H.Q. Medical Officer went on leave two days ago though normal leave is still in abeyance.[21]

The Boche seems to be achieving very much less than their aims with the new submarine piracy. The number of ships sunk is not alarming & rumour has it that we have accounted for quite a number of the hostile craft.[22] I heard (though this has not been officially announced) that some days ago one of our transports carrying Kaffirs for labour in France, was torpedoed in the Channel & practically all on board lost – the first loss of its kind we have sustained in the Channel. I also hear that the need for speeding up railway construction is so great that guards at GHQ are to be abolished, and that the Artists are to be taken away to work on doubling the railway line. Lloyd George's speech on Friday, with most drastic proposals regarding restrictions of imports and the increase in home production, seems to have been a momentous utterance & is being well received.[23]

Yes: the Boche is retiring on a large scale – how large it is difficult to say. Rumour has it tonight that we are now in Bapaume. Though it is good that we are thus gaining at no expense so much valuable ground, it is generally recognised that the Boche in accomplishing this retirement secretly and successfully has done a very clever thing, foiling our offensive plans. He has probably big reserves ready to fall on us if we advance too carelessly. Col Repington in yesterday's Times warned his readers that the Boche might have 800,000 new troops this summer.

Along with the news of our advance on the Ancre (and the fall of Bapaume if it is true) comes official intimation of the fall of Kut.[24] Had a very interesting time yesterday with Neil Munro,[25] first at tea in the Hut, then at dinner where he, Gen Charteris, & I were the guests of Mr & Mrs Stevenson in Mr S's studio.

March 4th 1917

I felt last Sunday that the Chief looked much older than I had ever seen him before. Mr Stevenson would not have this: he said that if there was any foundation in fact for this impression the explanation was to be found in the dull day – which makes us all look older. Whatever be the true nature of the case, this morning (a bright spring morning) the Chief looked his old self, fresh & alert.[26] I spoke on the Transfiguration – a great subject and (as I felt when I selected it) relevant to him in the present situation: but my preparation had gone all agley and I am afraid there was little either of vision or of exaltation about my discourse. But all the same I got a very cordial and approving smile from the Chief as he left. Talking of Christ's going up the mountain, I could not help saying what a spiritual asset it was for us at G.H.Q. to be set for our work in such a place as Montreuil – a place that speaks of far distances and of things the eye hath not seen or the ear heard. Truly the landscape here on such a spring day is fair & "speaks of heaven".

Two 17th Lancers officers were present with the Chief today: and Lindsay & Sir Harry Verney MP[27] (now a Colonel & with Lindsay in the Director of Labour's office) were also in the congregation. Lindsay was also there at the evening service – the only officer present. I saw that he got his heart's desire by including both Ps 95 & Ps. 30 in the praise list! The Chief I believe left the Chateau this afternoon. He is said to have gone to Beauquesnes till Friday.

March 5th

Yesterday we were rejoicing in the arrival of spring. This morning the ground was thickly covered with snow, which began last night about 11.30 & went on till 6 a.m. or so. Most of it has now disappeared: and tonight the stars are out & the air is warm.

I dined tonight at the "Labour" Mess in a back parlour of the Hotel de France – with Col. Sir Harry Verney, Col. Wace,[28] Col. Marshall,[29] Capt. Wood & Lindsay. Verney is a most charming man – & Christian gentleman every inch, so one felt: rich in faith, hope & love. He said he was delighted with the service yesterday morning, and heartily agreed with what I had said about Montreuil. There was a good flow of sail over the dinner table, our conversation being concerned largely with the German temper and the hope of a permanent peace in Europe (& the world) after this. I raised the question of disarmament. Verney thought one might hope for it, but Wace could not hear it was possible yet, however much as we might desire it. Appealed to by Col. Wace as to my view & whether there was anything in Scripture to justify the hope, I said I felt I was like the old lady who, on being informed to cultivate the faith that could move mountains, spent a whole evening in earnest prayer that an offending hillock opposite her window might be removed & who after pulling up the blind with eager anticipation next morning merely remarked "I thought as much."

March 11th

There was a heavy rain-shower at 7 am but by the time the service began a summer sun was glowing. The Chief looked much as usual – a bit preoccupied, perhaps. Irles was captured yesterday.

In the evening I gave the first of a series of addresses on "Reconstruction from the Christian standpoint" – a big congregation, eager clearly to learn and anxious for guidance. Our discussions on After the War Problems, held at the Y.M.C.A. on Tuesday Evenings, are creating a very great interest and draw a very large crowd. We have been especially fortunate in having Pte Horabin of the Artists (Board of Trade) to open on certain occasions with most careful & fairminded papers. Thunder has now begun to roll. 10 p.m.

March 12th

Baghdad fell yesterday.[30] Sursum Corda.

March 16th

These are stirring days – though news is scanty. For the last day or two we have had Bapaume at our mercy and I suppose we could enter it (or what is left of it, which can be little more than the site) at any time we wish. But probably the place is mined & we are proceeding cautiously. Besides, the mere occupation of a town (even if it be more than a mass of ruins) is of relatively little importance: what is of importance is to deal with the enemy's forces. It is announced that the Germans are wantonly burning up what is left of the town. While yesterday the replacement of Gen. Lyautey, French Minister for War,[31] was announced, much more stirring news has come through tonight regarding Russia.[32] The Government is overthrown, the Czar has abdicated, a Regent has been appointed and assassinations have taken place. The news began to go round in the early evening: but it was difficult to get details (the Continental Daily Mail had nothing to say of the matter & there were no French papers to be got). But it was clear there had been a revolution, and what we wanted principally to know was: "to whose interest would it turn out, the Bosches or the Allies?" In many quarters there was a natural view of pessimism – ("no hope now of getting this beastly business over for years & years yet!"). But when we saw the English newspapers which had long accounts through it, as I said, the French Daily Mail was silent: we began to feel this might indeed be a "Win the War" movement. May it indeed be so. One wonders how far the recent Allied Mission, including Gen. Castelnau & Lord Milner – to Petrograd for a Conference may have paved the way[33] – Col. Burns' visit may have had something to do with it.[34] And in the absence of anything like authoritative news (for I have been able to read nothing more than the headlines in the English newspapers) one begins to speculate what the leanings of all this will be in the future history of Russia & of Europe. Is this the downfall of Russian autocracy? By a strange coincidence I have just come across the following in a chapter from Fisher's "Napoleon" which I took up at the close of my day's work: "Francis could hardly be expected to look with gentle curiosity at the dethronement of the Spanish Bourbons. There is a sense of comradeship – a kind of tacit trades union among crowned heads which renders the misfortunes of kings especially significant & lamentable to their brethren." (p. 180)[35]

Duncan MSS, St.A. MS 37090/3/61

34

Haig to Lady Haig

Friday, 16th March 1917

I do feel that the Higher Power has been good to me in so many ways, especially in giving me health and strength to carry on.[36]

Haig MSS, NLS, ACC. 3155, No. 146

35

Duncan Diary

March 18th

There is little more definite news about Russia – except that the announcement of the Czar's abdication would seem to have been premature.[37] I have not seen a newspaper today (yesterday's or today's) but yesterday evening I heard we were now in Bapaume. A Zeppelin was brought down by the French in flames at Compiegne & it's said one of those that raided the Kent Coast on Friday night was also brought to earth (our gunners here stood by from 3 to 4 a.m. on Saturday morning). Since midday all sorts of advances have been announced – most astonishing progress has been made between Arras & Baupaume and south of Peronne. In Champagne the French are said to have made a 4 mile advance on a 14 mile front. At several points the cavalry are in action.[38]

There was a "foo kirk"[39] this morning. Gen. Birch, Col. Burn, Col. Fletcher, Major Thompson, Major Heseltine & Sir P. Sassoon were all with the Chief: there was quite a parade of Artists from Ecuires: Col. Marshall, too, was present & Mrs. Van der Veyden. I do not know how others felt: but I enjoyed the service. The subject of the sermon was Christ on the "long long trail" up to Jerusalem (Luke 9:51) – "Lead thou me on" – the secret of the power to carry on. The Chief looked fresh & hearty – as well he might do with such news to cheer him. After the service he, Col. Burn (followed of course by the others who seemed to wonder what was "up") all went off up to the Citadel – & of course

stumbled upon the Machine Gunners in various stages of
deshabille, shaving, etc. Lieut. [?Power] overran the august visitors
as he was returning from late breakfast!

March 19th

Yes: the Boche are in full retreat to the Hindenburg line. Peronne,
Chaulnes, & Nesle are now in our hands: while the French are
once more in possession of Noyon & at some places their advance
is to a depth of 20 miles. So much the newspapers report. And
how much more is going on? – for those who know are reticent.
The enemy is retreating in a masterly way & is leaving us few
prisoners to boast of and – call it systematic or call it brutal as you
wish – he is destroying most things of value that he leaves behind
him. Artists in arson, artists in cattle-driving, artists in poison – so
the pictural Beach Thomas of the Daily Mail describes them
asserting that 300 villages are burned to a cinder and that the
wells, esp. near Peronne, have been infiltrated with arsenic &
probably other poison. "One of our first acts in the advance", he
says, "was to send a sample from the wells at Barleux to one of our
analysts. I am informed on good authority that he found in the
water sufficient arsenic to kill any man or horse who drank it."[40]
How much more ground is he going to give up? He seems to be
making for St Quentin & Cambrai: he will likely hold Lille. And
will he try to attack in force up north to run his new line on
towards Calais?[41]

The German official report says: "Between Arras & the Oise
the English & French have occupied our old positions and several
localities including Bapaume, Peronne, Roye, & Noyon."
Unpalatable news served up as simply as possible! But to hear in
one week that Baghdad was captured, that the Augean stables of
Pan-Germanism in Russia were being thoroughly cleared out, that
their glorious armies had retreated before the contemptible British
and French on a front of 82 miles, surrendering fortresses like
Bapaume & Peronne without a struggle,[42] that the removal of the
Zeppelin has meant the loss of another airship, that for all their
wild hopes, the U-Boat piracy was not apparently beating Britain
to her knees, that China had broke off diplomatic relationships, &

that the day seemed ever drawing nearer when the United States could range themselves definitely among the armed antagonists of Hunnism – such news must come as a serious crown of sorrow to a people that numbers its dead & wounded by millions and is denied the simple gift of daily bread.[43]

The one cloud in the sky is that the whole of the French Government has resigned and M. Ribot is trying to form a ministry. The withdrawal of M. Briand from the Presidency of the council is, I take it, a very real loss to the Allied Cause.[44]

March 20th

The retreat still continues – but there isn't much in the way of definite news tonight. For such news as is available these days we are dependent almost entirely on the newspapers. The French are now well beyond Ham, and some of their outposts appear to be fairly near St. Quentin.

We had a good time at the Y.M.C.A. tonight when Sapper Cox opened a discussion on the pathological condition of Britain before the war. He had some strong, rather unbalanced, denunciation of England's false sentimentalism (witness the Sign of the Cross, & Chas Dickens' death of Little Nell and of Paul Dombey), but it was his plea for sound thinking that evoked (in the subsequent discussion) the most wholehearted support from the audience. What to me is especially interesting is to see how, in sheer honesty, the men who take part in these discussions are brought up against the need for some sort of educative, driving, & regenerative force without seeming – I must say – to believe but are we to imagine that is precisely why we supply such a force that (so to speak) religion exists.

March 23rd

Snow came on yesterday (Thursday) morning – not very much but I shd say there is more still to come. During the showers reconnaissance work can be impossible: but while unfavourable to our advance I suppose the weather must in some ways be unfavourable to the enemy. The enemy is now putting up a stiff resistance between St Quentin & Arras.

Where is Advanced G.H.Q. to move? Still no word of it: but Evans set off somewhere today (without a word to us) and is not returning tonight.

March 25th

The Chief was not at service this morning. Just when he was about ready to come out he was prevented from leaving (I think it was a case of a guest arriving – I heard the new French War Minister.)[45]

March 28th

Progress in the advance is now stiff & slow. One feels that a move to an Advanced G.H.Q. may be made next week but there is very little talk & nothing at all authoritative to go on. Evans has not returned.

April 2nd

These are days of great interest. One feels we are on the verge of some big move: yet few know anything definite. The secret this time is being magnificently kept. Evans came back on Friday evening from <u>England</u>: it seems to have been simply a case of leave, but leave which it was evidently desired in a way to keep dark. I hear from one of the clerks in Operations A office (who has just returned from special leave altho he had ordinary leave about Xmas-time) that <u>all</u> the members of that office have in the last few weeks been sent on special leave as if in preparation for a hard summer. (Evidently G.H.Q. is expecting to keep fit for this summer's ordeal: a month or so ago the offices in the Ecole all received a message from the C. in C. pointing out to them that it was advisable that as far as possible they should close down each night at 10 p.m. Formerly 11 to 11.30 seems to have been a usual hour: now many officers leave at 10, & others at least leave earlier than they used to).

While anything like definite news was entirely lacking, and even rumours had little that was definite about them, there was an impression abroad last week that this week might see the opening of our offensive. Such an impression could not be without its effect on our worship yesterday morning. The C. in C. was present: also Heseltine, Sassoon, Gen Birch, Col Burn, Dr Simms and – thanks especially to a big parade (big for us) of Artists – there was an "unco. foo kirk." It was the Sunday before Easter: and after singing "O God, our Help in ages past", that great hymn of confidence & strength, followed by prayer, I read most of Math 27 1–35. This I followed immediately by a short exposition in which I pointed out that the death of Jesus, the crucifixion of the Perfect Son of God, not by criminals, but by men like ourselves – was a fact of history which from being historic became superhistoric, showing us as against a white background the real blackness of our natural life & puts every man at the foot of the Cross as one who has helped to drive Christ there. Thus nothing explored the depths of a man's soul so much as the Cross did: and much as we like to sing "Fight the good fight", our deepest depths were touched when, in all honesty, we sang "When I survey the Wondrous Cross". Then quietly & feelingly the congregation sang that great hymn of X^{ian} dedication. Prayer followed: then came a break for intercession & the collection, after which I resumed my discourse with a message of hope. The Cross, I said, put every honest man at the foot of it: but it was also God's supreme appeal to all that was best in a man to hate the natural life that was thus so glaringly shown up, & so to yield himself to the love that thus appealed to him & to join himself to the armies of the crucified with a devotion that knew no reservations. Then I spoke of the Cross' appeal to the nations. Once again the Cross was set up: and all the nations were at the foot of it. . . . Where was Britain? We had as a nation little conscious realisation of Christ: yet if the same Spirit was in us still as there was when in August 1914 we spontaneously as a people sided with the Crucified nation, if still we were going on, not in the pride of our might nor in a lust for power, but rather seeking thru willing sacrifice & in a general hatred of war, to live & die to make a better world possible, we might, like Constantine, see in a rift in the storm clouds a Cross, & a sign by which we should conquer, and thus feel that we went as Christian soldiers "with the Cross of Jesus going on before". Then I asked the congregation to stand while we had a short prayer of dedication & intercession: and then while we stood we sang as a closing Hymn "Stand up, stand up for Jesus", followed by the National Anthem and the Benediction. Many seem to have felt the service appropriate & impressive. Dr Simms, who was present again in the evening, said he wished to thank me for it. I had thought it was just possible that the C. in C. might give some hint as to whether by next Sunday he was likely to be at an Advanced GHQ: but nothing was said nor have I yet heard from him. Is there to be an Advanced G.H.Q? I did hear last night that meanwhile there were to be only advanced <u>Army</u> Head-Quarters and that as this general attack developed G.H.Q. would move to the most effective quarter. Evans today at table followed up some remark about a move by saying quietly: "You all talk about moving: I don't know that we are going to move." Yet I know that at least one place (perhaps there are others) is ready as an Advanced G.H.Q.: but the exact place is a secret. Beauquesnes one assumes is ready: but it is now far back from the line and it does not seem likely that our main attack will be made from positions occupied since the German retiral. There is known to be an immense concentration of artillery around Arras: for myself I take it that it is round there (both north & south of Arras) that our chief offensive will be launched. The Germans have been stoutly resisting our attack on Croisilles, but I hear tonight that we have at last got into that town: if so it means that the Germans north of Arras will catch it badly both now & more especially when they are driven to retire. Further south the pressure is still being relentlessly kept up: Each day brings news of more villages captured & we are said now to be within 2½ miles of the centre of St Quentin.

Yesterday was a cold day with a good deal of rain. This morning there was snow on the ground and there was a heavy storm with quite a fog of thick, big flakes in the afternoon. Now (11.30 pm) a gale has arisen. A Zepp.[46] crossed our lines near Arras this evening at 7.40: if it is out in this wind, it must be having an unhealthy time. Whenever is spring going to come?

April 3rd

The weather is too much with us. Late last night, as I said, a gale
sprang up. About 4 a.m. there was (I am told) thunder. Then came
snow, which by the time I got up this morning was a few inches
deep. Midday brought a thaw and the streets ran rivers. Despite
the wet under foot I had my weekly walk with A. D. Lindsay. He is
a gem. We talked (he opening the subject) on the Crucifixion. I
had said on Sunday evening that the Crucifixion was wrought not
by criminals but by ordinary men. He admits that such a
"reaction" as I display here is in the right direction: but he
deprecates the impression being created that therefore the men
who crucified Jesus were not "wicked" – that we should say of
them "Oh, they were no worse than we are." "They didn't know
what they did", he said, "No, but they jolly well ought to." "They
are wicked: and we are no better than they were?"

Discussion at the Y.M.C.A. tonight on "What is to give us the
driving force for Social Reconstruction?" was opened by Cpl.
Spencer[47] of the Signals with a very fine manly broadminded
statement regarding Christianity as spirit & life.

Sunday April 8th

Easter Day. The sun has shone beautifully all day: & the music of
the birds & the freshness of flower & grass & trees all told that
spring has come: and made men more receptive of the message
that Christ has risen.

The C. in C. was at service this morning. So also were Gens
Birch & Charteris & Col Burns. The chief looked preoccupied,
again one saw on him traces of ageing. We had a simple Easter
service, closing with the singing of "For All the Saints". As he left
the Church, an officer was waiting (so I had heard) to hand him a
telegram:[48] and after glancing at it he dismissed his staff and went
off quite pleased-like, with Gen. Birch around the Ramparts to the
right. He is small in height compared with Birch but as I caught
sight of them one could not help noting again the huge breadth of
shoulders & the firm bold step.

This evening at table there came to me a note from Major
Heseltine (Aide de Camp) saying the Chief suggested I might go up

for some days to a Cas. Clearing Station as so many Scottish troops were to be in the fighting. This is the first official news I have got. The note added: "We are all off this afternoon," & I got the C. in C.'s address in case I wanted to phone. It is clear now that many officers know, or suspect, that big fighting is about to commence, but few know details & almost none, I should think, outside those to whom such knowledge is necessary know where Advanced G.H.Q. is. So I mean to go off tomorrow & I shall get a car from the C. in C.'s. Evans is still with us. At the mess Evans had nothing to say about a departure, and I, too, was silent. – it's better.

Wednesday morning brought in news of President Wilson's first speech summoning the United States to side with the Allies in the cause of humanity against the German despotism. The speech was very favourably received, so far as I could make out in the Army. Now war has been officially declared. The French people are very enthusiastic and flags are out everywhere.

Duncan MSS, St.A. MS 37090/3/61

36

Haig Diary

Sunday, 8th April 1917 (EASTER SUNDAY)
I attended Church of Scotland at 9:30 a.m. Rev. Mr. Duncan took the service. He spoke about the certainty of life hereafter, and prayed for us to be given an "unconquerable mind".

Haig MSS, NLS, ACC. 3155, No. 112

37

John Heseltine to George Duncan[49]

8.4.17
The Chief suggested that as there were such a lot of Scotch Regiments taking part in the Fighting you might like to go out and

stay at some Casualty Clearing Station tomorrow for a few days. He suggested in the XVII Corps area.[50] I don't know if you know anyone up there who you would like to go & stay with or should I get in touch with the XVII Corps Padre who is I believe a very good fellow.

We can send you out anywhere in a car.

Gen Butler suggests your consulting the A.G. We are all off this afternoon. So either ring up Alan Fletcher at C in Cs house HEUCHIN[51] or if you can make your own arrangements ring up Sgt Crouch here at BEAUREPAIRE he will send a car to take you out.[52]

Duncan MSS, St.A. MS 37090/3/80

38

Duncan Diary

Monday, April 9th

The offensive (around Arras) began this morning – at 5.30, I believe.[53] I am told it had been arranged for yesterday, but had to be postponed. I am tonight not far off from the scene of it – at Aubigny. In the course of the day I have been a good few miles further still up the line.

I left Montreuil this forenoon in a glorious Daimler of the C. in C.'s: called on R. G. MacDonald en route at St Pol: finally introduced myself at No. 30 C.C.S. at Aubigny. Scarcely had I arrived than I met Lord Beauclerc[54] (Aide-de-camp to the C. in C.) on a round of enquiries as to how things were going at the C.C.S.'s: then on my first sight of one of the hospital wards I caught Sister Brooks beaming at one of the windows: and as I chatted with her a doctor entered, Nicol of Dundee, whom twice before I had met at C.C.S.'s. Such is the fraternity (& the littleness) of the mighty B.E.F.!

In the afternoon I went off in my car with the Rev. Herbert Reid, now a Col. Corps Chaplain with the 17th Corps. We first went to Haute Avesnes where the Corps hospitals were (3 hospitals of the 9th, 34th & 57th divisions) and those we found surprisingly empty. Then on to the Corps Collecting Cage for German Prisoners (at Etrun), which were surprisingly full: I should say there were 2000. But lonely fellows most of them were – many belonged to the Bavarian Corps, a crack corps (which seems to have cracked right enough). None enjoyed the sight of them more than the French women. Our Tommies swarmed round the cages bartering for souveniers – for bully beef or cigs: many a package of the latter being too light weight to carry against a strong head wind over the 10 or 12 feet of intervening barbed wire. Then after a visit to Rev [?Bevy] Preston at Etrun Y.M.C.A. we came home thro Maroeuil (pretty badly shelled). At one point we saw 2 Nissen Huts & alongside the side of a third which 2 nights ago had been caught by a chance German shell: it had been occupied by the officers of one company of the 6th Gordons, the company that was to lead the attack: 4 of them were killed & the other 4 wounded. Part of the roof of the hut still stuck up a neighbouring tree. We had to pass endless transports on the way back.

What has been the result of the days fighting? It now seems to have been <u>very</u> successful. Our corps here (the 17th) has gained all its objectives. Except Balleul, where the 57th Div. was held up by machine gun fire: but the sharp salient here caused on the Boche line cannot hold out long. Vimy Ridge has been also captured by the Canadians. The casualties are said not to be heavy: probably smaller than the number of prisoners taken.[55]

Duncan MSS, St.A. MS 37090/3/61

39

Reverend Professor Main[56] to George Duncan

12 April 1917[57]

Many thanks for your letter. I shd have replied to it sooner, but I have thought much of it & have not been idle.

I am perturbed, greatly perturbed by it. I know a good deal about St. Andrews College, Sydney.[58] In fact some Sydney friends of mine thought wd there be a vacancy in the Principalship a while

339

ago & were pulling strings for me. But it is <u>not</u> the St. Andrews which is to be yours. <u>You are coming here</u>. Please don't commit yourself till war is over. Scotland needs you, & we in St Andrews specially need you. You know, & have power over, students: & I make no secret of this that we need your knowledge & your power. The St. Mary's[59] traditions have not been good, & I want you to help me in big changes. Our Church needs men of your kidney, & especially the Church needs to see Chaplains who have not been failures. Everywhere I go I hear galling things said about Chaplains at home & abroad, & we must have you back.

I saw Herkless.[60] He is on your side, & though he can't definitely promise that your appointment is secure, he has empowered me to write to you (confidentially) that everything that can be done will be done to bring you here. Do you not realise what a tremendously strong candidature you have now? Sir Douglas Haig is our Lord Rector;[61] your fame has reached us; the appointment will not be made on political grounds; & our leaders will support you strongly. I don't wish to minimise the claims & the opportunities of the Colonies – far from it – but Scotland is the home of Presbytery, & the times are ripe for big things. <u>Do think carefully before you let this chance go by</u>. You wd get time for original work here, for inspiring, human work, for taking a hand in Ecclesiastical Enterprises. It is good to be alive in these momentous days, & we shall see a rosy future dawning <u>if</u> we get the right men. And you are one of these. Let me make a special appeal to you as a NT[62] scholar. We are not strong in that department. Who is to lead us in the days to come? Our old Church needs scholars, & you have spent many years in scholarship. Our Colonial students almost invariably, & of necessity, have devoted themselves to other matters than scholarly work. If you go to Sydney, you wd begin a new life work & one for which a training wh was different from yours would be just as suitable – I hope I don't offend. Forgive me if I write too strongly, but I feel strongly. We want you to collar the Student Movement (for Scotland), to get a new class of student for the Church, to prepare men for the glorious days in store for us, & to make St. Andrews University lead once more.

Duncan MSS, St.A. MS 37090/3/75

40

Duncan Diary

Thursday evening[63]

There seems to have been a real lull in the fighting. The 8th Division, advancing ahead of the glorious 9th had a hard time in some attack it made on Tuesday – and again yesterday an attempt which it made in conjunction with the cavalry to push on past the railway towards Roeux was badly held up by machine gun fire on the flank. In this last attack the 2nd Seaforths suffered badly. Many of them went on tonight by hospital train to Etaples – most of them with hard memories of the hellfire from which they had so painfully escaped: but there was one of them – a gardener from Wick, Donaldson, I think was his name – whose bright ruddy countenance and clear sparkly eyes arrested me as a perfect picture of bodily & mental health: "Yes, sir", he said, "I never felt better in my life." "I got hit in the knee. I was the sorriest bloke that got knocked out yesterday. I was just beginning to enjoy it." And clearly he was quite honest: he meant what he said. But he must be almost unique in his point of view. What most men felt was put very well by another to whom I spoke today: "There'll be lots of conscientious objectors in the next war, sir."

There are some very sad cases in hospital. There was dear Easton, a boy from Abbeyhill, Edinburgh, shot thru the stomach, whose frank bright eyes compelled one to love him. "I have wandered sir", he said: but then with a fine sincerity he added: "but I have never disowned Him though". I held up before him a little Crucifix, and he took hold of it & kissed it saying "He died that we might live": and then he asked me to kiss him. And today there was McDougall from Port Ellen lying in the ward for hopeless cases, still quite conscious but smelling badly with gas gangrene. His wounds were in the elbow & both thighs – not in themselves so severe: but he had lain out for 13 hours.

The weather has, I suppose, hindered operations: it certainly has made it hard on the poor fellows who were exposed to it – waiting to attack or lying out wounded. There were occasional heavy blizzards on Tuesday (snow & sleet) and yesterday a real snow storm came on about 5 p.m. and the rain was very heavy I believe most of the night. A visit which I had hoped to meet with Rev. Herbert Reid up the line on Tuesday was postponed till yesterday. An ambulance car took us up to St. Nicholas (suburb of Arras) where we found Rev. Johnstone of Paisley (9th Division) and with his two Coffee Bar Caravans dispensing coffee, etc. at his Field Ambulance. A mile or two along the Bailleul road I met an old New College friend, Cameron, now a chaplain with the 9th Division: and the saddest sight of all some fifty of our boys lying side by side while a "labour party" was digging them graves – stark & stiff as they had been picked up on the battle field, their arms sometimes held up as if imploring help or seeking to stave off a fate they felt overwhelming them: one had his arm linked in his comrade's. By the side of another there lay a sheet of a letter written in a woman's hand. It was full of the anxieties of war: one brother had been wounded, another had fortunately been transferred to a timber-cutting detachment and had prudently renounced his leave lest in his absence he should lose their "safe" job: and it went on in this strain: "Cannot you get a transfer dear: it would be much safer if you could get on the roads or something instead of the trenches. Oh, how I wish this awful war was over."

After returning to Johnstone's Caravan, – where we had a tinned pork pie heated up and coffee, duly served by his orderly who in civilian life is beadle at Tollcross U.P. Church Glasgow – we set off to look for Lt. Oswald Milligan who we knew was engaged with a burial party. The walk took us along the road to the south of the Bailleul road: it was alive with men coming or going (especially wounded returning from the unsuccessful attack toward Lieven that had been begun at midday) & with labour parties. Soon we were on the ground recaptured on Monday morning. One need not recount the desolation of it all – the upturned ground, the ruined walls, the mounds of bricks that used to be houses. Yet St Laurent Blangy was not such a dust-heap as I believe Fricourt was: at least some walls still stood. I saw no dead bodies about – but here & there one came on a dead horse and at one point there was one poor beast in whom life was not yet extinct. Beyond Blangy the railway bridge over the road still stood. But another bridge a little to the right which spanned the river had been destroyed by the Boche on their retreat. At the village we cut off to the left to the little cemetery, to find that Milligan had just gone: and we chased him without success down to German dug-outs, one which was now the battalion headquarters (8th Black Watch), the other the abode of the padre & the doctor. Back then to Johnstone's place while the snow came down in a steady downpour. The labour parties were still busy – few things impressed me more amid these scenes of destruction than the reconstruction work of the engineers & labour-men busy with stones & planks & wattles in re-converting these mud-paths into a worthy highway of traffic. It was a weary trudge thru snow & mud on past St Catherine, with its big collecting station for wounded and its ruined Church (the plaster cast above the altar of Christ on the Cross, was bereft of the head) until we got a motor which carried us while the snow still descended in a blizzard past Anzin and Artillery Corner to Maroeuil, there we had tea at a part of the ruined Mairie which now did duty as a Scottish Churches Club, and while the kettle boiled I had a chat with the Secretary of the Maire – her family next door, into whose house while they sat by the fireside, there had once burst a shell which demolished all the upper story of the house & then pitched beside them – it was a dud (!) & lay there untouched for some weeks until the Artillery Authorities requiring the house for a billet were constrained to remove it by the aid of a long wire which slipped & brought the shell toppling down the stone steps outside, without any untoward consequences.

As I write, a fair deal of shelling goes on: it sounds like Boche shelling. On Tuesday afternoon the first 3 shells out, Frevin Capelle, 1 mile or so from here, which fell 30 yards away from the railway, harmlessly in the fields.

14/4/17 Saturday Evening

What is happening? News, authentic news reaches us slowly here. Did the French begin their attack yesterday, as rumours yesterday said they did?[64] We are said to have advanced beyond the village of Bailleul & taken Oppy: if so, surely Lens is doomed, and the rumours that it is in flames or that it is even in our hands, can only err, if they err at all, by being premature. The 9th Division have again been in, with (I think) doubtful success. Yesterday & today has seen a steady improvement in the weather: it is much clearer, calmer, & warmer. The Boche has not been forgetful of Aubigny these days. The big shells dropped harmlessly near Corps Head Quarters yesterday about 9 a.m.: and while last night as I was jumping into bed there were 2 loud reports as of falling bombs accompanied by the noise of splintered wood, (as a matter of fact I believe they were caused by our Archies,[65] & one shell fell on a shed within a few yards of the C.C.S. Theatre: and it is averred that they were firing at one of our own planes). I dressed this morning to the accompaniment of an Archie firing prolifically at a Bosche plane that seemed to be immediately overhead.

The Hospitals are having a fairly quiet time. A large number of sick came down today and have been evacuated. It looks as if it were the calm before another storm burst.

Duncan MSS, St.A. MS 37090/3/61

41

Haig to Lady Haig

Friday, 20th April 1917

As to the Battle of Arras, I know quite well that I am being used as a tool in the hands of the Divine Power, so I am not at all conceited, and you may rest assured that I am not likely to forget to whom belongs the honour and glory for <u>all</u> our good work and success.[66]

Haig MSS, NLS, ACC. 3155, No. 146

42

Duncan Diary

27/4/17

Since my last entry in my diary I have been nearer the firing line than ever before. On the 17th I went up to St. Nicolas, a suburb of Arras, to act as padre at a Walking Wounded Station there. Contrary to expectations, I had a very slack time there. The renewal of the offensive planned for somewhere about the 19th, was postponed till the 23rd. The storm broke on the Monday morning (i.e. the 23rd) at 4:35 after a terrific bombardment. The story of that day's fighting has yet to be told: but it would seem that our men, going forward in something of that Bank Holiday spirit of exultation that had been with them ever since their great & uninterrupted onrush on Easter Monday, came up against tremendous Bosche resources in men & guns (have the Bosche been preparing an offensive against us?) and hence ensured perhaps the fiercest battle of the whole war. Little was gained by us in the way of ground, though we were able to move forward at two points capturing Gavrelle & Guemappe: but if we inflicted heavy losses on the enemy, and if (as may have been the case) we ruined his plans for an offensive, then the military gains were still considerable. Neither the Walking Wounded Stations nor the Cas-Clearing Stations had any very special rush of wounded: Yet the losses on our side must have been considerable, though some of the pessimistic tales of the wounded, who often spoke as if 3/4 of their battalion had been wiped out, were doutless due to the fact that they went over the parapet with too easy hopes of victory & were aghast at their apparent failure to make headway.

Many memories stand out: Visits to ruined Arras in search of provender for the mess – what a ghoulish town Arras would be by night if it were deserted: but as a matter of fact many of the inhabitants are there, shops are being opened again & crowds of British soldiers throng its streets till they are like the Strand. Scottish bonnets are especially conspicuous: & one cannot go far without meeting kent faces. I had 2 good evenings addressing men at the Y.M.C.A.: an evening service for the 1st Gordons on the eve of the 23rd offensive in the Sale des Concert a big dark concert hall, its gallery empty & considerably demolished for a shell had come thru the roof: a long service at my own station for a party of bearers who left that Sunday afternoon to go up the line for work on the morrow, a service which was disturbed by the rattle rattle of a machine gun, as a Boche plane attacked one of our sausage-balloons & forced the observer to descend in a parachute. One day an aeroplane, another day a balloon came down in flames: on Wed. afternoon a "dump" went up near Arras.

But a truce in all this for the hour is late. I left St Nicolas yesterday afternoon meaning to return to Montreuil to see what was happening there: but at Aubigny I received a wire saying that the C. in C. wanted me to take services at Advanced G.H.Q. on Sunday next. So this evening, thanks to Gen. Charteris, I came across by car from Aubigny to Adv. G.H.Q. which is at Bavincourt, a tiny village a little off the Arras Doullens road. I arrived in time to see Wood before dinner regarding a Church & a billet. This doesn't seem much of a village. I have got a bare room as a billet and a wire bed has been rigged up for me. As I approached the village this evening, one of its first sights that greeted me was a chauffeur out in a field cleaning a magnificent car that carried the familiar little Union Jack (the C. in C. car): and then entering the village, I came upon those other familiar insignia, the two sentries & the little Union Jack over the gateway: for the C. in C.'s house this time stands not out in the country, but in the village street, separated from the street by a wee bit of a garden, but plain & open there for all passers by to see.[67]

Duncan MSS, St. A. MS 37090/3/61

43

Haig Diary

Sunday, 29th April 1917

I attended Church of Scotland. Mr. Duncan preached from the story of St. Paul's shipwreck. He urged us to have a personal and practical religion. First pray to be told what is God's will.

Secondly, believe that God is working in us for a particular purpose. Thirdly, that being so, have no fear lest any evil may befall you.

Haig MSS, NLS, ACC. 3155, No. 112

44

Duncan Diary

Sunday Evening: April 29th, '17

On Friday evening I arrived in Bavincourt, our Advanced G.H.Q., a tiny village a mile or so north of the Doullens Arras road – a decent clean village as it seems to us who have just arrived, but to those who saw it in the mud of a fortnight ago its filth seemed to make it impossible. But the Chief is not nearly so fastidious for himself as his friends are for him: and Col. Fletcher (Chief Aide de Camp) allayed their fears and assured them that if the place got a decent clean-up the Chief would settle down in it all right. Since I arrived the sun has been shining brightly: today the weather has been quite hot: and Bavincourt looks a place where one who loves country peace might spend a few weeks very contentedly.

A good part of yesterday was spent in having our orderly's mess room converted into a Church. The mess room in question is one half of an old French military hut – formerly used by British Tommies as a theatre. The theatre curtain, with its slight attempts at scenic representation had to be obscured by matting, as had also one side where our orderlies had their [?meat]-safe. We finally got it made into quite a quietly reverential place of worship.

The sun shone brightly at 7.30 this morning. . . . The service was none too hearty: the congregation was small (about 30), the singing was not hearty and one heard the traffic passing to & fro on the main highway: yet it wasn't a bad service! I spoke on Paul's personal religion – "There stood by me this night the angel of God, whose I am & who I serve, saying: Fear not, Paul." The Chief looked uncommonly fit. I ventured to congratulate him as he arrived on the events of these last weeks and he looked as if he fully admitted that great things had been accomplished, but he added in his usual modest way: "But it isn't me."[68] As he left I got an uncommonly hearty greeting from him.

After the service Col. Fletcher waited behind saying the Chief would like me to come around to lunch – he evidently wanted to have a talk with me about my best arrangements for these next few weeks, for of course he wants me to be here on Sundays no matter what I do during the week. I had a good talk with Fletcher – he is very approachable & open. He told me how the Chief had been summoned off the other evening to Paris,[69] for the French politicians were frightfully jumpy after the failure of their offensive (it was a real failure), & how if they were to retain office they would get rid of Nivelle, & substitute Pétain – a change which would not be at all welcome to D.H. for he did not at all like Pétain.[70] Evidently the French put great faith in D.H. and at present they are full of excited appreciation for the British & their doings. "The French are always nicest when they are down", said Fletcher: "when they are up they are horribly conceited." And it is not merely the French who are changing their opinion: it's the same with Lloyd George. Formerly it was always "the French, the French, let us copy the French": and so he was always interfering, – eg in his advocacy of long range guns over howitzers, though guns could not fire over some of the intervening heights. Then we talked of Russia: discipline in the army has naturally disappeared, while there was revolution in the state: we could expect Russia to do no more than hold on, if she could even do that. And so we reflected on how precarious a thing the Entente was, how but for Britain it would all go to pieces & be at Germany's mercy.

I went round to the chateau for lunch. After I had had a chat with the Aide de Camp, the Chief appeared, coming out in his usual hearty way & shaking hands to wish me good morning again & forthwith led me into the dining room where he proceeded with his own hands to dish out a cutlet for me from the good things that were set out on the cupboard. He asked me lots of things about myself & the time I had had up the line, about the spirits of the wounded, about the physical condition of the Bosche prisoners (did they show any signs of food shortage? For we knew that on such & such a date, which he mentioned, their rations were further reduced).[71] He was most interesting when at one point he opened out & said "I was in Paris the other day." "They're a fickle people, the French," he added & remembering what Col. Fletcher had told me I could see what a time he had had with them trying to steady them in their jumpiness. "They're going to get rid of Nivelle", & when I expressed surprise and disappointment, he added, "Oh, yes, they are." It seems that Nivelle had given himself away by speaking pretty freely & with much detail of what he was to do & where the French would be 48 hours after the offensive began and all that increased the disappointment & gave his critics a handle against him. So the Chief told me, & Col. Fletcher had told me in the morning that there had been practically no organisation behind the line for evacuation, etc. It was clear, too, the Chief went on – that too many secrets had leaked out, & that the Bosche knew all about the French offensive. "How do you account for their failure?" I asked him and he added at once: "Simply because they are French." I told him I was surprised at the answer – and he said that the French as such were bound to fail in an offensive. Oh, they're all right once the army are drawn back a bit, but you asked me why they failed, & I answered 'Just because they are French' – they are a decadent race. They haven't it in them. I never thought much of them and I have had a great deal to do with them since the beginning of the war. We had a terrible time with them on the retiral. It's a wonder our people & they have managed to remain friends so long."[72] When we talked about my own arrangements he was very keen that I should during the week go further up the line – "that's where you get the real thing", he said: & arrangements would be made for me to come here for the weekends. I ventured to show him a cutting I had received regarding his taste for sermons – the quotation from "Current Opinion" . . . It amused him highly. "What is meant by the Presbyterian temperament?", he asked with a smile (the paragraph said that he was a Scottish Presbyterian with the Presbyterian temperament very pronounced in his character) and when I ventured to [unintelligible] him about the library well stocked with works of polemical divinity he smiled & said, there were plenty of polemical books there but I'm afraid they weren't divinity!"

It was a perfectly delightful time we had at lunch – so unrestrained & natural. The meal over, we rose & shaking hands said he would say goodbye. But before going he talked again about my coming back Sunday by Sunday & asked Col. Fletcher to make any arrangements necessary for my going further up the line, & hoped I would have a good time there, adding "For, as I have told you before, you could make anyone fight!"

Truly he is a great soul. What I learned today about his dealings with the French made me realise fully that just as we are by far the predominent party in the Entente, so he is the biggest man on the Allied fighting side. And when one reflects that the present situation – when Germany has had almost more than she can bear & is yet threatening us very seriously with her submarines[73] & the Entente is only with difficulty holding together – what above all is needed for us is a great military success, there dawns on one a new consciousness of the vast responsibility that rests on that man's shoulders. And one turns & looks in amazement at the apparent ease with which he bears it. Some of the French villagers remarked to me this afternoon on his fine appearance, and a Tommy who has just joined G.H.Q. expressed just what all of us feel when he said to me today: "when one thinks of the awful load of responsibility there is on his shoulders, I don't know how he can bear it. But it fills one with respect for him just to look at him."

In the evening I had a chat with Gen. Charteris in his office – kind & amiable as ever. I asked him about the Cadaver verarbeitende anstalt of which the Daily Mail has had so much to say of late. He said the evidence wasn't conclusive, but he was quite prepared to believe it possible. He said that quite a long time ago we had evidence the Bosche transported train loads of dead through Belgium, but whether to cremate them or to make use of the bodies was never proved. – I had raised the same subject with the Chief at lunch, and he said then: "Charteris doesn't believe it. He thinks they had got hold of the wrong end of the stick. But all the same we had evidence months ago that from their Zeppelins the Germans were using more —skin (I didn't catch what the name was which he used) than could be supplied from animals.[74]

Continuing the subject with Charteris – the latter said it was not at all unfathomable or improbable. The German is so utterly materialistic that he could quite well tolerate such treatment of the dead & even rejoice in it. They haven't denied the charges, he said, it is questionable if they would want to or if they would mind them. And then he began to generalize on the German mentality, in some ways extraordinarily intelligent, yet in others not much removed above the beasts. He said he had been in Germany not many years before the war when he kept his eyes open: & he was much struck by the lack of moral discipline, eg. in the education of children. Certainly in the family he knew it was considered no sin on the child's part to tell a lie: if the child lied successfully the father applauded & approved: if unsuccessfully, he said, you silly little boy. And as for their efficiency, he said: that is a bubble that has been pricked again & again.

Duncan MSS, St.A. MS 37090/3/61

3

May to December 1917

45

Duncan Diary

Monday: May 14th

During the first week of May I was at Montreuil, winding up matters there – with visits to Boulogne, & to Etaples. At the latter place there was a memorable "Presbytery" meeting when Rev J. R. P. Sclater introduced the subject of discussion "Is God to blame (for the war)?" & the subsequent discussion was practically monopolised by Scottish Presbyterians – the one "outsider" who ventured to join in (an English Congregationalist) putting forth the impossible thesis that God was the author of evil & sin. I arrived back at Bavincourt on the Saty. There was some talk then of Mr. Lloyd George coming that evening: but finally his arrival was postponed till Sunday afternoon at 3.30, so I missed him both at Church & at lunch. He left again on Monday morning, quite early (about 8.30). He was quite troubled about the submarine menace (so Col. Fletcher told me afterwards), and while he was here he had a wire about Russia, where the situation was clearly critical. On Monday morning about 10 I saw the Chief & CGS go off by car – to Doullens, I learned afterwards, where there was a large conference of our generals & Mr. Lloyd George was also present.[1] I had lunch on the Sunday (6th) with the Chief. He seemed more preoccupied than in the previous week. The fighting along that line was very severe, and an attack we had made on the previous Thursday morning had had only a very partial success. I heard afterwards of one officer who alleged as two reasons, among others, why his men had completely failed 1) the Boche knew fully

352

that the attack was coming off 2) the attack was made too soon – before dawn and the troops could not see. Clearly too our men are feeling the strain of attacking, attacking, attacking, when heavy losses are incurred & no appreciable advance made. Several places have resisted attack after attack (like Roeux), or, like Oppy & the Chemical Works north of Roeux, have been taken & lost several times. For a time we held Fresnoy, but lost it again.[2]

May 14

Yesterday (Sunday) I had again lunch at the Chateau. Brig. Gen. Crow[3] had just arrived from a special mission to Italy, so he absorbed most of the Chief's attention. It was interesting to hear him talk of the "Macaronis." Their offensive had been due to start on the 6th but had been postponed.[4] They were naturally apprehensive of what was happening in Russia: a separate peace on Russia's part might mean that the released German divisions would be flung against Italy. The Italian staff could not abide the French, whose cocksureness & overbearing manner they deeply resented, but they had warm feelings of appreciation towards us.

Owing to Gen. Crow's presence I sat on the Chief's left, next to the C.G.S.[5] What a truly admirable man he is. One wonders how many people there are at home or even in the army, who could tell you his name or on learning his name could truly say that they had even heard of him. Yet there he is, with no glamour of fame about him, but a master mind, a real student, a tremendously devoted worker and withal one of the kindest & quietest of men.

His mind seems to be engrossed by the war – & how to win it. He showed the same desire as the Chief has done on other occasions to learn in what sort of spirit I found the men (I had been in Arras again for one day last week). I told him that I felt they were a bit gloomy at their repeated fruitless efforts to make headway. He quite understood that this might be so but added that the Boche were having an infinitely worse time (they were getting no respite & had to use up division after division) and in the last few days they had begun to show signs of softening. (Attacks on Friday evening at 7.30 and on Saty morning had been particularly successful & we were in possession of Bullecourt, the Chemical

Works, & the outskirts of Roeux). So far as the military situation on our front was concerned he was quite hopeful: he felt that the Boche might quite well crack up all of a sudden, but other factors were less hopeful. – Russia especially & the temper of our people at home. He was deeply stirred about the Munitions Strike that is going on[6] (& spreading at present[)]; spoke about the governmental fear of Labour & said that when he reflected on what our men had to suffer out here & how many of them had perished, he would himself gladly pull a trigger to settle some of these strikes. There was no real government: it was only government by consent: it could not continue in office if it displeases the people. Yet he admitted that the heart of the people as a whole was sound, & that the Anglo Saxon was characterized by a wonderful sanity & particularly, "What a chance poor K.[7] missed!" he added regretfully. "He could have done anything." But he tried to do too much himself (whereas a great man always delegates functions to men whom he can trust.) and his judgment seems to have been at fault.

Duncan MSS, St.A. MS 37090/3/62

46
Leaflet advertising Presbyterian services, Montreuil

CHURCH NOTICE

SERVICES ARE CONDUCTED BY THE PRESBYTERIAN
CHAPLAIN
IN THE CHURCH HUT EACH SUNDAY:–

Morning Service – – 9.30 a.m.
Evening Service – – 6.15 p.m.

Holy Communion – After the Morning Service
on the Second Sunday of each month and after
the Evening Service on the Last Sunday of
each month.

ON SUNDAY EVENINGS AT 8 P.M. there will be A SERIES OF LECTURES (with open discussion) ON:–

Some Great Religious Questions arising out of the War.

May 13th – How can we say that GOD is love?
May 20th – Who is to blame for the war – God? or Man?
May 27th – Is the world becoming a better place?
G. S. Duncan, C.F.,
Presbyterian Chaplain.

Duncan MSS, St.A. MS 37090/3/87

47

Duncan Diary

20/5/17

The end of a busy day. Four services at G.H.Q. to-day – an early Communion (the first I have ever had: Major Heseltine & an Artist were present) at 7.30, the usual services at 9.30 & 6.15 & a series of lectures with discussion at 8 p.m. (subject this evening: "Who is to blame for the war? God or man?["]]. In addition I had an open air service (with two or three hundred men present) at Gouy at 5.15.

Esher was with the Chief at Church today. Derby was here yesterday.[8] Is the war situation in Paris giving trouble that these two are across (a few days ago it was officially announced that Pétain took Nivelle's place as C. in C. of the French Army). At 2 pm I met quite a crowd of Portuguese officers leaving the Chateau in two cars – some of them had lunched at the Chateau. I was not present at lunch today. The Chief looked much as usual this morning – fairly happy-like. The guns have been going strong since early morning. – an attack by us was, I believe, on at the junction of the 3rd & 5th Armies.

On Wednesday afternoon last we were all startled here by terrific explosions – a fire beginning at the railhead at Wangeutin caught a dump there. On Wednesday the Boche made a terrific attack & temporarily regained Roeux & the Chemical works, but were soon ejected. The attack seemed like a real attempt to break through. The Boche attacked in 7 waves, each man arranged (something quite new) in full kit. The cavalry was massed behind, & Hindenburg was said to have been on the spot. I have heard no news of the affair here but several stories were current in Arras. The Boche are said to have reached the Headqtrs of the 8th (?) Argyles, where the situation was saved by the resource & pluck of the staff. The C.O. himself killing 4 men. 3 6th Gordons boys with whom I had a long talk in the Y.M.C.A. Library Room at Arras told me that they owed their salvation to a German prisoner who, when some of our men were inclined to have him shot, ran at full speed towards H.Qrs crying "Valuable information", viz. that a German battalion was advancing up by a gap in our line. Machine gunners were accordingly sent out & never, said one of these boys, "have I seen machine gunners do such excellent work" "But for that German", said he continuing, "our whole Brigade (152) would have been captured."

Two or three days ago came news of the Italian offensive. Query? Will it go on? The latest returns show a diminution of one half in the weekly losses by submarines. The American destroyers etc. are now operating with ours over by the Channel in tackling the problem. The latest news from Russia continues more favourable. 5 or 6 days ago it seemed very bad, when M.G.[9] – Minister of War, resigned, a consequence of the attitude of the Workmen's Committee. Since then the same Com. has declared emphatically – "no separate peace". A Socialist Congress is due to come off soon at Stockholm,[10] & it is not unlikely to be used (so some think) as an occasion for the interchange of real peace proposals re conditions of peace . . .

Duncan MSS, St.A. MS 37090/3/62

48

Haig Diary

Sunday 27th May 1917

I attended the Church of Scotland. The Rev. George Duncan conducted the Service. Today being Whit Sunday he spoke about the spirit of the Lord entering into those who are desirous of it. We thus get a power which is not our own.

Haig MSS, NLS, ACC. 3155, No. 113

49

Duncan Diary

Wed. May 30th

Sunday was Whitsuntide – a day of beauty & light when the great Quarter Master showered his good gifts with liberal hand on the evil & on the good. In other respects it was a day of some solemnity so far as worship was concerned: for a great offensive would seem to be preparing "up north" (as the phrase is), & the storm may burst this week.[11] Yet the Chief was buoyant, almost boyishly buoyant. There was a gleam in his eye and a more than wonted spring in his step as he came along to Church: & also when 1 p.m. he welcomed me & another guest at lunchtime. The other guest, a small unimpressive major in an A.S.C. uniform, he introduced to me as "Mr. Orpen, the artist you know".[12] Orpen had the seat of honour on the Chief's right: I was on his left next to the C.G.S. who had first arrived back from leave & who, as always, asked me about the spirit of the men (i.e. up Arras way). I told him I felt they were a bit tired – as a result of continual fighting by the same divisions: & he admitted they might be, then added (but with no lack of sympathy of what they had gone through) that the strong heat must have been very trying for them. I asked the Chief about Russia: & he seemed to think things were improving, thanks to the influence & efforts of the new War Minister.[13]

I reminded him that the General Assembly[14] was then in session: and he said, "Oh, yes. I received just the other day a telegram (of good wishes) from 4 churches." He remarked on the fact of the telegram coming from a united meeting of the Churches: and when I said that the modern eccles. situation in Scotland was characterised by a very considerable amount of charity he said "I'm glad to hear it, there was need for it." This led him to speak of the C. of E. – which seems to him to suggest a policy of splendid isolation, "I always tell Bishop Gwynne that it will never do for them to sit still in this way, if bodies don't reform themselves from within they get a ruder reform from without. People won't be content now to listen Sunday to Sunday to an old man mumbling prayers from a book." Then he went on to talk of the new form of education in the clergy and a broad liberal education apart from their more particular training. "I used to notice at Oxford what a scanty education some of the fellows had who were to become parsons."[15]

Duncan MSS, St.A. MS 37090/3/62

50

Haig to Lady Haig

5th June 1917

Everything seems going satisfactorily as far as our preparations are concerned. We ought to take the ridge[16] without much difficulty, but then as you already know, nothing is certain in war. Success lies in a Higher Power than me.

Haig MSS, NLS, ACC. 3155, No. 147

51

Alan Fletcher to George Duncan[17]

June 5th, 1917

You must be here at 9.30 am tomorrow 6th – to see C in C as he leaves at 10 am. We will then leave at 10.30 am or 11 am.

Duncan MSS, St.A. MS 37090/3/68

52

Haig Diary

Sunday, 10th June 1917

I attended the service of the Church of Scotland in a hall in the village. Mr. Duncan officiated. He came to dinner in the evening.

General Robertson (C.I.G.S.) left after having a talk with me and Kiggell after Church. A night's reflection and Duncan's words of thanksgiving for our recent victory seemed to have had a good effect upon him. He was less pessimistic and seemed to realise that the German Army was in reduced circumstances.[18]

Haig MSS, NLS, ACC. 3155, No. 114

53

John Heseltine to George Duncan

16.6.17

The Chief is going to England tomorrow[19] for a week or so – after church – & asked me to tell you that you could do the Leave if you cared to. I don't know yet how long the Chief will be away but he said you could go off for 10 days or whatever you like.

Duncan MSS, St.A. MS 37090/3/81

54

Duncan Diary

June 18th.

Much has happened since the last entry. In the course of the days immediately succeeding it I learned that the great attack was sure to commence on the 7th & that we were to remove from Bavincourt to Blendecques on Sunday, 3rd: that tho the "move" would begin on Sunday morning early; the Chief would not leave Bavincourt till after lunch & that, therefore, I might have the morning service as usual. "The Boche know all about this coming fight?", I ventured to ask Lt Col. Fletcher: "Oh, yes, of course they do," he answered, "the Kaiser has told his troops this is to be the decisive battle of the war". With these things in mind I looked forward to a Sunday morning service with more than usual solemnity: but on Saty morning, without my knowledge, notices were sent out by the C. in C.'s orders cancelling all my Sunday services (viz. Hol. Communion at 7.30 & Morning Service at 9.30). Why? I learned later the reason. Not at all because of the move. It was because on Saty forenoon Col. Ryan[20] had taken the opportunity to mention to the Chief that my throat was bad: & with magnificent kindness, he immediately called Capt Straker & told him to see that the services were cancelled.

I was able to leave Bavincourt on Sunday morning & travelled to Blendecques with Col. Ryan in his car. Having missed the Chief on Sunday through the cancelling of the service I felt I should like to see him before he left to go up to his forward G.H.Q. (he & his personal staff were due to leave at 10 or so on Wed. morning June 6th, to live in a train near Boeschepe): & so I was asked to come round to the Chateau at 9.30 a.m. When I got there I was told that Gen. Nash (Railways, etc.) was with him & that Gen. Charteris must see him next. So I hung about in the Aides de Camp room while Gen. Kiggell, Butler, Davidson, Charteris, etc. were all coming out of & going in to other rooms near by. At 10.30 or so I was told the Chief could see me so in I "popped". There he was at the side of his green table and he came forward to greet me with outstretched hand & smiling eyes: & thanked me for coming to see him. His head, you could see, was full of thoughts of all kinds: but he chattered away in his usual kind way, & showed me his contour maps with all the divisions, etc. duly marked. "This is where we are to be on the train & you can come over to see us", said he, pointing to a point near Godewaersvelde, near Mont des Cats: "& here's where Gen. Gough's headquarters are", he added, pointing to Lovie Chateau n.w. of Poperinghe. This was the first intimation I had had of Gen Gough's presence in the neighbourhood, and as I was soon to learn, it meant that the 5th Army had moved north.[21] "You are making this an Irish battle", I said to him with a smile, with reference to the fact that the attacking force that morning was to include both the 16th & the 36th Divisions: "Oh, but the Irish are all Scots now", he replied with even a greater smile. He means that the Irish divisions were drawing their reinforcements from troops of other nationalities, but it was my experience next morning that the Irish element in them was still quite strong. Then he asked me what I wanted to do and where wd I like to go to up the line for the engagement: and in my raising the question of a pass to get into the 9th Corps area, he rang the bell for Major Heseltine & he ordered him to take me up in a car to Cassel where I could get a pass, learn about hospitals, etc. and decide where I wanted to go to. After a minute or two, again by ourselves, I left him. His goodbyes are never perfunctory: as we shook hands & again as I passed to the door & still again as I was closing the door after me he followed me with smiling kindly eyes & another "goodbye". I was sorry not to be in the spot at the the actual minute of his departure, but I felt I had now no justification for staying on & my presence might be an intrusion so I left the Chateau: but half an hour afterward as I turned in for a side lane to the main road heading from Blendecques Church to Arques, two cars came flying along. The first was carrying the Union Jack: and as it passed I saw the face of D.H. & his Chief of Staff.[22] He spotted me, too, and returned my salute. He was off to [?win] Battle of Messines.

At 12.30 Major Heseltine & his brother, [?Tim] Heseltine,[23] the old Hants bowler & soon one of the King's Messengers, came in a Rolls Royce for me. We had lunch with Heseltine's brother-in-law, a Brig. Gen. of the Guards: then the Major & I journeyed onto Cassel and hence to Loker.

<u>Written up on July 8th</u>

Much that is deeply impressed on my memory & experience I must dismiss in a few phrases in this diary – my experiences at Loker & Kemmel at the time of the great Wyschaete Messines fight; my visit on the morning of June 9th to the Chief's train, etc. Next morning (June 10th) the Chief was at Church (at Blendecques) with Sir Wm. Robertson[24] and I had dinner with him (D.H.) in the evening. When I ventured to offer him my congratulations, he waved his hands in his usual way & said: "It's you: it's you <u>all</u>". We talked that evening of Willie Redmond,[25] of Seeley (they felt that in politics he was like the rest of them, and wd do anything to catch a vote: but in the army – "He's a man" said the C.G.S.): Haig told me how he had had a visit from a French general regarding the French troops up north: he (DH) was much "bucked" that the French troops were to be at <u>his</u> (DH's) command. He talked freely of the Belgians "what worth can they be after standing <u>looking</u> at the enemy all these years?"[26] – and of the Portuguese – "I wd gladly be without <u>them</u>." The talk that evening (as on [?one] other interesting occasions) got on to education. Kiggell had referred to a circular which had come round some time ago advocating scientific education. The Chief remembered it & asked what he had done with it. "Oh, I just sent it off as it was" to which the Chief, turning to me, said with a comic leer: "He knew there was no use asking my signature to <u>that</u>". This interested me immensely: & I asked him to explain. "Why, where are you going to get your teachers from?", he asked me. "Scientific education will give you men who know science but it will not produce men who are able to teach others – capable instructors."[27] A novel & cogent argument – especially interesting from the mouth of a military man. "I have come across so few who really inspire me," he went on. Kiggell reminded him of his attempt to introduce Univ. Extension Lectures in the Army: & he told me how he felt that by some such scheme they might educate their junior officers, esp. to discover likely talent for Staff work.

July 8th

We had a good service this morning. Some sisters from the Scottish Hospital at St. Omer, two officers from the train, Munro (chaplain)[28] & another officer from the Canadian Hospital at Arques: DH, Col Burn, Gen Birch & the aides de camp. Col. Fletcher has been away for the last few days & also Major Thompson[29] who is no doubt waiting on the King (the King & the Queen are both in France at present: they are running separate "tours": the Queen was here on Thursday, the King yesterday).[30]

At the service I read John 21 & spoke on the Recurrence of Experience, with reference to the parallelism with Peter's experience (Luke 5 & John 21). I felt there was a parallelism suggested by Blendecques, by the events of July a year ago, by the conflict round Ypres (which might be to us what the lands of Tiberius were to Peter, the place where not once only, but once & again we found that God was a reality in this war): – a parallelism, too, with the Napoleonic wars (not merely victories, but long patience & dogged determination: England then saved herself by her exertions & was to save Europe by her example): and with the life & death of our Lord, who taught his brethren & inspire[d] to suffer & to die. (We safely trod where God has trod). Our hymns were: "O for thou are my God alone", and "Praise to the Holiest on the Heights". and (after the address) "Sometime a light Surprises". We took up a collection for St Dunstan's Hospital for blind soldiers & sailors & got 125 francs!

As usual, I had lunch with the Chief. Col. Burn[31] sat on his right, I on his left, while Major Orpen was between Col Burn & Sir P. Sassoon. I learned then for the first time that the King had just made D.H. a Knight of the Thistle, an extraordinary honour which naturally pleased the Chief immensely – I think this is only the 2nd occasion it has been given to a Commoner. The most interesting part of the lunch conversation to me was begun when the Chief told Col. Burn that he had seen Field Marshal French in London on his recent visit (the Chief was in England from 17th–27th June attending meetings of the War Cabinet, it wd seem almost everyday), & French said to him that he realises now that the change of command was altogether for the good of the nation. Col Burn said he was delighted to hear it, for evidently French had behaved none too well just at the time. The Chief corroborated, remarking how badly French had taken his recall: but now French had generously said to the Chief that he felt he had said many things & done many things that he ought not to have said. And he was sorry for them now.[32]

We were talking about our Scottish Territorials, & Col Burn told how one man claimed friendship with him. "I know you, fine sir, but I have voted Liberal!". "Very sensible, too", added the

Chief, with a smile,[33] and then with more seriousness he referred
with some contempt to Bonar Law. The exact point of this came
out later: viz. that Bonar Law, alone in the War Cabinet, was keen
on the air defense of London & wished aeroplanes for the purpose
which D.H. felt were wanted in France. The Chief had no
sympathy with a policy of reprisals. He spoke, of course, entirely
from a military point of view: but he objected to taking away
aeroplanes for that work which might rather be employed to a
work of military advantage & to the great risk our aeroplanes ran
in proceeding to German towns, travelling all the way by land so
that there were all sorts of chances of being shot down or cut off,
whereas the Boche aeroplanes are not observed during their
journeys by sea to Britain until they arrived over land.

July 22nd[34]

I see I have no entry for last week. On July 12th I went up to the
Fifth Army area & finally settled down for 2 nights with Harry
Miller who was doing temporary duty with the 19th Corps as
D.A.P.C. On the Friday evening we had dinner with Neville
Talbot in Poperinghe. On Sunday morning, 15th inst., I spoke
simply on Faith, illustrating from Heb. 11, 8, 27, 29. The Chief
seemed thankful for the service. I had lunch with him afterwards:
and I was the only "guest". It was a quiet & uneventful lunch. The
Chief was hard on Jowett[35] of Balliol for the politicians he had
turned out – some of the Curzon type,[36] who went to India
inspired by Jowett "with a turn the other cheek policy" which the
Chief felt wouldn't work there – "so different from the manly X[nty]
you preach to us" – (a doubtful compliment, I felt: – I tried to put
in a word of defence for the other). After lunch we sat out in the
garden where we had coffee – & the Chief had some hard things to
say to himself for forgetting to give me my usual glass of port at
table (he generally saw that I had a most ample supply of the
beverage at the conclusion of lunch: for like him, I generally drank
aerated water during the meal). At the close of our coffee & our
garden talk he rose to go back to work. I asked if I might speak
with him for 2 minutes. So on our way back from the garden to the
Chateau I asked if he couldn't stay behind some Sunday for

364

Communion. I'm afraid I took him unawares: for his natural shyness overtook him & he could just mumble "No; no; I don't think so": and when, with perhaps the appearance of pressing him, (though I meant only to convey the impression that it would be a great pleasure to me to see him there), "You know, sir", I said. "You treat me in such a way that I speak to you as I would to an ordinary Tommy". He replied, "Yes, but you know I must be the judge of that." By then we were well off the stairs of his chateau. He seemed disinclined to continue the conversation, & simply shook hands again & said goodbye & disappeared into his room.

Today (Sunday) I felt we met on the threshold of big things. It seems certain that the big battle up north will begin this week.[37] At the morning service I spoke on Hope, and I ventured to say that, speaking as one who has no knowledge of military secrets, but as one who has great faith in the human spirit, I believed if we here, & the people at home, all went forward in the next months with a glowing hope that we were to carry this thing through, the war would be over this year. The Chief seemed very happy at the end. Major Heseltine, acting on orders received before the service, said the Chief wanted me to come to <u>dinner</u> (not lunch as is usually the case). When I arrived at the Chateau at 7.45, I met Gen. Kiggell outside at the base of the steps: and I chatted with him there. Unfortunately the Chief was already in the ante room without our knowing it: so that before we knew we saw him leading the company into dinner. And what a company! I was sorry to miss the friendly preliminaries of introductions before dinner. The Chief sat in the middle of one side with Gen Pershing on his right, & Col Harbord, (American Chief of Staff) on his left: then going round the table from Pershing were Gen Butler, Col Fletcher, Capt. Straker, the C.G.S.,[38] Gen Sir Wm Robertson, myself, Gen Charteris . . . Most of my conversation during the meal was with Charteris. Homely & kind he generally is. He was especially human as he talked about the tragedy of the war. – "[unintelligible] what a tragedy it is, look at the widows & children": and then he added "I got a letter the other day from the widow of my best friend: it's so <u>sacre</u>. I oughtn't speak about it, but I'll tell you this in confidence and she said, referring to her husband: 'I feel he has stolen a march on me.'" A beautiful sentiment. I told him I liked it so and he added, "Yes, a beautiful thought. I oughtn't to break a confidence but I felt you would like it." This led me on to say how I sometimes feel a process of selection was going on by which the best were being picked out for some special service beyond the grave: & he added, "Yes, I think it is like that." Sir Wm Robertson was busy with the C.G.S. on his left – but he was as simple as can be in his talk with me. I asked him about his son: & he told me he had just met him. He was celebrating his 21st birthday. He is now with Haking (?) – at the 11th Corps. he was only 18 when he first came out here: & what's the good of sending a boy of 18 to the trenches: he'll just get killed. So I kept him with me as A.D.C. Afterwards he went up to be a Sapper, but Sir Douglas took him on as an A.D.C. He went from there to a Corps, then to a Brigade and now again he is with a Corps: but his heart all the time is with the Sappers. You know a boy doesn't like being always with Generals: that's what he used to say when he was with me: "You're all brass hats here, and I'm quite out of it." I corroborated from my own experience: & he asserted very readily: "Yes, I am sure you must feel that very much:" (You must want more scope, he hinted): but then you know, padre, we must all do what we are told in this war and your job is here." "Look at me", he went on, "stranded away in London – and I sympathised with his being amongst those "damned" politicians & missing the free heart of a soldier out here. . . . You must have so many things to do that you don't want to", I said. "I hardly ever have anything to do that I want to", he replied.

As I write at 11.30 we have had an air raid. No bombs dropped: but much firing from Archies & occasionally from machine-guns. From my window I can see ½ dozen searchlights all near one point: and one plane full in the glare of one of them, flying pretty low. The wretches were in the neighbourhood a few times last night & we had our Archies polting at them at 2 o'clock this morning, while a little further afield the guns were going for them about 9.20 a.m. A big fleet of them were also over in England this morning (Harwich & Felixstowe): but I haven't heard much about that yet.)

After dinner we moved out to the garden where a long plank table was set in the gravel just under the window of D.H.'s working room. Charteris was to introduce me at once to Pershing: but the Chief got hold of me & introduced me first to Harbord & then with his usual eulogy ("He could make anyone fight") he introduced me to Pershing. There were lying back wicker chairs about the middle of the table & one small table chair toward the end, & the Chief wouldn't have it, but that he would take the small chair at the end & that I should chat to Pershing. . . . My talk with Pershing did not develop much, for Sir Wm Robertson came up to him on the other side & bagged him for a private talk.

But this just meant that the Chief & I had a collieshangie. He was in an uncommonly gay mood.[39] Charteris leant over from the other side of the long table to tell the company of how I had introduced that morning at Church a new Collection Plate that had been presented to me with the inscription carved on it: "Fill this with a tenth part of the chief spoils." I protested with a smile that that was much too strong, for the real inscription was less graphic, being "To whom Abraham the patriarch gave a tenth out of the Chief Spoils", but even so there was a general laugh, the Chief going on most beautifully while he drew a picture of the spoils of the coming fight – the big guns, etc. being all [?polished] & put into this poor little collection plate & then to be taken by me & put up for auction. The Chief insisted I had been in great form this morning – personally I hadn't thought so for I had had nothing approaching finish in my preparation: and I told him I had broken for quiet time yesterday evening but an officer had dropped in to talk to me after dinner (this was [?De Hailes][40]) & we talked till after 11 when I had to ask him to go: then I had to try and do some preparation till midnight & later these wretched Archies began to fire so this morning my head was quite dull. His only reply was: "You oughtn't to be sitting up after eleven." Then he began to tell me he had had the Archbishop of York[41] calling on him at lunch time, along with Bp. Gwynne (I suppose that was one reason why I was asked out to dinner rather than to lunch). He was rather taken with Lang. He <u>looked</u> quite old, about 65, but "he went up to Oxford in the year I went down (1882) so he is younger than me", said the Chief. "I told him that the church would have to alter its ways after the war: and one would like to see one great Church for the British Empire: and he was quite open & sympathetic" (I told the Chief this was not the Cosmo Lang that we unfortunately knew in Scotland). "I told him, too, that before I was made Com. in Chief I used always to go round:[42] and that for 3 Sundays or so afterwards I did so out here: but one fellow told me what to do with our spare money, but it was only Duncan who told us straight what we ought to do and to be regarding the big things of the present." The Archbishop said he had heard about Duncan. I said I was surprised, for no one ever heard of me before this war. "Oh, well" he added, "You see how your fame is spreading."

Then as I still sat next to him – & he was quite on the outskirts of the little company (the C.G.S. had gone, & there was a good deal of coming & going on the part of the others) – he chatted on to me & told me that the 15th & 51st Division were to be in the coming fighting: He meant, of course, that I would probably care to go up & see them. I told him that I had already been booked by the A.P.C. 51st Army to do temporary duty at a C.C.S. near Proven: but once that duty was over I should like to go up & be with some of the Scots boys. "I should like to get further up," I said. "Oh, you were far enough up last time", he remarked, probably with reference to the H.E. that nearly got me at Kemmel.[43]

After a little bit he rose up to go, saying he must see the telegrams: and he did not again appear outside. He was really in great form. He has, I feel sure, aged quite considerably in the last 18 months: but there is never a burdened look on him. I have often seen him with his eyes flashing with the joy of action for which he was ready: tonight (as on so many other occasions now) there was rather a steady straight look on his face as of the man who had much to meditate on before the action began: but one <u>never</u> sees him oppressed by his meditation: He was really happy tonight & hearty – pleased to be among friends, and kind & thoughtful of them as ever. One never feels there is anything self-centred about D.H. – or ultra self-conscious.

Later Col Fletcher came & took the Chief's seat beside me: and chatted about next Sunday's arrangements. At present he said he couldn't in the least say what would be best but so far as he could see there was almost no chance, 1 in a million, of the Chief's being at Blendecques. But he told me various things about the Chief's train,[44] etc. & asked me to get onto them by phone there on Friday. He, too, was happy that the Chief was so fit. Then, open and communicative as he always is, he began to tell me various things about the coming attack – esp. about the great attack that is to come later – things which I cannot put down on paper, they are so deadly secret, & which I was surprised to hear him disclose especially with Charteris sitting so near, just across the table from me.

Later I had a chat with Harbord, the C.G.S. of the American forces. He had a kindly face, but a bit soft one felt.[45] Pershing, on the other hand, is made in the same mould as Haig – a man of quietness & confidence. He has got a square face, with an almost vertical profile. I know how tremendously our Staff is impressed by him – (they are less so by his C.G.S.). He looked, as I said, a man of ability & force of character: what impressed me even more was his quite genuine simplicity & modesty. There was no Yankee bumpishness about him – if there ever was, it was gone now. Both he & Harbord told me how they were overwhelmed by the magnitude & elaborations of our preparations. It was the Queen of Sheba over again – & what they said they honestly felt.

Duncan MSS, St.A. MS 37090/3/62

55

Haig Diary

Sunday, 22nd July 1917

At 9:30 a.m. I attended Church of Scotland. The Rev. Duncan officiated. He preached from St. Paul's letter to the Hebrews. "By Hope are we saved."

The Archbishop of York (Lang) with Bishop Gwynne came to lunch. The former spoke to me privately about the necessity for opening the doors of the Church of England wider. I agreed and said that we ought to aim at organising a great Imperial church to which all honest citizens of the Empire could belong. In my opinion, Church and State must advance together, and hold together against those forces of revolution which threaten to destroy the State.[46]

General Pershing and his C.G.S. were at dinner also the Rev. George Duncan.

Haig MSS, NLS, ACC. 3155, No. 115

56

Memo by the Reverend Duncan to the Chaplain General[47]

PRIVATE AND CONFIDENTIAL
In writing on this subject one must generalise, and in generalising there are two things one must keep in mind (1) that the Army is no longer a mere section of the nation, representative of one or two classes, it is the nation in arms, (2) that after well nigh three years of war, it is possible to get a truer conception of the whole situation than it was in those earlier days of the war, when men turned to the Unseen in sublime confidence, or in helplessness and bewilderment. It may well be maintained that the attitude of the Army today towards religion is fairly indicative of the normal attitude of the British people as a whole towards religion. The day has declared it.

The first thing one wants to testify to is the glorious Christian spirit that animates the great mass of our men in the ordinary relations of Army life – all the more glorious because they are so little conscious of it as being Christian. The army is a great brotherhood. It is part of the army code that men stand by one another, and don't let one another down if they can help it; a stranger in khaki is welcomed as a friend and brother, without being first called upon to explain himself; there is everywhere a spirit of cheerfulness, not incompatible with a deep seriousness (the most rollicking fellow I have known out here, an R.A.M.C. officer, confided once to a friend of mine – "when I was up the line, I settled my account with my Maker"), and even when men are genuinely anxious or sad at heart or dead tired, they still feel it is "up to" them to keep smiling. As for the way in which men stick it out amid conditions that constitute almost as big a strain as any the human spirit was ever subjected to, bear up under excruciating pain, accept with fortitude the prospect of broken and maimed lives, or give themselves ungrudgingly to death – words are'nt good enough to describe it. What some of us professing Christians feel about these things is not merely that our men have in them Christian qualities beyond what we have looked for in them, but that their's is a Christianity which we have not found, no not even among Christians. Their good fellowship, their optimism, their courage, their self-sacrifice, impress us because they have more of these things than we have ourselves. And we turn away, inspired and hopeful, yet also feeling what a pathetically poor thing much of our modern Christianity is.

On the other hand there is much in the whole situation that is profoundly disquieting. There is firstly the plain fact that the great mass of men are out of touch with the Christian Church, and do not look to it as being in any vital relation to life as they know it, either in peace or war. There is the deeper and sadder fact that to a very large proportion of them God Himself means little or nothing, or means something that is very unchristian. What is a Christian to feel about these things, if they are true? a) Even from the point of view of the present he must recognise the pathos of the situation. The men are up against the terrible forces of sin, death, fate – as indeed they were, in scarcely less terrible fashion, in peace time – and, to put it quite simply, they haven't a chance. One remembers how our Lord on one occasion 'saw much people, and was moved with compassion towards them, because they were as sheep not having a shepherd', and he began (we are told) to teach them many things. And that situation has its parallel to-day. And (b) this state of affairs must lead us to have grave misgivings with regard to the future, for, despite all that can be said about the unconscious Christianity of our men, can christian character be long maintained unless it be rooted and grounded in a personal relationship towards the Christian God? The apocalyptic effects of these last three years on the average Britisher – a practical soul, who when he is honest, does God's will and knows it not – are to be seen much rather in a nobler conception of social duty than in a fuller appreciation of the reality and the nature of God. Many of our men have been deeply stirred in heart and will, amid the testing experiences of war: but the days of action will be succeeded by others more conducive to calm reflection: and unless they come to see that there is an eternal background to the daily life of man and that, in the very constitution of the universe (or as we should say, in the heart and purpose of God) there is something that corresponds to – and therefore justifies, and may stimulate afresh – such heroism and devotion as they and their fellows have displayed since the outbreak of the war, and will likely be called on to display for long after it is over, there is grave danger that in many quarters bitter resentment, both towards other members of the community and towards the heartless, helpless, tyrant of Heaven, whom they call God.

What is the explanation of this separation between our splendid soldier-souls and the God whom in their daily lives so many of them ignorantly worship?

(1). Far more than most of us realise, the stumbling block lies in an un-christian church and in un-christian christians. The Britisher is rarely a visionary or a theorist; the God whom he is most likely to come to know, is a God who takes flesh and dwells among men; and there is no good telling him that in the person of Jesus Christ, God did this in Galilee 1900 years ago, if in the men and women, individually and collectively, who form the body of Christ in our own land and in our own day, he sees little that reminds him of God. Sometimes men's grounds of opposition to the Church are fairly well defined – it favours wealth, privilege, class distinctions and it does not lead, it follows: it fosters a life that is cabined and confined; its services are, to many, unreal and unintelligible; it seems to educate men, not in citizenship, but in a hypocrisy which shrouds their native selfishness, and so on. Especially one ought to add, do they criticise our Church divisions, which seems to them almost always to imply mutual rivalry, competition and even opposition. More often their alienation from the Church is due to less well-formulated reasons; they feel they miss in the Church the two things which might attract them there, viz. Reality (whatever that may be), and Fellowship.

But the offence of the Church is not the only reason why Tommy so often sits loose to Christianity. To a man who has had a good Christian education and has known in his own life a developing Christian experience, it comes as a shock to realise how weird are the misconceptions as to the nature of religion entertained by "the ordinary man" outside the Church. Here are some of the views of religion seriously entertained by many, and these are not always the uneducated or the unthinking.

It is essentially a "<u>profession</u>". Those who go in for it profess that they believe certain truths, seek for certain blessings, or have attained to certain heights of character. They thus differentiate themselves from other people. but after all their profession is a piece of hypocrisy, and the only difference between them and other people is that the latter are too honest to make any such profession. The outsider is accordingly only too ready to seize on any lapse, or supposed lapse, on the part of the professing Christians, and declare "<u>There</u>, I told you:"

2. or it is confounded with a system of beliefs, to which the outsiders attitude is, either (a) "all this is bunkum; I don't believe these things" – and because he cannot accept some wonderful tale of the Old Testament, he is ready to close his mind to all belief in God and eternity, or (b) "it's all too mysterious and subtle for me, too much in the air, too remote from the sort of life I have to lead", – (a criticism one may add for which there is only too much justification in many of the sermons and addresses, that claim to be presentative of religion).

3. or it is regarded as a sort of insurance by which men seek to win bliss in another world (a world, by the bye, of which existence

our critical friend is very sceptical) by the sacrifice of all happiness in <u>this</u>. Christianity from this point of view involves much unnatural worrying about what is right & [?wrong], becomes a series of prohibitions and disapprovals, it means long faces instead of smiles, repression of life instead of expansion and far away calculations which smother all the joy of the present. Christianity regarded in this light, is certainly not attractive; it is worse, it is repulsive; for, to put the case bluntly, it seems a cowardly business, unworthy of a manly independent spirit – this ultra-concern for saving one's soul.

4. It is a sort of slavish devotion, (based on fear), to a most unattractive Deity who sits in glorified ease in a far away Heaven – "almighty", men say he is, but it does'nt look like it, for he does nothing to help matters on – does'nt even care enough for us down here, to relieve human suffering. Even H. G. Wells seems to imagine that we Christians are stupid or hypocritical enough to worship a God of that kind: and in this he is simply representative of a great mass of ignorant opinion outside the Church. . . .

In all this however I do not desire to write pessimistically if there is "Godlessness" in the army, do not let us mistake its nature. The godlessness one finds revealed there is not of that tragic type which springs from a love of vice. There is immorality of various kinds among our men out here in France but on the whole the immorality does not so much engender, as it is engendered by, the lack of any vital relation on their part to the Spiritual and the Unseen. Nor again is its primary cause to be found in doubt and disbelief. The world will doubtless always have its sceptics – men who have sought God and found Him not, or have sought Him and found (as they think) that He is not, or while conscious of His existence, but unwilling to meet Him on His terms, have either refused to seek Him, or have run away from Him; but nine-tenths of the godlessness that exists in the Army or [*sic*] in measure that Men have lost the sense of God.

Now the hopeful side to all this is that, while so many have lost the sense of God, they have not lost their consciousness of their need of Him; neither are they without the honesty and heroism of spirit that would respond if they realised that He needed them. Where there is a living presentation of religion men are responsive – extraordinarily so. Take the matter of their need of God. There are in particular three things (I have heard it said, and from my own experience I endorse it), about which tommy wants a word of God if any word of God on them is to be found and they are (1) How does God allow this war if, as you say, He is almighty and really cares. (2) Is my chum who was killed, dead and done with?. (3) Is there any thing that will make me more than a match for temptation? Now, if these are Tommy's needs, we may well say to each other. "Be of good cheer", for is'int he ripe for the Christian gospel of God, Father, Son and Holy Spirit?. But alas: as matters stand at present, the Being whom he pictures to himself when on occasion he speaks or thinks about God, the Being whom he thinks we christians worship, is'int in the least little bit like that. As for the other matter the qualities of the heart and soul that will respond, if only religion, too often regarded as providing merely refuge from the storm and an insurance of selfish blessings to come, sounds the appeal for unselfish service.

I have said that I feel that the "irreligion" real or apparent, of many of our men is due, not so much to immorality or unbelief as (a) to their antipathy to the Church, and (b) to their lamentable misconception of what men are to believe concerning God and what duty God requires of men. Even with regard to these misconceptions I have no doubt that many of them would disappear if Christians gave unconscious testimony in their daily life and conduct of what their religion meant to them, and if the organised church showed more courage and sincerity in working for the spiritual uplift of mankind, concerning herself less with unrealities and trifles than with 'the weightier matters of the law, judgment, mercy and faith! (St. Matthew XXIII/23).

. . . there is a very great place in the present day Church for the preacher who is also a prophet; – one entrusted with a word from God. But this means that in many cases we must have a new ideal of preaching. There can be but little place in the Christian pulpit for the literary essay or the exposition of subtle psychology. One learns too that out here at least, there is small place for the sermon that is slavishly read from manuscript. The preacher must be direct and simple: He must not content himself with moral exhortation, which is often so futile (what's the good of urging men to fight' when they are trying to do that in their own humble way far more earnestly, it may be, than the preacher is in <u>his</u>) – no, instead of merely exhorting them to be good he must try, if he can, to show them <u>how</u> it is to be done, by getting them to open their lives to the influence of the divine; to do this he must appeal to such experience as they have and build on that, must proceed from the known to the unknown; and especially he must deal with the great simple things that are really vital to men. As I have watched the rows of eager faces in a soldier congregation it has sometimes impressed me that many of the things about which we preachers speak so easily (e.g. the divine providence, the forgiveness of sins, the life beyond the grave, the strength that comes from above) mean a thousand times more to them than to the preacher. If these things <u>are</u> true, they are among the greatest truths man can know; and men ought to feel that, who proclaim them.

And what is the Gospel which the prophet is called to preach? Undoubtedly it must begin with a proclamation that like all honest men they have natural religious instincts: only these instincts require to be fed. Hence we are not called upon to begin at the beginning and prove that God exists: neither is it nearly so needful as we might imagine to set ourselves apologetically to justify His way (though I grant there is a place for that – especially in lectures, followed by discussion) The preacher's first duty is rather to <u>proclaim</u> God's existence. His Nature and His Will. Read Psalm 139 to men, and they recognise at once with out argument, how true it all is, and (for the time at least) they feel His Reality, and doubts as to His goodness etc. disappear. Or take them back to the story of the prodigal son, depict to them the Father, and show them that personal religion consists in hankering after home and in arising and going to the Father; and you will get them to arise and go with you.

And inasmuch as men's minds are saturated with an idea of God that is not at all Christian, so that even while the preacher's soul turns within him many of his congregation sit unmoved, for the God whom they have in their mind's eye is not one likely to evoke their enthusiasm and how He can evoke such enthusiasm on the part of the preacher passes their comprehension – there is need for simple, but definite and emphatic preaching about God . . .

It is when one thinks of these things that one feels how emphatically we are called to give to our men a new conception of Almighty God – not a Giant Being endowed with an omnipotent might, (exercised alas: too often to crush and too seldom to save) but rather a Spirit whose might lies in His love, a love that is leading on to a great and final triumph. He is less the All-mighty than the All-conquering.

The greatest need of the times, I feel, is for a Gospel of <u>Hope</u>. And it is because I feel <u>that</u> that when I come to ask myself "What is the cutting edge of the Gospel?" I find that for the present at least, it is less in the fact that Christ died than in the fact that He who died rose and lives for evermore. The Cross still remains at the very core of our Christian Gospel; and the Resurrection is a triumph just in proportion as it is recognised as the resurrection of One who was obedient right up to death. But too often the Gospel we have preached is one that has stopped short at the Crucifixion; it has lacked the note of triumph, and has failed to lead me into apocalyptic vision of God and His Purpose. . . .

Perhaps it is true of us that as yet we are too much under the shadow of our 20th century cross to be able to appraise its meaning as we ought. But the time will come, and a few years hence the world will be ready for a new St. Paul if the Church can produce him. But meantime the Church that is to produce him is first called to enter into a deeper baptism of the Spirit and to give herself to deeper thought. The world knows the hollowness of much conventional religious talk; and inasmuch as it takes a big man (one with a big heart and a full experience) to present to others the place of the Cross of Christ and the divine economy, might it not be well that until the Church has entered more fully into fellowship with Christ's sufferings, our preachers should seek rather to awaken the Christian assurance <u>of the reality of eternal life</u>, without indulging too much in a exposition (which with many is pretty sure to be hackneyed) of how that life is mediated through the <u>death</u> of Christ?

To come back to where we started. What is the influence of the war on the spiritual life of the troops. Why more than half of the men out here came out with the most meagre spiritual experience or religious training; so that in danger they are like infants crying in the night, and out of danger they are pretty much what they used to be. The people who are really on their trial are those who, both out here and everywhere else, were already 'religious', so to speak – our Church-members and adherents, and not least the padre and the home-minister. Are <u>we</u> being shaken and so led to deeper depths of faith and truer Christian life? If the multitude is, through the war, to be led back to God, there is an intermediate step which will in general be vitally necessary, that our Christians be Christianised and our preachers learn to prophesy.

Duncan MSS, St.A. MS 37090/3/60

57

Reverend John Simms to George Duncan

4 August 1917

Yours of the 1st[48] fills me with dismay – I trust you are not going to follow in poor Pagan's footsteps.[49] Where would our non-Combatant services be if every man in your position – thought likewise. To my mind the chaplains are going to do more to win this war [?in their own proper place than any other unit]. Trying times lie ahead & if the courage of our men is to endure to the end, the bitter end a chaplain will be a greater asset than a young officer with a revolver in his belt.

P.S.

I have reread yr note & possibly in the hurry I may have misinterpreted it. Do you mean you want sent forward as a <u>Chaplain?</u>

Even then I beg of you to steady your brain. I look on you as a gift of God to our great Chief. Do you not think that that is duty grand enough for any chaplain, to stay & strengthen & uphold his hands in this titanic struggle? Who needs it more, who deserves it better, what more splendid work, God knowing & man helping could any chaplain at this crisis in our fortunes put his hand to?

I know of absolutely <u>none</u>.

Duncan MSS, St.A. MS 37090/3/78

58

Reverend John Simms to George Duncan

8 August 1917

I wish every chaplain out here could feel as calmly confident that his existence has been justified up to the hilt as fully as yours will have been when the day comes for you to lay down your trust. I feel very sure that Aaron had no greatness of conscience as to the propriety of his actions when he std on the mountain top upholding his great leader's arms while the battle raged below. Stay & strengthen your soul with that old world story. No one in this Campaign has the sacred claim to our very best as our Chief, for he bears a well nigh crushing burden, & I bless God night & day that he has found a chaplain whom he is not afraid to say does help him to bear up under this load. And how mortal man can desire a better, nobler, greater task for his war work I cannot imagine. That the man he delights to honour is a Presbyterian is to me a double cause of thanksgiving for I look upon it as the noblest, strongest form of religious influence that I know on this earth.

Duncan MSS, St.A. MS 37090/3/77

59

Harry Miller to George Duncan

11. Augt. 1917.

I am still here, elaborately idling . . . I wonder shall I see you before I go away?[50] As the end of my months draws near I am filled, like [?Auriel], with a deep and grey sadness, with a saffron light in it of hope & prayer. What failure! What business without effect! What crowds, without any issue from the "word preached"! And the sense behind everything is that all of us – chaplains, men & women workers, have got caught in the stream of restless and ineffective activity, and the Master has been hidden. That another side of it is also true, I believe &, in measure, see: but the discontent, the criticism, the gossip all point to failure to believe in prayer. I condemn myself truly. Jaffray[51] and I have criticized the H.Q. often. We have not once knelt down and prayed for our Chief[52] together. With Aveling[53] there, we can't. No wonder we grow cynical, & sarcastic, and bitter. For the healing of criticism is intercession. Oh, Man! We want far more of Christ's Spirit. One thing, in these last weeks & after them, I hope I shall continually do – & that is to pray constantly for "all in authority". and if we can say as St. Paul says, "always in every prayer of mine for you all making request with joy", then there will be new life in the Chaplains Department. Far more than new organisation, we need a deeper sense of God & a quieter faith in prayer.

Duncan, MSS, St.A. MS 37090/3/73

60

Haig Diary

Sunday, 2nd September 1917

I attended Church of Scotland at 9:30. Rev. Duncan officiated. He preached from the 25th chapter of St. Matthew – the story of "the Talents". It is noticeable that there was no equality in the distribution of the talents. The war has taught us, at any rate in France, that we are all servants. Each has his appointed task. The Corporal's work is as important as the Colonel's etc. How long must the war go on before people at home realise that there is a duty for each one to perform in order to win the War, in accordance with God's will?

Haig MSS, NLS, ACC. 3155, No. 117

61

Reverend Cecil Simpson[54] to George Duncan

Sept 14th – 1917

The deep problems of religion – not the petty foibles of men are what interests you – is it not so, my friend? And yet I am not altogether serious when I say that. As a matter of fact, I do not know anyone to whom the words – nihil humani etc. – can be more appropriately applied.

Duncan MSS, St.A. MS 37090/3/74

62

Duncan Diary

Sept. 18th, 1917

Much, very much has happened since my last entry: yet not nearly so much as we had hoped for. Contrary to Col. Fletcher's confident expectation, the Chief was still at Blendecques on July 29th, so instead of a service up the line (which I had hoped & provisionally arranged, that Harry Miller would take) I had to come back to Adv. G.H.Q. on the 28th and spoke (none too well) next day on David & Goliath. The Chief suggested I might come into lunch if I cared: but I knew he was due to go off in the afternoon up to "the train", and in any case I myself had to leave by 1.30 to conduct a funeral at Millam of a Scotch boy who had been accidentally killed by a lorry: so I declined. The offensive began on the Tuesday morning (July 31st), and for 3 days we had drifting rain. When, on Friday morning, I rang up Col. Fletcher at the train, and as I expected I found that the Chief & he & all the others had returned to Blendecques on Thursday Evening; so that was a shortlived offensive. So back to Blendecques I came (from Proven) about 8.30 on the Sunday morning (Aug. 5th) as I was preparing for an anniversary service, Cpl Roberts came round with a note to say that the Chief would not be at Service: and I learned afterwards he had a touch of influenza and had been ordered by

Col. Ryan to stay indoors. All the same he was out by afternoon. On Wednesday he went off for a few days holiday to Trouville(?) near Havre, returning on Sat'y afternoon. Next day Dr. Kellman[55] conducted the service & he & I were invited to lunch. One looked at the Chief & marvelled. He wouldn't allow one to speak as if he had been ill ("I must have caught some of these doctor's microbes".): but what was most surprising of all (though not surprising either in him) was his perfect calm despite the disappointment of his foiled offensive.[56] "He's the cheeriest of the lot", said Col. Fletcher to me & then he went on "Kiggell was just saying to me 'He doesn't show it one bit, but by God doesn't he feel it?'"

The same optimism has continued since then. On Aug 26th he chatted to me about the military situation, explaining how we were using up the German divisions at our unprecedently rapid pace.[57] "There are roughly 148 German Divisions on the Western Front: and since the Spring offensive, 124 of these have been up against us at some point where we have attacked (or they were forced to counter-attack), & were withdrawn, exhausted, in some cases with 50% losses: of the remaining 24, 16 are poor divisions with an inferior type of man: & the total remaining (8) is being reduced every day. Or take again artillery. Gen Gough has 1570 guns up in his army and the Germans have only 147. (These were approximately at least the numbers he quoted) [Col. Fletcher, with whom I had a talk next day, was willing to agree about the men: but was very sceptical about the guns, angry that we had no very sure means of arriving at Boche statistics & feeling that the proportions of guns in our favour were much more nearly 3 to 1.][58] At the same lunch Capt Botha (son of Louis Botha[59]) sat on the Chief's left as I did on his right: the Chief had introduced him to me at Church. "It's very nice to have Capt. Botha with us" were the Chief's first words to me over the lunch table.

. . . the Chief remarked of how there had just arrived in Paris an old lady whose chateau the Crown Prince recently occupied: & before she was released by the Germans to come across to this side of the line, the Crown Prince said to her: "You must tell the French authorities that we must have peace this autumn: the people at home don't have food, and to go on fighting longer is sheer murder: we mustn't mind that silly old father of mine" (Little Willie evidently wanted to pose as a keen advocate of peace in contrast to his father).[60]

Was it that same Sunday that there appeared in the newspapers of the previous day an account by Lord Haldane of his official mission to Berlin?[61] I suggested to the Chief that Haldane was not a persona grata in military circles and his reply came straight: "I don't agree with you a bit. Haldane was the best man to work with we ever had": & he went on to explain how, after the clause in the Army Act relating to the military necessity for maintaining the balance of power in Europe had been deleted so that the Army was left with no defined function except to be a sort of police, Haldane gave it a definite raison d'etre by saying that the Army must maintain an Expeditionary Force of 6 Divisions for service wherever required. "Oh no", he raves, "that case against Haldane is worked up by the National Review".[62]

Sept. 19th

At lunch we had a sit down meal. The guests including Rawlinson, Byng (3rd Army), Simms, W.W.[63] & myself. The Chief bethought himself of a Grace, & looked across the table to me. I sat next to Rawlinson. He told me of the huge Hotel with over 200 rooms which was his H.Q. & it was not large enough to accommodate his 2nd Echelon which had gone elsewhere. (It had been bombed but much to their annoyance, the Boche probably "mistooke the part for the whole!") "But we can't stay there during the winter", said Rawlinson, referring, I think, not merely to his H.Q. accommodation (the walls, no heating arrangements – a "purely seaside summer" building) but also to the military situation – ground, etc.[64] Byng is a big cheery weather-beaten faced sort of fellow. "This is the passive army", said the Chief with a smile: & Byng summed up the situation from his point of view admirably by saying "Yes, we get along by Christian science down our way: We haven't the men or the guns. We just believe we have them."[65]

The Chief has had a bad time with politicians of late. On

Monday morning, Sept. 3rd, he was summoned to London. I saw Col. Fletcher that morning arranging for the departure: & he was most annoyed about it. "Why cannot they leave him alone? I know what they're wanting: Lloyd George will be wanting to send guns off to the Italian front (the Italian offensive at this time was going strong). I asked, "Isn't Sir Wm. strong enough to keep matters right at that connection?", but Col. Fletcher felt he was disposed to listen to them (i.e. Lloyd George and Co.) too much. "It will upset the Chief for a month", Fletcher went on. "It did so last time".[66] The Chief came back on Thursday. On the following Sunday I introduced him to Cecil Simpson [the R.E. Cecil Simpson, C of Elgin][67] – just as a week before I did to Nurse Hutchinson, a sister who said she came from Kennoway, Fife, & that the two families had many relations.[68]

But to return to the politicians, last week Winston Churchill came (self-invited), lived at the Chateau (most annoying for the Chief: so we gathered from Fletcher). He came about Wednesday.[69] On Friday Asquith & Carson rolled up. Carson has with him Sir R. MacNeill[70] who flung the "Hansard"[71] at Winnie in the [?lounge] one day. By a strange coincidence Sir MacNeill & Winnie were at the [unintelligible] Chateau together on the Saturday, one upstairs, the other down: and some wag of the Intell. Department suggested to MacNeill that if he wished another hefty tome to shy at the foe, they wd provide a liberal supply. Out here we have no use for politicians and not merely because they talk, but also because they are felt to be dishonest: but in this respect an exception is sometimes made in the case of Carson.[72]

What is likely to happen soon? One would naturally expect a resumption of the offensive this week.[73] The weather has still been quite uncertain – dull in the mornings, but with strong sunshine afterward (which is all in favour of our Armies & against the Boche, who have then the p.m. sun in their eyes). Today after a good deal of sunshine, it got quite overcast in the evening, with some thunder clouds & now it rains a trifle. Will the attack be tomorrow? No one knows – or at least no one says. The papers tonight aver that the Boche are liberal in their reply to the Pope's note, to suggest a willingness to evacuate Belgium & renounce all claim to it, & the German papers have had much to say in the last days about a British Peace Proposal.[74]

Sept. 20th (Thursday)

Our offensive, we hear, was begun afresh this morning over a wide front extending well into the S. of Ypres. There is still no detailed news, but one learns that in the 2nd army all our objectives (& more) have been taken, and that the 5th Army got most of what it set out to get. There was rain last night: & even yet the weather is unsettled – an uncertain sort of wind is always rising now & then: but during all the hours of daylight today the sky was clear. At 2.15 p.m. the Chief passed me in his motor, obviously on his way up to the line. I understand he has now had another politician visitor, Lord Derby, who has just returned from a tour to the Italian front. Does this mean they still want more of our guns there?[75] So far as we back here are concerned the secret of this attack has been well kept. As yesterday, so again today, bus load after bus load of Australians has come down the hill from Heuringhem direction and turned off toward Arques as if going up the line: and a long procession of New Zealand Transport passed through about 2 p.m. The latter knew nothing of the attack and were interested to get news of it: most interested, too, when I told them that the car which passed them with flag waving contained Sir Douglas.

This morning I had a walk with Cpl. Howard Spring,[76] a clerk in the Intelligence Office, and talked with him about religious truth (he had once thought of the ministry, but had been put off it by theological doubts, esp. on the question of miracle) and also on his future (he will probably take to journalism). . . . In the evening Lt Harding joined us at dinner and he talked much, & well, to us about the future of the Empire. He told us there was accumulating proof that the prestige of the white man in India & the general respect he commands from the natives were very seriously on the wane: and he felt that when these go, the British rule in India collapses, as a result not of an armed rising but of the general uncertainty of life for a few Europeans among so many million

385

natives. He was also pessimistic enough to believe that the war was to see the breakup of the British Empire. Australia, eg, would have her own problems, arising esp. from her antipathy to the yellow races: would British troops willingly go out there to fight for Australians, & would not Australia naturally find an alliance for herself, say with America?

Sep. 21st, 17.

Another day of good sunshine. On my way into St. Omer in the morning I called at the Intelligence office, & got from Mr. Isaacs some news of yesterday's victory: and on coming downstairs was met by Gen. Birch with his usual hearty greeting. "How are you, young fellow?" As I looked at his blood shot eyes I could not help saying: "How are you? That is more important." "Ah, well", he said. "there's a lot to think about these days." But he was full of cheer over yesterday's success: & busy as he was he went back with me into his room & showed me his contour maps showing how we had gained all the high ground south east of Ypres.

It seems to have been a clean cut victory – better even than Messines.[77] Will there come another halt in the operations? Time is short & the weather is good.

Sunday: 23rd Sept

Yesterday an uneventful day. It was one of those sad days when my spirit was frozen within me, and much as I tried I could get into no real preparation for the morrow. When Dr Simms & Dr Wallace Williamson & Rev. J. H. Miller turned up without warning in the afternoon on their way back from the line to Montreuil & Etaples they found me in my shirt sleeves preparing to desecrate our church with a game of Badminton!

This morning with the thought of last week's victory as a promise & pledge of final success if only our spirit did not fail, I went back to my old favourite chapter: Joshua 1: and was rewarded when Gen. Birch, shaking hands on going out said: "That's the best I have ever heard you preach". He is a great fellow, is General Birch. Of late he has been looking a bit ill – his eyes swollen – clearly a result of too much work. On Monday last, as I was strolling outside his office with two other chaplains for Arques, he appeared on the Chateau steps with another of his officers, then seeing me, hailed me in his usual cheery way: "How are you, young fellow?" "I wish you could come & speak to these officers of mine" he went on, with his arm round my shoulder. "& tell them not to work so late at night": then, slapping me on the back, he went off while the officers told me it was no good: with the amount of work on hand it meant midnight or later every night. I ventured to suggest that the General, too, was always working to which he replied: "Oh no, the General does no work: I wouldn't work either if I were a General & had a staff to do the work for me: but he is always thinking – always. I gobble down my egg in the morning & get off before he appears in case he should come on me with 'I've just been thinking. –' and I am not prepared for that at breakfast." He & I had a chat for a few minutes outside Church this morning while we waited for the Chief. "I was sorry not to be here last Sunday", he said: "I make a point never to be absent: but I had some papers to be ready for a man who was going to catch the boat: and Winston, too, was coming to see me." [Dr. Simms told me last Sunday that he had received a letter from Gen Birch apologising for his enforced absence: & adding that though he was a member of the Church of England, he was a convert to Presbyterian from the war.]

I congratulated him on the great work that his branch of the service was on all hands admitted to have performed in the last days.[78] "There's nothing else for it. I tell my fellows: 'When you have to deal with a bully, you must just hit him & hit him hard & keep hitting him, & give him no rest'. But it's hard on our fellows, too, this ceaseless strain. I try to get them back a bit for a rest but it is not an easy matter."

As he chatted, he pulled out his pipe for a smoke, remarking, "I smoke too much. I know it: but I find it soothes me at times, especially at night when one wants to think. I have knocked it off for a year 3 or 4 times. And I've been a tee-totaller 4 times in my life. I once made a compact with a sergeant of my battery – a fellow I liked & who was drinking too hard: I said to him: 'I'll give it up if you do': & he agreed. And four months afterwards he was sent to the base with D.T.s. He had been getting spirits secretly". "That's very disheartening", remarked Gen Black,[79] who was now with us: to which brave, cheery Birch replied, "If we allowed these things to dishearten us where would we be?" I asked him about the battle, but he told me there was nothing more doing at present.

Our party at lunch at the Chief's included Gen. Asser & Admiral Bacon. Gen. Asser, in charge of L. of C., had had a long interview with the Chief regarding the recent riot at Etaples. According to him, the troops mainly concerned were Scottish – "The scum of the earth, from the slums of Glasgow." But he was down on the management that had allowed the affair to develop as it had: "Fancy a boy of 17 as a ringleader: it's absurd: and now he gets 10 years: it ought to have been a case at the beginning of his getting his backside kicked!" He was more severe on another ringleader, a corporal – a regular army man with 8 years service, choke full of socialistic ideas, who had advised the men to disarm a picket & heave the officer over a bridge![80] I had this talk with Asser before lunch. At that time, too, I had a chat with Col. Fletcher. His view of the Russia situation (and he said it was M. Painlevé's) was that Kerensky was a rogue, and that he had enveigled Korniloff into that revolution deliberately to overwhelm him, and that Korniloff had been foolish in not seeing into the game & having a large force at his disposal. [Alexieff has now resigned his position of C.G.S. under Kerensky as C. in C., holds that Kerensky's ban on so many generals of the Korniloff party means an embargo on military efficiency. It looks as if it might yet be a case of the Army v. the "People in Russia".][81]

Admiral Bacon appeared in the ante-room with a breezy smile – "breezy" is the true word for it. But he seems to have no delusions regarding the task that lies ahead. "I am bombarded with suggestions for destroying Zeebrugge", he said.[82] "They forget that to demolish the mole at Zeebrugge, if we fired, say, 640(?) rounds of 15 inch shells would wear out so many guns & even so the vital part, which is under the water, would remain untouched." The question was raised of sinking a ship in Z. harbour. All such proposals forget, he said that any such vessel would be sunk by gunfire miles before it got there. "Then it would have to be a submarine", said Kiggell. But Bacon replied that that would not be big enough. The Chief quotes how effectively Boulogne has been blocked for over a month: but the difference, Bacon pointed out, was that at Boulogne passage had to be cleared for big ships, a comparatively narrow passage (for submarines & torpedo boats) was all that would be wanted in the other case. The point one could not get over was the rise and fall of the tide – which could make a passage so very much easier. If a fairly big vessel, protected by concrete sides against gun-fire, were to reach the harbour & there sink herself, a working party would still be able to clear a sufficient passage to let the submarines, etc. come out at high tide. Kiggell still held on to the attack, suggesting now that bombs might be used to prevent any salvage operation on the part of the enemy. "But any bomb that could do that would blow up the ship, too", said Bacon. "Then in that case," said Kiggell, "couldn't you have a number of smaller bombs that would do no effectual damage to the ship but would frighten off the working party." Bacon admitted that was a new suggestion which might have something in it. (These difficulties and the strength of the Boche coast defences meant, said Bacon, "that the Boche must be driven back by land. Only with Army cooperation can the Navy do anything.") From Zeebrugge, we got on talk of the submarine menace. Kiggell remarked that there were some open references to our use of the microphone: weren't these indiscreet? or did the Boche know quite well that we were employing such instruments. Bacon corroborates that the Boche did know. Besides, the microphone, though it did excellent work, it could not effectively squash the submarine peril, for a submarine could quite well continue its course with engines off (& so make no sound) & still go 3 or 4 knots. "No, you are dealing with the problem of an object which you cannot see, smell, or hear: and there's no one right road to dealing with it. But we can deal with it sufficiently. It is quite clear now that the submarine can never be the decisive force against us. That hope of the Boche is squashed. Besides, as I always say, they will never sink the last ship. Even if things got very much worse then they are at present, things would right themselves by a new adaptation of our needs. We would just strike a new balance of our supplies."[83] The new steam [unintelligible] ships, he explained in answer to a query, were not torpedo proof.

"Is the weather to hold, Admiral?", someone asked: & his reply showed he was anything but hopeful. However, it was a case of a conflicting cyclone & anti-cyclone (?), & if the anticyclone coming north were to come out top, it could be all right. "But you ought to know", he went on "You have got the best weather man with you here for the B.E.F. – (that's Gold): "his reports are always infallible." We all rejoiced to hear this testimony, & said we must pass it on to Gold: but D.H. (with memories of July 31st & subsequent days still fresh) said he felt that Gold always safeguarded himself: "he hedges."[84]

I put in a word at this point for my friend, Capt. Geddes[85] of the weather department: & so we easily got on to talk of Sir Eric & his brother.[86] It was a surprise to Kiggell & to Asser to know that Sir Eric was a Scot: Asser said he always thought he was a real New Yorker! Bacon hopes that the devotion to accurate facts, statistics, etc. which was an essential in the makeup of a railway manager or a scientific thinker (professor) would not lead the Geddes brothers into error when they came to deal with concrete problems. "I was just telling Carson", said Haig, "that I was afraid the Navy was going to bag all the steel. There's the Navy going to have £80 million spent on aeroplanes for it," and we all felt round the table the £80 million was an enormous sum – how many planes would likely turn out with that? "And America is to spend £123 million". But as Asser pointed out, America is starting practically from the beginning. Haig & Bacon found themselves at one on their praise of Carson. "He's sound", they both said, again and again: and proceeded to contrast him unfavourably[87] with "Winston" (it is always by that name that D.H. alludes to the gentleman in question).

In the course of the talk, mention was made of the numbers of German prisoners killed or wounded in the German bombing raids: And it was felt that the Boche might place our prisoners up in Ostende & Zeebrugge. The cases, as D.H. pointed out, were not really parallel. Belgium was different from Germany, & in the cases where the Boche had got them, our men the prisoners were far back from the lines. "No place, of course, is safe from bombing".

D.H. looked again as fit as could be. He has every reason to be pleased, it wd seem with the victory of Thursday last. He told of one Boche sergeant who, when captured, said that things had come to a pretty pass "when brave ones like me have to come in from the fight, and the private soldiers skulk behind in shell holes."

Monday, 24th Sept.

Met Scotland[88] (Intelligence Officer) this morning. He said many of the Boche Divisions we had been up against were pretty poor: but there had been one really good one to the north, "but it did not fight any better than the poorer ones" (I infer that he meant the standard was uniformly "under par") He corroborated what he had told me some days ago that the Boche suffered tremendous losses in the 4 days preliminary bombardment.

It has been a beautiful day – hot & rather "close": bright sunshine & clear sky. Is the good anticyclone to win the day?"

Tuesday 25th Sept.

The Anniversary of Loos. A day of bright sunshine & rather oppressive heat. Saw Geddes (Meteorologist office) this afternoon. And he explained to me that a cyclone from the coast of Ireland was pressing on with great persistence & some success, but we ought to have good weather for two days yet at least & maybe more. The Boche, I understand, attacked heavily this morning at 6 a.m. & succeeded in winning back quite a few positions, but doubtless our counterattacks will drive them out again. The big operations would seem not yet to have been renewed.

Friday: Sept. 28th

Since my last entry I have been away from Blendecques. On Wednesday morning I went up to the Corps Main Dressing Station on the Elverdine road . . . From there I came on to Aire – to a Conference of Chaplains of the 1st Army,[89] & was there with them this morning. Well over 100 chaplains were present (of all denominations excepting R.C.[90]) and the conference was in every way a treat, marked by a fine spirit both of devotion & of camraderie, thinking that was at once honest, acute & lofty and a sincere desire both to understand better the various denominational positions, and to improve the efficiency of our work as chaplains. The Conference owed much to the presence and the Christian utterances of Gen. Horne at the opening session and of Gen. [unintelligible] on the forenoon of the 2nd Day, & to the presence (more so than to the remarks) of the D.M.S. (Gen. Thomson[91]) at the meeting where the various denominational standpoints were put forward & criticised. Gen. Horne, speaking as the Army Commander, said just the right things in his short 10 minutes address. Morale & religious emotions, he reminded us, are very closely bound up, & while we were out to beat the Germans, we must be in all earnest in seeking to qualify ourselves to best them. Every blow at the Germans is a blow for the Kingdom of Christ. He recalled the great work which had been done last winter in his army in connection with the National Mission,[92] and said he wanted this winter's campaign to be prosecuted with even more thoroughness than last year's. Major Gen. Thrushing's address was a masterpiece of genuine Christian thought & sentiment, its earnestness being reinforced by the genuine humility & unaffected tenderness of the man. With no attempt at eloquence against all that was contained in the word Prussianism, we were engaged in a Crusade, not now to snatch the tomb of Christ from infidel hands, but to rescue the life & the Spirit of Christ from the dark forces that would seek to overwhelm it. And the whole of that victory was not to be won on the battlefields of France. He had some wise words to us on Reconstruction after the war, & some equally wise advice to give us as chaplains regarding our special duties, etc. In one memorable sentence he reminded us that simplicity is the keynote to all successful dealings with the soldiers. Rev. J. Kelman spoke on the religious outlook of the soldier & spoke in a way that quite captivated the conference: he was to my mind much less happy when at a service (?) primarily for the personnel of the school & our batmen,[93] he "out Beach-Thomased" Beach Thomas in the gloomy picture he drew of what he saw in Italy, America, etc. & did little more. To many, the most memorable meeting was that in which many reps from the Church of England, the Presbyterian, & the Free Churches stated their respective positions from a positive point of view. I ventured in the course of a few remarks in the subsequent discussion to point out that so far as the democratic glories of our Presbyterian system were concerned, I had never heard the case of Presbyterianism better put than had been unconciously done the previous evening by a C. of E. Chaplain from Canada – a fervent plea he made for emancipation from the trammels of a clerical order & a fuller representation of the laity. The discussion towards the end tended to recognise that if the Church of England became more democratic the other churches might readily accept (in some form or other) Episcopal government, and when both Free Churches & Presbyterian stated clearly that they could not agree to reordination, a way seems to open up for what was called conditional reordination.

The weather these last 3 days has been fair with much sunshine. We have no grudge against the weather this time. The attack was renewed on Wednesday morning, (the day after the anniversary of the opening of the Loos Battle) when we advanced considerably beyond our line of last Thursday, making our line secure at Tower Hamlets, gaining the whole of Polygon Wood, & storming Zonnebeke.[94] The enemy has been forced to counterattack heavily (he made 7 counterattacks yesterday), & his losses are bound to be heavy.

On Wednesday, before I set off up the line, I saw Sir Wm Robertson & Lloyd George at the Chateau (whatever does that little Welshman want now?)[95]

Duncan MSS, St.A. MS 37090/3/62

63

Haig Diary

Sunday, 30th September 1917

I attended Church of Scotland at 9:30. Mr. Oliver (who is still staying here) accompanied me, and was much struck with Rev. Captain Duncan. the text was from Isaiah, and Duncan laid stress on our believing confidently that <u>at the right time</u> the Lord would bring about a great victory, not only in this war but in the whole arrangements on the Earth. Only we must be able to endure and not be impatient.

Haig MSS, NLS, ACC. 3155, No. 117

64

Duncan Diary

Monday morning: Oct 1st

Saturday was a bit of a wash-out day with me, as I felt seedy & finally went off to bed with the general <u>scheme</u> of my Sunday address in my head but with nothing clearly thought out. I had hoped to speak on the War as an Apocalypse, a) of the reality of the distinction between good & evil, & a summons therefore to choose when we would serve, b) of the inevitability & glory of sacrifice in the conflict that must ensue from the inducement of right, c) of the reality of God, who though He may long hold His peace, yet at last arises in His might to achieve His Holy Purpose. And that was more or less what I <u>did</u> speak of next morning, taking as my foundation Isaiah 42 1–16. We had a big congregation – it seems to grow & grow (I shd say about 80): and with the Chief was Mr. Oliver (author of "Ordeal by Battle"). I saw more of Oliver at lunch, when he was the only guest besides myself (J. Ian Macpherson[96] was at the Chateau on Saturday & I called to see him then, but he was up the line somewhere yesterday). Oliver is a tall figure, with a face that suggests reserve & refinement – a touch of the Woodrow Wilson in it, though more pleasant & less ascetic-looking. He told me at once (on my arrival at the Chateau) that he had enjoyed the service: and I frankly told him I hadn't! . . . Our lunch was not <u>particularly</u> interesting, so far as our <u>general</u> conversation was concerned. The old question of education came up – when Oliver ventured the opinion that "that among civilised countries, the general education in England was about the worst & Scotland was among the best." The Chief, less by any definite remark than by that appreciative look he can convey with his eyes, corroborated.[97] (He had already remarked that at the time of their introduction "there was really no necessity for School Boards in Scotland; their work was already being done.["]) but with a mischievous leer he said in reply to Oliver: "Ask him over there (nodding towards Kiggell): he ought to know, he's 3 parts Scots!" Kiggell received the butt with his usual reserve,[98] & after a pause remarked that he had no right to speak on these things – which obviously took Oliver aback, for the Chief's remark had clearly led him to expect that in Kiggell we had an authority. (I asked Kiggell after lunch about the "3 parts Scots": but he said he was afraid that was more than he could claim: his mother's people were from Scotland, but that was 100 years ago – (or was it 300? G.S.D.)) Australian education was touched on, & the Chief (with his wide interest & knowledge) said he understood that their primary education was extraordinarily good, but they were distinctly weak on the prosecution of more advanced study.

But if the <u>general</u> conversation was not particularly interesting, some of the Chief's remarks were uncommonly so. Talking at one point to Oliver regarding a certain officer (Greenway,[99] was it?) who had gone from a Staff (I think) job to be in command of a Cavalry Division & was now restless to be in command of an <u>Infantry</u> Division, the Chief commented on the fact that he was a man who was rarely satisfied, & then, turning to me (I sat on his immediate left) & looking straight into my eyes with a sort of twinkle, he added: "He hasn't the faith that we can go through these people & beat them with bladders". (So it looks as if <u>he</u> hadn't lost his faith in the use of the Cavalry, though most people seem to have done so).[100] Later in the conversation he showed how little was his appreciation of the French. "What sort of a people are they that are exhausted after a year & then fight the war with words." I felt called on to put in a plea for them: they did great work in the first year when we were not ready & so on. But he wouldn't have it. Clearly he didn't seem to think they had fought with brains. In that first winter they had hammered away to no purpose at the enemy in the Ardennes, & didn't realise that the Boche was standing firm there & working his way round the weakened French to the left in an attempt to separate them from the British & turn the flanks. Later came the frightful waste of life at the Labyrinth, & a similarly useless effort in Champagne. As the great man talked you felt it was the talk of a man who knew his job and realised what it meant by then to be robbed of his legitimate support from an Ally who in her previous campaigns showed such surprising lack of military judgment & now was letting him down through sheer lack of character. It was the talk of a man who realised that though nominally we had Allies in Russia & France, Russia was now (by her own choice) hors de combat, & France was not doing anything like what she might do & what the hour required: at Ypres he & his army were fighting as it were alone against the might of Germany – & even so were winning, though we ought not to have here all the fight to fight alone."I began with a high appreciation of the French", he went on "as was only natural, being a Scotsman: but events proved too much for that. In the retreat from Mons (I notice he does not scruple to call a "retreat") they thought only of themselves. After leaving us hanging in the air, a French commander tried to keep for himself the only road along which my men & their transport, etc. could go. So I simply sent word to him that I was to have that road and I put a whole division right along it to serve as a picket, and he gave way.[101] I would have fought him for it if he hadn't. That's a nice sort of way to treat your Allies, isn't it?" And then he broke off to tell of one incident in 1914 when the French really <u>had</u> played the game: when a force of old Poilus was suddenly brought up & sent into the fight, & on they went with their coats waving, full of spirits, as if they could carry anything before them, and his eyes smiled as he told of the confident jaunty way they went forward (Poor old Joffre, he told us, was practically prisoner – guarded so closely by the French lest, in those troubled days of the Republic, he should be made a military dictator!)

Tuesday: Oct. 9th

Much of the above was written this afternoon. It has been difficult of late to sit down of an evening to write up a diary, firstly because of the nocturnal visits of the Boche planes, & secondly because of

the cold. On Sunday evening, Oct. 1st, I conducted the service at
St. Andrews Church, St. Omer, speaking on "Fear not, Paul": and
that evening, after I had returned to Blendecques, & while with
my friend Munro, a Canadian chaplain, I was having a frugal
supper at the White House, the Boche came on in strength. It was
a perfectly beautiful evening – full moon, stars, & not a cloud: and
searchlights were of little use. They attacked the Scottish hospital,
where there were some 20 killed (including 6 nurses) & 50
wounded.

Duncan MSS, St.A. MS 37090/3/62

65

Haig Diary

Monday, 15th October 1917
I cannot think why the War Office Intelligence Department gives
such a wrong picture of the situation except that Gen. McDonogh
(D.M.I.) is a Roman Catholic and is (perhaps unconsciously)
influenced by information which reaches him from tainted (i.e.
Catholic) sources.[102]

Haig MSS, NLS, ACC. 3155, No. 118

66

Duncan Diary

Oct. 23rd
I am writing again after a long break. Was it on the 11th that
another great attack was launched, which had to be broken off
prematurely owing to the breakdown of the weather.[103] On
Monday the 10th the Chief went off to live at Cassel in
preparation for this attack: then towards the end of the week he
decided to come back, and his return took place accordingly on
Sunday afternoon (so that on the 16th he attended service at

Cassel). Last week he was visited here by the Portuguese Premier, & also by the Duke of Connaught.[104]

On Sunday (21st) he was in his place as usual at Church. There was a very small congregation – A.A.C. & Signals being both on special sandbag fatigues in view of moonlight air-raids.

At lunch (when Gen Rawlinson sat on his right, I on his left) he said that my remarks at the service, regarding the struggle at Ypres 3 years ago had sent him on his return to consult his notes of what was happening at the corresponding date of that year. The 1st & 2nd Divisions were attacking Poelcapelle & Passchendaele. When the enemy were already retiring from Poelcapelle village, the French cavalry on our left flank were, without any warning to us, ordered to return West of the Canal because the enemy were attacking from the direction of Clercken[105] in strength – about a Division! "The General Commanding the French Div. immediately on Lomax's left at once declined to obey the order when it was repeated: he refused to uncover our flank without "une ordre formelle!"[106] But the order came & he had to retire. The French were evidently in a great difficulty in those days. As he went on telling me of the uncertainty they caused him at every turn, I remarked to him: "Then the Boche weren't the sole source of your troubles in those days, sir": and with a most knowing look, he replied with the significant monosyllable – "No."

Then Rawlinson & he got on to talk of those days – immensely interesting to see these two men sitting calmly at lunch fighting their battles over again – so different from the actual [?instance] of 3 years ago. I told them how immensely interesting it was for me to hear their firsthand knowledge: & asked them what there was published that was at all a good account of those days. They said there was nothing . . . Then Kiggell broke in: "I'm afraid the real story can never be told until after another war when the French & we are on different sides!" But this enquiry of mine had one most interesting sequel. The lunch part over, the Chief handed to me his book of notes on the "Ypres fighting, October 17th to 21st, 1914" (a diary he kept at the time) & saying I might care to read it. I have it by me now: was there ever a more interesting document?

The Chief's notes say that Rawlinson came to see him on the

day of the fight already referenced to (Wednesday, Oct 21st, 1914) at Hotel [?Chapelere], Ypres, where D.H. had his H.Q. Next day they got "wind" from interrupted wireless message of the enemy that the German Corp Commander were to press their attack to Zandvoorde – Beselare first & Rawlinson said that a similar message came to him also from the War Office – wherever the War Office had got its information from!

The Chief looked tired. As he shook hands with me after the service, he looked me straight in the face, without any approach to a smile (had my reference to Ypres by any chance anything to do with his solemnity?). And so too at lunch. The jauntiness of other days had gone: he was kind as ever: but I noticed e.g. that when he helped me to anything (or invited me to help myself) he did not season his kindness, so to speak, by any grace of smile or manner: and when he filled my glass with port he did not, as so often, joke about it.[107] Yet he was clearly happy in Rawlinson's company: and he opened out (quite early in the lunch) to tell a story which the Duke of Connaught had told against himself (i.e. the Duke) the day before – how at Balmoral one year the Duke was summoned by a stalker, at Queen Vic's orders (!) to go off stalking, he'd reluctantly obeyed, he'd trudged & clambered over rocks until he was dead tired, then when the eager stalker got him into a sheltered nook with a lovely shot before him & he hopelessly missed, the stalker seized the gun angrily from his hand, exclaiming, "God, man: you've spoilt the whole damn thing."

But clearly the Chief has much to worry him. I suppose Russia's affairs must cause him grave anxiety . . . but above all his troubles, I should say, are more immediate, and arise less from the straight, the arduous, job he has of beating the Boche than from the unstable & unreliable French and interfering and character-less politicians. "When Sir Wm. Robertson went home," he said, "I told him we should have to finish this war, & he must prepare to give us 2,000,000 men: and we have only got <u>one</u> year."[108]

I ventured to remark that just as in the days of Napoleon, so again: if all our European Allies failed us, we could fight to a finish alone & win, & this time we would have America[n] help. He felt we could, & would, fight on alone if need be: but he clearly was not inclined to value American help too highly. He doubted if America was whole-hearted: & Rawlinson, quoted the opinion of someone who knew America well, that so far as Wilson was concerned, he had done no master-stroke by coming into the war when he had done: he had come in reluctantly, because he could no longer keep out.

On Sunday evening I went to No. 7 General Hospital to conduct a service there at 6.30: a fine moonlight night (the first really dangerous night of this spell of moonlight), and the service was rudely disturbed by our Archies before the sermon came on, & the congregation was asked to disperse. The previous evening (as on some other occasions last week) Dunkirk & neighborhood came in for a bad bombing: Rawlinson told how the nearest bomb fell within 20 yards of his Chateau smashing the windows: so that apart from the danger of bombs, the Chateau, which had no fires & no fireplaces, & was now windowless, was much too cold for habitation, & the H.Q. was now removing. We were much cheered over the weekend by hearing that of the Zeppelins which had visited England [unintelligible] on Friday evening, 4 & perhaps 5 had been brought down in France.

Yesterday (Monday) our troops made a useful advance near Poelcapelle – doing all, (or practically all) that they set out to do, but it was nothing big. Today (Tuesday) the French attacked west of Chem. des Dames, & acc. to present accounts have captured 7000 prisoners & 60 guns. It is good news. One does not grudge the French their success: but one hopes that this success, & their success with the Zeppelins, as contrasted a) with our strong advance near Ypres, b) our failure even to fire a shot at the Zeps, c) our naval inactivity, e.g. our failure to combat the German success in the Baltic, & the sinking of a large merchant convoy with its two destroyers escort may not be worked up by an unscrupulous Press & unscrupulous politicians & a cynical & jumpy public so as to create distrust at home. Surely our people will remember that so far, at least as the French military success is concerned, all the German regiments that were up against the French have previously received a severe hammering from us at Ypres.

I had a long talk with Fletcher – open & straight as ever. He . . . said he felt certain that the politicians would try to make peace this winter.[109]

Duncan MSS, St.A. MS 37090/3/62

67

Haig Diary

Sunday, 28th October 1917

I attended the Church of Scotland at 9:30. Duncan officiated. Text from 91st Psalm. "Fear not for He will give angels charge over thee, whithersoever thou goest." This morning I am somewhat anxious regarding the change of plans at Home and the large demands now being made on this army for a Field Force to go to Italy to fight the Italians' battles. Certainly Duncan's sermons are most comforting and give one "peace of mind" in these days![110]

Haig MSS, NLS, ACC. 3155, No. 118

68

Douglas Haig to George Duncan[111]

Dec. 28. 1917

With my best thanks for your kind letter and all good wishes for 1918.

Duncan MSS, St.A. MS 37090/3/72

4

1918 and After

69

Haig to Lady Haig

28th February 1918

Many thanks for all you say in yours of yesterday about the "quiet way in which I tackle all". I must say that I feel quite confident, and so do my troops. Personally, I feel in the words of 2nd Chronicles, XX Chap., that it is "God's battle" and I am not dismayed by the numbers of the enemy.[1]

Haig MSS, NLS, ACC. 3155, No. 149

70

Haig to Lady Haig

Tuesday, 11th April 1918

If one has full confidence that everything is being directed from above <u>on the best lines</u>, then there is no reason for fussing. Do the best we can, and I am confident that every thing will come out right in time. But we must be patient, fully realising that <u>our</u> ways may not always be the ways chosen by the Divine Power for achieving the wished for end.

Haig MSS, NLS, ACC. 3155, No. 150

71

Douglas Haig to George Duncan

Tuesday, 16 April 18.

One line to thank you most truly for your letter. I am very grateful for your thinking of me at this time, and I <u>know</u> I am sustained in my efforts by that Great Unseen Power, otherwise I c'd not be standing the strain as I am doing.

I missed my Sunday morning greatly. But it c'd not be helped.[2]

Duncan MSS, St.A. MS 37090/3/29

72

Haig Diary

Sunday, 4th August 1918

I attended a Special Service of Thanksgiving at 9:30 a.m. in the Square in the "Ecole Militaire" in which G.H.Q. offices are established.[3]

A hollow square was formed of British Officers and clerks of G.H.Q. as well as well as of the Battalions forming the Guards (the Guernsey Militia), W.A.A.C. and a large number of French Officers and a few Americans.

The service was carried out by the Rev. George Duncan (Church of Scotland) and the Rev. Bateman Champain[4] (Church of England). The Roman Catholic Priests were not allowed by their regulations to take part in the ceremony, but many R.C. officers attended. The attitude of the R.C. clergy over this service should open our eyes to what the R.C. religion in our empire really is. They must be R.C. first, and English afterwards, if their Church discipline permits.[5]

The service was very impressive, and was much appreciated by all.

The Bishop of Kensington[6] and Rev. Bateman Champain came to dinner. I did not allow the Bishop to take part in our Thanksgiving Morning Service because I wished our own Military

Chaplains to conduct the service. The Bishop, however, gave an address this afternoon. I was not able to go. I thought him rather an ordinary type of man, and scarcely up to the standard of Intelligence which ought to be expected in a Bishop.

Haig MSS, NLS, ACC. 3155, No. 130

73

Haig to Lady Haig

Thursday, 8th August 1918

Who would have believed this possible even 2 months ago?

How much easier it is to attack then [than] to stand and await an enemy's attack!

As you know, I feel that I am only the instrument of that Divine Power who watches over each one of us, so all the honour must be his.

Haig MSS, NLS, ACC. 3155, No. 152

74

Haig to Lady Haig

Tuesday, 3rd September 1918

I am glad that you had Duncan to lunch. He is very shy but is a wonderful preacher and has such influence over his hearers.

Haig MSS, NLS, ACC. 3155, No. 152

75

Alan Fletcher to George Duncan

Oct 17th, 1918

Many thanks for your letter – I will be sure to let you know re Sunday service but C in C is generally out most days now flying round –

Come to lunch any day here if you can get a lift – out – Thresher may be coming out or somebody – Warn us on the telephone before coming & we will try to find out if C in C is likely to be in –

All news is A1 & we have them at last <u>clean beat</u>!

Duncan MSS, St.A. MS 37090/3/70

76

Haig Diary

Sunday, 20th October 1918

Doris[8] and I attended the Church of Scotland, Pont Street (St. Columba's[9]) at 11 a.m. The Rev. Dr. Fleming[10] preached the sermon. He spoke of vengeance and punishment with reference to making peace with Germany. We could not wish to see our Armies entering Germany to destroy a German town for a town in France, in conformity with the Scriptural passage "an eye for an eye, a tooth for a tooth". On the other hand, the punishment must be adequate to the crimes committed.

Colonel Wigram talking to Doris on the telephone states that a telegram just rec'd states that cholera in a bad form has broken out in Berlin. It looks as if the prophecy of 11 Kings is to be fulfilled re the Assyrians being slain in battle and many thousands by the Lord in pestilence!

Haig MSS, NLS, ACC. 3155, No. 132

77

Haig to Lady Haig

Monday, 11th November 1918

Hostilities are to cease at 11 a.m. today!!

How pleased you will be. And my first thought is to thank that Power that has guided and guarded me well these anxious years, and to thank <u>you</u> too for being such a good true little wife to me through these long black days since I left you at Aldershot in August 1914.

Haig MSS, NLS, ACC. 3155, No. 152

78

Haig Diary

Monday, 11 November 1918

We heard this morning that the Kaiser is in Holland. If the war had gone against us, no doubt our King would have had to go, and probably our Army would have become insubordinate like the German Army. cf, John Bunyan's remark on seeing a man on his way to be hanged, "But for the Grace of God, John Bunyan would have been in that man's place!"

Haig MSS, NLS, ACC. 3155, No. 133

79

Haig to Lady Haig

Friday, 15th November 1918

General Horne and others in high appointments here regard the sudden great success and absolute disintegration of the Enemy as "the act of God". This is indeed satisfactory that they realise how vain our efforts would have been unless the Lord had been with us.

Haig MSS, NLS, ACC. 3155, No. 152

80

Haig Diary

Sunday, 17th November 1918

I attended Church Parade at 11 a.m. The Rev. George Duncan went with me to the parade and said a prayer, but the Chaplain of the Division (51st) preached the sermon and I fear missed a grand opportunity of saying what we all feel and desire to say to Almighty God – our heartfelt thanks for giving us Victory.

Haig MSS, NLS, ACC. 3155, No. 132

81

Douglas Haig to Reverend John Simms

Sunday, 17th November, 1918

Please accept my very grateful thanks for your most kind letter. I value very much your friendly words of congratulation. But I really feel that my share in all this great work has been such a little one. I have been only the instrument in the Almighty's hands for, as you quote in your most excellent "Epistle to the Chaplains", "the battle is not yours but God's." This I have truly felt and so my courage and belief in Victory have never failed me. I insisted always in keeping as much Cavalry as possible, because I believed in Victory, and that arm alone can reap the fruits of Victory![11]

Strengthened as I know I and the whole Army have been by the Divine Power, I cannot adequately express the gratitude which I owe to you and all our chaplains for the grand work which they have rendered to our Cause. – And to you in particular, my dear Dr. Simms, I thank you with all my heart.

Duncan MSS, St.A. MS 37090/3/63

82

Haig to Lady Haig

Sunday, 17th November 1918

The vast majority of our countrymen are fully alive to what has been done by the Army under my orders, and are grateful to me in a very surprising way. But I scarcely feel that I deserve the gratitude, for as the Old Testament says, "the battle is not your's but God's", and I feel that I have only been the instrument to carry out the Almighty's intentions.

I am disappointed to see that our rulers are entirely given up to electioneering now,[12] apparently forgetful of all our War truths. In my opinion they should be on their knees, thanking God for having preserved the Old Country and our liberties in spite of the Government.

Haig MSS, NLS, ACC. 3155, No. 153

83
Haig Diary

Sunday, 1st December 1918

I attended Church of Scotland Service at 9:30 a.m. The Rev. George Duncan preached about the Patron Saint of Scotland. St. Andrew, the Apostle, was evidently a kindly, broadminded man in his religious views; practical in all his actions; and of quiet retiring disposition who shunned publicity. Mr. Duncan thinks that the patron Saint of Scotland has been a great influence on the character of our people, due no doubt to the character of the Church of Scotland. The Scots, like St. Andrew, carry their religion more into their every day life and there is much less pomp and show in their religious services than is the case in other Churches.

Haig MSS, NLS, ACC. 3155, No. 132

84
Memo by Douglas Haig

25th March 1919

If, as I confidently believe, there will be few among the men stationed at MONTREUIL who will not carry away with them as one of their most pleasant recollections the memory of the Scottish Churches' Hut on the Ramparts, I feel that I too owe it a debt of gratitude. I therefore thank warmly Mr. and Mrs. Stevenson, Mrs. MacDonald, Miss Urie and Miss Spiers for all that they have done to enable the Hut to take so high a place in our affections, and especially the Rev. G. S. Duncan, by whose teaching and example a right spirit has been so well maintained among those who frequented it.

I know that the influence for good exercised by the Scottish Churches Hut during the past three years has been immense. I trust that its spirit will live among all who now leave it, and its influence outlast the Ramparts of MONTREUIL.

Duncan MSS, St.A. MS 37090/3/88

85

Douglas Haig to George Duncan

Monday, 11th August 1919.

I was delighted to read in the papers that you had at last been appointed to <u>the</u> Chair at St Andrews. Though Rector, I really had nothing to do with the selection. It was your own worth, and hard work which got you the place. And I well know that no better man could have been found if one searched the whole world through, than yourself for the job. So it gives me the greatest pleasure to congratulate you, and to wish you long life and happiness, though I hope it won't all be spent in a Chair of Biblical Criticism. But I am really glad that you are starting your great work at St Andrews. I somehow feel that there is a genuinely friendly atmosphere there, and I shall look forward to dropping in and having a chat with you there during your leisure moments.

I am proposing to take my title from the homeland![13] A kind of compliment I hope folk will think to what our brother Scots have done in the Great War. This seems to me more preferable than to describe myself as of some small spot in the far flung Battle line of our great Armies in France and Flanders. What do you think?

Duncan MSS, St.A. MS 37090/3/31

86

Douglas Haig to George Duncan

31 January 1921.

Yes – It was very difficult to keep going <u>all</u> the time of the long War. And I am frequently asked now how <u>I</u> managed to do it!! Well – I can truly say that you were a great help to me, when I was C. in C., in putting things into proper perspective on the Sundays. But I had a hard trial before I came across you at St. Omer – and I have a little half sheet of writing paper sent me by some unknown friend who apologises for writing to me saying "People generally jib at Bible quotations. But these are sent in no "tract"-giving spirit etc." and he writes – Fear thou not for I am with thee; be not dismayed etc—as far as "with the right hand of my righteousness".

"They shall renew their strength: they shall mount up with wings" etc. as far as "they shall walk and not faint".

"Only be thou strong and very courageous".

Duncan MSS, St.A. MS 37090/3/30

Notes

Unless otherwise expressed, the place of publication of books and articles mentioned is London.

Notes to the Introduction

1 Many biographies of Haig have been written. The most useful are G. DeGroot, *Douglas Haig: 1861–1928* (1988) and John Terraine, *Douglas Haig: the Educated Soldier* (1963).
2 Rachel Haig to Douglas Haig, 25 February 1879, Haig MSS, NLS, ACC. 3155, No. 3(a).
3 Haig's early career is covered extensively in DeGroot, *Douglas Haig: 1861–1928*.
4 Haig to Lady Haig, 27 December 1915. Haig MSS, ACC. 3155, No. 141.
5 Haig Diary, 2 January 1916. *Ibid*, No. 104.
6 G. S. Duncan, *Douglas Haig as I Knew Him* (Allen and Unwin, 1966), p. 43.
7 *Ibid.*, pp. 21–2.
8 Haig Diary, 17 September 1916. *op. cit*, No. 108.
9 Duncan Diary, 29 April 1917. Duncan MSS, St.A. MS 37090/3/61.
10 Biographical information on Duncan taken from *Dictionary of National Biography* (1961–1970) and from personal knowledge.
11 Duncan, *op. cit.*, p. 18.
12 Duncan Diary, 24 July 1916. *op. cit.*
13 Duncan Diary, 4 March 1917, *op. cit*. Duncan was referring to the way Haig had looked on the previous Sunday.
14 Duncan Diary, 25 February 1917. *Ibid*.
15 Haig Diary, 23 April 1916. Haig MSS, ACC. 3155, No. 105. Douglas Duncan to G. DeGroot, 25 February 1989.
16 Haig Diary, 16 July 1916. Haig MSS, ACC. 3155, No. 107.
17 Haig Diary, 19 March 1916. *Ibid*, No. 105.
18 Haig Diary, 5 October 1916. *Ibid*, No. 108.
19 Haig Diary, 4 June 1916. *Ibid*, No. 106.
20 *Ibid*.
21 Haig Diary, 8 July 1916. *Ibid*, No. 107.
22 Haig to Lady Haig, 5 June 1917. *Ibid*, No. 147.
23 Haig Diary, 30 September 1917. *Ibid*, No. 117.
24 Haig to Lady Haig, 11 April 1918. *Ibid*, No. 150.

25 Haig to Lady Haig, 30 June 1916. *Ibid*, No. 144.

26 Duncan Diary, 29 April 1917. *op. cit.*

27 Haig to Lady Haig, 20 April 1917. Haig MSS, ACC. 3155, No. 146.

28 Haig to Lady Haig, 17 November 1918. *Ibid*, No. 153.

29 See especially Chapters 12–16.

30 Haig to Lady Haig, 30 June 1916. Haig MSS, ACC. 3155, No. 144. For a more extensive discussion of this subject, see G. DeGroot, '"We Are Safe Whatever Happens" – Douglas Haig, the Reverend George Duncan and the Conduct of War, 1916–1918', in N. Macdougall, ed., *Scotland and War: AD 79–1918* (Edinburgh: 1991), pp. 193–211.

31 Haig Diary, 5 November 1916. *op. cit.*, No. 109.

32 Haig Diary, 10 September 1917. *Ibid*, No. 117.

33 Haig Diary, 10 October 1917. *Ibid*, No. 118.

34 Haig Diary, 11 February 1917. *Ibid*, No. 110.

Notes to Section One

1 Haig replaced Field Marshal Sir John French as Commander-in-Chief of the British Expeditionary Force on 10 December 1915.

2 Gwynne was anxious to weed out unsuitable men and send them home, but Haig's idea of the chaplain's role would not have appealed to the majority of chaplains.

3 The advice was given to Army Commanders during a conference at St. Omer.

4 Correct spelling: 'Babur'. His real name was Zair-ud-din Muhammed, King of Kabul. On 16 March 1527, in a field near Khanua (west of Delhi), he defeated Rana Sangram Singh, Rajar of Mewar. The quote is verbatim from *Memoirs of Babur* (trans. J. Leyden and W. Erskine, 1921), Vol. II, p. 286. This suggests that Haig was reading the *Memoirs* at the time. Babur was preaching *jihad*, or holy war, an idea which appealed to Haig, even though he may not have appreciated its fullest implications. My thanks go to my colleague Professor Bruce Lenman for advising me on this point.

5 The theme of moral purification through the sacrifice of war was a favourite one of both Duncan and Haig.

6 From September 1915 until his arrival at GHQ, Duncan had been stationed in St. Omer where he was an assistant to the Presbyterian Chaplain W. J. McConnell. He worked mainly in the four hospitals in the region. When Haig moved his GHQ to Montreuil at the end of March 1916, he arranged for Duncan to accompany him. It appears that Duncan began his diary upon arrival at Montreuil.

7 Reverend Douglas Falkland Carey, Chaplain 3rd Class. Was responsible for assigning chaplains to posts once they arrived in France.

8 Many Church of England chaplains at the front worked closely with other denominations, including holding joint services. This was frowned upon by

the Church of England clergy at home, who were horrified by the thought of joint communion services.

9   One suspects he meant Henry Sargent, who was actually Q.M.G., I Corps.

10 Duncan's son Douglas, in a letter to this editor, speculated that this is an example of Haig hearing what he wanted from Duncan's sermons. Douglas Duncan does not think he would have referred to death in such a matter of fact way. 'He was an excessively emotional man who until the end of his life bitterly lamented the early death of his parents and elder brother, not to mention many of his friends in the war.' (Douglas Duncan to G. DeGroot, 25 February 1989.) This seems a reasonable assumption.

11 Most Reverend Randall Thomas Davidson, Archbishop of Canterbury, 1903–30.

12 Revd John Macmillan, later Bishop of Dover.

13 Major-General Sir Charles Macpherson Dobell, commander of the Allied forces in the Cameroons.

14 An example of Haig's tendency to embroider his past. He was hardly a serious student at Oxford. He credited Walter Pater with teaching him to write, but since his written expression was in no sense remarkable, Pater's effect could not have been profound. Haig passed his exams, but did not actually earn a degree, since he spent insufficient time in residence. G. J. DeGroot, *Douglas Haig: 1861–1928* (Unwin Hyman, 1928), pp. 18–26.

15 This was Haig's brother John, who was four years older than him.

16 Note in the margin: 'He acknowledged this to me in a later period of the conversation "I micht hae gaen ye first 'a guid day' or 'a [?] day': but I saw you were a thinkin sort of a fellow: that's why I opened my mind tae ye."'

17 The wrong date. He meant June 4th.

18 The reference is to the inconclusive Battle of Jutland of 31 May 1916. Haig wrote: 'General opinion . . . is that we have not won a great victory at sea, so we are a little disappointed.' Haig Diary, 3 June 1916.

19 Duncan was indeed a candidate, but he had no intention of leaving the Army until the war was over. Chaplains were only required to serve one year, but Duncan considered his responsibility to be 'for the duration'. He joined the St. Andrews faculty in July 1919.

20 Simms naturally included Haig among the 'many others'.

21 Duncan meant Monday June 5th.

22 Perhaps Phillip Reginald Margetson.

23 A detachment of the Artists Rifles was stationed near St. Omer as an Officers Training Unit.

24 Captain Guy Straker had been an ADC of Haig's since 1912, when he took over the Aldershot command. Lieutenant-Colonel Richard L. B. Thompson was an ADC who joined the GHQ staff in February 1915.

25 Kitchener, the Secretary of State for War, was on the *Hampshire*, en route to Russia, when it struck a mine off the Orkneys on 5 June 1916.

26 A reference to Field Marshal Lord Roberts, who died in 1914.

27 A reference to General Brussilov's offensive in Galicia, which was

impressively successful at the beginning but did not achieve the strategic success which would have justified the eventually enormous Russian losses.

28 Haig had been in London since 6 June. He had a brief meeting with the King, in which they disagreed over the continued value of cavalry, and also attended a meeting of the War Committee, at which French political and military representatives were present. It was agreed that the British would take steps to relieve the pressure on the French at Verdun.

29 Colonel Charles Rosdew Burn, sometime member of H.M. Royal Bodyguard.

30 Reverend Gavin Pagan, minister of St. George's parish Church in Edinburgh, enlisted in 1914 as a private in the Royal Scots and by 1916 was an officer. Haig heard of his story and suggested that he should become a chaplain, but he would have none of it. He did not survive the war. His story is told (briefly) in Duncan, *Douglas Haig as I Knew Him*, p. 46 and in John Charteris, *At GHQ*, p. 148. Charteris was 'a sort of cousin' of Pagan's.

31 A Protestant Liturgy. The important points are that the phrase means 'Lift up your hearts', and that its placing in the Roman Mass and in the reformed communion services have always associated this thanksgiving with the idea of sacrifice, hence it is very appropriate for Duncan to use it. My thanks go to my colleague Dr Steve Spackman for helping me on this point.

32 Duncan was referring to the artillery preparation for the Battle of the Somme.

33 William Henry Bragg (1862–1942). Renowned physicist and chemist. Received Nobel Prize for Physics (in conjunction with his son) in 1915. President of the Royal Society, 1935–40. William Lawrence Bragg (1890–1971). Technical Adviser on Sound Ranging, GHQ, 1915–19. Director of the Royal Institution, 1954–66.

34 In order to be closer to the fighting on the Somme, Haig moved to the Château at Val Vion and quartered his staff at Beauquesne. Fletcher was referring to Haig's desire that Duncan should be with him at Beauquesne. It is an indication of Duncan's importance to Haig that he was taken along.

35 Written at bottom of page in pencil by Duncan: "Before the opening of the Battle of the Somme."

36 A reference to preparations for the Battle of the Somme. In his diary Haig wrote: 'The men are in splendid spirits. Several have said that they have never before been so instructed and informed of the nature of the operation before them. The wire has never been so well cut, nor the Artillery preparation so thorough.' (Haig Diary, 30 June 1916) The reality was, of course, quite different.

37 An indication perhaps that Haig had become somewhat sobered by the massive losses on the Somme since 1 July.

38 'Decisive results', according to Haig, meant a significant breach in the German line which would allow the use of cavalry. He never quite came to terms with the inevitability of stalemate.

39 Should be spelled Beauquesne.

40 Duncan seems to have believed the optimistic reports circulating at GHQ. There is no mention of the 57,000 casualties suffered on 1 July, nor of the miniscule gains.

41 Duncan was referring to Rawlinson's night attack of 14 July which advanced to a depth of 1500 metres on a front of five kilometres – perhaps the most successful action of the entire offensive. Haig initially opposed the plan and agreed to it only reluctantly.

42 The Battle of Neuve Chapelle (10–13 March 1915) and the Battle of Loos (25 September–14 October 1915) were both judged by Haig to have failed because sufficient reserves were not pushed forward at the climactic moment. Duncan seems to have absorbed this logic.

43 Later Baron Robertson of Oakridge. The square brackets are Duncan's.

44 According to Haig, Northcliffe 'was much struck with the Rev. Mr. Duncan and his sermon'. Haig Diary, 23 July 1916.

45 The square brackets are Duncan's.

46 He meant the Queen's Edinburgh Rifles.

47 Captain W. A. R. M. McRae.

48 Lieutenant-Colonel James Thomson Rankine Wilson.

49 Actually Major Douglas Craig M'Lagan.

50 These were inserted on a loose sheet in Book One of Duncan's diary. They seem to have been notes for the discussion on the afterlife which took place on 27 July 1916.

51 Stevenson, who served as Duncan's beadle, ran the social activities in the Scottish Churches' Hut, what he called the St. Andrews Soldiers Club. On this occasion, he was writing to Duncan from Montreuil, while the latter was with Haig in Beauquesne.

52 The Reverend Bruce Nicol, a padre based at Étaples, stood in for Duncan, while the latter was in Beauquesne.

53 The École Militaire in Montreuil housed the main GHQ offices, including those of Operations and Intelligence, the Quartermaster-General, Artillery Adviser, Adjutant-General and Engineer-in-Chief.

54 Frank Andrew Munsey, owner of the New York *Sun* and the Baltimore *News*, among other publications.

55 Duncan provided no explanation for why he abandoned his diary for nearly four and a half months. One can only speculate that the pace of events at Advanced GHQ afforded few opportunities for introspection.

56 Haig liked Duncan's absences to coincide with his own, another indication of how he depended on the padre.

57 A reference to the preparations described in Document 25.

58 Reverend Simms was technically a Major-General, though Duncan seldom used that title.

59 Named after Sir Eric Geddes, Director-General of Transportation.

60 During his theological studies, Duncan spent three summer terms in

Germany and in fact returned from Heidelberg in 1914 a week before the outbreak of war.

61 On 12 December 1916, the German Chancellor issued a 'peace note' which called for negotiations but arrogantly implied that the Central Powers should be treated like victors. The Allies understandably rejected the note.

62 On 6 December 1916, Lloyd George replaced Asquith as Prime Minister in a new coalition government. Lord Derby became Secretary of State for War.

63 A Greek pun. Translated literally, it means 'Friday, the day before Saturday.' But 'paraskevy' also means preparation and 'prosabbaton' is the Greek word for the Sabbath. One assumes, therefore, that Duncan meant 'preparation for the Sabbath'.

64 Duncan was referring to the French attack on 15 December, spearheaded by Nivelle's artillery, which advanced the French line by over three kilometres and resulted in the capture of 11,000 prisoners and 115 guns. French casualties were light.

65 Haig was in London where he had his first meeting with the new Prime Minister. Lloyd George forcefully expressed his doubts about the possibility of achieving progress on the Western Front; Haig was equally assertive in his condemnation of 'alternative' strategies.

66 Lieutenant-Colonel J. E. N. Heseltine, one of Haig's ADCs.

67 The École Militaire.

68 This was a reference to an accident which occurred at the National Shell Filling Factory at Barnbow, near Leeds. A shell which was in the process of being fused exploded, causing a chain of detonations. Thirty-five women were killed instantly and over 100 were injured.

69 This is presumably the case which Haig referred to in his diary on 6 December: 'this is the first sentence to death on an officer since I became C. in C. Such a crime is more serious in the case of an officer than of a man, and also it is highly important that all ranks should realise that the law is the same for an officer as for a private'.

70 C. Company.

71 These were the poems which were incorporated into Buchan's *Poems, Scots and English* (1917).

72 It is safe to suppose that this information came to Duncan from Charteris, who sometimes paid excessive attention to the physical and emotional state of German troops, always hoping to show that they were ripe for a knockout blow.

73 According to Haig, Joffre was the source of this rumour. Haig Diary, 15 December 1916.

74 Duncan apparently meant 'notes', not 'name'. He wrote the former in the margin later. He is referring to the note by Woodrow Wilson of 18 December calling upon the belligerents to define their war aims.

75 Duncan presumably meant armoured tanks. If so, this is an interesting reference to the attempt to disguise the weapons as fuel tanks when they were carried by rail. The name stuck, and 'tanks' they were thereafter called.

76 The day had been designated by the King to be observed as a National Day of Prayer.

77 Rumania had declared war on the Central Powers on 28 August 1916. Bucharest fell on 6 December.

Notes to Section Two

1 blockading: Duncan's misspelling.

2 The King notified Haig of the honour on 28 December 1916.

3 Later the 7th Baron Balfour of Burleigh.

4 Nivelle had replaced Joffre as C-in-C in mid-December 1916.

5 Haig's leave was in no sense a holiday. At a series of bruising meetings with the War Committee, it was decided that the BEF would take over a section of the French line and that it would do its utmost to support the offensive proposed by the new French C-in-C, Nivelle. Lloyd George made it clear to Haig that he thought the French Army was superior to the British.

6 Reverend Thomas Martin Lindsay was Principal of the theological college at Glasgow University and a historian of the Reformation.

7 Germany declared unrestricted submarine warfare on 1 February 1917.

8 A series of attacks by the 5th Army on the Ancre front had begun in the first week of February.

9 The monk Rasputin, who had a sinister influence over the Tsarina Alexandra, was murdered on 29 December 1916.

10 Duncan thought the boy was reading Adam Smith.

11 The pen-name for Major General John Hay Beith, author of *The First Hundred Thousand* (1915).

12 (Joseph) Hilaire Belloc (1870–1953). Prolific author, political commentator and poet. Liberal MP 1906–10. Wrote a number of books on the war.

13 Château Beaurepaire was Haig's residence when GHQ was at Montreuil.

14 On 1 February 1917, Haig was interviewed by three French journalists. He made some rather controversial statements on the shortage of ammunition, the necessity for concentrating effort in the West and the need to prepare for a very long war. The articles were censored by Charteris from a military, but not from a political point of view. When the interviews were reprinted in *The Times*, Lloyd George, who was sensitive to the damaging effect which Haig's views would have at home, was furious. There is no doubt that he exploited the episode to the full, but also no doubt that Haig had misunderstood the mood at home – both among politicians and ordinary citizens.

15 Probably a reference to Reverend Richard Hanson, a temporary chaplain, 1917–19.

16 On 17 February II Corps, with the 2nd and 18th Divisions attacked on a front of 2.5 kilometres, to a depth of approximately 1000 metres.

17 Colonel George Alexander Malcolm (1872–1933).

18 Duncan accurately predicted Haig's reaction. Haig told his wife: 'I am doing

my best and have a clear conscience. If they have someone else who can command this great army better than I am doing, I shall be glad to hand over to him and will be so *happy* to come back to my darling wife and play golf and bring up the children.' Haig to Lady Haig, 22 February 1917.

19 The first reference to the German evacuation to the Hindenburg Line, a move designed to shorten the length of the line which the Germans had to defend and thus to free troops for employment elsewhere. The new line was also better constructed, with extensive use of concrete emplacements. As Duncan's reaction reveals, it was not immediately realised around GHQ that the Germans had carried out a brilliant strategic retreat.

20 Duncan's batman possessed some extraordinary knowledge since Kemmel was near the Advanced GHQ for the Battle of Messines, which would not begin until 7 June 1917.

21 When an officer such as the one Duncan mentioned went on leave 'mysteriously' it was usually assumed that he was on a secret mission, and therefore that big events were imminent. The incident indicates how easily rumours spread at GHQ.

22 A curious statement and perhaps an indicator of the blind optimism prevalent at GHQ. In fact, the British government and the Royal Navy were severely alarmed at the depredations of the U-boats. Food stores were becoming perilously low. The scant number of U-boats sunk did little to allay concern.

23 Duncan was referring to Lloyd George's speech to the Commons on 23 February 1917, in which he warned that food stocks were 'alarmingly low' and urged a massive increase in home production.

24 Duncan was referring to the re-capture of Kut-el-Amara from the Turks by Lieutenant-General Sir Stanley Maude.

25 Munro was a Scottish author and journalist who was visiting GHQ.

26 An interesting observation since Haig had every reason to look more aged than he had the previous Sunday. This was the first service after the Calais Conference, at which Lloyd George decided to place Haig and his Army under Nivelle's command. Haig, in response, offered his resignation to the King, which was rejected. It is intriguing that neither the conference nor the controversial decision were mentioned by Duncan.

27 Verney had been Liberal MP for North Bucks since 1910 and was a temporary Lieutenant-Colonel stationed at GHQ.

28 Edward Gurth Wace, later Brigadier-General, a General Staff Officer.

29 Perhaps Hugh John Miles Marshall, RE.

30 After routing Kut, Maude moved on to Baghdad and captured it on 11 March 1917.

31 Sceptical of Nivelle's plans, Lyautey resigned and was replaced by Painlevé. Lyautey's resignation destroyed Briand's government. Ribot became the new Premier.

32 The Russian revolution began on 12 March 1917.

33 Milner was the British civilian representative on the Allied Mission to Russia in February 1917. The conference in Petrograd took place from the 1st to the 20th. It was part of an attempt by Lloyd George to establish closer links with Russia and ascertain her needs. It came too late to help the Russians.

34 Burns' visit had nothing to do with the revolution and the speculation that it might have had is an indication of how ignorant most people were of what was going on in Russia.

35 H. A. L. Fisher, *Life of Napoleon* (1913).

36 He was undoubtedly referring to the 'strength to carry on' after the humiliation he had to endure as a result of the Calais Conference. A few days earlier he confessed to his wife, 'As regards . . . resigning, any *weak* man can do that.' (Haig to Lady Haig, 10 March 1917).

37 The news was not premature. The Czar abdicated on 15 March 1917.

38 Duncan was still referring to the German retreat to the Hindenburg Line. The French 'advance' was on the Aisne, not in Champagne.

39 Scots for 'full church'.

40 This was not just propaganda. Villages were destroyed and wells were poisoned.

41 The Germans held St. Quentin, Cambrai and Lille. There was no movement 'up north' toward Calais.

42 It is interesting to note how Duncan stubbornly continued to believe that the retreat to the Hindenburg line was a victory for the Allies.

43 The paragraph was written very unintelligibly, as if in great excitement at the Allies' tremendous 'progress'.

44 Officers at GHQ were suspicious of the new government because they doubted its commitment to the Western Front. Both Ribot and Painlevé were strong supporters of a Balkan strategy. It did not help that Painlevé was a socialist. 'Such are the people under whom the British Army has been placed for the forthcoming offensive operations', wrote Haig. Haig Diary, 16 March 1917.

45 Haig wrote that he found Painlevé ('an extreme Socialist') a 'pleasant bright little man . . . He is most anxious to keep on the most friendly terms with the British. . . . I thought it was nice of him coming to see me so soon, and I was most friendly.' Haig Diary, 24 March 1917.

46 Zeppelin.

47 Captain F. A. Spencer.

48 Probably the telegram from Sir William Robertson (CIGS) wishing him luck on the eve of the Battle of Arras.

49 Written across the top margin in pencil: 'Before the opening of the offensive (beyond Arras) that opened on Easter Monday, April 9, 1917. (Written after the Morning Service)'.

50 The VIII Corps was stationed near Aubigny.

51 He meant Heschin.

52 The last paragraph was added as a postscript.

53 The British offensive in the Arras sector was to be three-pronged. The First Army was to push toward Vimy Ridge, the Third was to aim at the spur around Monchy-le-Preux, and the Fifth would attack near Bullecourt.

54 Misspelled – Beauclerk. Osborne de Vere Beauclerk, 12th Duke of St. Albans, was a Captain in the 17th Lancers and ADC to Haig, who called him 'Obbey'.

55 The attack, launched by Allenby's Third Army, was the most successful to date. Two hundred guns and 13,000 prisoners were captured on the first day. But, as in previous battles, the British could not find a way to exploit the early success. It lasted until 23 May, being prolonged (contrary to Haig's original intention) to relieve pressure on the French. British casualties were about 85,000, German slightly lower.

56 Archibald Main (born 1876) was Professor of Ecclesiastical History at the University of St. Andrews.

57 Written by Main in margin: 'You people are giving us glorious tidings these days. Keep it up. Remember me to Sandie Lindsay.' He meant A. D. Lindsay.

58 Duncan had been offered the post of principal of St Andrews College in Sydney at the same time that a post at St Andrews University was being discussed. He turned down the offer from Australia.

59 St. Mary's is the Faculty of Divinity at St Andrews.

60 Very Reverend Sir John Herkless, Vice-Chancellor and Principal of the University of St Andrews.

61 Haig was chosen Lord Rector in October 1916.

62 New Testament.

63 The date was 12 April 1917.

64 The French attack on the Chemin des Dames began on 16 April. Nivelle's plans had been known by the Germans for at least a month. By Great War standards, the attack was not a disaster, but because it did not produce Nivelle's promised results, it was perceived as such.

65 Anti-aircraft batteries.

66 An unintentionally ironic comment, given that Haig did feel rather smug after Nivelle's failure and his own relative success.

67 This is the last entry in Book One of Duncan's diary.

68 Meaning, of course, that it was the work of God.

69 Haig went to Paris on 26 April, where he saw Ribot and Painlevé. According to Haig, Painlevé tried to get him to persuade Ribot to drop Nivelle. In his interview with Ribot, Haig was non-committal. He would not be drawn on the merit or demerits of Pétain. Haig was mainly interested in securing French assurance that they would support his planned offensive in Flanders. Haig Diary, 26, 27 April 1917.

70 There is no evidence that Haig and Pétain had formally met by this stage (Haig confessed on 26 April that he knew him 'very slightly'). Fletcher's claim therefore was mere gossip. When Haig met Pétain on 3 May 1917 he found him 'most clear-headed and easy to discuss things with'. Haig Diary, 26 April, 3 May 1917.

71 This was a matter of keen interest to Haig. Many of Charteris' intelligence reports dealt with it.

72 Some typically Haig anti-French feeling. He was referring to the retreat from Mons in 1914.

73 On 26 April 1917 Robertson told Haig that 'The situation at sea is very serious indeed. It has never been so bad as at present, and Jellicoe almost daily pronounces it to be hopeless.' Robertson to Haig, 26 April 1917, included in Haig Diary.

74 The *Daily Mail* had accused the Germans of recycling human skin, an accusation which was without foundation. The material (which probably originated from the government's propaganda mill) nevertheless served its purpose which was to stir up anti-German hatred.

Notes to Section Three

1 Haig was at a conference in Paris on 3–4 May at which French and British senior political and military figures were present. By this time Pétain had replaced Nivelle. Lloyd George was acting decidedly pro-Haig in his attempts to persuade the French to support Haig's offensive plans for the summer. Lloyd George was not at the conference in Doullens, where Haig informed his Army Commanders of the decisions made in Paris.

2 These attacks, agreed upon at the Paris Conference, were partly an effort to relieve pressure on the French.

3 Misspelled – Crowe.

4 One of the many battles on the Isonzo.

5 Duncan wrote in the margin "[Kiggell]".

6 Relatively minor strikes often inspired a paranoid reaction at GHQ.

7 Kitchener.

8 Haig wrote after the meeting with Derby: 'I can't think how he can get through his work if he wastes so much time talking on matters of secondary importance.' Haig Diary, 19 May 1917.

9 A. I. Guchkov, the War Minister, had been the most committed to war. His resignation resulted in the formation of a new government, which pledged itself to make peace without annexation.

10 An international Socialist conference was scheduled to take place in Stockholm. It was intended that representatives from all the combatant (and neutral) countries would attend. The British left split over sending a representative. Arthur Henderson, at the time the Labour Party member of the War Cabinet, was adamantly in favour of sending a representative. In the end, the British delegates were denied passports.

11 He was referring to the planned attack on Messines, which was launched on 7 June 1917.

12 Orpen was at the time painting Haig's portrait. 'He now says that if he were

to paint me twenty times he could not make a better job of it! All the same, the likeness is not good.' Haig Diary, 30 May 1917.

13 The new War Minister was Kerensky, who was in favour of continuing the war, but was not, in the end, able to carry his country with him. Haig was, of course, being overly optimistic.

14 The General Assembly of the Church of Scotland.

15 Haig made a similar remark in the diary he kept at Oxford, on 18 April 1883.

16 Haig was referring to the planned assault on the Messines–Wytschaete ridge, which had been eighteen months in preparation. The attack was launched on 7 June. Its most impressive feature was the explosion of 19 mines at the moment of assault. The action was one of the most successful of the war.

17 Written across the top of the letter in Duncan's hand: 'Immediately before the attack at MESSINES which opened on the morning of June 7, 1917 I was privileged to see D.H. as arranged at his Chateau at BLENDECQUES before he set off for the front, and later I was at hand as his car passed on his way about 11 am.'

18 On the previous day, Robertson urged Haig to 'realise the difficult situation in which the country would be if I carried out large and costly attacks without full cooperation by the French.' (Haig Diary, 9 June 1917). Haig thought Robertson was being unwarrantedly pessimistic.

19 Armed with his recent victory, Haig went to London to gain War Cabinet approval for his next offensive (3rd Ypres) which was designed as an attempt to clear the Belgian coast by a northward assault from Ypres. After a tortuous series of meetings between the 17 and 25 June, he was finally able to secure Lloyd George's acquiescence, but not his support.

20 Colonel Eugene Ryan, RAMC, Haig's Medical Officer at GHQ.

21 Gough's Fifth Army replaced Rawlinson's Fourth Army in the sector around Ypres on 10 June. Haig desired the change because Gough was considered a 'thruster'.

22 It was actually Butler in the car with Haig, not Kiggell.

23 He presumably meant Lieutenant-Colonel Christopher Heseltine who later served on the MCC committee between 1925 and 1943.

24 See document 51.

25 Major William Redmond. Brother of John Redmond (Chairman of Irish Parliamentary Party). Nationalist MP for East Clare. Killed in action, 1917.

26 On 18 May Pétain agreed that a corps composed of six French divisions and six Belgian would be at Haig's disposal during the offensive in Flanders. It would be commanded by King Albert of the Belgians, with General François Anthoine as Chief of Staff.

27 Haig's antagonism toward scientists was typical of his generation and his class. See Jay Luvaas, *The Education of an Army* (1964) and Brian Bond, *The Victorian Army and the Staff College* (1972).

28 A chaplain attached to the Canadian Corps and a friend of Duncan's.

29 Duncan may have been referring to Richard L. B. Thompson, who was in fact a Brevet Lieutenant-Colonel.

30 Queen Mary, who visited on 5 July, was the first woman to dine at Haig's GHQ. The King saw Haig in Cassel on 3 July where he presented him with the insignia of a Knight of the Thistle.

31 Duncan wrote in the margin: '[King's Messenger (of Fyvie)]'.

32 Haig and French had worked closely together since 1891 and Haig had benefited greatly from French's patronage. By 1914, however, they were rivals and a deep antagonism developed. (See G. DeGroot, *Douglas Haig, 1861–1928*.) The 'reconciliation' took place on 27 June 1917. Haig had not seen French since December 1915, when he took over command.

33 As this is the only known incident of Haig expressing a party political preference, it is difficult to tell if he was merely being ironic. In truth, he held most politicians in contempt.

34 The entry was written on 22 July, but deals with the fortnight previous.

35 Benjamin Jowett, Master of Balliol, 1870–91. Asquith was another of the politicians Jowett 'turned out'.

36 A strange reference given that Haig earlier wrote of Curzon: 'I quite admire him and am only sorry that he is not at the head of the Govt. in these troublous times. He has all the brains, and also the ability to decide on large issues.' (Haig to Lady Haig, 6 February 1916).

37 The battle was to have begun around the time of this entry, but was, for a variety of reasons, delayed until 31 July.

38 Kiggell.

39 The gay mood might be explained by the fact that he was about to launch an offensive which was exclusively his, and one which he had been planning virtually since the beginning of the war.

40 He might have been referring to Captain J. P. De Hailes.

41 Most Reverend Cosmo Gordon Lang.

42 Haig meant, presumably, that he did not go to a specific church each Sunday. He often, in fact, attended Church of England services before he came across Duncan. See Duncan, *Douglas Haig as I Knew Him*, pp. 17–22; 119–32; and Document 86.

43 This would have happened while Duncan was in IX Corps area during the Battle of Messines.

44 During the Flanders offensive Haig's Advanced GHQ was situated in a train, which had the obvious advantage of mobility.

45 An impression which Haig shared: Harbord was 'quite ignorant of the problems of modern war . . . a kindly soft looking fellow with a face of a punchinello'. (Haig Diary, 20 July 1917).

46 Haig was seriously worried about the possibility of a socialist revolution in Britain and even worried that Lloyd George was conspiring to establish a republic. See DeGroot, *Douglas Haig: 1861–1928*, pp. 338–9; 359.

47 The memo has no date, but given the passage about the British fighting for 'well-nigh three years', one assumes that it was written shortly before the launch of the Flanders Offensive on 31 July 1917.

48 Duncan's letter to Simms has not been found.

49 See document 12 and note 30. Simms thought at first that Duncan wanted to follow in Pagan's footsteps and join an infantry unit. Pagan had by this stage been killed in action.

50 Contrary to expectation, Miller remained as a chaplain of XIX Corps in France until 1919.

51 Reverend William Stevenson Jaffray, Chaplain to the Forces, 1st Class. Eventually became Assistant Principal Chaplain, Fifth Army.

52 He was referring presumably to Haig.

53 Reverend Francis Arthur Powell Aveling, Acting Chaplain to the Forces, Second Army H.Q.

54 Note on envelope in Duncan's handwriting: 'Killed in Action'. Simpson is identified by Duncan in Document 62.

55 A reference to the Reverend Dr John Kellman, a Free Church minister who was not an Army chaplain but did visit the front and wrote a volume of sermons connected with the war. Duncan was rather inconsistent in the spelling of Kellman's name.

56 Haig had expected to be well toward his goal of clearing the Belgian coast by this stage. Instead, his forces had advanced hardly more than a mile. The weather (incessant rain) was partly to blame, but in truth Haig's strategic objectives were totally unrealistic given the state of the German Army and the tactical realities of this war.

57 When it became clear to Haig that he would not achieve his objectives he suddenly began to talk of the offensive as if it were a campaign of attrition, which it was never intended to be. DeGroot, *Douglas Haig, 1861–1928*, chapter 13.

58 The square brackets are Duncan's.

59 Louis Botha was the South African Premier. Haig and he fought on opposite sides during the Boer War, but afterwards got on splendidly.

60 Crown Prince Rupprecht, the son of Kaiser Wilhelm, commanded an Army Group during the Battle of Arras.

61 Virtually since the beginning of the war, Haldane had been the victim of a scurrilous hate campaign organised by the right wing press. It was alleged that he had pro-German sympathies, an allegation based on the fact that he had been a keen student of German philosophy.

62 Haig had a genuine fondness and admiration for Haldane, but it has to be understood that his defence of the ex-War Minister was in effect a bit of self-congratulation since he was one of Haldane's chief advisers in the Army reforms of 1906–09. What Haig never quite accepted was that domestic political considerations were more important than continental strategic issues in determining the shape of these reforms. See E. M. Spiers, *Haldane: An Army Reformer* (Edinburgh, 1980).

63 The Right Reverend Andrew Wallace Williamson was Moderator of the Church of Scotland 1913–14 and the Minister of St Giles, Edinburgh.

64 Rawlinson's Fourth Army was holding the sector from Nieuport to the sea.

65 Byng's Third Army was defending the line in the vicinity of Cambrai. Since it was this unit which would take part in the battle launched on 20 November and since the initially impressive gains in that battle were not exploited due to a lack of reserves, Byng's comments carry a certain irony.

66 Haig went to London on 3 September to discuss a proposal by the French General Ferdinand Foch to transfer 100 guns from Anthoine's force to the Italian front. Haig insisted that the guns were essential to the continuance of his offensive in Flanders. Lloyd George, who agreed with Foch, put pressure on Haig, and the latter eventually agreed to review the situation with a view to sending 50 guns.

67 The square brackets are Duncan's.

68 Kennoway is a short distance from Markinch, where Haig grew up.

69 Churchill, the new Minister of Munitions, arrived on 12 September and stayed at GHQ for two nights. He discussed strategy with Kiggell and armaments with Birch and Butler and told Haig that he and Lloyd George were doubtful of the chances of beating the Germans on the Western Front. Haig Diary, 12–15 September 1917.

70 Ronald MacNeill, (Mr not Sir) was Unionist MP for St. Augustine Division of Kent. On 13 November 1912, during the debate on the Home Rule Bill, MacNeill, an Ulsterman, threw the Speaker's Copy of the Standing Orders at Churchill, who was leaving the Chambers after having made a speech in support of the bill. The book hit him on the head and drew blood. Randolph Churchill, *Winston S. Churchill*, Vol. III, p. 473.

71 Duncan apparently couldn't read his own handwriting and, on later editing, guessed 'Hansard'.

72 Duncan was echoing Haig's feelings. The latter wrote: 'Sir Edward Carson . . . is quite a rest to deal with . . . after Winston! He is so straightforward and single-minded. He is convinced that the military experts must be given full power, not only to advise, but to carry out their plans. He is all opposed to the meddling now practised by the Prime Minister and other politicians.' Haig Diary, 7 September 1917.

73 The offensive was resumed on 20 September when Plumer's Second Army (to whom the main burden of the assault had been transferred) attacked the Gheluvelt Plateau, with some success.

74 The Papal Peace Note was released on 1 August and called for restoration of occupied territory, especially Belgium. Germany, reluctant to surrender her trump card, was non-committal, as were the other belligerents. The 'British Peace Proposal' must be an effort by the Germans to turn the British response to the Papal Note into a favourable piece of propaganda.

75 Derby was more concerned that Lloyd George apparently wanted to be rid of him and Robertson. He also told Haig that the Prime Minister and

Painlevé were interested in establishing an Allied General Staff, an idea which Haig rejected outright.

76 Howard Spring (1889–1965) was a poet, novelist and newspaper correspondent. His time at GHQ is briefly told in his autobiography, *In the Meantime*.

77 This is an exaggeration. The battle was a success, but not of the order of Messines. It was significant that all but one of the four tanks employed were immobilised in the muddy, shattered ground before they reached their first objective.

78 The 20 September attack on the Gheluvelt Plateau was preceded by a bombardment lasting three weeks which consisted of 750 guns, a third of them heavy.

79 Perhaps Major-General Walter Clarence Black, Indian Army.

80 The mutiny is described in D. Gill and G. Dallas, 'Mutiny at Etaples Base in 1917', *Past and Present* (1975).

81 L. G. Kornilov (1870–1918), who had earlier arrested Nicholas II, was C-in-C of all Russian forces in August 1917. Realising the danger of a Bolshevik coup, he took steps to suppress the Soviets, against the will of A. F. Kerensky (1881–1971), head of the Provisional Government. Kerensky had him arrested. This 'Kornilov Affair' resulted in the further weakening of the provisional government and the strengthening of the Bolsheviks. Kornilov escaped from prison in December 1917 and formed with General M. V. Aleksiyev the first anti-Bolshevik volunteer units. The square brackets are Duncan's.

82 Earlier in the year Haig and Bacon had agreed upon an amphibious operation to coincide with the Flanders offensive. Even though the land operations had so far failed, both men remained hopeful that the naval action could still be implemented. (Haig Diary, 23 September 1917). Bacon was under pressure to find a way to prevent German submarines from leaving their bases, thus the reference to Zeebrugge. In December 1917 he would be replaced at Dover Patrol by Admiral Sir Roger Keyes.

83 Bacon was remarkably more optimistic than the First Sea Lord, Jellicoe, who had been in a constant state of panic since the resumption of submarine warfare. Nevertheless by this stage the Allies were coming to terms with the problem. Losses in the fourth quarter of 1917 were about half those endured in the second quarter.

84 Surely a case of blaming the messenger. Gold's forecasts were imprecise, but that was the fault of the available technology, not of the man. Haig, it seems, could not come to terms with the fact that his grand plan had been foiled by the weather and was therefore desperate to blame someone. D. Winter, *Haig's Command: A Reassessment* (1991), p. 90.

85 It is not clear to which Captain Geddes Duncan was referring.

86 The brother in question was Sir Auckland Geddes.

87 Duncan later put a question mark in the margin, which suggests that he actually meant 'favourably'.

88 Lieutenant A. P. Scotland.

89 The conference was organised by H. W. Blackburne, addressed by Dr Kellman, and attended by Gwynne.

90 The Roman Catholics refused to attend joint conferences.

91 Major-General James Thomson, later Deputy Director of Medical Services, BEF.

92 In 1915 Archbishop Davidson launched the National Mission of Repentance and Hope which called the British people to the 'earnest and honest repentance of our sins and shortcomings as a nation'. Special Services of Intercession were combined with group discussions of Mission literature. Services were held in schools, village halls and out-of-doors, in an attempt to attract those reluctant to attend Church services. The Mission is widely judged to have been a failure.

93 This might be the service Kellman gave at GHQ which Duncan refers to on 18 September 1917.

94 The attack, a carbon copy of the action on 20 September, was launched on the 26th, with a similar, limited success.

95 Lloyd George suggested to Haig that since the Belgians, Russians and French were not fighting, it made sense for the British to go onto the defensive until next year. Haig replied: 'We should go on striking as hard as possible with the object of clearing the Belgian coast.' (Haig Diary, 26 September 1917). Lloyd George was not convinced.

96 The Liberal MP for Ross and Cromarty and Under Secretary of State for War.

97 Given Haig's antagonism towards English public schools, it is interesting to note that his son Dawyck (born 1918) was sent to Stowe, though it is possible that the decision was not Haig's since he died in 1928.

98 It was quite common for Haig to poke fun at his self-effacing staff officers, who were helpless to react.

99 This might be a reference to Major-General Walter Greenly.

100 He certainly had not lost his faith in the cavalry, which he retained to the end of his life. DeGroot, *Douglas Haig, 1861–1928*.

101 The story, suitably embellished, related to an incident which occurred on 27 August 1914.

102 Major-General Sir George MacDonogh, Director of Military Intelligence, had shortly before produced a report which refuted Haig's claim that the German Army was on the brink of collapse as a result of the Flanders operations.

103 It was actually on 12 October that the Second and Fifth Armies renewed their attack.

104 The third son of Queen Victoria.

105 Usually spelled 'Klerken'.

106 Haig Diary, 14 October 1914.

107 It was around this time that Haig finally, reluctantly, gave up on his idea of clearing the Belgian coast. This might explain his solemnity.

108 He was referring to Robertson's visit to GHQ on 26 September.

109 This is the last entry in Duncan's diary. Whilst it seems inconceivable that he would have suddenly abandoned it, there is little to suggest that a subsequent volume existed. Volume II of the diary ended with approximately ten blank pages which would presumably have been filled had Duncan continued to keep a diary.

110 On 27 October Haig received a telegram informing him that the Government had decided to send two divisions to Italy, a move prompted by the enormously successful German attack at Caporetto on the 24th.

111 According to the envelope, Duncan was at the No. 8 Convalescent Home for British Officers, Cap Martin, at the time.

Notes to Section Four

1 This was Haig's favourite and most often quoted Bible passage.

2 The last sentence was added as a postscript.

3 The occasion was the fourth anniversary of the British declaration of war.

4 The Reverend J. N. Bateman Champain, Minister of the Church of St Mary, Redcliffe, Bristol, was the Church of England Chaplain at Montreuil, 1917–18.

5 Throughout the war, Catholic chaplains were ordered not to take part in joint services.

6 The Right Reverend John Primatt Maud.

7 He was referring to the successful attack at Amiens, the beginning of the end for the German Army.

8 'Doris' was Haig's wife, whose actual name was 'Dorothy'.

9 After the war Haig attended this church when he was in London and became an elder of it.

10 The Reverend Archibald Fleming.

11 The sentence is one of the best indicators of Haig's undying faith in the cavalry, and also of his blindness to the real nature of modern warfare.

12 A General Election had been called for 14 December.

13 He was to become Earl Haig of Bemersyde.

Biographical Notes

Other persons mentioned in the transcripts are indentified in the Notes.

Asser, Joseph John (1867–1949). Previous service in Sudan, 1897–9; retired 1914; restored to active list 1916. Major-General, GOC line of communications, Western Front, 1916–19. Governor and C-in-C, Bermuda, 1922–7. Knighted, 1917.

Asquith, Herbert Henry (1852–1928). Prime Minister 1908–16. Liberal MP 1886–1918; 1920–4. Served Home Office, Exchequer, War Office before 1914. Earl of Oxford and Asquith, 1925. Haig preferred him to Lloyd George.

Bacon, Reginald Hugh Spencer (1863–1947). Commanded Dover Patrol from 1915. Haig's favourite Admiral, cooperated in plans for Passchendaele offensive. Removed from command late 1917.

Birch, (James Frederick) Noel (1865–1939). Previous service in Ashanti Campaign, 1895–6; and South Africa, 1899–1902. Artillery Adviser at GHQ, 1916–1918. Knighted, 1918. Retired, 1927.

Black, George (died 1918). ADC to Haig. Commanded 17th Lancers escort which attended Haig. Left GHQ early 1918, in order to join the Tank Corps because he "wanted to fight". Killed in action a short while later.

Bonar Law, Andrew, (1858–1923). Conservative MP 1900–23. Served Board of Trade, Colonial Office before 1914. Chancellor, 1916–19; Member of War Cabinet, 1916–19; Prime Minister, 1922–3.

Bourne, Francis, 1861–1935. Archbishop of Westminster 1903–1935. Cardinal, 1911.

Briand, Aristide (1862–1932). French Politician. Prime Minister, 1909–10; 1913; 1915–17; 1921–2; 1925–6; 1929. Nobel Peace Prize 1926.

Buchan, John (1875–1940). Prolific novelist and poet. On GHQ Staff, 1916–17, temp. Lieutenant-Colonel. Wrote GHQ despatches during Somme campaign. Director of Information, 1917–18. Conservative MP, 1927–35.

Butler, Richard H. K. (1870–1935). Deputy Chief of General Staff, 1916–18; GOC, 3 Corps, 1918. Rejected by the government as a replacement for Kiggell in 1918.

Byng, Julian Hedworth George (1862–1935). Previous service in Sudan, South Africa. GOC, 3rd Cavalry Division, 1914–15; Cavalry Corps, 1915; IX and XVII Army Corps, 1916; Canadian Corps, 1916; 3rd Army, 1917–19. Governor-General of Canada, 1921–6; Commissioner Metropolitan Police, 1928–31. Major-General, 1909; knighted, 1915; Baron, 1919; Viscount, 1926.

Carson, Edward Henry (1854–1935) Unionist MP 1892–1914, 1918–21. Served as Solicitor-General before 1914. Attorney-General, 1915; First Lord of the Admiralty, 1917; member of War Cabinet, 1917–18. One of Haig's favourite politicians.

Castelnau, Edouard de (1851–1944). Commanded 2nd French Army, 1914; Chief of Staff to Joffre, 1915–17; commanded Eastern Group of Armies, 1917–18.

Cavan, 10th Earl of, Frederick Rudolph Lambart (1865–1946). Commanded Guards Division, 1915–16; XIV Corps, France and Italy, 1916–18. Served on British Delegation to Washington Conference, 1921; CIGS, 1922–6. Field Marshal, 1932.

Charteris, John (1877–1946). Chief of Intelligence at GHQ, 1916–18. Haig discovered him in India in 1909; stayed beside Haig until 1918. A very intelligent man, but no formal training in Intelligence work. His reports reflected the wishes of his master. Accurately predicted timing and place of German 1918 spring offensive.

Churchill, Winston Leonard Spencer (1874–1965). Conservative MP 1900–4; 1924–64. Liberal MP 1904–22. Served Board of Trade, Home Office, Admiralty before 1914. Minister of Munitions, 1917–19. Served Colonial Office, Exchequer, Prime Minister, etc. after 1918. Haig detested him.

Connaught, Prince Arthur of (1883–1938). Major and Lieutenant-Colonel, Scots Greys, 1907–20. Later ADC to the King, 1936–8.

Crowe, John Henry Verinder (1862–1948). Commanded RA, East Africa, 1915–17; General Staff, 1917–18. Retired as Brigadier-General in 1919.

Curzon, George Nathaniel (1859–1925). Conservative MP, 1886–98. Viceroy of India, 1898–1905; Lord Privy Seal, 1915–16; President of the Air Board, 1916; Lord President of the Council, 1916–19; Member of War Cabinet, 1916–19. Foreign Sec., 1919–24. Baron, 1898; Earl, 1911, Marquis Curzon of Kedleston, 1921.

Davidson, General Sir John. (1876–1954). Chief of Operations, GHQ, 1915–18; Major-General, 1918. One of Haig's many lacklustre staff officers. Nicknamed "Tavish".

Derby, 17th Earl of, Edward George Villiers Stanley (1865–1948). Conservative MP, 1892–1906; succeeded father, 1908. Director-General of Recruiting, 1915–16; Under-Secretary for War, 1916; Secretary for War, 1916–18, 1922–4.

Esher, Reginald Baliol Brett (1852–1930). Liberal MP, 1880–5; succeeded father as 2nd Viscount Esher, 1899. Permanent member of Committee of Imperial Defence, 1905–18. Very pro-Haig.

Fletcher, Alan Francis (born 1876). ADC to Haig. Came to Haig's notice when latter took command of 17th Lancers in 1901. With regard to Fletcher's intelligence, Haig remarked 'All I require is people of *average intelligence* who are keen to do their work properly. Alan is well up to this standard and is most unselfish and tactful, so that I find it a pleasure to go about with him.' (Haig to Henrietta Haig, 1 September 1904, Haig MSS, Acc. 3155, No. 6).

Fowke, George Henry (1864–1936). Entered Royal Engineers, 1884. Engineer-in-Chief, BEF, 1914–16; Adjutant-General in France, 1916–19. Knighted, 1916.

French, John Denton Pinkstone (1852–1925). Service in Sudan, South Africa, before 1914. CIGS, 1911–14; Field Marshal, 1913; C-in-C, BEF, 1914–15; C-in-C, Home Forces, 1916–18. Viscount, 1915; Earl of Ypres, 1921. Once Haig's mentor, the two cavalrymen fell out when Haig replaced French as C-in-C in 1915.

Geddes, Auckland (1879–1954). Professor of Anatomy at Edinburgh until 1916. Director of Recruiting, 1916–17; Minister of National Service, 1917–18. Brother of Eric Geddes.

Geddes, Eric Campbell (1875–1937). Railway Engineer. Deputy Director-General of Munitions, 1915–16; Inspector-General of Transportation, 1916–17; Conservative MP, 1917–22; First Lord of the Admiralty, 1917–19; War Cabinet, 1918. Knighted, 1916; Hon. Major-General and Vice-Admiral, 1917.

Gold, Ernest (1881–1976). Meteorological Officer at GHQ. Began with a staff of three, ended the war with 120 assistants. Haig often blamed bad weather (and thus his failed offensives) on Gold.

Gough, Hubert de la Poer (1870–1963). GOC 3rd Cavalry Brigade, 1914; 2nd Cavalry and 7th Cavalry Division, 1915; I Corps, 1916; 5th Army, 1916–18. General, 1922.

Griffiths, John Norton (1871–1930). Served in Matabele War and South Africa before 1914. Engineer-in-Chief, GHQ, in charge of Tunnelling Companies, 1916–18.

Gwynne, Llewellyn Henry (1863–1957). Deputy Chaplain General in France, 1915–18. Bishop of Khartoum, 1908–20; of Egypt and the Sudan, 1920–45. Volunteered as a regular chaplain with the BEF in 1914 and was shortly afterwards promoted in order to relieve the pressure on the Chaplain General.

Haig, Douglas (1861–1928). Service in Sudan, South Africa, India before 1914. GOC, Aldershot, 1912–14; 1st Army, 1914–15; C-in-C, BEF, 1915–19. Knighted, 1913; Field Marshal, 1917; Earl, 1919.

Haking, Richard Cyril Byrne (1862–1945). Served Burma, South Africa before 1914. GOC, XI Corps, 1915–18; Chief of British Section, Armistice Commission, 1918–19. Brigadier-General, 1908; knighted, 1916.

Haldane, Richard Burdon (1856–1928). Liberal MP, 1885–1911. Secretary of State for War, 1905–12; Lord Chancellor, 1912–15 and 1924. Viscount, 1911.

Harbord, James (1866–1947). Chief of Staff to Pershing. Later in charge of supply for American Expeditionary Force.

Hindenburg, Paul von Beneckendorf und von (1847–1934). German Field Marshal. Hero of Battle of Tannenberg, 1914; Chief of German General Staff, 1916. With First Quartermaster-General Erich Ludendorff, came to dominate German military policy.

Horne, Henry Sinclair (1861–1929). Royal Artillery. Served South Africa, before 1914. Commanded Artillery, 1st Corps, 1914; 2nd Division, 1915; XV Corps, 1916; C-in-C, 1st Army, 1917–18. Major-General, 1914; knighted 1916; Baron, 1919.

Joffre, Joseph Jacques Cesaire (1852–1931). Served Franco-Prussian War, China, Indo-China, Formosa, Sudan, Madagascar before 1914. Chief of the French General Staff, 1914; C-in-C, French Armies, 1915–17.

Kiggell, Launcelot Edward (1862–1954). Served in South Africa before 1914. Chief of Staff to Haig, 1915–18. Sent to Guernsey as GOC after his nerve cracked. Knighted, 1916; Lieutenant-General, 1918.

Kitchener, Horatio Herbert (1850–1916). Served in Sudan, South Africa before 1914. Secretary of State for War, 1914–16; responsible for expansion of Army from 20 to 70 divisions. Drowned off Orkneys en route to Russia, 1916.

Lang, Cosmo Gordon (1864–1945). Canon of St. Paul's, 1901–08; Archbishop of York, 1908–28; Archbishop of Canterbury, 1928–42. 1st Baron Lang of Lambeth, 1942.

Lindsay, Alexander Dunlop (1879–1952), 1st Baron Lindsay of Birker. Jowett lecturer in Philosophy, Oxford before 1914. Master of Balliol, 1924–49; Vice-Chancellor, Oxford University, 1935–8.

Lloyd George, David (1863–1945). Liberal MP, 1890–1945. Served at Board of Trade, Exchequer before 1914. Minister of Munitions, 1915–16; Secretary for War, 1916; Prime Minister, 1916–22. Earl, 1945.

Lyautey, Hubert. French General. Minister of War, December 1916, resigned March 1917. Sceptical of Nivelle and his plan.

Miller, John Harry (1869–1940). Free Church Minister. Warden of New College, Edinburgh, 1908–35; Chaplain in France, 1915–19; Asst. Principal Chaplain, 1917. Principal of St. Mary's College, St. Andrews, 1935–9. Moderator of the United Free Church of Scotland, 1928.

Milner, Alfred (1854–1925). High Commissioner for South Africa, 1897–1905; member of War Cabinet, 1916–18; Secretary for War, 1918–19. Knighted, 1895; Baron, 1901; Viscount, 1902.

Nash, Philip Arthur Manley (1882–1968). Director, National Filling Factories, Ministry of Munitions, 1915–16. Deputy Director-General of Transportation, BEF, 1916; Director-General, 1917; Inspector-General of Transportation, 1918. Knighted, 1918.

Nivelle, Robert Georges (1856–1924). French General. Colonel in Artillery in August 1914; became hero during Battle of Verdun. Replaced Joffre as C-in-C, 1917. His failed offensive led to his replacement by Pétain in May 1917.

Northcliffe, Viscount, Alfred Charles William Harmsworth (1865–1922). Publisher of *The Times*, 1908–22. Chairman of the British War Mission to the USA, 1917; Director of Propaganda, 1918. Baronet, 1904; Baron, 1905; Viscount, 1917.

Oliver, Frederick Scott (1864–1935). Barrister, 1899. Political journalist. Author of *Ordeal by Battle* (1916). Great admirer of Haig.

Orpen, William (1878–1931). War Artist and portrait painter. Painted one of the better portraits of Haig. Knighted, 1918.

Painlevé, Paul. French socialist. Minister of War, March 1917; opposed Nivelle's plan; supported Pétain. Premier (and War Minister), September to November 1917. Supporter of alternative strategies, i.e. Balkans.

Pershing, John Joseph (1860–1948). US Army, served in Apache and Sioux campaigns, Spanish-American War before 1914. C-in-C, American Expeditionary Force in Europe, 1917–19. General, 1906.

Pétain, Henri-Phillipe Benoni Omer Joseph (1856–1951). Hero of Verdun siege, 1916; CGS, 1917; C-in-C, French Army, 1917–18. Negotiated truce with Germany, 1940; Chief of State, 1940–4. Condemned to death after liberation, but sentence commuted to life imprisonment.

Plowden-Wardlaw, James Tait (1873–1963). Chaplain, 1916–18. At various times an advocate, preacher and religious philosopher. Wrote, among other works, *The Test of War* (1916) and *Religious Reconstruction After the War* (1916).

Rawlinson, Henry Seymour (1864–1925). Served in Burma, Sudan, South Africa before 1914. GOC, IV Corps, 1914–15; 1st and 4th Armies, 1915–19; British Representative at Supreme War Council, 1918. Knighted, 1914; General, 1917; Baron, 1919.

Repington, Charles a'Court (1858–1925). Served in Afghanistan, Burma, Sudan, South Africa, before 1914. Military Correspondent of *The Times*, 1904–18; *The Daily Telegraph*, 1918–25.

Ribot, Alexandre. French politician. Finance Minister, 1914–16; Premier, March 1917, succeeding Briand. Fell from power in September 1917. Strong supporter of Balkan strategy.

Roberts, Frederick Sleigh (1832–1914). Served in many Imperial engagements. C-in-C, Madras, 1881–5; India, 1885–93; GOC, Ireland, 1895–9; C-in-C, South Africa, 1899–1900; C-in-C, 1901–4. Baron, 1892; Field Marshal, 1895; Earl, 1901.

Robertson, William Robert (1860–1933). Served in Chitral, South Africa before 1914. QMG to BEF, 1914–15; Chief of Staff, BEF, 1915; CIGS, 1915–18; GOC, Eastern Command, 1918. C-in-C, British Army of the Rhine, 1919–20. Knighted, 1913; Baronet, 1913; Field Marshal, 1920.

Sassoon, Philip (1888–1939). Haig's private secretary. Useful connection to the wealthy and powerful at home. Millionaire and sometime Conservative MP. Cousin of Siegfried Sassoon.

Sclater, John Robert Paterson (1876–1949). Chaplain, 9th Battalion Royal Scots, 1909–23. War service, Forth Defences and France YMCA, 1915–17.

Simms, John Morrow (1854–1934). Regular Army Chaplain, served in Nile Expedition and South Africa before 1914. Principal Chaplain, BEF, 1914–20. Moderator, Presbyterian Church of Ireland, 1919–20.

Stevenson, R. Macaulay (died 1952). Landscape artist who lived in Montreuil and was an active volunteer at the Church Hut. Served as Duncan's beadle. The latter described him as a 'weird genius'. (*Douglas Haig as I Knew Him*, p. 31)

Talbot, Neville Stuart (died 1943). Chaplain (First Class) in France, 1914–19; Bishop of Pretoria, 1920–33. Wrote *Thoughts on Religions at the Front*, 1917.

Thomas, William Beach (1868–1957). War correspondent of the *Daily Mail*, regular contributor to the *Observer* and *Spectator*. Knighted, 1920.

Wigram, Clive (1873–1960). Assistant Private Secretary to the King, 1910–31; Private Secretary to King George V, 1931–6. Knighted, 1931; Baron, 1935.

Wilson, (Thomas) Woodrow (1856–1924). President of Princeton University, 1902–10; Governor of New Jersey, 1911–13; Democratic President of the USA, 1913–21.

Select Bibliography

(all books published in London unless noted otherwise)

Books and Articles

Arthur, G., *Haig* (1928).

Blake, R. (ed.), *The Private Papers of Douglas Haig, 1914–1919* (1952).

Boraston, J. H. (ed.), *Sir Douglas Haig's Despatches* (1919).

Charteris, J., *At G.H.Q.* (1931).

—, *Field Marshal Earl Haig* (1929).

—, *Haig* (1933).

Churchill, R. and Gilbert, M., *Winston S. Churchill* (1967–88).

Cruttwell, C. R. M. F., *History of the Great War* (1982).

Davidson, J., *Haig: Master of the Field* (1953).

DeGroot, G., *Douglas Haig, 1861–1928* (1988).

—, "Educated Soldier or Cavalry Officer?", *War and Society* (1986).

—, "'We Are Safe Whatever Happens' – Douglas Haig, the Reverend George Duncan, and the Conduct of War, 1916–18", in N. Macdougall, *Scotland and War* (1991).

Duff Cooper, A., *Haig* (1936).

Duncan, G., *Douglas Haig As I Knew Him* (1968).

Farrar-Hockley, A., *The Somme* (1964).

Fox, F., *Battle of the Ridges* (1918).

—, *G.H.Q.* (1920).

Fraser, P., *Lord Esher* (1973).

French, D., 'Sir Douglas Haig's Reputation', *Historical Journal* (1985).

Gill, D. and Dallas, G., 'Mutiny at Etaples Base in 1917', *Past and Present* (1975).

Keegan, J., *The Face of Battle* (1978).

Lees-Milne, J., *The Enigmatic Edwardian* (1986).

Leyden, J. and Erskine, W., *Memoirs of Babur* (1921).

Liddell-Hart, B. H., *History of the First World War* (1972).

Lloyd George, D., *War Memoirs* (1938).

Luvaas, J., *The Education of an Army* (1964).

Lytton, N., *The Press and the General Staff* (1920).

Macdonald, L., *Somme* (1983).

—, *They Called it Passchendaele* (1978).

Morgan, K., *Lloyd George* (1974).

Protheroe, E., *Earl Haig* (1928).
Robertson, W., *From Private to Field Marshall* (1921).
—, *Soldiers and Statesmen* (1926).
Secrett, T., *Twenty-Five Years with Earl Haig* (1929).
Sixsmith, E. K. G., *Douglas Haig* (1976).
Spiers, E. M., *Haldane: An Army Reformer* (1980).
Terraine, J., *Douglas Haig: The Educated Soldier* (1963).
Travers, T., *The Killing Ground* (1987).
—, *How the War Was Won* (1992).
Wilson, T., *The Myriad Faces of War* (1985).
Winter, D., *Haig's Command: A Reassessment* (1991).
Woodward, D., *Lloyd George and the Generals* (1983).

Series

Official History of the War.
Parliamentary Debates.
Who's Who.

Index

Abbott, James, 73, 103, 113, 120, 166, 169, 171–2, 177–9, 194, 206, 217, 244, 254

Aberdeen, 289–90, 317

Adair, William, 61

Addison, Joseph, 4

Adjoodhia Pershaud, Dewan, 152, 251

Agassiz, Miss, 99, 100, 127, 140, 243

Agra, 226

Aire, 391

Akbar Shah, 131, 228, 248

Akora, 195, 227

Albemarle, Lt.-Gen. George, Earl of, 14

Aldershot, 291, 405

Alexsiyev, M.V., 388

Allahabad, 86, 227

Amritsar, 94, 96, 196, 227

Ancre, 320, 324, 326

Anderson, William Andrew, 72, 153, 159, 178, 206

Anson, Cpt. George RN, 65

Anstruther, Acting Maj. Robert, 30, 64

Antigua, 11, 13, 54, 57

Araul, 86, 227

Armiger, Col. Robert, 61, 64

Arques, 341–2, 385, 387

Arras, 273, 330–2, 335, 338, 342, 344–7, 356

Asquith, Herbert, 384, 429

Asser, Maj.-Gen. Joseph, 388, 390, 429

Attock, 74, 125, 132, 169, 175, 178, 182, 192, 215, 228

Aubigny, 338, 344, 346

Auckland, Lord, 139, 249

Aveling, F.A.P., 380, 424

Babur, Emperor of India, 278, 412

Bacon, Adm. Reginald, 296, 388–90, 429

Baghdad, 328, 331

Bailleul, 310, 342, 344

Bakrala, 194, 228

Balfour, Lord, 318

banks,
North Western Bank of India, 147, 250
Union Bank, 151–2, 250

Bannockburn, 284, 293

Bannu, 146–7, 159, 183, 228

Bapaume, 326, 328, 330–1

Barbados, 11, 29–30, 43, 47

Barrington, Maj.-Gen. John, 5, 11, 13, 23, 39, 45, 47–8, 52–3, 57, 61, 63, 65–8

Barrington, William, Viscount, Secretary at War, 5, 8, 63

Basseterre, 12, 13, 34–9, 41, 53

Bavincourt, 346–7, 352, 359–60

Bayley, Edward Clive, 220, 259

Beadon, Cecil, 199, 258

Beatson, Robert, 5, 11, 12, 60

Beauclerk, Lord Osborne, 338, 420
Beaufoy, Mark, 14
Beauquesne, 293, 295, 305, 309, 312, 318, 327, 335
Beaurepaire, 322, 338
Belgium, 350, 362, 390
Belloc, Hilaire, 322, 417
Benares, 87, 155, 228
Berlin, 286, 383, 405
Bhawal Khan, Nawab, 159–60, 171, 252
Bhimbar, 91, 228
Birch, Gen. Noel, 306, 330, 334, 336, 362, 386–7, 429
Black, Col. George, 287, 296–7, 310, 429
Black, Walter, 388, 426
Blendecques, 359–61, 363, 369, 381, 391, 397
Bligh, Lt.-Gen. Thomas, 9
Bokhara, 139, 228
Bombay, 102, 186, 193, 228
Bompart, *Chef d'Escadre* Maximum de, 66, 68
Bonar Law, Andrew, 364, 429
Botha, Louis, 382
Boulogne, 322, 324, 352, 389
Boume, Archbishop Francis, 429
Bowie, Charles Vincent, 177–8, 182, 256
Bragg, Prof. William, 292, 414
Briand, Aristide, 322, 429
British Army,
    financial administration, eighteenth century, 7–8
    First Army, 391
    Third Army, 322, 355, 383
    Fifth Army, 355, 360, 364, 385
    IX Corps, 361
    XI Corps, 366

XVII Corps, 338–9
XIX Corps, 364
2nd Division, 398
8th Division, 341
9th Division, 338, 342, 344
15th Division, 368
16th Division, 361
32nd Division, 298
34th Division, 338
36th Division, 361
51st Division, 339, 368, 406
57th Division, 338–9
8th Argylls, 356
Army Service Corps, 298, 357
Artists Rifles, 287–8, 290, 308–9, 312–14, 328, 330, 334, 355
8th Black Watch, 343
Cameron Highlanders, 282
Glasgow Highlanders, 279, 297
1st Gordons, 346
6th Gordons, 339, 356
Guernsey Militia, 403
16th Highland Infantry, 323
17th Lancers, 327
London Scottish, 324
Order of Battle in the Martinique/Guadaloupe expedition, 11, 31, 64
Regiments of Foot,
    3rd, 11, 64
    4th, 11, 64
    38th, 11, 64
    42nd, 11, 30, 63–4
    61st, 11, 64
    63rd, 11, 64, 66
    64th, 11, 64
    65th, 11, 64
Royal Army Medical Corps, 310, 371

Royal Artillery, 11, 66, 315
Royal Engineers, 281, 312, 315
Royal Scots, 298
Royal Signals, 279, 336, 398
Seaforth Highlanders, 284
Staffordshire Regiment, 284
British Legion, 273
'British Peace Proposals', 385
Brooke, Dr Thomas, 47–8, 66
Brown, Lewis, 135, 186, 248–9
Bruce, Herbert, 199, 258
Bruyeres, Annie Jessie, 99, 128, 243
Buchan, John, 314, 429
Bullecourt, 353
Bunyan, John, 406
Burke, James Henry, 102
Burn, Col. C.R., 288, 291, 306, 320, 329, 334, 336, 362–3, 414
Burn, Henry Pelham, 210–11, 217–18, 259
Burt, William Matthew, 39, 64–5
Butler, Lt.-Gen. Richard, 338, 360, 365, 429
Byng, Admiral John, 65
Byng, Gen. Sir Julian, 383, 427

Cadogan, Thomas Charles, 72, 84, 164, 166, 168, 240, 253
Calcraft, John, 8, 9, 59
Calcutta, 72, 84, 94, 97, 164, 229
Cambrai, 331
Cambridge, 271, 307
Campbell, Robert, 148, 191, 250
Canora, Col., 73, 169, 171, 173, 253
Carey, Revd Douglas, 279, 287, 412
Carson, Edward, 384, 390, 430

Carty, Patrick, 201, 203, 208, 259
Cassel, 361, 397–8
Castelnau, Edouard de, 329, 430
casualty clearing stations, 269, 337–8, 345, 368
Cavan, Lord, 282, 324, 430
Cawnpore, 86–7, 229
Champain, Revd Bateman, 403, 428
Charteris, Brig.-Gen. John, 291, 315, 318, 326, 336, 346, 350–1, 360, 365, 367, 430
Chattar Singh, 73, 171–3, 175, 177, 178–80, 183, 191, 254
Chaulnes, 331
Chesterfield, Philip Dormer Stanhope, 4th Earl, 134, 248
China, 331
Chuk Janoo Khan, 190, 229, 257
Church Army, 303
Church of England, 279–80, 282, 291, 307, 358, 370, 387, 403
Church of Scotland, 270, 273, 277–9, 281–2, 284, 289, 293, 301, 319, 321, 337, 346, 357, 359, 367, 380, 393, 401, 403, 408
Churchill, Winston, 384, 387, 390, 430
Clavering, Lt.-Col. John, 13, 23, 52, 63–4, 67
Cocks, Arthur Herbert, 189, 257
Colebrook, James, 62
Colgong, 88, 229
Compiègne, 330
Connaught, Duke of, 398–9, 430
Corbett, Sir Julian, 10
Courtenay, Francis Foljambe, 139, 249

439

Croisilles, 335
Crowe, Brig.-Gen. John, 353, 421, 430
Crump, Lt.-Col. Byam, 13, 52, 54, 64, 66–7
Cunningham, Lt.-Col. James, 39, 65
Cunninghame, Lt.-Col. William, 12, 39, 65
Cureton, Charles Robert, 182–3, 256
Currie, Frederick, 74, 146, 160, 165, 170, 172–4, 178, 201–2, 217, 250
Curzon, George, 364, 430

Daily Mail, 329, 331, 350
Dalhousie, James Andrew Broun-Ramsey, 10th Earl of, 75, 139, 249
Dalip Singh, 139, 171, 249
Davidson, Maj.-Gen. Sir John, 360, 430
Davidson, Most Revd Randall, 282, 413
Deering, Cpt. Daniel RN, 64
Delhi, 155, 229
Dera Ghazi Khan, 160, 230, 252
Dera Ismail Khan, 146, 230
Derby, Lord, 335, 385, 430
Devon, William Courtenay, 10th Earl of, 139, 249
Dhamtaur, 172, 230
Dobell, Sir Charles, 282, 413
Dominica, 13, 33, 52–3, 55–6, 64, 67
Dopatta, 184, 230
Doullens, 295, 346–7, 352
Duncan, Revd George S. 277–9, 281–2, 284, 286, 293, 295,

301, 303, 305, 319, 337, 346, 357, 359, 369–70, 393, 401, 403–4, 406, 408
career: pre-war, 271; at GHQ, 277–9; post-war, 273–4.
character: education, 271; personality, 271; relationship with Haig, 270–4; religious background, 271; religious beliefs, 272, 274, 281, 286, 292, 295, 299, 300, 303, 305–6, 313, 319, 327–8, 334, 336–7, 340–1, 346–8, 352, 363, 369–78, 380, 386, 392–4, 397, 408; death: 274; on the war: 273–4
Dunkirk, 400
Durant, George,
his journal described, 3–5; birth and family, 5; love affair with Elizabeth, Lady Lyttelton, 6–7; clerkship in Pay Office, 7–8; appointed Deputy Paymaster to Martinique/Guadaloupe expedition, 9–10, 17, 59; joins the *St George* man-of-war, 17; experiences a storm at sea, 19–20; comments on clergymen and sermons, 23, 27–8; experiences a strange dream, 25–6; comments on corruption and harsh discipline aboard the *St George*, 26–7; arrives at Barbados, 29; arrives at Martinique, 30–3; describes and

comments on the abortive attack on Martinique, 30–3; arrives at Guadaloupe, 33; describes the bombardment of Basseterre, 34–5; describes the destruction ashore and in the fleet, 35–9; plunders a painting, 39–40,; joins in the fighting, 40; observes an attack, 41–2,; makes love to a 'French Negress', 43; attends 'King's Auction', 44; comments on the death of General Hopson, 45; becomes seriously ill, 46; recovers, 48–9; reflects on the death of Cpt.-Lt. Gunning, 49; convalescent, 50; observes operations ashore, 51–2; describes scenery at Guadaloupe, 54; concludes duties in the islands, 14, 61; appointed Deputy Paymaster to the Havana expedition, 14, 61; his Havana fortune, 14–15, 61; relationships with the Lyttelton family in later life, 14–15, 61; later career and death, 14–15

Durant, Revd Josiah, 5, 6, 30

Eckford, James, 174–5, 255
École Militaire, 302, 403
Ecuires, 298, 309, 313, 341
Eden, Hon. Emily, 139, 249
Edinburgh, 269, 298, 313, 341
Edlmann, Adine, 75, 107, 128, 157

Edlmann family, 75, 107, 128, 157
Edlmann family, 75, 100, 107, 127, 157, 243
Edwardes, Herbert, 72, 146, 159–61, 165, 167, 170–1, 175
Ellenborough, Edward Law, 1st Earl, 74, 181, 246, 256
Elliott, Henry Miers, 210, 220, 259
Esher, Reginald, 283–4, 306, 355, 430
Étaples, 290, 301, 321, 323, 352, 386, 388
Evans, Mr 325, 333, 337

Fategarh, 117, 230, 246
Fenton, Thomas, 151, 250
Ferozepore, 165, 191, 196, 230
Fife, 269, 384
Fisher, Lt. Garrett, 323
Fisher, H.A.L., 329
flat-bottomed boats, 46, 66
Fleming, Archibald, 405
Fletcher, Col. Alan, 293–4, 296, 304, 318, 330, 338, 347–9, 350, 352, 358, 360, 362, 365, 369, 381–2, 384, 388, 401, 404, 430
Foote, Samuel, 3
Fortescue, Sir John, 5, 11
Fox, Henry, Baron Holland, Paymaster-General, 8, 9, 10, 14, 17, 59
Fox, Sir Stephen, 8
Fowke, George, 284, 430
French, Field Marshal Sir John, 270, 273, 277, 363, 431
French Army, 331, 344, 348–50, 355, 362, 395–6, 398–400

Fricourt, 343
Fry, Miss, 133, 248

Gambier, Cpt. John RN, 20, 62
Garbett, Hubert, 174, 255
Gardiner, Cpt. Richard, Royal Marines, 3, 12, 13
Gardiner, R.D., 289–90
Garhi Habibullah, 180, 230
Garton, J., 65
Gaton, Cpt. Clark RN, 26–7, 62, 63
Geddes, Auckland, 390, 431
Geddes, Eric, 390, 431
General Headquarters (GHQ), 269–71, 274, 279, 281, 285, 293, 295, 307, 311, 322–3, 326–7, 333, 335, 337, 346, 350, 355, 381, 403
George V, King, 320, 362–3, 406
German Army, 273, 295, 314–15, 320, 324–6, 329, 331, 335, 339, 343–5, 350–1, 353, 356, 360, 382–3, 389–91, 395–6, 398–400, 406
German Peace Proposals, 309–10, 315
Germany, 'His Britannick Majesty's Army in', 8–9
Gidha Gulli, 195, 231
Glasgow, 319, 322, 342, 388
Gorée, 44, 65
Göttingen, 291
Gough, Gen. Sir Hubert, 360, 382, 431
Gough, Hugh, 75, 183, 189, 196, 242, 254, 256–7
Govindgarh, 191, 196, 227, 231
Grandcourt, 320
Grandeterre, 12, 46, 53, 55, 57
Greathead, James Henry, 198, 258
Greathead, William, 113, 245
Greathead family, 198, 199, 258
Griffiths, Col. Norton, 315, 431
Guadaloupe, 10–13, 33, 52, 54, 68
Gulab Singh, 73, 91, 104, 110, 125, 155, 157, 192, 194, 243
Gulab Singh Pohuwindia, Sardar, 177, 255
Gunning, Cpt.-Lt. William, 49, 67
Gwynne, Bishop Llewellyn, 278, 282, 288, 358, 367, 370, 431

Hagley, 5–7, 15, 41
Haig, Lady Dorothy, 272, 277, 294, 306, 318, 330, 344, 358, 402, 404–7
Haig, Field Marshal Sir Douglas, 277–80, 283, 285, 287–9, 291, 293, 304–5, 307, 310, 314–15, 317–18, 320, 323–7, 330, 333–4, 336–8, 346–9, 352, 355, 357, 359–65, 367–9, 378–9, 381–3, 387, 390, 394–5, 397, 399, 431.
  career: pre-war, 269, 283, 291; becomes Commander-in-Chief, 270; appointed Field Marshal, 317–18; post-war, 274.
  character: upbringing, 269; education, 283; personality, 270; religious beliefs, 270–5, 277–8, 280, 282, 292, 330, 344, 358, 397, 401–9.

Haig, Lt. John, 283, 287
Haking, Richard, 366
Haldane, Col. George, 3, 4, 11, 61, 64, 66
Haldane, Richard, 383, 431
Hansard, 384
Hanson, Revd Richard, 323, 431
Harbord, Gen. James, 365, 367, 369, 431
Harding, John Ward, 71, 199, 240, 258
Hardinge, Henry, 74–5, 89, 139, 173, 199, 201, 241
Haripur, 73, 154–6, 169, 206, 231
Harkishangarh, 148, 152–4, 231
Hassan, Abdal, 195, 204, 231
Hastings, Warren, 63
Havana, 14–15, 61
Hawke, Rear-Adm. Edward, 65
Hay, Ian, 321
Heidelberg, 271
Herbert, Charles, 182, 256
Herkless, Very Revd Sir John, 340, 420
Hervey, Andrew, 174, 255
Hesdin, 287, 312
Heseltine, Maj. John, 310, 325, 330, 334, 336–7, 355, 359, 361, 365, 416
Hewitt, Maj. Shuckborough, 68
Hindenburg, Gen. Paul von, 356, 431
Hindenburg Line, 331
Hira Singh, 111, 244
Holland, 315, 408
Holmes, Lt. Lancelot RN, 28, 63
Hopson, Maj. Gen. Peregrine, 4, 11–13, 17–18, 22, 29, 33, 35, 39, 43, 45, 60, 62, 65–6

Hormuck, 192, 231
Horne, Gen. Sir Henry, 392, 431
Hoshiarpur, 163, 231
Hughes, Cpt. Sir Robert RN, 20, 22–4, 53, 55, 62, 68
Hyde, Henry, 107, 244

India, 364, 385
International Socialist Conference (1917), 356
Ireland, 391
Irish Waste Land Improvement Society, 129, 247, 249
Italian Army, 353, 385, 392, 401

Jaffray, Revd W.S., 380, 424
Jalalabad, 138, 231
Jalalpur, 130, 189, 204, 232
Jamaica, 15
Jammu, 109–12, 233, 232, 246
Jamrud, 195, 232
Jarl, 157–8, 232
Jena, 271
Jews, 303
Jhunder Singh, Sirdar, 171, 254
Jindan, Rani, 154, 251
Jindrai, 89, 232, 241
Joffre, General Joseph, 289, 318, 396, 431
Johnstone, Revd, 342–3
Jonas, Sarah, 113, 245
Jonas, William Knapp, 113, 117, 178
Jones, Jenkin, 102
Jowett, Revd Benjamin, 364, 423
Jullundur, 191, 196, 232
Jutland, Battle of, 285, 287

Kabul, 125, 139, 165, 183, 232
Kangra, 72, 95, 232

Karachi, 94, 233
Kellman, Revd John, 382, 392, 424
Kemmel, 325, 361, 368
Keppel, Cdre Hon. Augustus RN, 65
Kerensky, Alexander, 388
Kerr, Charles, 162, 164–5, 168, 193, 240
Khanor, 110, 233
Kiggel, Lt.-Gen. Sir Launcelot, 359–60, 362, 365–6, 368, 382, 389–90, 432
Kimball, Gertrude Selwyn, 5
Kipling, Rudyard, 289
Kitchener, Field Marshal Lord, 288, 318, 354, 432
Knott, George Alexander, 132, 135, 140, 149, 156, 196, 248
Kohat, 177, 182, 233
Kooree, 143–6, 233
Korniloff, L.G., 388, 426
Kotla, 95, 233
Kut, 326

Labour Party, 354
Lahore, 94, 96, 134, 172, 191, 206, 233
Lang, Cosmo, 367–8, 370, 432
Laughton, John, 86, 241
Laurenson, George Simson, 86, 240
Lawrence, George St. Patrick, 177, 218
Lawrence, Henry Montgomery, 74, 111, 153, 178, 180–1, 195, 245
Lawrence, John Laird Mair, 153, 174, 251
LeCras, Cpt. Edward RN, 23, 57, 63

Leeson, W.J., 204, 259
Leeward Islands, 11
Leiah, 160, 233
Lens, 344
Leslie, Cpt. Lachlan RN, 31, 44, 64
Ligonier, Gen. Jean-Louis, 63
Lille, 331
Lincoln, Abraham, 293
Lindsay, Alexander, 321, 327, 376, 432
Linday, Revd Thomas, 319, 417
Littler, John Hunter, 174, 254
Lloyd George, David, 271, 326, 348, 352, 384, 393, 432
Longueval, 295, 300
Loos, 294, 391, 393
Louisburg, 10
Lucknow, 227, 234
Ludhiana, 191, 234
Lumsden, Peter Stark, 207, 259
Lyautey, Hubert, 329, 432
Lynn, Cpt. [?] RN, 64
Lyttelton, Revd Dr Charles, 6–7
Lyttelton, Lady Elizabeth, *née* Rich, 5, 7, 14, 61
Lyttelton, Sir George, later Lord, 5–7, 14, 15, 61
Lyttelton, Lady Lucy, *née* Fortescue, 5
Lyttelton, Hon. Thomas, 9–10, 13, 15
Lyttelton, William Henry, 'Governor', 6, 15, 61

Macdonald, R.G., 338
MacDonogh, Sir George, 274, 397
McGuffie, T.H., 15
Maclean, Cpt. Francis, 64
MacNeill, Ronald, 384, 425

Macpherson, J. Ian, 394
McRae, Cpt. W., 298, 415
Madras, 234
Mahmud of Ghuznee, 131, 248
Mahtab Kumar, 129, 247
Main, Revd Prof. Archibald, 339,
420
Malcolm, Col. George, 324, 417
Man, Cpt. Robert RN, 65
Mankiala, 122–3, 234
Mansehra, 173, 234
Marburg, 271
Margala, 74, 169, 234
Margetson, Lt. Philip, 287
Marie Galante, 13, 56, 68
Marshal, Col. Hugh, 327, 330, 418
Martinique, 10–12, 20, 30–3, 55
Maud, John, 403, 428
Meerut, 72, 88–9, 108, 234, 240
Melville, Maj. Robert, 64
merchants and agents for India in
England,
Fletcher, Alexander & Co., 166,
168, 253
George Dollond, 161–2
Henry & Thomas Peat, 97, 242
Mordan (Sampson) & Co., 140,
249
Reid, Irving & Co., 133, 248
merchants and agents in India,
Allan, Deffell & Co., 121, 143,
163–4, 168, 180, 246
Bagshawe & Co., 166, 168, 253
John Hutcheson Fergusson,
199, 246, 258
Saunders, May, Fordyce & Co.,
85, 133, 240
Messines, 272, 361, 386
Milford family, 81, 106, 240
Miller, Frederick Francis, 113, 245

Miller, Henry Newdick, 94, 102,
186, 193, 242
Miller, John Harry, 289–90, 364,
379, 386, 432
Miller, Sarah, 136, 186, 249
Miller family, 89–90, 113, 136, 241
Milligan, Oswald, 342–3
Milner, Lord, 329
Minorca, 8, 11, 65
Mirpur, 181, 234
Mirzapur, 88, 235
M'Lagan, Maj. Douglas, 298, 415
Monckton, Maj.-Gen. Robert, 12
Mons, 396
Montreuil, 269, 275, 281–2, 285,
305, 307, 310, 314, 327–8,
338, 352, 354, 386, 408
Montserrat, 11
Moore, Cdre. John RN, 11, 12, 41,
46–7, 53, 57, 60, 65–8
Morse, Leonard, 19, 28, 59, 62, 65
Muhammad Khan, Dost, 177,
190–1, 255
Multan, 72, 153, 157, 165, 169,
174–5, 186, 191, 206, 235
Munro, Neil, 326, 362, 397
Munsey, Frank, 304, 415
Murray, Robert, 199, 258
Mussoorie, 103, 197, 235
Mutual Life Assurance Society,
154, 251
Muzaffarabad, 181, 235

Nadir Shah, 131, 247
Namier, Sir Lewis, 15
Nangal Dunna Singh, 119, 235
Napier, Robert Cornelius, 75, 174,
191, 201–3, 206, 255
Napoleon, 329, 399
Nara, 170, 172, 235

Nash, Philip, 360, 432
National Mission of Repentance and Hope, 392
National Review, 303
National Shell Filling Factory, Barnbow, 311, 416
Naushahra, 195, 235
Nawashahr, 177, 235
Nesbitt, Arnold, 62
'Neutral Islands', 33, 64
Nicholas II, Tsar of Russia, 320, 329–30
Nicholson, John, 74, 110, 169, 171–2, 190, 254
Nicol, Revd Bruce, 301, 338
Nivelle, Robert, 318, 322–3, 348–9, 355, 432
Northcliffe, Viscount, 296, 432
Noyon, 231
Nurpur, 91, 95–6, 98–9, 101, 103, 236

O'Connell, Daniel, 98, 118, 242
Oliver, Frederick, 393–5, 432
Oppy, 344
Orpen, William, 363, 432
Oxford, University of, 283, 319, 358, 368

Pagan, Revd Gavin, 290, 378, 414
Painlevé, Paul, 388, 432
Pallaravam, 81, 236, 240
Paris, 348–9, 355, 382
Passchendaele, 272, 398
Pathankot, 89–93, 236
Paymaster-General, 7–8
Pencraig, 114, 246
Peronne, 331
Pershing, General John, 365, 367, 369–70, 433

Peshawar, 91, 137, 153, 171, 177, 182, 190, 193, 195, 236
Pétain, Marshal Henri-Philippe, 348, 355, 433
Petrograd, 320
Pinfold, Charles, 29, 63
Pitt, William, Secretary of State (South), 8, 10
Plowden-Wardlaw, Revd James, 307–8, 310–11, 433
Poelcapelle, 398, 400
Poincaré, Raymond, 304
Polygon Wood, 393
Pope, the, 384
Poperinghe, 364
Portuguese Army, 355, 363, 398
Potwar, 183, 236
Poziers, 296–8, 300
Presbyterianism, 270, 340, 349, 352, 354–5, 393
Pukli, 172, 177, 236
Punch, 181, 236

Rajmahal Hills, 236–7
Rajoia, 141–2, 237
Ramgarh, 109, 237
Ramnagar, 182–3, 189, 237
Ranbir Singh, 110, 111–12, 126
Randell, Cpt. James RN, 33, 46, 64
Rasputin, 320
Rawlinson, Gen. Sir Henry, 383, 398–9, 400, 433
Rawalpindi, 124–5, 196, 207, 223, 237
Redwood, William, 362, 422
Reid, Revd Herbert, 338, 342
Repington, Charles, 326, 433
Ribot, Alexandre, 332, 433
Rich, Gen. Sir Robert, 5
Roberts, Lord, 288, 413, 433

Robertson, Cpt. Brian, 296, 366
Robertson, General Sir William, 274, 296, 359, 361–2, 365–7, 384, 393, 399, 433
Robinson, Charles Francis, 76, 100–1, 107, 118, 127, 149–50, 162, 165, 170, 185, 192–3, 243, 247, 252, 254
Robinson, John Harding, 76, 100, 122, 156, 162, 193, 240, 243, 251
Robinson, Maria de Guadaloupe Anna Antonia (Ninetta), 76, 93, 116, 130, 132, 134, 135, 143, 145, 152, 156, 198, 239, 251
Rodney, Rear-Adm. George, 12
Roman Catholics, 280–1, 308, 391, 397, 203
Royal Marines, 11, 26–7, 31
Royal Navy,
    Composition of the Fleet in the Martinique / Guadaloupe expedition, 11
    HM Ships,
        Bristol, 31, 64
        Britannia, 52
        Burford, 62
        Falcon, 12
        Grenada, 12, 67–8
        Griffin, 53, 67
        Infernal, 12
        Kingfisher, 12
        Lancaster, 41, 65
        Panther, 29, 63
        Rippon, 12
        Roebuck, 31, 47–8, 55, 64, 66
        St George, 4, 17, 33, 38, 62–3
        Winchester, 31, 57, 63–4

        Woolwich, 31, 64
    Transports,
        John and Mary, 48
        Ruby, 47
Rumania, 315–16
Russia, 315, 320, 329–30, 352–4, 356–7, 388, 396, 399
Ryan, Col. Eugene, 360, 382, 422

St Andrew's, University of, 271, 273, 286, 340, 397, 409
St Kitts, 11, 50, 54
St Lucia, 30
St Mary's College, 273, 340
St Omer, 279, 311, 362, 386, 397, 409
St Pop, 338
St Quentin, 331–2, 335
'Saints', The, 33, 64
Sassoon, Sir Phillip, 283, 330, 334, 363, 433
Sclater, Revd John, 313–14, 352, 433
Scotland, A.P., 391, 427
Scots Churches' Hut, 275, 290, 295, 300, 307, 309–10, 312, 314, 317, 357, 408
Seeley, J.E.B., 362
Serre, 320, 325
Shah Jahan, 131, 248
Shamsabad, 137, 204, 237
Sherwan Khurd, 158–9, 163, 167, 169, 237
Shield, Mary, 83, 99, 240
Shuldham, Cpt. Molyneux RN, 63
Simla, 237
Simms, Dr John, 282, 286, 302, 306, 317, 323–4, 334–5, 378–9, 383, 386–7, 407, 433

Simpson, Revd Cecil, 381, 384
Sind, 102, 237
Skene, Lt.-Col. Robert, 51–2, 55, 68
Sobraon, Battle of, 72, 242
Somerville, Mary, 145, 250
Somme, 318
Sorrus, 285, 308
Spencer, F.A., 336, 419
Spiller, Berry, 26–7, 63
Spring, Howard, 385, 426
Stevenson, R. Macaulay, 280, 290, 307, 310, 312, 317, 323, 326, 408, 433
Stockholm, 356
Straker, Cpt. Guy, 287, 360, 365, 413
Sudan, 270
Sydney, 339–40

Talbot, Neville, 364, 433
tank, 146–7, 159, 238
Tatchum, Revd, 62
Taylor, Alexander, 88, 241
Taylor, Peter, 8–9, 59
Taylor, Robert Paris, 8–9, 59
Taylor, Cpt. Thomas RN, 53, 67
Temple, Revd Sir Richard, 22, 62
Thomas, Edward, 196, 258
Thomas, William Beach, 331, 392, 433
Thomson, Maj.-Gen. James, 392, 427
Thompson, Richard, 287, 330, 362, 423
Tong Castle, 14, 61
Touchet, Samuel, 8
Townshend, Cpt. Roger, 29, 39, 63
Trapaud, Lt.-Col. Cyrus, 61, 64
Treil, M. Nadau du, 53, 67

Tremenheere, George Borlase, 144–5, 250

U-boats, 320, 331
United States of America, 304–5, 315, 320, 332, 337, 365, 399–400
Urie, 181, 186, 238
Usman Khattar, 151, 238
Uvedale, Cpt. Samuel RN, 55–6, 68

Vans Agnew, Patrick Alexander, 72, 153, 159, 178, 206, 251
Ventura, Jean Baptiste, 122, 246
Verdun, 310
Verney, Sir Harry, 327–8, 418
Vernons Hill House, 152, 251
Victoria, Queen, 399
Vimy Ridge, 339

Wace, Col. Edward, 327–8, 418
Walpole, Horace, 6
Waterloo, 288
Waugh, Andrew Scott, 201, 209, 223, 259
Wazirabad, 115–17, 127–8, 189, 196, 204, 238
Whish, William Sampson, 74–5, 174, 254
Wigram, Clive, 405, 434
Wilhelm II, Kaiser, 360
Williamson, Right Revd Andrew Wallace, 383, 386, 425
Wilson, Lt. Col. James, 298, 312
Wilson, Woodrow, 337, 394, 400, 434
Woodcock, Samuel Charles, 87, 241

YMCA, 280–1, 308, 312–14, 328, 332, 336, 339, 345, 356

Young, Ralph, 98, 103, 109, 120

Ypres, 308, 385–6, 398–400

Zandvoorde, 399

Zannebeke, 393

Zeebrugge, 388–90

Zeppelins, 330–1, 335, 351, 400

ARMY RECORDS SOCIETY
(FOUNDED 1984)

The Society has already issued:

Vol. I:
The Military Correspondence of
Field Marshal Sir Henry Wilson 1918–1922
Edited by Dr Keith Jeffery

Vol. II:
The Army and the
Curragh Incident, 1914
Edited by Dr Ian F.W. Beckett

Vol. III:
The Napoleonic War Journal of
Captain Thomas Henry Browne, 1807–1816
Edited by Roger Norman Buckley

Vol. IV:
An Eighteenth-Century Secretary at War
The Papers of William, Viscount Barrington
Edited by Dr Tony Hayter

Vol. V:
The Military Correspondence of
Field Marshal Sir William Robertson 1915–1918
Edited by David R. Woodward

Vol. VI:
Colonel Samuel Bagshawe and the
Army of George II, 1731–1762
Edited by Dr Alan J. Guy

Vol. VII:
Montgomery and the Eighth Army
Edited by Stephen Brooks

Vol. VIII:
The British Army and Signals Intelligence
during the First World War
Edited by John Ferris

Vol. IX:
Roberts in India
The Military Papers of Field Marshal Lord Roberts
1876–1893
Edited by Brian Robson

Vol. X:
Lord Chelmsford's Zululand Campaign
1878–1879
Edited by John P.C. Laband

Vol. XI:
Letters of a Victorian Army Officer
Edward Wellesley
1840–1854
Edited by Michael Carver